Dying for Faith

*Religiously Motivated Violence
in the Contemporary World*

EDITED BY
MADAWI AL-RASHEED AND MARAT SHTERIN

I.B. TAURIS
LONDON · NEW YORK

Published in 2009 by I.B.Tauris & Co Ltd
6 Salem Road, London W2 4BU
175 Fifth Avenue, New York NY 10010
www.ibtauris.com

Distributed in the United States and Canada Exclusively by Palgrave Macmillan
175 Fifth Avenue, New York NY 10010

Library of Modern Religion: 6

ISBN: 978 1 84511 686 6 (hb)
         978 1 84511 687 3 (pb)

A full CIP record for this book is available from the British Library
A full CIP record is available from the Library of Congress

Library of Congress Catalog Card Number: available

Printed and bound in Great Britain by CPI Antony Rowe, Chippenham
from camera-ready copy edited and supplied by the author.

FSC
Mixed Sources
Product group from well-managed
forests and other controlled sources
Cert no. SGS-COC-2953
www.fsc.org
© 1996 Forest Stewardship Council

Contents

Acknowledgements

This book would not have been possible without the support of various people and institutions. We would like to thank the British Academy for a conference grant that allowed us to hold an international conference on *Dying for Faith*. The School of Humanities and the Department of Theology and Religious Studies at King's College London, provided a comfortable and hospitable surrounding, in addition to grants in support of the event. The Head of the Department, Professor Oliver Davies, has been a constant source of encouragement and support throughout the project.

We are grateful to many academics who participated in the conference, even though the space limit did not allow us to include all their papers in this volume. We would also like to thank Professor Cathy Wessinger for her valuable comments during the editorial process.

Our special thanks go to Carys Alder and Wendy Pank whose tireless work ensured the smooth running of the conference. We also owe a debt to the future generation of academics, our students who enthusiastically supported us during two days of academic discussion and debate.

We would like to thank Mr Iradj Bagherzade of I.B.Tauris, who realized the importance of this project and the need to disseminate its outcome to a wider audience at an early stage. Without his financial support during the preparation for the conference, many valuable contributions would not have been included in this volume. The manuscript benefited greatly from the meticulous and patient copy-editing of Mary Starkey.

Contributors

MADAWI AL-RASHEED is Professor of Anthropology of Religion at the Department of Theology and Religious Studies, King's College, London. Her main research interests include history, society, politics and religion in Saudi Arabia. She has worked on Arab migration, religious minorities, globalisation and transnational connections. Her latest publication is *Contesting the Saudi State: Islamic Voices from a New Generation* (CUP, 2007).

EILEEN BARKER, OBE, FBA, is Professor Emeritus at the London School of Economics and Political Science. Her main research interests are new religious movements, and the social reactions to them; and the religious situation in post-communist countries. She has over 250 publications. In 1988, she founded INFORM, www.inform.ac.uk. She is a frequent advisor to governments, other official bodies and law-enforcement agencies.

JONATHAN BIRT has published several academic papers on British Islam. In 2007 he directed a study of the beliefs, ideologies and narratives of violent radicalization in Britain, commissioned by the European Commission. He is national Director of the City Circle, *www.thecitycircle.com*, a Research Fellow at the Islamic Foundation, and a member of Islamica Magazine's Editorial Board.

DAVID G. BROMLEY is Professor of Religious Studies at Virginia Commonwealth University. His most recent books include *Cults and Religious Movements: A Brief History* (Blackwell, 2007), *Teaching New Religious Movements* (Oxford, 2007), *Cults, Religion and Violence* (Cambridge, 2001), He is former president of the Association for the Study of Religion and former editor of the *Journal for the Scientific Study of Religion*.

SIMON DEIN is a Senior Lecturer in Anthropology and Medicine at University College London. He has published widely on religion and health, responses to failure of prophecy. He is the editor of the *Mental Health, Religion and Culture* and the author of three books, including *Religion and Healing among the Lubavitch Community of Stamford Hill: A Case Study in Hasidism*

ABDELWAHAB EL-AFFENDI, Ph.D., is Senior Lecturer and coordinator of Democracy and Islam Programme at the Centre for the Study of Democracy, University of Westminster. His publications include *Who Needs an Islamic State?* (1991), *Rethinking Islam and Modernity* (2001), and *The Arab Human Development Report* (co-authored, 2004). He is the 2006 winner of the Allama Iqbal Award for Creativity in Islamic Thought.

JOHN R. HALL is Professor of Sociology at the University of California – Davis. His research spans the sociologies of culture and religion, epistemology, social theory, and economy and society. Recent books include: *Cultures of Inquiry* (1999); *Apocalypse Observed*, with co-authors; and *Sociology on Culture*, with co-authors (2003). Currently he is studying apocalyptic terrorism and modernity.

MARK HUBAND is an award winning journalist and writer on the Middle East, Islam and global security issues. A former correspondent for the Guardian and the Financial Times, he oversaw the FT's coverage of terrorism, intelligence and security issues. His publications include *Warriors of the Prophet: the Struggle for Islam (1998), and Brutal Truths, Fragile Myths: Power Politics and Western Adventurism in the Arab World* (2004)

FOUAD IBRAHIM holds a Ph.D. in Near and Middle Eastern Studies from School of Oriental and African Studies, University of London (2004). He is an editor of Saudi affairs magazine and author of a number of books on the Saudi politics, and cultural, historical, and religious legacy of Shi'ism, including *The Shi'is of Saudi Arabia* (2006).

MASSIMO INTROVIGNE is managing director of the Center for Studies of New Religions (CESNUR) headquartered in Turin, Italy, and is currently vice-president of the Association for the Sociology of Religion of Piedmont (APSOR). He is the author of forty books and more than one hundred articles in several languages on the sociology of religion and the relations between religion and violence.

NOHA MELLOR is Senior Lecturer in Media and Cultural Studies at Kingston University, London. She is the author of *The Making of Arab News* (2005) and *Modern Arab Journalism: Problems and Prospects* (2007).

J. GORDON MELTON is the director of the Institute for the Study of American Religion based in Santa Barbara, California and a research specialist with the department of Religious Studies, University of California in Santa Barbara. He is the author of a number of books on new religions and has written widely on issues of persecution, discrimination, and violence relative to new religious movements.

PASCAL MÉNORET is post-doctoral research fellow at the Institute for Transregional Study of the Middle East, North Africa and Central Asia (Princeton University). He holds a PhD in history from the University of Paris-La Sorbonne (the title of his disseration is "Thugs and Zealots: The Politicization of Saudi Youth 1965-2007). He is the author of *The Saudi Enigma :A History* (London: ZedBooks, 2005).

IAN READER is Professor of Japanese Studies at the University of Manchester and is the author of several books, including *Making Pilgrimages: Meaning and Practice in Shikoku* (2005) and *Religious Violence in Contemporary Japan: The Case of Aum Shinrikyô* (2000). His research focuses on religion and violence in global contexts, and on pilgrimage in the modern world.

MARAT SHTERIN is Lecturer in the Sociology of Religion at King's College London. He holds a Ph.D. from the London School of Economics and Political Science. His research interests and publications are concerned with religion in Russia and Britain, new religions and other religious minorities, and religion and law.

AZAM TAMIMI, Ph.D. is Director of the London-based Institute of Islamic Political Thought (IIPT) and co-founder of the London-based Alhiwar Arabic satellite channel. His books include *Rachid Ghannouchi, Democrat within Islamism* (2001), and *Hamas: Unwritten Chapters* (2006), and co-editor of *Islam and Secularism in the Middle East (2000)*. He is a regular commentator for Arabic satellite channels and contributor to UK news programmes.

NEIL WHITEHEAD is Professor of Anthropology at the University of Wisconsin – Madison. His research interests include violence and the cultural order; shamanism and sorcery; vampires, zombies and the body. His regional specialization include South America and the Caribbean. Among his numerous publications are *Violence* (2004) and *Terror and Violence – Anthropological Approaches* (ed.) with Andrew Strathern and Pamela Stewart, 2005.

STUART WRIGHT is Professor of Sociology at Lamar University (Beaumont, Texas). He holds a Ph.D. from the University of Connecticut. He has published four books, most recently *Patriots, Politics, and the Oklahoma City Bombing* (Cambridge University Press, 2007), and authored over forty publications in scholarly journals and edited volumes. He is internationally recognized for his research on religious movements, domestic terrorism and conflict/violence.

Foreign Words

'ahirat al-rum ('Roman prostitutes', female American soldiers (in Saudi Arabia))
ahl al-bayt (the House of the Prophet)
aimat al-da'wa al-najdiyya (Najdi religious scholars)
ajnabi (foreigners)
aliya (emigration to the land of Israel)
amir (leader, prince)
al-amr bi'l-ma'ruf wa al-nahy 'an al-munkar (commanding good and forbidding evil)
'aqida (creed)
al-badiya (the countryside)
al-bara' (disassociation)
bay'a (oath of fealty)
dar al-iman (land of faith)
dar al-islam (land of Islam)
dar al-kufr (land of unbelief)
dar al-shirk (land of polytheism)
da'wa ('summons' to allegiance)
din (religion)
din rodef (the duty of a Jew to kill another Jew designated a traitor)
dira (homeland)
drubynon ('crazy wisdom')
dunya (world)
fajr (dawn [prayers])
falaqa (bastinado)
faragh (vacuum)
fasad (iniquity, corruption)
al-fi'a al-dhalla ('those who have gone astray': Kharijites)
fiqh (Islamic jurisprudence)
fitan madhhabiyya (doctrinal discord)
dayuuth (a pimp)
fatwa (pl. *fatawa*; individual legal opinion)
fitna (sedition)
gharbzadaghi (those who were awestruck, intoxicated, or bewitched by the West)
hadith (Prophetic tradition)
hadith sahih (sound Prophetic report)
hajj (pilgrimage)
hajwala (street culture)
halaqa (circle, informal group)
al-hara (the neighbourhood)

hijra (migration of the Prophet and his followers from Mecca to Medina; protection)

himla salibiyya (a crusade)

hukm 'adil (just rule)

hurra (a free woman)

'ibadat (religious observances)

'ilm ahl al-bayt (the knowledge of the Prophet's descendants)

imamiyyun (supporters of the imamate)

intizar (waiting)

jihadan kabiran (struggle with the utmost strenuousness)

jihad defa'i (defensive *jihad*)

jihad ebteda'i (offensive *jihad*)

jizya (tax paid by non-Muslims who reside in a land conquered by force)

jumhur (fans of *mufahhats*)

kafir (pl. *kafirun/ kuffar*: unbelievers, those that are thankless or those that reject faith)

kafira (unbelieving)

kasrat (*tafhit* songs)

khawarij (Kharijites: secessionists)

khawarij al-'asr (contemporary Kharijites)

khuruj ('rising' (against tyrants))

kiddush haShem (sanctification of God's name)

al-kitab wa 'l-sunna (the book and the deeds of the Prophet)

kyôsaku (Zen 'waking stick')

mabaheth's ([Saudi] secret service)

madrasa (Qur'an school)

maharim (taboo female relatives)

mahrumin (deprived)

malal (boredom)

marji' taqlid (religious authority)

mitzvot (the commandments God gave to the Jewish people in the Torah)

mufahhat (one who drives in the style of *tafhit*)

mufaraqat al-hayat (leaving life)

mujaddid bi-'l-fikra (intellectual innovator)

mujahid (pl. *mujahidin*; warrior, struggler)

mujtahid (authorized to perform independent judgment on religious matters)

mushaf (a copy of the Qur'an)

mushajje'in (fans of *mufahhats*)

mutazawwij arba' (married four times)

nashid (pl. *anashid*: religious chant)

natla (lateral skid)

nifaq (hypocrisy)

olam haba (the world to come)

qaba'il ('tribesmen', settled agriculturists)

qital (kill, slay)

raj'iyyun (reactionaries)

as-sahwa al-islamiyya (the Islamic awakening)

salat (prayer)

sangha (spiritually advanced individuals (Aum Shinrikyo))

sayyid (pl. *sadah*: Hashimites, descendants of the Prophet)

schluchim (emissaries)

sefirot (divine emanations)

al-shahada (profession of faith; martyrdom)

shahid (martyr)

shari'a

shirk (polytheism)

shmagh (headdress)

tafhit (street culture)

tahawwur wa 'abath (temerity and nonsense)

ta'ibun (repentant skidders)

ta'ifiyya (sectarianism)

takfiriyyun (those who declare other Muslims unbelievers)

taqiyya (dissimulation)

tawaghit (despots)

tawhid (monotheism; unity of God)

tufush (a sense of despair that drives one to deviant behaviour)

'ulama (sg. (*'alim*: religious scholars)

umma (the Muslim community)

waqf (religious/charitable foundation)

wasta ([social or family] connections)

wir' (pl. *wir'an*: a beautiful boy)

wir'anjiyya (the love of young boys)

zaddik (holy man)

zaffat al-shahid ('the martyr's wedding': the celebration of a martyr)

zakat (alms tax)

Introduction
Between Death of Faith and Dying for Faith: Reflections on Religion, Politics, Society and Violence

Madawi Al-Rasheed & Marat Shterin

It was only recently that the link between faith and violence looked like a thing from the past. What many loosely defined as globalization seemed to promise a new world of cohesive culture, economic prosperity, interconnectedness, redundant nation-states with their visa regimes and border controls, strengthened multinational presence across the globe, and, as a result, easy movement of people and capital. It was a vision – and now nearly a cliché – of the global village with deterretorialized free enterprise optimistically expected to bring prosperity to all. Faith was hardly noticeable in the grand globalization narrative, even though it was included in some of the original theories of globalization (Robertson 1992). The promise was partly realized and partly thwarted. Opening a bank account or travelling to New York for business or pleasure, carrying an ornamental nail clipper or a sophisticated perfume in hand luggage are technically easy as ever, but have also become nightmare scenarios that threaten to make or break the global village.

In another area of the utopian global vision was the newly emerging world citizen, described as empowered, self-contained, educated, cosmopolitan, transnational, and connected by the latest communication technology gadgets – the model man of the twenty-first century. There was little apprehension, however, that all these gadgets could be used against us. It was not anticipated that some citizens of the new 'global society' would be willing to die for faith, assisted by the latest inventions. The recent events seem to have urged us to rethink the idea of a new, free-floating global citizen liberated from the constraints of identities and loyalties that revolve around religion, sect, and ethnicity. Instead, what we are witnessing is both a resurgence of familiar identities and loyalties and an emergence of new, hitherto unexplored ones, whose expression can at times take violent turns.

The previous generation of scholars of religion predicted the death of faith, but it seems that *dying for faith* is undergoing a revival in the contemporary world. There is a need for explanations as to why the common wisdom about the role of religion in society failed to account for the revival of this aspect of religion. How do we make sense of people who seem to be using faith *against* a globalized world, and who endorse violence in a world where weapon production and sales are still the monopoly of states, corporations, and arms dealers? How do we make sense of the survival of faith, and even its strengthening to the extent of dying for it in a world dominated by images of pop stars, footballers, and scandalous and sensational stories? Is there some disheartening truth in the view that this violence may be seen as a plea to reinstate the religious narrative in a world increasingly seen as secular, disenchanted, and lacking moral values?

Dying for Faith is intended to explore a number of issues related to acts of religiously motivated violence. In recent years, this phenomenon has caught considerable public attention throughout the world, as part of the political strategy of militant Islamic groups and, consequently, as one of the central issues in the 'war on terror'. In a broader context, after the end of the Cold War in 1989, religion has become increasingly significant as an identifiable source of violence, both independently and in combination with other sources (economic, ideological, political, or ethnic). However, we should remind ourselves that for centuries, individuals and groups have been prepared to sacrifice their lives for a religious cause, from the Jewish defenders of Megiddo through the Russian Old Believers to the more recent cases of mass suicide in new religious movements (or 'cults'), such as the Branch Davidians or Solar Temple. This extremely complex social phenomenon has so far mainly attracted sensational media coverage, but insufficient academic attention. In fact, one of the key questions to be addressed is the extent to which we can discern patterns and make generalizations from different cases of 'dying for faith'; in other words, whether there is a sense in which such cases can be seen as expressions of a *phenomenon* or whether they should rather be regarded as disparate *phenomena*.

This volume reflects the variety of academic disciplines from which these cases have been discussed, and is intended as a step towards a more systematic multidisciplinary approach. Historians document ancient and modern incidents of 'dying for faith'. Scholars of religion tell us that various religious traditions have accommodated theological and ethical justifications for sacrificing individual lives in the name of faith. Anthropologists describe incidents whereby violence against the self and others can be part of the religious and ritualistic aspects of cultures. Sociologists investigate dynamics of social interactions that may result in acts of individual or group suicide or homicide. Political scientists analyse such violence in the context of political conflicts, national interests, and ideological commitments. Psychologists delve into the depths of the human psyche to discover personal motivations and 'pathologies' that may push the individual to overcome the basic instinct of preserving human life. Experts on terrorism have also appeared, who theorize the phenomenon with the hope of identifying its underlying causes and possible prevention.

In the public arena, however, understandings produced by academics interact – and often compete – with other accounts and portrayals. The mass media broadcast words and images that terrify and disgust many. Statesmen flex muscles and vow to combat the menace and its causes. One can also find a great deal of manipulation and misguided statements, perhaps out of a sense of helplessness and defeat in combating the new terror. The perpetrators themselves and their sponsors glorify acts of suicide and homicide by defining them as martyrdom, and celebrate the sacrifice of exceptional martyrs. Ordinary people watch in horror as the dramas of 'dying for faith' unfold in different parts of the world.

For our present purposes, it is useful to distinguish between three different acts. First, dying for faith as a sacrifice that involves annihilating the self for a religious cause. This act is a result of a personal or group decision, the consequences of which involve only the actors, such as the mass suicide of the Peoples Temple in the jungles of Guyana in 1978. Second, annihilating both the self and the enemy of the faith. This act leads to the death of the actor and many others. Thus, Jewish Zealots and Sicarii adopted a strategy of violent attacks to provoke massive uprising against the Roman occupation. In modern times, Japanese kamikazes were members of the regular armed forces who used suicide attacks for military purposes. It has been argued that in this sense, al-Qaeda's acts of violence committed in different parts of the world can be seen as an expression of such old strategies. Third, annihilating others for one's faith without going as far as dying with the victim. This act is usually part of warfare that is intended to kill the enemy, and may or may not lead to the death of the perpetrator together with his victim. The Crusades is one example.

In this volume we discuss all three types of violence, with faith as their common denominator; hence the subtitle *Religiously Motivated Violence*. Faith appears in martyr/terrorist rhetoric, televised performances and iconography, motivations, policy recommendations and formulae promising an end to the menace, and indeed in academic explanations. However, contributors to this volume tend not to assume a linear causal relationship between rhetoric of faith and violence in its name; rather, they consider possible wider causes, for example social, political, economic, ideological, or personal. Also, we see this specific violence as sharing many characteristics with that committed under different motivations and rhetoric.

In discussing this complex phenomenon, we must not forget that throughout history people have died and killed others for secular reasons too. Dying for nation and state is but one example. Dying for honour is another. This requires us to ask what sets dying for faith apart from dying for freedom, dying for one's country, or dying for the moral values of a secular democracy. While people have found many reasons for dying and killing others either individually or communally, in this volume we will focus on one variant, namely acts of violence against the self and others in pursuit of a goal defined as a religious obligation. In this respect we use the perpetrator's iconography, rhetoric, and discourse, which describe this violence. We do not impose the label 'faith' on such acts but use the actors' own description.

Having said that, many contributions in this volume highlight the connection between religiously motivated violence, on the one hand, and economic, political, social, psychological, and international contexts, on the other. All contributors situate this violence between victims and perpetrators, thus incorporating in the analysis the wider context in which violence is enacted. As social scientists, most contributors do not hold essentialist views about religions, and certainly do not consider religion – or some religions – to be intrinsically violent. All major religious traditions involve a text that is interpreted and enacted in specific historical, social, and biographical contexts. The contributors to this volume aim to identify and interpret the intersections between these contexts, group dynamics, and personal biographies, which affect how religion is appropriated, manipulated, and propagated by various groups and individuals. We know that wars have been fought under religious rhetoric and pretexts. We also know that, in the name of religion, people have coexisted and lived peacefully for centuries.

It is unfortunate that theorizing religiously motivated violence has not benefited from cross-fertilization between disciplines and scholarship on a variety of religious traditions and movements. In this volume we will not focus on one religious tradition, but we hope to be able to present a comparative approach across cultures, societies, and religious traditions. We hope that multidisciplinary approaches will offer useful methodologies, theoretical perspectives, and data to capture both the diversity and complexity of what the world faces today in distant geographies, cosmopolitan cities, tourist resorts, busy airports, and train stations.

Religion, politics, and violence

Political scientists concentrate on the strategies of groups that often delve into religious discourse to mobilize their followers in specific national struggles, group emancipation, identity politics, and ethnic conflict. Robert Pape identifies the strategic logic of suicide terrorism in terms of three levels, involving the political, the social, and the individual (Pape 2005: 22–3). Religious discourse is seen as a tool for other political and economic struggles rather than a force in its own right, capable of mobilizing people to act for religious as well as other causes.

Thus, according to Pape, suicide attacks in Iraq became common after the country's occupation by the coalition forces in 2003. A secular nationalist ideology shaped the Iraqi polity throughout the twentieth century. As this ideology was undermined, but perhaps not totally defeated, with the overthrow of the Saddam regime, violence against the occupier and the struggle between various power contestants in post-Saddam Iraq draw on religious rhetoric, allegiances, and the logic and practice of suicide bombing – not only to liberate the country from the occupation but also to carve political space on the elusive power map of the country. Similarly, Hamas and its resort to suicide bombing, under the umbrella of *jihad*, is another example of the use of religiously motivated violence in the pursuit of political goals, the understanding of which is incomplete if framed without reference to both the Israeli occupation and the failure of the Palestinian secular nationalist ideology. However, those who engage in these struggles insist that their acts are a religious obligation before it is a tool for national liberation.

Reflections on the links between politics, religion, and violence involve focusing on the process of 'othering' and assertions of identity that may result in using violence as a strategy. Scholars have focused on how violence produces and enhances social solidarity in the group's quest not only for recognition but also for entitlement to rights. Elizabeth Picard outlines how violence by the marginalized Shiites of Lebanon evolved over several decades. Religious discourse was used to mobilize the community and give meaning to its struggle against both exclusion from the Lebanese state and the Israeli aggression on Shiite villages in the south of Lebanon. The traditional Shiite annual mourning ritual, 'Ashura, evolved from a religious celebration into a political performance, galvanizing collective mobilization (Picard 1993: 4). Religion gives groups what Picard calls 'mytho-logics', which structures the discourse of their emancipation, especially at a time when nationalist and Marxist ideologies declined. However, the decline of these ideologies does not necessarily mean that they cease to inspire groups who resort to traditional religious discourse to justify violence. Historically an acquiescent community, the Shiites revolutionized their traditional theology, especially the concept of martyrdom, only after cross-fertilization with modern Marxist interpretations. While the religious rhetoric remains potent, it is clear that the political emancipation of the Shiites was the ultimate purpose behind the various acts of violence committed by the group between 1974 and 1990. Violence committed under a religious umbrella serves as political means.

While acknowledging that external pressure may force groups to adopt violent strategies in pursuit of specific goals, we must not overlook the internal schisms faced by groups that often use violence. Fawaz Gerges points to the importance of internal disputes, fragmentation, and often violent struggles within groups that may lead to one splinter group globalizing violence, thus deterretorializing aggression under a global religious discourse (Gerges 2005). In his analysis of why al-Qaeda's violence went global, Gerges draws attention to the internal disputes and the failure of various Islamist movements to score success nationally – that is, in the local struggle of each group against secular regimes in Algeria, Egypt, and other Muslim countries. In this case, external pressure has led to fragmentation and even conflict within groups, with one of them resorting to global religiously motivated violence to salvage itself from total annihilation. Religious rhetoric that goes beyond the locality and appeals to a constituency wider than the nation-state becomes a last resort to increase recruits and cast sanctity on violent acts.

Notwithstanding internal disputes and conflicts within Islamist movements, al-Qaeda's violence, while certainly the most visible aspect of its *jihad*, is also linked to a whole world of beliefs and practices that remains invisible in much scholarly writing on the subject. According to Faisal Devji, this 'invisible world of ethical, sexual, aesthetic and other forms of behaviour is far more extensive than the Jihad's realm of violence' (Devji 2005: xvi). Devji argues that al-Qaeda's militancy must be situated in the fragmentation of traditional structures of Muslim authority within new global landscapes. There is more to al-Qaeda's discourse than resisting Western hegemony. As al-Qaeda's violence developed over the last decade, 'Jihad abandons the authorities and heartlands of Islam by taking to the peripheries, assuming there a charismatic, mystical and even heretical countenance that dismembers the old social and religious distinctions of Islam' (Devji 2005: 61).

Analysis of the so-called 'new terrorism', a form of deterritorialized violence drawing on historical religious traditions and obligations, often depicts these acts as meaningless, aimless, destructive, elusive, and indiscriminate. Such descriptions do not actually help understand this violence. Moreover, they can be used to justify state measures against terrorism, for example indeterminate detention without charge or trial, abandonment of presumption of innocence and the reversal of the burden of proof, and ethnic profiling (Eckert 2005: 4). It is easier to justify state measures if the enemy is defined as an omnipresent threat. However, a closer examination of these violent acts may reveal that they often have clear and identifiable aims – even rather territorial ones. Transnational Islamist terrorism is but one example (Eckert 2005). States fighting this terrorism can deliberately or inadvertently overlook the causes of this kind of violence, thus depoliticizing it. For example, we can observe that one of the aspects of the 'war on terror' is the 'culturation' of violence and its situation in realms other than politics, for example in an innate culture or religious tradition. As this violence is enacted in different places under transnational religious rhetoric, it is often a reflection of specific local political concerns. Bringing those political concerns as important variables behind the outbreak of violence would implicate the states that claim to fight it. The culturation of contemporary religiously motivated violence can be a strategy that achieves this evasion.

Religion, society, culture, and violence

The relationship between religion and violence (inflicted on the self and others) remains a central question occupying the minds of social scientists, in particular sociologists and social anthropologists. The theorization by anthropologists of human sacrifice, mass suicide, ritual killing, and examples of violence in the context of contemporary religious movements makes it clear that understanding of the relationship is still far from complete. Theoretical accounts range from contextualization of violence within wider socio-economic and political terms to asserting its significance and meaning as a strategy adopted by religious groups and organizations.

Regardless of the reasons that 'cause' groups to resort to violent acts under religious rhetoric, it seems that violence, in addition to empowering individuals and groups, tends to empower religion itself. According to Mark Juergensmeyer, violence has given religious organizations and ideas a public importance that they have not enjoyed for many years, as it served to increase their visibility – often at the expense of their secular rivals (Juergensmeyer 2000: 218). Moreover, groups that deploy violence have come to realize that the media will capture their acts and disseminate their message across the globe, thereby enhancing their visibility and 'soft power'.

Case studies indicate that the link between violence and religion tends to emerge at times when authority is in question, since it can be used for both challenging and replacing authority. According to Juergensmeyer, with the rationalist Enlightenment narrative assuming hegemonic status, religion retreated from the public sphere as societies transferred sacredness from God to the nation. Initially the Western nation-state and later colonial states embodied this transferral (Juergensmeyer 2000: 218). Subsequently postmodern religious rebels have arisen and resorted to 'cosmic wars' to counter the prevailing modernism, the ideology of individualism and scepticism that emerged in the last 300 years. Religiously motivated violence has provided a fundamental critique of the world's post-Enlightenment secular culture and politics (Juergensmeyer 2000: 228; see also John Hall's contribution to this volume, chapter 1).

In contrast to the above approach, Neil Whitehead proposes a hermeneutical rather than analytical approach to violence, in which the anthropology of meaning, experience, and bodily practices becomes central (Whitehead 2004). Relying on Appadurai's notion of ethnoscape, which describes the social worlds where local ethnic identities flourish and gain momentum, he situates violence in what is referred to as the economically and politically marginal ethnoscapes. Violence becomes a forceful, if not inevitable, form of cultural affirmation and expression of identity in the face of a loss of tradition and dislocation of ethnicity. On the relationship between religion and violence, Whitehead sees violence as a meaningful relationship with divinity. However, much of this violence seems to be a response to state violence, in particular the failure of post-colonial states, and their aggressive methods, often inherited and learned from the colonial era. Violence of the state includes death squads, special action units, torture chambers, and checkpoints, all of which must be taken into account when thinking of and dealing with religiously motivated violence in the modern world.

States also create counter-narratives that demonize and devalue an imaginary barbarous and rebellious enemy and so place it beyond the empathy that those violent narratives otherwise might create. However, to understand religiously motivated violence requires incorporating in the analysis the narratives of both victims and perpetrators; in other words, violence must be constructed through participation of victim, perpetrator, and witness. As Andre Girard argued in his *Violence and the Sacred* (1977), violence does not originate in difference but is situated in mimetic rivalry, competition between groups, cultures, and countries who desire to imitate each other. On the violence that destroyed the Twin Towers in New York, Girard offers a perceptive comment: 'By their effectiveness, by the sophistication of the means employed, by the knowledge that they had of the United States, by their training, were not the authors of the attack at least somewhat American? Here we are in the middle of mimetic contagion.'[1]

Sociological perspectives on religion and violence: lessons for the study of new religious movements (NRMs)

By the nature of their trade, sociologists have always been interested in patterns of social interaction – and violence can be seen as, among other things, an extreme way in which people interact with each other. Irrespective of whether interactionism is employed as a theoretical and methodological perspective, sociological analysis of religion and violence inevitably focuses on interactions between social institutions, between and within groups, and between a group and the wider society. Moreover, there is a rich and intellectually stimulating legacy of analysing the link between religion and violence, going back to the founding fathers of sociology, such as Marx, Engels, Durkheim, Weber, and Simmel.

For some time, however, that legacy lay largely dormant, as sociological attention had moved towards secular totalitarian ideologies, such as revolutionary Marxism and Nazism, which seemed to be primary triggers of violence in the twentieth century. However, in 1978 the mass suicide and homicide of nearly 900 members of the Peoples Temple in the jungles of Guyana served as an alarm bell (Hall 1987). In the 1990s, this was followed by a number of other tragic events, such as the 1993 siege near Waco, Texas, that resulted in the death of 80 people, including 76 members of the Branch Davidians (Wright 1995; Wessinger, 2000). In October 1994 and the subsequent months the world was shocked by the group suicide and murders of dozens of members of the Solar Temple in Switzerland, France, and Canada (Introvigne and Mayer 2002). In March 1995, before the dust had settled over that tragedy, members of the Japanese Aum Shinrikyo released gas in a Tokyo underground station, causing 11 deaths and hundreds of injuries (Reader 2000). Two years later, the tragic news came from San Diego, California, about the suicide of 39 members of Heaven's Gate (Balch and Taylor 2002). Finally, in 2000, the emerging assumptions that events of this nature were confined to new religions in the 'developed' world' were shaken by the events in Uganda, where nearly a thousand people died in what seemed like a mixture of homicide and suicide in the Movement for the Restoration of the Ten Commandments of God (Mayer 2001a). In addition, there have been less widely known and smaller scale instances of lethal violence in newer religious groups (Richardson 2001: 107–8, Mayer, 2001b).

For sociologists, the extraordinary nature of these events called for a general reassessment of the role of religions in the contemporary world, with the additional urgency of addressing the policy issues posed by them. Governments, and in particular law-enforcement agencies, seemed to be ill prepared analytically and logistically for comprehending and dealing with what seemed like an emergent serious problem (Wright 1995; Hall et al. 2000; Mayer, 2001b; Barker 2002). There was an additional urgency, however, to do precisely with the fact that these events mostly occurred in developed and well-run societies. As Barker and Introvigne point out in their contributions to this volume (chapters 4 and 5), the notions of brainwashing and mind control that had already been widely utilized in explanations of membership in 'cults' were now routinely applied in mass media coverage, public campaigns, and official statements. What such accounts had in common was the assumption that the tragic incidents of violence in several NRMs were only extreme manifestations of the destructive properties inherent in all 'cults', thus making all of them potentially prone to violence. By contrast, the refutations of the brainwashing claims by the empirical studies in the 1980s (Barker 1984; Galanter 1989; Levine 1984, Richardson, 1994) allowed scholars of NRMs to focus their attention on other possible explanations of violence associated with some of these groups.

The studies of the last nearly three decades clearly suggest that no mono-causal explanation will be viable as an analytical tool in studying the link between religion and violence in NRMs. Surely, the attempts to differentiate between religious traditions in terms of their propensity to violence do not provide sound answers, as the violent NRMs have been associated with different traditions and some of them mixed and matched various belief-systems. Sociological accounts of earlier historical instances of violent religious groups have also shown that they came from a variety of traditions, including Christianity, Islam, Judaism, and Hinduism (Rapoport 1984; Richardson 2001). Nor does it seem viable to boil everything down to the issue of social background and deprivation: while many – but by no means all - members of the Peoples Temple and Branch Davidians came from relatively modest and underprivileged backgrounds, Aum Shinrikyo and the Solar Temple attracted predominantly upper-middle-class and well-educated individuals. Certain lines of analysis, however, have emerged as most promising; these included focusing on beliefs, organization, leadership, relationship with the wider society, and contingencies in the sequence of events. In many ways, the Weberian tradition of analysing ever-changing systems of meaning and their complex relationships with particular social groups at particular historical junctions came back to bear on the study of NRMs and violence (Weber 1978, chap. 6; see also Robbins 1997).

Some studies of NRMs have pointed to a link between religiously motivated violence and apocalyptic millenarian beliefs that run *across* different religious traditions. Scholars of millennialism have developed useful typologies of apocalyptic beliefs, groups, and behaviours with some types more likely than others to encourage or justify violence (Wessinger, 1997, 2000; see also Robbins, 2002). Wessinger argues that millenarian beliefs should not be seen as uniform and static, as they involve a variety of interpretations and can encourage a range of behaviours. In particular, it is useful to distinguish between 'catastrophic' and 'progressive' millenarian expectations. In the 'catastrophic' scenario, the violent destruction of earthly corruption and evil will come primarily as the result of a transcendental intervention before the perfect world is established. Although such beliefs are likely to encourage those who hold them to draw sharp boundaries between themselves as elected ones destined for salvation and those immersed in earthly evil, only some groups may, in certain circumstances, take a violent stand against the evil world. Thus, some of them may have a heightened sense of being persecuted by the doomed world and therefore arm themselves for protection; they may fight back when outsiders come to be seen as doing Evil's work and closing in on them. Wessinger also points to a possibility of 'revolutionary' catastrophic millennialism by those who feel compelled to assume the role of divine agents and destroy the evil world, thus creating the space for the Kingdom on Earth. Progressive millenarians, on the other hand, are inclined to put their trust in a divine agent guiding their hard work towards the advent of the millennium. However, in certain circumstances some of them may attempt to accelerate the pace of progress and engage in the cosmic struggle against the forces of Evil for the building of the perfect world; Wessinger describes this stance as revolutionary progressive millennialism. (Mark Juergensmeyer's notion of the cosmic war is one eloquent expression of this stance). It seems that taking account of the millennialism found in some new Islamic movements, such as Al-Qaeda, would sharpen our understanding of these groups, analysis of which is currently almost entirely focused on their geopolitical and terrorist dimensions (for a useful discussion, see Mayer, 2001; Wessinger, 2006; also John Hall's contribution to this volume, chapter 1).

The available empirical studies have suggested that millenarian beliefs *per se* are not absolute predictors of religiously motivated violence, nor will revolutionary millenarian ideologies necessarily lead to harmful acts against the rest of society. These beliefs are subject to reflection and change by those who hold them; hence the focus of the sociological studies on a range of internal and external factors that may encourage transformation of millenarian beliefs towards justification of, and engagement in, violent acts. This includes issues such as totalistic organization, charismatic leadership, relationship with the state, and reactions of the wider society, which are discussed in contributions to this volume (see also Hall et al. 2000; Bromley and Melton 2002; Wright 1995; Richardson 2001).

Some sociological studies of tensions between NRMs and the wider society have usefully employed the notion of deviance amplification, which describes a spiral of conflict constantly reinforced by the mutual negative expectations and consequent actions of the sides involved in it (see Richardson 2001; Barker 2002). The term is derived from the seminal study by Stanley Cohen (1972) in which he describes the *deviancy amplification spiral* created by the media hype in reporting on a phenomenon defined as an instance of anti-social behaviour even though this behaviour may be unconventional and socially deviant but not necessarily unlawful or dangerous. The analytical value of this notion is that it helps to avoid assumptions and rushed conclusions about the degree of threat from certain religious groups while allowing analysis and monitoring of their evolution through focusing on both their internal dynamics and interactions with the wider society. It is particularly important as an element in understanding of what Melton and Bromley call 'polarization', i.e. the escalation of tensions caused either by group extremism or control agency unreasonable pressure, or by mutually reinforcing interaction between these two aspects (Bromley and Melton 2002: 243).

Contributions to this volume

Patterns and dynamics of religiously motivated violence
In this volume, John Hall (chapter 1) argues that what we may be observing now is 'epochal violence' used by 'bands of true believers' attempting to destroy the currently dominant institutionalized secular liberal modernity and to shape the postmodern world according to their religiously inspired utopian visions. Despite their numerically insignificant numbers, these 'bands', such as al-Qaeda or Aum Shinrikyo, tend to claim a higher ontological status and hence more legitimacy than the currently dominant social institutions, precisely because they see themselves as implementing God's will in pre-apocalyptic times. Hall suggests that in some – and to many quite an uncomfortable – sense, we should take such claims seriously as they reflect two competing types of projects – that of secular modernity and those of religiously motivated utopians. He points out that the modus operandi of the new sectarians can only be understood by taking full account of the interactive nature of their relationships with modern states. The latter face an extremely complex task of protecting their citizens and avoiding being seen as participants in the apocalyptic scenarios of the utopians themselves (see also Hall et al. 2000).

Stuart Wright's contribution to this volume (chapter 2) draws on a considerable body of sociological work on the ways in which the meaning of events is conceived through a process of 'framing', whereby certain aspects of personal and collective experiences are selected, blended, and integrated into seemingly consistent ideologies capable of creating internal group solidarity and inspiring action vis-à-vis those defined as enemies. This process is particularly evident in war situations when human beings from conflicting sides are locked in a spiral of mutual dehumanization by defining each other as enemies and attributing to each other qualities that justify infliction of harm and ultimately killing. Wright demonstrates that while being a potent source of solidarity, progress, and reconciliation, religion also has the tremendous ability to frame earthly – political, economic, and social – grievances in ways that provide ultimate justifications for the most atrocious acts of violence. Echoing Hall's observation, Wright shows how, facing the necessity to respond to the challenge of religious violence, the state can inadvertently become implicated in this kind of conflict framing by employing a rhetoric that mirrors that of the opponent.

The theoretical possibilities of the interactionist approaches become particularly apparent in Gordon Melton and David Bromley's discussion of the acts of homicide committed by Aum Shinrikyo in Tokyo in 1995 and the mass suicide of Heaven's Gate in San Diego, California, in 1997 (chapter 3). The authors enhance the explanatory power of the previous theoretical models, which had stressed the significance of interactions between groups and the wider society, and identify some internal characteristics of cultic movements that may account for such tragic events. To put it simply, the question is why these groups did what they did, while most other apocalyptic–millenarian movements that apparently shared many essential features with them did not and do not seem to be prone to doing so. Melton and Bromley point to the three major internal characteristics that tend to predict the likelihood of violence: apocalyptic millenarian ideologies that imply rejection of the established social order and encourage both symbolic and physical separation from its vices; charismatic leadership that hinges mainly on a precarious balance of acceptance and rejection by its followers; and the totalistic organization that can facilitate confrontational stance towards the established social order. However, their analysis identifies some additional characteristics that may contribute to violent outcomes of millenarian trajectories: the high degree of improbability of a movement's goals; the extreme isolation from the wider society that results from uncompromising pursuit of these goals; and the escalating reinforcement of confrontational stance through interpreting successive events as justifying the movement's improbable goals. Although applied to manifestly different groups, the methodology of this analysis raises interesting possibilities for understanding some contemporary Islamic movements.

Massimo Introvigne (chapter 4) argues that one most useful lesson from the studies of NRMs that can be applied to our understanding of new Islamic movements concerns the social profiles and motivations of those involved in violent groups and acts. He points out that the notion of brainwashing that is often used to explain suicide terrorism has long been discredited by social scientific research and is likely to obfuscate our understanding of such acts currently done in the name of Islam, as it once has with respect to the issue of 'cults'. Another assumption, that economic deprivation can account for the propensity to engage in religious violence – either 'cultic' or 'Islamic' – also finds little evidence in academic research. According to Introvigne, empirical evidence from research on both violent NRMs and terrorist Islamic groups suggests quite a different profile of their 'typical member': mainly middle class, better off, and more educated. We may, however, pause before making definitive conclusions: after all, members of the Peoples Temple did come disproportionately from underprivileged backgrounds. Drawing on the supply-side theory of religious participation, Introvigne calls for more attention to the issues of organization and beliefs as the key factors accounting for appeal of violent groups.

Eileen Barker's discussion of a case study of individual involvement in a terrorist group (chapter 5) is particularly valuable precisely because it draws on the theoretical and methodological insights from her empirical studies of NRMs. It challenges any foregone conclusions about 'profiles' of those involved in violent actions and shows that such actions are results of complex interactions between a number of 'pushes' (e.g. dissatisfaction with the wider society, the family, personal circumstances), 'pulls' (e.g. the appeal of a group's beliefs, organization, personal attachments), and individual predispositions (e.g. idealism). However discomforting this thought may be for most of us, those who perpetrate or are prepared to perpetrate atrocities in God's name are not born terrorists, and may still possess a number of attractive human qualities. Nor are these people dupes who simply follow the commands of their gurus and lieutenants without experiencing any doubts. Steering outside the extremes of the largely refuted brainwashing and mind-control claims and the sociologically unsound notion of unbounded personal choice, Barker's analysis shows that any sound understanding of individual trajectories leading to terrorism should take into account *a number* of personal choices negotiated and mediated through interpersonal interactions within the group.

From the perspective of political sociology, Abdelwahab El-Affendi (chapter 6) discusses the complex relationships between religious and political motifs and motivations of the groups involved in terrorist actions, either suicidal or homicidal. He points to the paradox that while being inspired by religious imagery and ideology they can succeed only if they manage to legitimize their actions by reference to secular political causes that could increase their popular appeal. According to El-Affendi, this tendency is mirror-imaged by that within which secular states attempt to justify their anti-terrorist wars by presenting them as sacred causes in defence of civilization.

Case studies of religiously motivated violence

Case studies document both the discourses and practices of groups who have either debated 'dying for faith' or engaged in activities described as 'martyrdom operations' in the pursuit of various goals. Within Muslim contexts, Madawi Al-Rasheed (chapter 7), Azam Tamimi (chapter 8), and Jonathan Birt (chapter 9) analyse current debate among Muslim ideologues, political activists, and religious scholars who define for their followers the parameters of their national and religious struggles in terms of *jihad*, a struggle in the way of God. Notwithstanding the different contexts of Saudi Arabia (Al-Rasheed), Palestinian occupied territory (Tamimi), and Birmingham (Birt), dying for faith is the rhetoric of mobilization, invoked to pursue projects relating to purification of the land from blasphemy, national liberation, or solidarity with wider Muslim issues. The resulting violence in these contexts seems to take place within the parameters of nation-states or by groups aspiring towards becoming nation-states. In the Saudi case, jihadism developed into a culture with its own politics and poetics, with a performative aspect propagated in pamphlets, videos, and iconography. Jihadism developed into a gendered duty, defending women and honour. In the Palestinian context, the human bomb, used by Hamas, generated debates between religious scholars and is far from being a taken-for-granted religious duty. In Britain, the jihadi Salafists defined themselves in terms of belonging to the Muslim *umma*, seen as deviating from true Islam and consequently humiliated by Western powers. Dying for faith becomes a corrective mechanism and a defiance of structures of authority.

Fouad Ibrahim (chapter 10) calls neo-Shiism. Political repression by powerful states and their security agents seem to be a relevant context that breeds violence expressed in religious idioms. In contrast, Pascal Ménoret (chapter 11) show that it is not always the case that religiously motivated violence is the option chosen by groups who resist state oppression, marginalization, or depoliticization. Some male Saudi youth opt for other modes of resistance to emancipate themselves from an authoritarian public sphere. A 'street culture of resistance', manifesting itself in *tafhit*, acrobatic skids by young car drivers, potentially leading to death, is a product of depoliticization and a challenge to it. While jihadism has attracted a minority of Saudi youth, the authors show that far more young men are attracted to forms of non-ideological mobilization. *Tafhit* groups offer 'cool worlds' that exceed jihadi iconography, poetry, and media performances in their appeal. However, Ménoret does not rule out that the 'body capital' may in some instances turn into 'warrior capital' in pursuit of an 'authentic' Islamic state.

Outside the Islamic tradition altogether, Ian Reader (chapter 12) demonstrates how violence in Japanese Zen Buddhist temples is accepted and valorized as a worthy act intended to facilitate the attainment of spiritual goals and enlightenment. Temple practices are then appropriated to promote militarism and nationalism for the advancement of the nation. Simon Dein (chapter 13) discusses violence associated with Jewish millenarian groups, the Gush Emunim and the Lubavitch Hasidim. He shows how failed millenarian prophecies can reinvigorate religious activity, sometimes culminating in violence. This violence is often directed towards political process believed to have interfered in the materialization of prophecies.

While the mass media are unlikely to cause people to kill, they certainly disseminate the poetics by which killing can be made meaningful to an audience. Neil Whitehead (chapter 14) offers an anthropological perspective on what he calls our 'addiction to violence', leading to images of terror competing for our attention. He proposes to interpret violence as a discursive practice, whose symbols and rituals are as relevant to its enactment as its instrumental aspects. Noha Mellor (chapter 15) invokes the notion of 'market ideology' in media where humanizing the story becomes the norm and journalists are turned into an eyewitnesses and mediators. Mark Huband (chapter 16) shows how the Western media realms have become, without prior preparation, entangled with projects to explain al-Qaeda terror. In trying to answer the question 'why they hate us', most journalists have failed to seek adequate and sound answers. Instead, they have invoked a defensive position about 'our way of life', democratic values, and national sentiments.

Conclusion

Studying religiously motivated violence requires efforts across disciplinary boundaries, as it involves complex interactions between faith − or faiths − and geo-political and national contexts, group dynamics, and individual characteristics. Furthermore, in a globalized world, geographical boundaries are increasingly porous. Violence in one peripheral location may be a mirror reflecting a different type of violence originating in a more cosmopolitan centre. Analysing these new trends requires a re-examination of specializations and disciplinary frontiers.

This does not presuppose blurring interdisciplinary boundaries, let alone uncritically lumping together unrelated cases. On the contrary, we should avoid, as much as we can, unwarranted generalizations and assumptions that all cases of religiously motivated violence can be explained by a limited number of standardized references. Instead, we advocate detailed and rigorous case studies that will help to discern patterns and further develop typologies of what may seem disparate or similar cases. At the same time, our work will be enhanced by sensitizing findings from different disciplines and perspectives.

On a more practical note, the vast diversity of motifs, motivations, contexts, and dynamics of 'dying for faith' should perhaps make us slightly sceptical about the prospects for finding a uniform solution for this disturbing social phenomenon. However, we can draw a degree of hope from insights provided by our increased knowledge and understanding of the cases related to it. We suggest that one lesson is that any solution should not presuppose efforts for eliminating religion from public life; rather, the public sphere must show flexibility in accepting and recognizing that there is ample space for religious groups to contribute to public life and policy; exclusion will never serve as an incentive for moderation. Indeed, Mark Juergensmeyer has suggested that the cure for religious violence may ultimately lie in a renewed appreciation of religion itself (Juergensmeyer 2000: 243).

As for the groups that are *prone to* violence, there is no doubt that they require thorough security measures, including monitoring and prevention. However, part of the solution would also lie in creating a communal space within which at least some such groups would have incentives to re-enter the public sphere and gain recognition through renouncing violence. What those involved in the public debate and policy should try to avoid is actions and rhetoric that may reinforce the deviance amplification spiral. Although by no means an absolute warranty, knowledge and sensitivity to sound academic research seems the best available consultant on these matters. The warning against deviance amplification also applies to religious groups that seek acceptance and recognition. Prospects for preventing or defusing any conflict that may result in groups or individuals choosing to die for faith will, among other things, depend on all those involved accepting that violence is often an outcome of greater inflexibility, dogma, misunderstanding, and demonization of the other.

Part I
Understanding Religiously Motivated Violence

CHAPTER 1

Apocalypse, History, and the Empire of Modernity

John R. Hall

In 2006, the American cable television channel Comedy Central presented spliced-together clips from US television news coverage of the Apocalypse. So, finally we've come to it, the Apocalypse as news. Here is CNN's Paula Zahn posing the lead question: 'Are we really at the end of the world? We asked CNN's faith-and-values correspondent Delia Gallagher to do some checking.' Later, CNN *Live from* . . . anchor Kyra Phillips reports: 'At least a couple of those four horsemen of the Apocalypse are saddling up as we speak.' This leads the Comedy Central anchor to ask, 'Yeah, Wolf, can we get a live shot of that?' This is all very amusing to watch, but it gives me pause. Comedy Central masterfully deconstructs American news media's pseudo-earnest construction of the Apocalypse. However, we need to do more than trivialize media trivializations of the Apocalypse.

An Apocalypse, I submit, is a collectively experienced social crisis, a parting of the curtains of normal reality. As the ancient Greek meaning of the word's root suggests, an Apocalypse 'discloses' aspects of the human condition or historical moment that pierce the ideological screen of the established social order, which ordinarily masks ultimate reality. History is opened to new revelation not only in the statements of prophets but also in events themselves.

To investigate something as alien from everyday life as the Apocalypse, we need not just to shift *what* we study, but to reinvent *how* we study. A useful point of departure is phenomenologist Maurice Merleau-Ponty's 1947 essay *Humanism and Terror*, a reflection on Stalin's political trials of the 1930s via Arthur Koestler's novel *Darkness at Noon*. This topic is both dated and secular. Nevertheless, it suggests striking points for our times and for religion and violence. As Merleau-Ponty remarked then, so it is now: 'the questions that haunt us are precisely those which we refuse to formulate' (1969: 2). The questions that Merleau-Ponty addresses – against the refusals of others, both Communists and anti-Communists – concern whether and how humanist values operating under the sign of Reason should embrace *historical violence*.

- Merleau-Ponty contrasts the 'historical *period*' relatively free from political violence – 'in which political man is content to administer a regime or an established law' – from the '*epoch*', 'one of those moments where the traditional ground of a nation or society crumbles and where, for better or worse, man himself must reconstruct human relations....' Under these conditions, 'the liberty of each man is a mortal threat to the others and violence reappears' (1969: xvii).

- Epochal violence is inevitable so long as the dynamic forces of history remain in play. But 'we cannot imagine ... a consciousness without a future and a history with an end' (1969: 92).
- Thus, Merleau-Ponty remarks, 'We do not have a choice between purity and violence but between different kinds of violence' (1969: 107).
- No social truth is absolute. The (never absolute) meaning – that is, the legitimization or rejection – of violence becomes evident only after the fact, when the objective outcomes of historical struggle become apparent. Only then can violence be identified as *progressive* or merely *self-serving* (1969: 175).
- The end of violence justified through Reason (for Merleau-Ponty, Marxism) marks the end of meaningful history. 'After that', he asserts, 'there remain only dreams or adventures' (1969: 153). The absence of a philosophy of History 'would mean in the end ... that the world and our existence are a senseless tumult' (1969: 156).

Merleau-Ponty's discussion implies that to understand religion and violence, we cannot formulate questions from within positivism or Western liberalism, at least in so far as they may serve either to mask or demonize violence. Some forms of religiously connected violence occur *within* – and are legitimized by – the ideologically normalized established social order. Other forms manifest as conflicts *between* an established social order and some external counter-cultural movement (Hall 2003). We thus need a more encompassing intellectual vantage point, or at least a less encumbering one. To encourage a new approach to questions about relationships between religion and violence, in this chapter, I propose a *phenomenological/historical* analysis. In a very brief survey, I sketch: (1) a general socio-historical phenomenology; (2) a phenomenology of modernity; (3) a genealogy of apocalypticism; and (4) the contemporary temporal structures of apocalyptic war.

Prologue: a socio-historical phenomenology
Not only for present purposes, but in general, the prospect for a historical phenomenology of the social can be charted via the scholarship of three Germans: the historical sociologist Max Weber, the social phenomenologist Alfred Schutz, and Karl Mannheim, who developed a sociology of culture and knowledge. Fortuitously, because Mannheim focused on utopian ideologies, this triangulation makes it possible to come at the problem of religion and violence through a phenomenology of history.

Drawing on the work of Schutz and his colleague Thomas Luckmann (1973), we can identify two fundamental dimensions of phenomenological variation in structures of the everyday lifeworld of social experience: *time* and *social enactment*. Social time is a substrate of subjective and social action and its organization – in relation to irreversible unfolding physical time. Social temporality's possibilities are manifold, fluid, overlaid, and interpenetrating in their manifestations. Mannheim (1936) offers a basis for typifying ideologies temporally through the examination of specifically utopian idealizations. Formalizing Mannheim to study counter-cultural communal movements,

I have identified four variants in the phenomenological structuration of utopian social time:

- *synchronic time*, that is, the time of the here-and-now;
- *diachronic time*, treated as a 'thing', and organized via the clock and the calendar;
- *pre-apocalyptic time*, in which utopianists see themselves in the last days before a dramatic 'end of the world'; and
- *post-apocalyptic time*, a New Age of 'timeless' perfection in a heaven-on-earth.

As for the second dimension, again drawing on Schutz, I described three broad possibilities of social enactment:

- *natural*, that is, enactment under what Schutz described as the taken-for-granted viewpoint that assumes the world to be unproblematically centred in the actor's array of life experiences;
- *produced*, some socially or institutionally constructed and regulated enactment of the social; and
- a transcendental enactment, which sheds any cognitive or social construction of reality in favour of an absolute experience of unfolding *durée* (e.g. in Zen meditation).

The two dimensions of time and enactment, juxtaposed to each other, yield a typology identifying alternative utopian communal groups (Hall 1978: 202). Though the dimensions of the typology are phenomenological, the alternative ideal types can be elaborated in Weberian terms, as forms of social organization. Thus, there is the anarchic everyday sociability of the commune, as well as 'worldly utopias' of rationalized formal association and of the community, which are meant by their participants to provide practical models for everyday life.

But, obviously, these organizational forms are not inherently utopian. Rather, utopian communal groups – the diachronic utopia of a B.F. Skinner, the community of George Rapp's nineteenth-century Harmony, Indiana – when shorn of their utopian content, reveal a parallel mapping of the social world that aligns with more general Weberian types of social organization, for example, with legal–rational bureaucracy, and with the (ethnic or national or status-group) community. So translated, the typology of utopian communal groups can provide a general phenomenological basis for analysing the socio-historical world (see figure 1).

To recast the typology of utopias for a wider socio-historical analysis only requires broadening the categories of apocalyptic temporality, to shear them of their utopian ideological content. Thus, for utopian communal groups, I identified *pre-apocalyptic time*, when action builds during the Last Days. But pre-apocalyptic time is actually an extreme version of a much wider kind of temporality – *strategic temporality*, in which events are goal directed, and build on, or play off, one another. Strategic time is the unfolding time of biography and history. It might be theorized via game theory, and, substantively, the realm of conflict, notably in politics, and, ultimately, war. *Post-apocalyptic temporality*, on the other hand, is a truly utopian construction, a sort of vanishing point of temporality.

Figure 1: Structural phenomenology of the social world

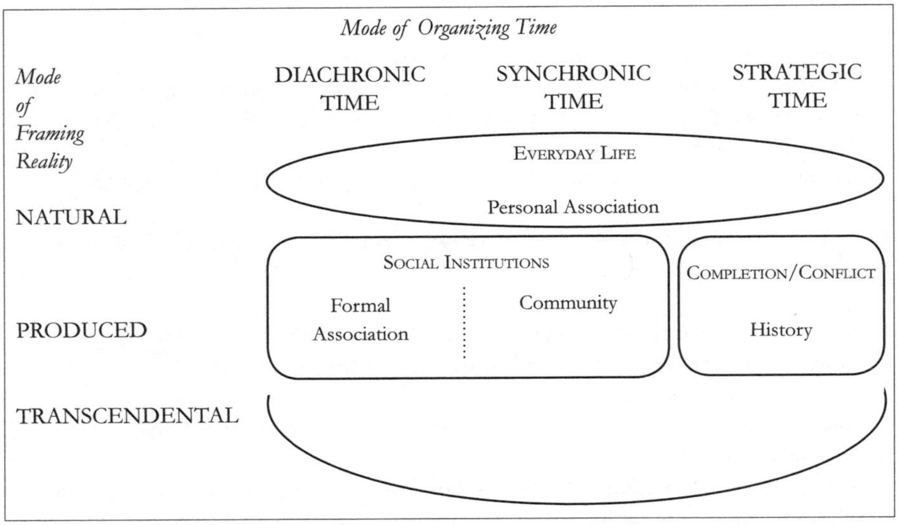

	Mode of Organizing Time		
Mode of Framing Reality	DIACHRONIC TIME	SYNCHRONIC TIME	STRATEGIC TIME

Shifting between two phenomenologically based typologies – one of utopian communal groups and a second of social organization – opens up the possibility of pursuing a historical phenomenology of modernity, a genealogy of apocalyptic movements, and an assay of the contemporary Apocalypse.

A phenomenology of modernity

First, let us consider a historical phenomenology of the modernizing established social order, in order to foreshadow the connections between history and Apocalypse. Among diverse writings on modernity, historical sociologist Peter Wagner (1994) offers a point of departure congruent with phenomenological assumptions, for Wagner talks not of modernity as a 'thing' or 'stage' of history, but of 'modernizing projects' – collective efforts realized only incompletely across space, that remain unstable over historical time. This approach avoids reification. It allows us to locate modernizing projects typologically as social complexes in relation to an emergent array of *natural* and *produced* enactments temporally organized through *synchronic* and *diachronic* schema. In turn, we can trace the relationships of these complexes to history and the apocalyptic.

* Along the *synchronic* temporal dimension can be found the realm of face-to-face daily life, community (ethnos), and their sacred events of communion. In contrast to the utopian possibility of transcendental ecstatic association, within the established social order, the experience of the transcendental typically is mediated by religious practitioners and experienced only indirectly or fleetingly.
* The *produced-diachronic* realm is that of the rational organization and administration of social life and its culture – what Jürgen Habermas (1987) describes as the '*system*' that *colonizes* the lifeworld of synchronic experience – either natural, or produced within communities.

Several intermingled streams of modernizing projects are especially important in structuring the social and cultural content of these phenomenologically mapped possibilities.

- One early modern stream of what might be called 'proto-colonization' can be located in the *diachronic infrastructural organization of lifeworldly action* via rationalization and routinization, for example agricultural practice (e.g. in the draining and consolidation of fields), road networks, market towns, and economic calculation and accounting.
- A second stream of modernizing projects is to be found in the *mass distribution of meanings and the reconstruction of the self*, both to sustain 'traditional' identities and allegiances on a mass scale (e.g. via the medieval Catholic mass) and, subsequently, to formulate and diffuse modern identities suited to gearing into a diachronically organized world, in the Protestant Reformation forging of an industrious work ethic appropriate to proto-industrial and industrial capitalism.
- In a third stream (theorized both by Habermas and by Foucauldian analysts interested in 'governmentality'), the locus shifts away from the self-disciplining individual of Weber's Protestant ethic and into power-centered and economic organizations concerned with the 'colonization of the lifeworld', and the 'containment' and 'regulation' of the new individual liberty so necessary to the functioning of emergent apparati of production and labour, social organization, participation in markets, and social institutions of private life.
- Fourth, following the work of Jean Baudrillard, what may be called postmodernizing projects establish *simulacra* that reorganize the relationship between diachronic system and synchronic simultaneity by shifting from colonization to a kind of *absorption* of lifeworldy gearing-in of action into an administratively and/or computer-created synchronic reality.

Diverse historical sociologists have analyzed these and related shifts. Their analyses would be important to consider; but even without doing so, we can offer an initial characterization of modernity in phenomenological terms.

Overall, modernity comprises a complex web of relations between fundamentally alternative forms of life. There is the intersubjectivity (and sometimes, as Schmalenbach (1977) noted, 'communion') of everyday social life, the administrative logic of legal–rational bureaucracy, and the (religious, ethnic, status-group, national, or even democratic/civic/state) community that engages in 'collective' action. Social life in the modern world largely unfolds in relation to a shifting set of natural and produced enactments, with individuals and groups only occasionally moving beyond, to the transcendental realm of experience. In that much of the character of this world is 'produced', that is, framed in relation to relatively durable institutional patterns and logics of action, we may speak of an *established social order*.

Yet modernity obviously is not exhausted by the possibilities I have mentioned so far. An adequate account additionally requires consideration of politics and war, colonialism and empire. In phenomenological terms, these considerations point to the temporality in which events build upon one another in competition and conflict, what I have called strategic time. Focusing briefly on world-historical strategic time, it is possible to locate theories of modern domination, empire, and world economy phenomenologically. What matters, to mention two major theorists – Lenin and Wallerstein – is that the international hierarchy of states in relation to economic organizations is structured not only by institutionalized patterns organized through economic, state, and extra-state regimes of formal association, but also by the strategic exercise of force via imperialism. The modern rise of diachronic time has facilitated economic calculation, routinized production, and the administration of rule-based organization and law. But it is the operation of imperialism that underwrites and expands the domains of calculable diachronic time. Central to imperialism is strategic conflict, which unfolds in the time of 'History'. Whereas diachronic temporality predominates in organizing modernity, modernity necessarily unfolds within multiple and intersecting temporal horizons, for which the strategic time of History is central to the uneven fates of various modernizing projects.

A genealogical phenomenology of the Apocalypse

Under normal circumstances, the term 'Apocalypse' would seem overwrought as way of referring to historical time, for Apocalypse is permeated with the idea of a cataclysmic conflict resulting in the 'end of history' and the beginning of a timeless utopia. However, if and when utopian mentalities spread broadly in concrete social movements, this very duality offers a basis for theorizing the temporal structurations of such movements. Thus, German social critic Walter Benjamin (1968: 263) noted that a historical moment can be shot through with 'chips of messianic time'. Yet messianic time is not all of a piece; there is the time leading up to a decisive conflagration and the time afterwards, what I defined above as pre-apocalyptic and post-apocalyptic time.

- *Post-apocalyptic* time is, ideologically, the dreaming of a world of perfection so complete that time, especially the strategic time of history, is erased. In utopian efforts to enact such a circumstance, life is orchestrated as a supposedly timeless heaven on earth. While such a tableau is the putative goal of many revolutionary movements, in practice it is mostly enacted by small 'other-worldly sects', and even there the tableau is typically most important as a *legitimization* of social arrangements that bear a quite different temporal character.
- On the *pre-apocalyptic* side, in relation to strategic temporality, when there is a strong ideological construction of crisis, a situation is depicted as so dire that meaningful actions oriented toward that crisis become imbued with a sacred legitimization. One widespread pre-apocalyptic organizational form centres on religious repentance and conversion before the 'final day of judgement'. The more strategically intensive pre-apocalyptic trajectory is that of the 'warring sect', which engages in apocalyptic war to hasten the dawn of the New Age.

As utopianists under the latter dispensation see it, the end of history can come only through a conflict in real historical time, and the warring sect makes inaugurating such a conflict its sacred enterprise. As I described such a sect in *The Ways Out*:

A band of true believers, who become certified as charismatic warriors through a process of rebirth, acts alone or in concert with a wider underground network of sympathizers and similar bands. These warriors engage in the moment-to-moment coordination of guerilla-style action in pursuit of strategic, symbolic, and terrorist missions. The members of the sect come out of the quiescent masses to act in historical significance far out of proportion to their actual numbers. ... The successful execution of actions related to missions and contingency plans depends on interpersonal trust, the development of high proficiency at various technical and strategic skills, and acts of commitment and bravery which place mission ahead of personal survival. (Hall 1978: 206–7)

This, then, is the locus of 'holy war'.

Phenomenologically, all modes of temporality and enactment are socially contingent, and in this, the apocalyptic is no different from, for example, diachronic modernizing projects (which I took care to describe in terms that avoid reification). The Apocalypse thus is not an omnipresent reality; rather, it is an extreme, utopian form of temporal enactment that, when it arises, is experienced by those caught up in its mentality as enveloping their meaningful lives. Yet we would be mistaken to treat apocalyptic phenomena as imaginary or unreal, for they have the same ontological status as other socially constructed realities, in that individuals in concert with one another can act meaningfully in relation to them. Therefore, apocalyptic social realities can be considered in empirical terms in just the same way as 'bureaucracy' and 'community'.

There is a broad and deep history of apocalyptic 'awakenings' – ably traced by scholars such as Norman Cohn, Ronald Knox, and Gunter Lewy. These would include the ancient Jewish quest for a Promised Land, the historical experiences that must have accompanied the New Testament Apocalypse of Saint John the Divine, the medieval Christian Crusades in the Levant, and apocalyptic elements in the Protestant Reformation and the sixteenth- and seventeenth-century wars of religion. Of particular note, in the Crusades, there was a shift within Western Christianity toward legitimizing apocalyptic action by groups approximating the warring sect. Whereas theologians previously had insisted on keeping the carnage of war separated from the works of the Church, in the Crusades a specifically *religious* military organization – the Knights Templar – emerged. As St Bernard saw it: 'The soldier of Christ kills safely: he dies the more safely. He serves his own interest in dying, and Christ's interests in killing!' (quoted in Partner 1982: 8).

A religio-military social organization of the sort heralded by the medieval Knights Templar could have directed European history along the track of what Weber (1978: 1159–63) described as 'hierocratic' religious rule of the secular world. But as Lewis Namier has suggested, religion is a sixteenth-century word for nationalism (Hechter 1975: 67). With the Protestant Reformation, pan-national religious civilization became displaced by an emergent pattern of absolutist states legitimized through national religion that sometimes had a quasi-apocalyptic cast. In these developments, S.N. Eisenstadt (1999: 46) argues, it was the specific *combination* of class and religious intellectuals and their sectarian movements that propelled European revolutions towards modernity. Thus, England's seventeenth-century millennialist Fifth Monarchy Men anticipated the secular Jacobin totalistic urge of the French Revolution to make the world anew, according to a utopian plan.

One of the major modernizing projects has been to 'tame' apocalyptic and eschatological expectations – to 'close the book' on religious prophecy on the basis of procedures of rationalization and routinization that would, as Weber put it, 'demystify' social life. In the aftermath of the European sixteenth- and seventeenth-century wars of religion, by the late eighteenth century, religious apocalypticism became pacific, often channeled through utopian communalism, sometimes tied to migration, by which people sought to come to grips with the displacements and challenges of rapid social change. Emblematic of these possibilities is the apocalyptic retreat to an other-worldly utopia of Mother Ann Lee's Shakers, who, believing the Second Coming of Christ to be imminent, forswore procreation.

Yet religious pacification spelled not the end of the apocalyptic but its realignment. As Eisenstadt (1999) argued, certain religiously infused cosmologies and legitimizations of sacred violence that preceded modernity became inserted into modern terrorism. More broadly, by the latter eighteenth century, revolutionary violence became centered in political movements increasingly shorn of religious trappings – the American Revolution, the French Revolution, and, during the nineteenth and twentieth centuries, Marxist-inspired communist movements and revolutionary anarchism. Marx and Engels famously dismissed utopian communal socialism (which would include both other-worldly sects and secular demonstrations of 'worldly utopias') as distractions. The central axis of History would be class struggle in the unfolding strategic time of 'this' world.

These developments consolidated *secularized* apocalyptic struggle as a dominant feature of modern society. Within the core nation-states of the capitalist world economy, messianic religion as any conduit of violence lay largely dormant. With religious prophecy deemed closed, charisma, when it arose, played out within secular political movements. By the 1960s, some theologians would follow Nietzsche's lead, affirming the 'death of God' in the collapse of any sacred framework for social life under the sign of modernity. Others hoped for a rebirth of the sacred.

The re-enchantment of the world
If theologians of the 1960s could have foreseen the future, they might have pulled back from seeking re-enchantment of the world. For with hindsight we can see that over the course of the twentieth century two broad conduits of Apocalypse – secular–political and religious – again became intertwined, as they had been at the late medieval/early modern conjuncture, yielding a new, postmodern apocalyptic epoch. Modern secular political apparati and technologies of violence scaled up to a level of destruction that can only be deemed apocalyptic.

- The Nazi regime carried out mass, bureaucratically organized genocide, exterminating over 5 million people.
- The United States dropped atomic bombs on Nagasaki and Hiroshima in August 1945, resulting in a death toll of over 200,000.[1]
- The Cold War, frequently portrayed by Western protagonists as a struggle against godless Communism, became a global conflict shadowed by the potential for nuclear holocaust.

Communism crumbled, largely 'from within', in part due to the kind of corruption of violence that Merleau-Ponty anticipates in *Humanism and Terror*. Soviet violence lost its 'progressive' rationale, and a façade of ideology justified brutality empty of anything beyond the will to dominate. It was in the wake of the Cold War's end that Francis Fukuyama (1992) could boldly announce 'the end of history' and the inevitable triumph of free-market democracy.

How could Fukuyama have got it so completely wrong? In a nutshell, he failed to anticipate the power of religion to organize violence in a way that rises, as Merleau-Ponty puts it, to the level of History, that is, violence beyond any institutionalized framework of legitimization, that shakes the world to the roots of its inhabitants' understandings. Religious apocalypticism surged during the latter part of the twentieth century on two broad fronts – within the developed world, and in what used to be the Third World. In the West, even as theologians announced the death of God, the divine was resurrected – in oddly contradictory ways. The theologians correctly anticipated the increasing absorption of meaningful life into the sphere of consumption organized under the sign of commodity fetishism. But they did not anticipate the (largely American) apocalyptic dialectic between evangelical Christianity and the counter-culture.

The great irony of recent American history is that the once socially marginal religious movement of Christian fundamentalism trumped the death of God through a strange ideological admixture that juxtaposed millenarian anticipation of the 'end times' and antipathy towards government, nevertheless coming to exercise an extraordinary influence in mainstream American cultural and political life. In relation to the anticipated apocalyptic 'end times', the movement promoted the Second Coming to organize conversion projects, and it engaged in increasingly militant – and mainstream – political campaigns against practices culturally abhorrent to conservative values, such as abortion and gay marriage.

Conservative American apocalypticism gained energy in part by becoming a counter-reformation to the second broad movement of Western apocalypticism during the latter part of the twentieth century, the counter-culture of the 1960s and 1970s. Indeed, some elements of the conservative movement – the radical fringe of the anti-abortion movement and Christian survivalists – mimicked the violence initiated on the left. Broadly construed, the counter-culture encompassed both the New Left and alternative lifestyle movements – in their most concentrated forms in utopian communal groups. The potential for sacred utopian violence surfaced anew in both political and communal counter-cultural arenas. Politically, various groups approximating what I have termed the 'warring sect' emerged, advancing ideologies akin to Huey Newton's Black Panther Party doctrine of 'revolutionary suicide' – death to one's previous self constructed within racist capitalism, and rebirth to a revolutionary struggle that would end only in victory or death. Groups such as the Weather Underground and the Symbionese Liberation Army engaged in the exemplary violence of the warring sect, the actions of which they hoped would simultaneously further 'the Revolution' and inspire others to like-minded actions.

A different kind of violence sometimes erupted in relation to utopian communal groups. The most dramatic episodes, in the USA and elsewhere, concerned those groups that established the strongest boundaries dividing themselves from the everyday world of the established social order, namely, post-apocalyptic other-worldly sects. In such groups, participants came to believe that they had 'escaped' from the clutches of the old world left behind, sometimes not least importantly from their parents. In the most extreme incidents involving other-worldly sects, collective violence resulted from cultural conflict with group opponents centered on custody of children and accusations of cultural deviance (Hall, Schuyler, and Trinh 2000). Thus, 918 people died in the murders and mass suicide orchestrated by Peoples Temple at Jonestown, Guyana, in 1978. In a similar way, in 1993, 74 members of the Branch Davidians died in a fiery conflagration at Mount Carmel, Texas, when they refused to surrender to US government agents who had laid siege to their compound.[2]

As dramatic as counter-cultural apocalyptic violence could be, apart from attacks instigated from within the New Left, they involved relatively isolated groups and lacked much in the way of wider historical import. However, one religious movement, Aum Shinrikyo in Japan, demonstrated the potential of apocalyptic violence on a broader scale. In the 1990s the inner leadership of the group came to construe Aum Shinrikyo as a pre-apocalyptic warring sect that might achieve its grandiose goals of ridding Japan of the neo-colonial domination of the United States and ruling Japan themselves. Aum Shinrikyo gathered a far more imposing arsenal than either Peoples Temple or the Branch Davidians, including biological and chemical weapons. They regarded technologies of violence as tools not just to defend themselves during the Apocalypse, but as instruments to *precipitate* the public disaster that would *be* the Apocalypse. Compared with more secular New Left warring sects of the 1960s and 1970s – groups such as the Weather Underground and the Baader–Meinhof gang – Aum Shinrikyo was distinctly religious. And at least in its grandiose vision, it marked a transition from the *asymmetric* struggles of the Jonestown community and the Branch Davidians as small, geographically isolated communal compounds against a more powerful legitimized and territorially extensive state. Aum's was a putatively *symmetric* struggle as a sect that proclaimed equal legitimacy with the established order that it opposed (Hall, Schuyler, and Trinh 2000: 106–10). In these features, Aum Shinrikyo's programme begins to approximate the Apocalypse as, in Merleau-Ponty's terms, *historical* violence, and a harbinger of the possibility of world-historical apocalyptic struggle.

Quite independent from the strands of renewed apocalyptic violence that surfaced in the developed world after the 1960s, there are deeper roots of apocalyptic religion, and ones more directly linked to geo-political contestations, in the messianic movements that arose in opposition to colonialism – for example in the Mau Mau rebellion and in Rastafarianism. Mostly, such movements did not effectively challenge colonial rule. However, at the beginning of the twenty-first century, with the collapse of communism, and with the worldwide growth of radical Islamism, the curtains have parted on a new and unprecedented *globalized* epoch of apocalyptic violence.

Contemporary religious violence lies outside the normative institutional framework of modernity, but it just as surely has emerged under conditions of modernity, and as a distinctive modern form of collective action. Apocalyptic religious terror now portends a new construction of modernity's empire. In the eighteenth century, the Apocalypse became secularized; now, it has become reinfused with a sacred character.

The Apocalypse of the twenty-first century

The terrorism carried out by al-Qaeda and allied Islamist movements is quintessentially action by 'warring sects' that operate in pre-apocalyptic time. The ideology of al-Qaeda promotes a holy war to avenge sacrilege. As detailed in the September 1996 Declaration of Jihad against the United States, the sacrilege includes: the stationing of US troops in Saudi Arabia near the holiest Muslim cities; the US-led 1991 war against Iraq after it invaded Kuwait; Israeli control of the city of Jerusalem; and, most generally, the defeat of the Ottoman empire some 80 years ago. In the ideology of radical Islam, sacrilege requires a specifically religious response of military *jihad* – a holy war. Of greatest significance, with the emergence of al-Qaeda an earlier Islamist theology of struggle against the 'nearest enemy' became displaced by a broader war against the crusader infidels. This theological shift has relocated terrorism from subnational and national arenas to a global one.

If the *ideology* of al-Qaeda and allied movements is broadly apocalyptic, questions remain as to whether militant Islamist *organization* and *actions* are also apocalyptic, and in turn, whether specifically apocalyptic characteristics make any difference in the jihadist struggle against the United States and the West. The temporal structure of apocalyptic ideology promises transcendence to eternity through victory or death. But the temporal structure of action by the warring sect takes the form 'of a ... Manichean battle between the forces of good and evil' (Hall 1978: 206). Apocalyptic war is unconventional war, not just because it involves a struggle pursued by armies and police and intelligence operatives against networks of underground cells. Rather, the contemporary Islamist struggle exceeds conventional political violence, and it positions terror as a technique in civilizational struggle that targets the established global order itself.

Yet the religious yoke of apocalyptic war is lightly worn. As Max Weber observed concerning warriors for the faith – from Muslims and Crusaders to Sikhs and Japanese Buddhists – 'even the formal orthodoxy of all these warrior religionists was often of dubious genuineness' (1978: 475). Participants in a holy war will be a diverse lot, varying in their religious sophistication and commitment. The sources of *jihad* as a doctrine among alienated religious thinkers and members of Arab professional classes show that the movement did not originate among the ignorant, the poor, or the dispossessed. Still, like medieval Christian crusaders, frontline operatives of al-Qaeda and its allies participate in a struggle infused with religious meaning without necessarily being saints themselves.

What leverage do we gain by analysing contemporary global militant Islamism in relation to the concept of the warring apocalyptic sect? After all, military strategy substantially depends on the assets and vulnerabilities of parties to a conflict. For terrorism in general, manoeuvres are dictated by the realities of a situation in which one party comprises an underground network of operatives. In the case at hand, these realities do not depend on whether radical Islamist forms of organization approximate the warring sect as an ideal type.

Yet compared to more secular insurgent movements, the theoretical distinctions about warring sects do throw into relief three features relevant to understanding the distinctiveness of contemporary militant Islam: ideology, internal organization, and external context.

- As opposed to Carl von Clausewitz's formulation of war as 'the pursuit of politics by other means', the *ideology* of apocalyptic war is diffuse and utopian in its goals, and it thereby warrants actions by *religious martyrs*. (Although much research has been directed to suicide bombers, their seamless connection to apocalyptic war has not been well understood, and the tendency has been to psychologize or instrumentalize the phenomenon.)
- Organizationally, the diffuse *decentralized network* of al-Qaeda and its allies is sustained through the *charismatic community of a warring sect* warranted by an apocalyptic ideology; such charismatic cells are more durable and more flexible, and more capable of independent action than other military organizations.
- As a 'counter-cultural' phenomenon, apocalyptic war is sustained by the connections between warring sects and a wider *oppositional milieu*.

These three features – apocalyptic ideology, decentralized organization, and connection to a wider counter-culture – could simply be empirically noted. But they are not independent: they tend to reinforce one another as a meaningful logic of collective action by groups approximating the apocalyptic warring sect.

However, apocalyptic war does not unfold as a one-sided series of terrorist actions. Rather, it is an *interactive* process. As was suggested in *Apocalypse Observed*:

> States face a delicate situation: they are duty bound to control the acts of strategic apocalyptic war, but to the degree that they do so, they become apocalyptic actors themselves. The problem that states confront is how to act strategically without feeding images of the state as an actor in an apocalyptic drama. (Hall, Schuyler, and Trinh 2000: 200)

As events since 2001 have demonstrated, even an implicit 'holy war' undertaken by the USA and its allies creates formidable challenges of its own, for a Western holy war frames conflict in terms that mirror those of al-Qaeda and kindred networks. Because rhetoric – and, especially, events on the ground – construct the conflict in these terms, in the Islamic world the struggle increasingly has come to be viewed as a *symmetric* one between *two* apocalyptic parties – each claiming good, righteousness, and God on its side – rather than a conflict between a global modern social order in which Muslims share a stake versus a fringe Islamist movement whose acts of terror will be rejected as illegitimate by most Muslims. In the current situation, each side becomes party to a crusade, whether explicitly declared, as by al-Qaeda, or more ambiguously invoked and pursued, as with the US administration and its allies.

The military and diplomatic mobilization initiated by the United States against militant Islamist networks has been enormous. With the war in Iraq, the initial calculation was that the USA need not worry about whether its actions might legitimize the Islamist view that the USA is a 'crusader' state. In this calculation, overwhelming military force was supposed to 'render perception immaterial'.[3] Yet the miscalculation in this calculation is now painfully apparent. Military and diplomatic strategies – the crux of empire in modern theories – may not bring success against an apocalyptically oriented opponent. The warring sect's ideology of revolutionary martyrdom, its organizational decentralization, and its counter-cultural support make defeating Islamist terrorism militarily extremely difficult, if not impossible.

A number of observers have questioned whether the terminology of a 'war on terrorism' makes any sense. Yet the terminology is more ideological than anything else. The strategy of the USA and its allies in the conflict with radical Islam certainly includes a strong military component, but overall it cannot usefully be construed as 'war', and is better understood through the post-structuralist conception of 'policing' advanced by Martin Coward (2005). Coward argued that empire can be understood as a Foucauldian governmental regime. *Internally*, policing organizes the structure of empire on an increasingly global basis that transcends boundaries of national sovereignty. But empire must also be defined at its *boundaries*. Thus, a second kind of policing is practised in relation to the empire's 'barbarian others'. Rather than seek military victory, an empire deploys policing strategies that define the otherness of its enemies, and thus maintain 'the fiction of the universal civility of Empire by excluding the alterity that might expose such a fiction'.

In the conflict between the USA and its allies and radical Islam, this dual policing strategy operates on multiple fronts, many of which are relatively distant from any direct conflict with religious terrorists themselves – tightening security, controlling immigration, and aggressively gathering and filtering intelligence. Beyond these conventional policing activities lie the more diffuse Foucauldian policing practices aimed at (post)modern biopolitics – of 'nation-building' efforts toward the consolidation of national governments in Afghanistan and Iraq, and the development of institutions of governance that regulate and facilitate everyday life through state and NGO development projects.

However, to the degree that the contemporary conflict has become a *symmetric* apocalyptic war, the tidy formula of policing empire becomes under pressure. Under symmetric conditions, both parties are able to assert roughly equivalent but competing claims of legitimacy, typically operating out of different territorial strongholds. The very boundaries of an empire's state-like monopoly on legitimate violence thus are at stake in symmetric apocalyptic war. In Coward's terms, this development 'risk[s] exposing the universality of imperial rule as a fiction' (2005: 863). For the West, an Orwellian prospect is unveiled: *jihad* and the 'war' against it fuel one another in ways that erode civil liberties within empire and more broadly consolidate an international security state and a globalized and increasingly integrated apparatus of surveillance. In all this, the social fabric of institutionalized Modernity is substantially, and probably permanently, altered.

Phenomenologically, the temporal construction of 9/11 and its aftermath is now the hinge on which modernity and empire are constructed. For the empire of modernity, the challenge is not to 'win' an apocalyptic war. Rather, it is to move the historical moment *beyond* the contemporary epoch, in which apocalyptic war is the overarching temporal construction of History. An apocalyptic war cannot be won, at least without undoing the character of the very established order that is being defended. Thus, the task for the established order is to defuse the apocalyptic times, and reorganize modernity/ empire as a new configuration of relations among institutions of democracy and governance in relation to everyday life, and to accomplish this not just within nation-states encompassed by empire but precisely at the boundaries where the governing reach of empire is particularly problematic.

Yet just as certainly as the empire of modernity is best served by seeking to transcend the Apocalypse through governmentality, its Islamist opponents see such governmentality as a key target. We only need to note the strategies being followed by al-Qaeda operatives and their allies generally, and the insurgents in Afghanistan and Iraq specifically, to understand this point. In a conventional war, attacks against aid workers, tourist destinations, journalists, and representatives of NGOs would amount to senseless and barbarian violence, and certainly this is the incontrovertible view within the established social order. But in the Islamist war against the empire of modernity, victory in the first instance motivates challenging governmentality in all its forms, military and otherwise – manifestly in the destruction of the World Trade Center, but also in actions against the postmodern simulacratic construction of the world as a tourist destination, generalized source of entertainment, and available domain for the spread of Western culture – from Christian missions, to universities, to McDonald's. Truly, the dialectic of Apocalypse and modernity is the stamp of our epoch.

Conclusion

In this chapter I have proposed a phenomenology of social temporality to explore the interconnections of modernity, Apocalypse, and empire. This historical and structural phenomenology of modernity and the apocalyptic is still very much a sketch. But it has the merit of considering religion and violence directly, unencumbered by the normative assumptions of any given historical institutional complex. As Merleau-Ponty saw in Communism and its adversaries, regrettably, we must recognize the multiple sources of sacred violence in current geo-political struggles – coming from the West, especially the United States, as well as from Islamists. And like Merleau-Ponty, we must recognize that whether any of this violence is 'progressive' is an open question, not one that can be answered simply by referencing the values of Western liberalism or any putative 'essential' violence of Islam.

In Merleau-Ponty's terms, we have entered a new 'epoch' – according to his definition, a moment in which the 'meaning' of violence remains undefined, awaiting the 'objective' moment when victory and the return to (a different) normalcy define 'truth'. History, its agents and witnesses, and their failures and successes are now beginning to answer questions that are no longer anything close to 'academic'. Only with Reason can we avoid Merleau-Ponty's grim dystopian world of adventurism and a 'senseless' tumult, or what we might call 'the new dark ages'.

CHAPTER 2

Martyrs and Martial Imagery: Exploring the Volatile Link Between Warfare Frames and Religious Violence

Stuart Wright

In the growing climate of religious violence and terrorism we find at its core a belief-system charged with ubiquitous images of divine warfare. The freighted meanings underlying the construction of conflict as a holy struggle have potentially perilous consequences for prospects of peace and political stability, whether in the Middle East or in Western democracies. It is important to understand how religion can effectively fuel violence and exacerbate hostilities by invoking divine imprimatur on what are essentially ethnic, tribal, or political conflicts.

I want to suggest that the linking of religion to 'warfare' and the framing of political conflict in terms of a 'sacred struggle' elevates violence to a moral imperative. Under these conditions, violence becomes sacralized as a heroic act and a religious duty. Armed combat is defined as a sacramental rite and combatants cast as 'holy warriors'. The crusade, the inquisition, the *jihad*, or the intifada assume deep religious symbolism and meaning; they are launched as a defence of faith, to defeat and expel an enemy whose very existence poses a grievous threat. The political opponent becomes not merely a challenger or contestant in a struggle for material resources and power, but an army of evil minions charged with destroying all that is good. The conflict is rhetorically constructed as a war between good and evil, light and darkness, God and Satan. The danger here is that warfare is *sacralized* as an instrument of divine justice, and compromise is equated with selling out to the devil. Not to fight is to lose one's soul. To fight and to die is to become a martyr.

By exploring the link between religion and warfare framing, I hope to explain how parties in political conflict become polarized and how the spiral of religious violence is propelled upward, particularly when *both* sides in a conflict adopt this strategy of conferring martial imagery on a cosmic scale.

Framing and social construction of meaning

'Framing' refers to the process by which social actors engage in 'meaning-work' or 'signification' – the struggle over the production and maintenance of ideas (Snow and Benford 1992: 136). The verb denotes an active, process-driven exercise that infers agency and contention at the level of reality construction (Snow and Benford 1992: 136). It is derived from the conceptual referent 'frame', which is defined as 'an interpretive schemata that simplifies and condenses the "world out there" by selectively punctuating and encoding objects, situations, events, experiences and sequences of actions within one's present or past environment' (Snow and Benford 1992: 137). In social movement theory, 'collective action frames' are emergent action-oriented sets of beliefs and meanings that inspire and legitimize social movement activities and campaigns. They empower movement actors to articulate and align a wide array of events and experiences so that they are integrated and blended in a meaningful way. Collective action frames function as filtering and collating mechanisms to encode, decode, and 'package' portions of observed and experienced reality. Substantively, collective action frames may accentuate or amplify the gravity and injustice of a particular social condition that has previously been defined as merely unfortunate. Or they may redefine a circumstance, an event, or policy as unjust and intolerable, making salient something that was ignored by society or political authorities. A 'striking amount of convergence' regarding content or substance of collective action frames highlights the central theme of injustice, indicating to some that 'collective action frames are *injustice* frames' (Gamson 1992: 68).

The effective linkage of individual and social movement organization interpretive frames is a process referred to as 'frame alignment' (Snow et al. 1986). Frame alignment entails a subset of strategic mechanisms that include bridging, amplification, extension, and transformation. Frame bridging refers to the linkage of two or more ideologically congruent but structurally unconnected frames regarding a particular issue or problem. Frame amplification refers to the clarification and invigoration of an interpretive frame that bears on an issue, problem, or set of events. Frame extension denotes the expansion of a primary framework to encompass interests or ideas incidental to its primary objectives, but of considerable salience to potential adherents. Frame transformation involves alteration or reconstitution of the problem constructed by elites or dominant groups (Snow et al. 1986).

An implicit function of framing is assigning causality or blame for an unjust action, condition, or event. In this regard, Snow and colleagues contend that collective action frames serve as modes of attribution, which specify 'diagnostic', 'prognostic', and 'motivational' tasks (Hunt, Benford, and Snow 1994; Snow and Benford 1992). 'Diagnostic framing' assigns blame for some problematic event or condition by designating 'culpable agents'. It entails imputing characteristics and motives to those who are seen as having 'caused' or compounded the problem. Culpable agents are then cast as villains, culprits, or 'enemies'. 'Prognostic framing' identifies or outlines a plan of amelioration, including an elaboration of specific targets and strategies, and the assignment of responsibility for carrying out the action. Finally, 'motivational framing' provides the appropriate rationales for action or 'vocabularies of motive', which 'entails the social construction and avowal of motives and identities of protagonists' (Hunt, Benford, and Snow 1994: 191). Taken together, these framing tasks assign blame, impute motive, identify targets, and propose strategies for action.

War framing

War can be defined as open armed conflict between hostile parties or nations. War framing then delineates the rules of engagement in conflict. In the spectrum of conflict, war represents the most intense state of hostilities. Armies are trained to kill, and warfare is understood as a violent struggle to destroy an enemy. Violence is justified as a necessary force to protect one's nation or tribe and repel a threat. War framing designates culpable agents as soldiers or warriors, identifies targets and strategies to defeat the enemy, and memorializes those who give their lives in service to their country. Killing, which is ordinarily condemned in peace-time conditions, is lionized during wartime.

Social science research on killing during wartime suggests that soldiers have to be trained to create moral and cultural distance between themselves and a defined enemy. This entails a process of systemic desensitization in which soldiers are taught that killing the enemy is an act of justice. The enemy's culpability is determined so that he must be punished and the legitimacy of one's own cause affirmed. 'Moral distance establishes that the enemy's cause is clearly wrong, his leaders are criminal, and his soldiers are either misguided or are sharing in their leader's guilt' (Grossman 1995: 164). Whether for freedom, independence, self-determination, or democracy, war framing endows the struggle with virtue and moral courage in the face of killing, aggression, and violence. Cultural distancing accompanies moral distancing and involves a dehumanization of the enemy in preparation for inflicting harm or death. The more familiar or similar the victim of aggression, the more difficult it is to inflict harm. Conversely, the more dissimilar and unfamiliar the enemy, the easier it is to kill. According to military psychologist Dave Grossman, 'It is so much easier to kill someone if they look distinctly different from you. If your propaganda machine can convince your soldiers that their opponents are not really human but are "inferior forms of life", then their natural resistance to killing their own species will be reduced' (1995: 161).

Pulitzer Prize-winning journalist Chris Hedges, who has covered insurgencies and wars in Bosnia, Kosovo, El Salvador, Nicaragua, the Persian Gulf, the West Bank, and Iraq, makes a pertinent observation: 'We demonize the enemy so that our opponent is no longer human,' he writes. 'We view ourselves, our people, as the embodiments of absolute goodness. Our enemies invert our view of the world to justify their own cruelty' (Hedges 2002: 21). He cites Lawrence LaShan's work, *The Psychology of War* (1992), which differentiates between 'mythic reality' and 'sensory reality' in wartime. Mythic reality imbues the struggle with sacred symbols of a cosmic battle between good and evil. It elevates the conflict to a mythical level of cosmology, spawning images of a triumphant victory and a grand moment of individual and collective transformation. It is a narrative filled with images of heroic conquest and reworkings or reinterpretations of archaic warrior myths. The sensory reality of war, however, tears away at the mythic veneer and exposes the brutality, carnage, and destruction of war. The direct experience of war on the ground stands in stark contrast to the mythical war, producing legions of dead, wounded, and psychologically scarred individuals whose sacrifice fades with the passing of time.

Dehumanization or demonization of the enemy takes the form of what Grossman calls 'pseudospeciation': the classification of a victim as an inferior species (Grossman 1995: 209). This devaluation of the opponent's humanity decreases the inhibition to kill and inflict harm. Grossman found that military training during wartime often incorporated a systematic inculcation of this attitude. Denigrating terms used to identify an enemy (gook, slopehead, Kraut, towelhead, *Untermensch*) by military trainers and personnel illustrate the exercise of pseudospeciation. One consequence of this type of training is that American military missions abroad sometimes involve military crimes, human rights violations, or other atrocities (Chomsky 1991; Klare and Kornbluh 1988; Marshall, Scott, and Hunter 1987) that build up 'reservoirs of resentment' and can create a kind of 'blowback' (Johnson 2000: 5, 8) or retaliation by targeted groups. The American imperial impulse to control foreign political powers or protect economic interests often entails a propagandizing of troops to believe that the military mission is undertaken to 'promote democracy' and defeat its enemies, thus legitimizing brutal aggression and violence.

In my interviews with the Oklahoma City bomber, Timothy McVeigh, he told me that during the Persian Gulf War his army unit would intentionally run over wounded Iraqi soldiers they encountered in the desert with Bradley tanks. They referred to the Iraqi soldiers as 'crunchies' because their bodies crunched under the weight of the tanks as they drove over them. He later complained that the troops were 'falsely hyped up' to kill the Iraqis, but found out in combat that they were 'normal like me and you'. In another interview with a journalist in 1997, he said he 'felt the Army brainwashed us to hate them' (Franklin 1997: 138). A psychiatrist who later examined McVeigh for trial, Dr John Smith, suggested that the Desert Storm veteran may have returned home with post-traumatic stress disorder. McVeigh's increased anger at the federal government following his decorated military service abroad indicates that he struggled with his own 'reservoir of resentment'. His eventual adoption of the belief that the American government was 'at war' with its own citizens was a key motivation in his insurgent consciousness leading to the bombing of the federal building in Oklahoma City in 1995 (Wright 2007).

The degree to which McVeigh viewed the conflict between the state and Patriots as 'war' was expressed in his own words in a letter to Fox News on 26 April 2001, only a few months before his execution. In this letter, McVeigh offered a military rationale for the bombing and drew a comparison to US foreign policy in a manner that clearly evoked a form of blowback.

> Additionally, borrowing a page from US foreign policy, I decided to send a message to a government that was becoming increasingly hostile, by bombing a government building and the government employees within than building who represent that government. Bombing the Murrah building was morally and strategically equivalent to the US hitting a government building in Serbia, Iraq, or other nations (see enclosed). Based on observations of the policies of my own government, I viewed this action as an acceptable option. From this perspective, what occurred in Oklahoma City was no different than what Americans rain on the heads of others all the time, and subsequently, my mindset was and is one of clinical detachment. (The bombing of the Murrah building was not personal: no more than when Air Force, Army, Navy or Marine personnel bomb or launch cruise missiles against government installations and their personnel). ('McVeigh's April 26 Letter to Fox News')

Curiously, the injustice framing of this insurgent act against the US government bears a striking resemblance to some of the statements made by Osama bin Laden, as I hope to show. Both McVeigh and bin Laden strategically frame their political violence as a *defensive* action aimed at repelling enemy aggression. In another part of the letter, McVeigh states: 'This bombing was also meant as a pre-emptive (or pro-active) strike against these forces and their command and control centers within the federal government. When an aggressor force continually launches attacks from a particular base of operation, it is sound military strategy to take the fight to the enemy.' Similarly, bin Laden rails against the US bombings in Iraq, Afghanistan, and neighbouring Muslim states on the Arabian Peninsula and calls for 'defensive *jihad*' in response to the aggression of the USA and its allies (Wiktorowicz and Kaltner 2003: 80). 'So, as they [the USA] kill us, without a doubt we have to kill them', bin Laden has said, 'until we obtain *a balance of terror*' (2005b: 114, emphasis mine).

Religion, war framing, and violence

Mark Juergensmeyer in his seminal work, *Terror in the Mind of God*, makes a compelling case for the explosive link between religion and war framing. 'What makes religious violence particularly savage and relentless', he observes, 'is that its perpetrators have placed such religious images of divine struggle – cosmic war – in the service of worldly political battles. For this reason, acts of religious terror serve not only as tactics in a political strategy but also as evocations of a much larger spiritual confrontation' (Juergensmeyer 2000:146). Religion is a dynamic force that is frequently marshalled to mobilize aggrieved or disenfranchised populations against perceived enemies. From a social movement perspective, religious militants believe that the world is already at war and thus devise theological explanations for deprivation. By employing eschatological beliefs, political turmoil and economic hardship may be interpreted as having much broader significance. The felt oppression, suffering, and frustration of the disinherited breeds an impulse of violence which can then be channeled into a righteous crusade through the skilful frame-bridging efforts of movement leaders (Stern 2003). Young males in particular can be recruited as soldiers of God and are more likely to and act out their aggression towards a defined enemy.

While religion is often associated with reforms, awakenings, and more constructive forms of social change, it has also been at the root of some of the greatest evils and injustices – war, genocide, massacres, crusades, witch hunts, ethnic cleansing. The troubling paradox here is that religiously motivated violence can be fiercely barbaric and vicious precisely because it purports to be defeating evil. An explanation of this paradox is offered by James Aho in his book *This Thing of Darkness*: 'Evil grows from the quest to defeat the enemy, however understood. ... My violation of you grows from my yearning to rectify the wrong I sense that you have done me. Violence emerges from my quest for good and my experience of you as the opponent of good' (1995: 11). The invocation of God and religion lays claim to the use of violence as an instrument of divine punishment or judgment. The devout individual feels justified in acting violently towards that which is evil; joining a campaign to defeat evil becomes a high calling.

This principle can be seen in the statements of al-Qaeda leaders, particularly its founder, Osama bin Laden. Only a few weeks after 9/11, bin Laden issued a videotaped statement calling the perpetrators of the World Trade Center and Pentagon attacks 'a group of vanguard Muslims' at the forefront of Islam 'whom God has blessed to destroy America'. That he construed or framed the attacks as a visitation of God's judgment on America was made clear in his opening statement:

Here is America struck by God Almighty in one of its vital organs, so that its greatest buildings are destroyed. Grace and gratitude to God. America has been filled with horror from north to south and east to west, and thanks be to God. What America is tasting now is only a copy of what we have tasted. (Lincoln 2003: 102)

Bin Laden went on to describe the desecration of the holy sites Mecca and Medina by the 'infidel' US troops stationed in Saudi Arabia during the Gulf War. The literal Qur'anic denotation of the term infidel is 'enemy of the faith'. 'Every Muslim must rise to defend his religion,' bin Laden declared. 'The wind of faith is blowing and the wind of change is blowing to remove evil from the Peninsula of Muhammad, peace be upon him' (Lincoln 2003: 103). According to a study by Bruce Lincoln (2003: 28), of the 584 words bin Laden uttered in his 7 October statement, 101 were plainly religious and many more carried subtler Qur'anic meanings.

In fact, the warfare imperative framed in religious language and imagery characterizes bin Laden's jihadist campaign from the beginning. In his Declaration of Jihad issued on 23 August 1996, bin Laden was careful to ground in religious texts the call to war against the infidel alliance. According to bin Laden, martyrs are synonymous with soldiers in the jihadist war frame. The best holy warriors must hold the battle line and embrace death in faith.

And the Prophet said: 'There are one hundred levels in Heaven that God has prepared for the holy warriors who have died for Him, between two levels as between the earth and the sky.' And the *al-Jami al-Sahih* notes that the Prophet said: 'The best martyrs are those who stay in the battle line and do not turn their faces away until they are killed. They will achieve the highest level of Heaven, and their Lord will look kindly upon them.' (2005a: 29)

In this same declaration, bin Laden goes on to assure the faithful that martyrdom in the service of the holy war is precious in the sight of God and will be given special honour in the next life. Among the heavenly rewards cited by bin Laden is the now infamous reference to the seventy-two virgins awaiting the martyred:

The martyr has a guarantee from God: He forgives him at the first drop of his blood and shows him his seat in Heaven. He decorates him with the jewels of faith, protects him from the torment of the grave, keeps him safe on the day of judgment, places a crown of dignity on his head with the finest rubies in the world, marries him to seventy-two of the pure virgins of paradise and intercedes on behalf of seventy of his relatives, as related by Ahmad al-Tirmidhi in an authoritative *hadith*. (2005a: 29)

In another declaration proclaiming the formation of the World Islamic Front and co-signed by bin Laden's trusted lieutenant Ayman al-Zawahiri, the call to violence against the American infidels s is even more specific. Americans, both military and civilian, are cast as 'soldiers of Satan' and the decree to kill civilians freely in the name of God is clearly articulated:

To kill the American and their allies – civilians and military – is an individual duty incumbent upon every Muslim in all countries, in order to liberate the al-Aqsa Mosque and the Holy Mosque from their grip, so that their armies leave all the territory of Islam, defeated, broken, and unable to threaten any Muslim. This is in accordance with the words of God Almighty: 'Fight the idolaters at any time, if they first fight you'; 'Fight them until there is not more persecution and until worship is devoted to God.'

With God's permission we call on everyone who believes in God and wants reward to comply with His will to kill the Americans and seize their money wherever and whenever they find them. We also call on the religious scholars, their leaders, their youth, and their soldiers, to launch the raid on the soldiers of Satan, the Americans, and whichever devil's supporters are allied with them, to rout those behind them so that they will not forget it. (bin Laden and al-Zawahiri 2005: 61)

It is also important to note the propensity of bin Laden to invoke the concept of the 'crusade' in his statements and speeches, referring primarily to American and Israeli forces. The notion of the crusade linguistically captures the coalescence of religion and war, the advancement of religion through military means. Bin Laden offers a strategic framing of the jihadist position; he is able to point to the overt religiosity of Bush administration officials as proof of a religious war. In an interview with Taysir Alluni, one of al-Jazeera's most celebrated reporters, in October 2001, bin Laden makes this point explicitly. He appropriates Bush's own words to champion the radical belief that violence used to enforce Islam is justified. The idea of a mutually declared war by both parties framed in religious terms is invoked to remove any doubts about the necessity of violence:

So Bush declared in his own words: 'Crusade attack.' The odd thing about this is he has taken the words right out of our mouth [that this war is a crusade]. ... So the world today is split in two parts, as Bush said: either you are with us, or you are with terrorism. Either you are with the Crusade, or you are with Islam. Bush's image today is of him being in the front of the line, yelling and carrying his big cross. And I swear by God Almighty that whoever walks behind Bush or his plan has rejected the teachings of Muhammad, and this ruling is one of the clearest rulings in the Book of God and the hadith of the Prophet. (bin Laden 2005b: 121–2)

Later in the same interview, Taysir Alluni makes the following statement to bin Laden: 'Your constant use and repetition of the word "Crusade" and "Crusader" shows that you uphold this saying, the "Clash of Civilizations".' Bin Laden replies, 'I say that there is no doubt about this. This is a very clear matter, proven in the Qur'an and the traditions of the Prophet, and any true believer who claims to be faithful shouldn't doubt these truths, no matter what anybody says about them' (bin Laden 2005b: 124). Indeed, bin Laden uses the terms 'Crusade' or 'Crusader' nineteen times in the interview. In several instances he refers to the 'Crusader Wars', lest there be any doubt about the meaning of the crusade.

Religious vocabularies of motive pervade all of the statements by bin Laden and other al-Qaeda leaders. In the final instructions to the 9/11 terrorists found in the luggage of Mohamed Atta, the purported leader of the attack, repeated references were made to God and cited passages in the Qur'an. 'Pray during the night', Atta wrote, 'and be persistent in asking God to give you victory, control and conquest, and that He may make your task easier and not expose us.' Elsewhere, Atta invokes a more martial imagery to inspire the terrorists:

> When the confrontation begins, strike like champions who do not want to go back to this world. Shout 'Allahu Akbar', because this strikes fear in the hearts of the non-believers. God said: 'Strike above the neck, and strike at all of their extremities.' Know that the gardens of paradise are waiting for you in all their beauty and the women of paradise are waiting, calling out, 'Come hither, friend of God.' (Lincoln 2003: 93)

The same principle of warfare attribution applies to acts of domestic terrorism in the USA. I have already made reference to McVeigh's statements and beliefs. His thinking echoed the sentiments and fears of the militia and Patriot movements that emerged in the 1990s. I argue in a new book that these far-right anti-government movements mobilized in response to the state's increasingly militarized war on crime and drugs, particularly as it turned towards gun raids, producing such incidents of misfeasance as Ruby Ridge and Waco (see Wright 2007). The central premise in the book is that a *mutual* and *reciprocal* framing of the conflict as 'warfare' contributed to an upward spiral of violence: the state defining its efforts as part of a war on crime and right-wing anti-government groups defining their efforts as a paramilitary response to a state-imposed war on its own citizens. Patriot organizations and actors came to believe the government was 'at war' with them as the mode of enforcement of firearms laws increasingly took the form of gun raids by paramilitary police units and the number of those raids rose significantly over a brief span of time in the early 1990s (see Kraska 2001; Kraska and Kappeler 1996). Both parties to the conflict – challengers and state actors – perceived an increasing threat posed by the other and redoubled their efforts to repel the danger. The reciprocal threat attribution produced an escalation of violence as Patriot insurgents bombed the federal building in Oklahoma City believing it was the moral equivalent of the government's actions at Waco.

A survey of other domestic terrorist groups in the USA that have linked religion and warfare framing is revealing. Robert Mathews and the Order was one of the most violent. Mathews was an Odinist who infused the ideal of 'Aryan warriors' with mystical power and meaning. Order members formed a blood covenant marked by an oath which stated in part: 'My brothers, let us be his battle ax and weapons of war. Let us go forth by ones and two, by scores and by legions, and as true Aryan men with pure hearts and strong minds to face the enemies of our faith and our race with courage and determination' (Flynn and Gerhardt 1989: 126). The Order engaged in a fifteen-month campaign of violence that culminated in a shootout with the FBI. During that period, Order members robbed banks, several electronics stores, a truck stop, a video store, and armoured trucks. Mathews' group also bombed a synagogue in Boise, executed a

Patriot, Walter West, for failing to protect the secrecy of the group, and assassinated a Jewish talk-show host, Alan Berg.

Mathews formed his violent underground cell at the 1983 Aryan Nation World Congress convened at Richard Butler's Idaho compound. Butler was founder of the Aryan Nations and a key leader in the Christian Identity movement. He also established his own church, Jesus Christ Christian Church, based on Identity principles. At the 1983 Congress, the groups hosted by Butler declared the infamous 'War in '84' against the US government. In addition to Mathews' group, participants included former national Klan leader Robert Miles, who had his own Identity church in Cohoctah, Michigan; Louis Beam, who formulated the widely adopted 'leaderless resistance' strategy among anti-government groups; and James Ellison's Covenant, Sword and Arm of the Lord (CSA) of Arkansas. Ellison was also an Identity believer and founder of the Zaraphath-Horeb Community Church, out of which the CSA evolved. It was CSA member Kerry Noble who penned the War in '84 declaration at the 1983 Aryan World Congress. Like the Order, the CSA also engaged in a campaign of violence during this time. CSA members set fire to a gay church in Springfield, Missouri; bombed a Jewish community centre in Bloomington, Indiana; attempted to blow up a gas pipeline near Fulton, Arkansas; shot and robbed a pawnbroker; planned the assassination of a federal judge, a prosecutor, and an FBI agent; and killed an Arkansas state trooper. The FBI laid siege to the CSA compound on 19 April 1985, ten years to the day before Timothy McVeigh blew up the Murrah federal building in Oklahoma City.

Other domestic terrorist groups employing a religious warfare frame include William Potter Gale's Posse Comitatus, Colonel Jack Mohr's Christian Patriots Defense League, Identity minister James Wickstrom's Tigerton Dells Church, Matthew Hale's World Church of the Creator, Eric Robert Rudolph, a self-confessed soldier in the Army of God, Reverend Paul Hill, a Christian Reconstructionist linked to Operation Rescue, the Phineas Priesthood, and a host of Christian Patriots, militia, Freemen, white supremacy and Identity groups.

Conclusion

In all these cases I have described, the appropriation of religion for violence is a common theme. The linking of religion to 'warfare' and the framing of political conflict in terms of a 'sacred struggle' ennobles violence and treats it as a spiritual duty. Yet this is not solely a strategy of insurgents and terrorist groups; it is also a strategy of states in wartime in an effort to gain the higher moral ground. The Bush administration's affinity for religious framing of conflict after 9/11 bears this out, devising a putative 'axis of evil', among other things, in which the USA and its allies are engaged in a Manichaean struggle of apocalyptic proportions. Bruce Lincoln's thoughtful analysis underscores the problem of this tactical approach by the USA: 'Both Bush and Bin Laden indulge in "symmetric dualisms"' where 'Sons of Light confront Sons of Darkness, and all must enlist on one side or another, without possibility of neutrality, hesitation, or middle ground' (2003: 20). Bin Laden divides the world into two camps, the camp of the faithful and the camp of infidels. President Bush follows the same pattern, 'pressing a complex and variegated world into the same tidy schema of two rival camps. The orienting binaries of this structure – good/evil, hero/villain, threatened/threat – are much the same for Bush as for bin Laden' (2003: 20). It is this mutual and reciprocal demonization of adversaries through religious warfare framing that helps fuel an escalation and upward spiral of violence.

A strategy of conflict resolution and cessation of violence, therefore, must take into consideration a deconstruction of warfare framing and invocation of divine mandates. I believe scholars of religion can play a critical role in this regard by helping policy makers understand the harm they inflict on the cause of peace and political stability by engaging in religious warfare framing of conflict, particularly in the Middle East.

The advocacy of martial violence as a religious mission is problematic but not hopeless. The violent jihadist position is a contested minority view based in part on the premise that the USA and its allies are waging war against Islam and that their campaign of violence therefore is essentially a 'defensive *jihad*'. As such, it feeds off the reciprocal warfare language and actions of US political and military leaders. Since many Islamic scholars, parties, and organizations do not condone violence or support the jihadist approach (Wiktorowicz and Kaltner 2003), it would be advisable for the purpose of foreign policy strategy to de-escalate militaristic threats and rhetoric and redouble efforts to exact a *political* solution to the conflict. This strategy has the advantage of robbing extremists of propaganda for the *jihad* while leveraging Islamic reformists in their attempts to discredit groups such as al-Qaeda.

CHAPTER 3

Violence and New Religions: an Assessment of Problems, Progress, and Prospects in Understanding the NRM–Violence Connection

J. Gordon Melton & David G. Bromley

In attempting to assess the state of theory and research on religion and violence as it relates to new religious movements (NRMs), it is important to begin with the observation that this project has been historically and politically shaped. The systematic study of the connection between NRMs and violence emerged out of the incident involving the murder–suicides by the Peoples Temple in 1978. There was an immediate spate of media coverage and a series of popularized, largely sensationalistic books about the incident (Kerns with Wead 1979; Kilduff and Javers 1978; Krause and Johnston 1978; Mills 1979; White, Scotchmer, and Shuster 1979), with only a limited amount of scholarly commentary at the time (e.g. Galanter 1978; Moberg 1978). The possibility of a comparison with the Manson Family murders was noted, but scholars have always found limited analytic utility in treating the Manson Family as a religious movement (Melton 1979). Although there had been some prior incidents of violence involving schismatic Mormon groups and a mass suicide by the Old Believers, for example, it was some time before potentially comparative cases were identified and incorporated into scholarly analyses (Wessinger 2000; Robbins 1986, 2000). What did occur over the next several years was the publication of a series of scholarly treatments of the Peoples Temple that offered much more systematic, theoretically grounded analyses (Richardson 1980; Levi 1982; Hall 1987; Chidester 1988; Moore and McGehee 1989). Still, at this point the Peoples Temple episode was treated largely as an isolated incident and approached as a case study. It was a critically important case in the development of the study of new religions and violence, however, since it was fuelled by and in turn reignited the 1970s cult controversy. Indeed, one of the most important features of the initial popular media coverage of the Peoples Temple episode was the attempt to introduce violence as one of the defining characteristics of 'cults' (e.g. Carroll and Bauer 1979). The image of violent cults was to significantly influence subsequent popular commentary and scholarly research on violence episodes.

The salience of studying the connection between NRMs and violence changed dramatically twelve years later as several violent incidents occurred in rapid succession, beginning with the Branch Davidian murder–suicides at Mount Carmel outside Waco in 1993, and followed by the Solar Temple murder–suicides in Switzerland and Canada in 1994, the Aum Shinrikyo murders in Tokyo in 1995, and the Heaven's Gate collective suicide in California in 1997. Only three years later in Uganda the Movement for the Restoration of the Ten Commandments of God engaged in a major episode of murder–

suicide. This series of incidents simultaneously created additional cases for analysis and more urgency to consider possible NRM–violence connections. The agenda was, of course, to change again in 2001 as the study of the salience of violent Islamic groups moved to the forefront of attention.

In this chapter we trace the progress that has been made in theoretical and empirical work on the connection between NRMs and violence as well as issues that continue to be explored. Theory and research in this area have developed by working through a series of issues. As the 1990s progressed, scholars initially focused on the dimensions of the problem and the nature of the issues to be analysed. Once the focus of analytic interest was clarified, scholars began to propose theoretical models that would permit an integrated understanding of episodes of violence. The third set of issues, which are currently emerging, involves how to incorporate more recent groups and events into the study of NRMs and violence.

Specifying the focal issues

The study of the connection between NRMs and violence began with little context, and so there were a number of foundational issues to be addressed. Two of the most important have been distinguishing different forms of violence, with the objective of identifying the form that is of focal analytic interest, and assessing the dimensions of the new religions–violence connection.

One of the first problems new religions scholars encountered was how to conceptualize the form of violence to be explained. It is very important to recognize that there is no single explanation for violence generally, since there are many distinct forms and levels of violence. This is well recognized in the criminology literature, for example, where there are very different explanations for different types of homicide (such as mass murder, serial killings, mercy killings, murder-for-hire, passion killings) as well as different levels of intent (ranging from premeditated murder to accidental homicide). The same observation can be made for the suicide literature.

Religious violence is equally diverse. It may occur at an interpersonal level – violence committed against a member by another member, of a member by a non-member, or the reverse. To date there is no systematic evidence that would suggest that NRM members are more or less likely to engage in or be the victims of interpersonal violence. However, it is clearly the case that if violence involving an NRM member does occur, it is more likely that the member's religious status will become part of the public record than would be the case for members of more established religions. Violence, individual or collective, may or may not have a religious purpose. Examples of religiously relevant individual and collective violence would include assassination and schismatic killings. While interpersonal violence is not irrelevant to understanding the violence–NRM connection, it has become clear that the most immediate agenda is to understand collective violence. By collective violence we refer to violence that is undertaken by individuals in the name of the group, whether a religious movement or a control agency, and is legitimized in terms of some organizational purpose. In general, the study of collective violence has been limited to incidents in which there have been multiple fatalities, although there is no theoretical reasoning to support any particular level of fatality.

The other issue that presented itself to new religions scholars studying violence was the assumption, largely growing out of the cult controversy, that there is a simple, direct connection between new religions and violence. There are several aspects to this assumption. One is that violence is pervasive among NRMs. As the area of New Religions Studies has emerged, scholars have become increasingly aware of the large number of new religious movements both in Western societies and around the globe. There are now at least 2,500 distinct religious groups in the United States alone, with about half of those being non-traditional groups (Melton 1998). If the new groups in South America, Asia, and Africa are included, it is clear that the number of new groups would be many times greater. Despite this very large number of groups, there have been fewer than two dozen instances of collective violence over the last several decades, and these cases are quite diverse. In terms of incidents that have now been analysed in which movements have positioned themselves in opposition to the existing social order and engaged in some combination of homicide and suicide, there was one episode in Japan (Aum Shinrikyo), one in Europe (Solar Temple), two in the United States (Branch Davidians and Heaven's Gate), and one in Africa (Movement for the Restoration of the Ten Commandments).

The assumption of a direct link between NRMs and violence also rests on the presumption that new religions can be easily and categorically distinguished from established religions. In fact, most NRMs have some cultural and organizational connection to established religious traditions. For example, among groups involved in violence Aum Shinrikyo derives from Buddhism, the Branch Davidians from Adventism, and the Movement for the Restoration of the Ten Commandments from Catholicism. With respect to other well-known movements, Hare Krishna derives from Bengali Hinduism, the Church Universal and Triumphant from Theosophy, the United Order from Mormonism, Happy, Healthy, Holy from Sikhism, and Mahikari from Shintoism.

Finally, if one compares the episodes that have been used to support the violence pervasiveness among NRMs argument with cases of violence in which established religious groups are involved, it becomes clear that violence is much more frequent and deadly with respect to the latter. Through European history, for example, there was a long succession of crusades, persecutions of heretics, and witch-hunts. Currently there is ongoing violence involving Sunnis and Shiites in Iraq, Israelis and Palestinians in the Middle East, Muslims and Hindus in India; Muslims and Christians in the Sudan, Christians and Muslims in Indonesia, and Tutsi and Bantu tribes in Rwanda.

As scholars began to consider the NRM–violence issue, it became clear that there are in fact a variety of types and levels of violence, and that conflating these would hinder theoretical progress. A primary focus has developed on collective violence incidents, those in which violence is perpetrated under group auspices for organizational purposes and which result in multiple deaths. If episodes of collective violence are surveyed historically, it becomes clear that NRMs are not disproportionately represented among such cases, either in terms of frequency or scope. That is, there is no direct connection between religious newness and violence. Once this conclusion is reached, it becomes productive to examine cases that do occur for theoretical linkages.

Creating an analytic framework

As the nature and magnitude of the new religions and violence issue was clarified, scholars turned attention to identifying social and cultural factors that might be connected to collective violence. As opposed to conceptions of NRMs as violence prone, new religions scholars have developed models more consistent with the study of violence in other contexts. Violence is a form of social interaction, and new religions scholars have explored episodes of collective violence from an interactional perspective. This approach entails examining the ideologies and actions of the opposed parties and each party's interpretations of the other's ideologies and actions. Two of the most fully developed models analysing episodes of collective violence involving NRMs have been proposed by Hall, Schuyler, and Trinh (2000) and Bromley (2002).

Hall, Schuyler, and Trinh (2000) identify several movement characteristics that may create a tendency towards violent confrontation: an apocalyptic world-view; charismatic leadership; high levels of internal control; and intense internal solidarity that produces isolation from the surrounding society. However, they argue that such movement characteristics do not necessarily yield violence; they insist that it is the interactive relationship between a religious movement and social order that is the critical factor in whether or not violence eventuates. In this model, violence emerges out of tension between a movement and external opponents, who frequently have included relatives of converts, apostate members, and groups that oppose 'cults'. These opponents then may be able to mobilize media representatives, who can shape the public image of a movement, and political leaders, who possess access to sanctioning power. Since collective violence may be internally or externally directed, Hall, Schuyler, and Trinh specify two alternative apocalyptic scenarios. They term the first a warring Apocalypse of religious conflict. This type entails an escalating tension between movement and a coalition of opponents that ultimately results in a violent confrontation. The second type, a mystical Apocalypse of deathly transcendence, involves less external opposition (at least as perceived by outsiders), but the group chooses collective relocation to a transcendent realm where its legitimacy will from their perspective receive appropriate recognition.

Bromley (2002) develops a socio-historical theory that describes movement–society conflict as building through several stages: latent tension; nascent conflict; and intensified conflict. The escalation of conflict is contingent and not inevitable as both sides possess alternative options to contestation; either side may choose an accommodative response to defuse conflict by lowering demands, or acceding to demands, or a retreatist response that creates social or physical distance between the two sides. In the event that conflict does polarize and destabilize during a period of intensified conflict, both movements and oppositional groups heighten mobilization and radicalization, allies enter the conflict and form coalitions, and each side begins to regard the other as 'dangerous' rather than merely 'troublesome'. Various factors foster polarization and instability, such as symbolic and physical threats, internal radicalization, secrecy, organizational consolidation/fragmentation, and elimination of third parties. Under these conditions a climactic moment, a dramatic denouement, may transpire when one or both sides conclude that their core identities and collective existence are being subverted and that the situation is intolerable. This moment leads one or both parties to engage in a final reckoning that will restore their understanding of appropriate moral order. As in Hall, Schuyler, and Trinh's model, there are two possible responses: Exodus and Battle. The former involves an orchestrated, collective withdrawal to alternative space through which the exiting group rejects the established social order and asserts its moral superiority. By contrast, the latter consists of organized combat that represents an acknowledgement that the conflict will only be resolved through force. In both cases the parties reject continued coexistence in the same space under existing conditions.

Exploring the internal dynamics of violence

The creation of interactional models of collective violence has been useful in highlighting the dynamics of NRM–societal violence, delineating how each responds to the actions of the other as well as perceptions of the other's actions. At the same time, a number of scholars have pointed to the internal characteristics of NRMs that are associated with movement–societal tension, although not necessarily conflict. Among the characteristics of NRMs most consistently linked with violence are apocalyptic–millennial ideologies, charismatic leadership, and totalistic organization. For the most part, analyses have focused on these characteristics separately but have not identified a dynamic that would link these, or other, characteristics together. Galanter is one of the few scholars to have constructed a model around primarily internal characteristics of movements (1999: 179–84). He identifies four conditions linked to extreme cultic violence: isolation (through geographical separation or constant mobility); leader grandiosity (a high need for total control) and paranoia (a fear of loss of control resulting from paranoia) that leads to a siege mentality; absolute dominion (intense regulation of members' daily lives); and government mismanagement (primarily a failure of government agencies to exercise appropriate social control measures). However, there is little consideration of the dynamics that link these four conditions.

We argue that the kinds of interactional models developed by Hall, Schuyler, and Trinh and Bromley are critical to understanding collective violence because the interests and identities of parties to the conflict are developed and sustained relative to one another. At the same time, an emphasis on interactional dynamics does not obviate the importance of the internal dynamics transpiring within both parties. In order to advance the specification of internal dynamics, we first review theorizing on apocalyptic–millennial ideologies, charismatic leadership, and totalistic organization. We then examine the cases of Aum Shinrikyo and Heaven's Gate in search of a common dynamic.

Apocalyptic–millennial ideologies

Apocalyptic–millennial ideologies most generally share an expectation that there will be a categoric break in historical time and that transformational moment, attended by a struggle between transcendent forces of good and evil, will be followed by the initiation of a new chapter of cosmic history. Groups with apocalyptic–millennial ideologies are likely to regard the current social order as corrupt and doomed to destruction, reject it as illegitimate and evil, and separate themselves from it symbolically and physically. Such groups are also likely to envision a new order, one that displaces the values of the current order and one in which they will play a prominent role. There are various versions of apocalypticism–millenarianism. Wessinger (2000) identifies 'catastrophic millennialism', an extreme form in which the world is depicted as evil, degenerating, and on the verge of destruction by transcendent forces. A related concept is Anthony and Robbins' (1997) 'exemplary dualism', in which social, political, or religious groups perceive conflicts between them as representing a clash of absolute good and evil.

In general, the more radically polarized a movement's world-view, the more likely the group is to maintain a high level of tension with the outside world, to perceive itself to be persecuted or at risk, and to separate itself from what it regards as a corrupt and moribund social order. In addition, the way that the timing and relationship of transcendent and human influence in the transformative moment are constructed is also an important factor in apocalyptic–millennial ideologies. In the Christian tradition, distinctions often are drawn between 'pre-millennial' scenarios (in which transcendent intervention in the form of the Second Coming of Christ will precede the establishment of a divine kingdom because humanity has become incapable of saving itself) and 'post-millennial' scenarios, which envision human initiative preparing the proper conditions for transcendent intervention. Depending on how time before the transformational moment is shortened or lengthened and the balance between human and transcendent responsibility for initiating that moment, religious groups will perceive varying degrees of imminence and involvement in producing that change. While there is general agreement that apocalyptic–millennial ideologies increase polarization with conventional society, such conflict does not necessarily translate into violence. There are a great many religious groups, including those in the evangelical Christian tradition, that share major elements of apocalyptic–millennial thought but exhibit no proclivity to violence.

Charisma
Tracing back to the work of Max Weber (1964), charisma is a form of leadership that rests on individuals being perceived as endowed with extraordinary qualities, displaying those qualities, maintaining an intense personal relationship with followers, and organizing a highly cohesive group in which they possess great authority. The assertion that charisma is a perceived quality is critical, as this means that both followers and leaders play a role in creating and sustaining charismatic authority. Charismatic authority is regarded as more precarious and volatile than more institutionalized forms of leadership since it is not embedded in tradition or a stable social context. Given the lack of institutional and traditional legitimization, charismatic leaders and their followers are continuously involved in the process of shaping the nature and degree of charismatic authority.

The instability of charismatic leadership is often attributed to the psychological characteristics of these leaders. While such factors are hardly irrelevant, the charismatic form can be understood from an interactional perspective as presenting a number of management problems, as Dawson (2002) has pointed out. Leaders must maintain their charismatic personas. Preserving the requisite aura of mystery means that leaders frequently distance themselves from followers, which can produce isolation and the kind of instability that results from an inability to obtain realistic feedback. Followers may over-identify with leaders, which can lead to an escalation of tension with outsiders if the leader is publicly denounced. Charismatic leaders can resist institutionalization of leadership through such tactics as creating constantly changing conditions, creating crises, suppressing dissent, and increasing demands for loyalty in order to maintain authority. Such tactics can increase movement instability and the likelihood of extreme actions. Finally, since charismatic leaders are dependent on being perceived as possessing extraordinary qualities, they may experience pressure to produce ever more extreme performances, such as prophecies or increases in group membership, that solidify followers' belief in movement ideology.

As in the case of apocalyptic–millennial ideologies, charisma cannot be directly linked to violence. Virtually all institutions incorporate elements of charisma into leadership positions in some fashion, and there are countless charismatic leaders through history who have shown no inclination to violence. It does appear, however, that if charismatic leadership is destabilized or in the process of disintegrating, this situation can contribute to the instability within a movement and create the potential for more extreme actions. Since the charismatic leaders are the single most influential individuals in movements, their personal and positional stability is a significant factor in shaping increases or decreases in movement volatility.

Totalistic organization
There is a long history of studying organizations that set themselves off physically, socially, and psychologically and demand high levels of individual commitment. Convents, monasteries, communes, custodial mental hospitals, maximum security prisons, and elite military units are all examples of such organizations (Dornbusch 1955; Kanter 1972; Coser 1974). These groups employ a variety of resocialization mechanisms along with social encapsulation to heighten the commitment of members and create distance from the outside world. This kind of radical distancing from conventional society and intensified internal cohesiveness is one of the noteworthy characteristics of many new religious groups, particularly those that organize communally. When groups encapsulate individuals ideologically and socially, individuals may find it more difficult to sustain independent critical assessment of and reflection on their personal motives and actions as well as those of the group as a whole. If such groups have an unusually high capacity for unified action and reduction of dissent, there is a heightened probability for radical actions of various types. Particularly for religious movements that have developed an apocalyptic–millennial scenario and have adopted a highly polarized world-view, totalism may create a potential for violent confrontation that less unified groups do not possess. Totalism, however, is always a matter of degree, and groups typically empirically exhibit various mixes of characteristics. In fact, most totalistic groups, including those with apocalyptic–millennial ideologies, do not exhibit a propensity for violence.

Comparing the Aum Shinrikyo and Heaven's Gate cases
The Aum and Heaven's Gate cases are particularly instructive because they contain the three internal characteristics hypothesized as violence inducing: apocalyticism/ millennialism; charismatic leadership; and violence. In these cases, of course, violence did in fact ensue. However, in many other groups with the same characteristics, violence did not occur. Further, in these two cases the violence, while collective in nature, moved in opposite directions. From an interactional model perspective, the violent outcome in the Aum case approximates what Hall, Schuyler, and Trinh refer to as the warring Apocalypse and Bromley refers to as Battle; the violent outcome in the Heaven's Gate case approximates what Hall, Schuyler, and Trinh refer to as a mystical Apocalypse of deathly transcendence and Bromley refers to as Exodus. The question, therefore,

is whether internal dynamics can be identified that distinguish these two cases from others in which violence did not transpire, but that are common to these two cases despite the fact that the violence is differentially directed.

The Aum Shinrikyo is a useful example of the importance of internal dynamics in leading to a confrontational stance towards the dominant social order. The movement was established by Asahara Shôkô in 1984 after he became disenchanted with the Agonshû movement. Within a decade Aum had been transformed from a relatively mundane meditation and healing movement to a group that initiated lethal violence by placing nerve gas in the Tokyo subway system in 1995 (Reader 2000). Like many other NRMs, Aum developed a theology that rejected the dominant social order and anticipated an impending apocalyptic moment. Asahara taught that the pervasive materialism of conventional society produced negative karma that would consign individuals at death to the hells and to subsequent unfavourable rebirths in their future lives. The solution was to acquire psychic powers that would neutralize negative karma generated by life in materialistic society through the ascetic practices that Asahara taught. This basic orientation, while radical, was not particularly problematic either for the movement or for its relationship with the social order.

However, subsequent developments within Aum simultaneously heightened tensions within the movement and increased its confrontational posture towards conventional Japanese society. Aum taught that an apocalyptic confrontation between good and evil could be avoided and a new spiritual age could be realized peacefully only if Aum were successful as a movement. Asahara stipulated very specific criteria for success that had to be achieved by the dawn of the new millennium, establishing two centres in every nation in the world and creating 30,000 spiritually advanced beings. The movement began training a contingent of spiritually enlightened individuals (*sangha*) and establishing a network of communal villages where the *sangha* would reside. The movement had now placed itself in the position of having to achieve extraordinary success in a brief period and having predicted cataclysm if it did not. Given the movement's requirement for novitiates to sever contact with their families as well as all other past relationships, live communally, and engage in highly ascetic practices, it is not surprising that it was unsuccessful in either recruiting a large number of converts or establishing branches abroad. As it became evident that Aum would not be able to achieve its objectives, Asahara adopted a strategy employed by many movements: revising expectations. He asserted that the unresponsiveness to his message had condemned humankind to destruction and that only the Aum faithful could be saved. Thereafter, the severity and coerciveness of ascetic practices increased, and the new requirements were legitimized on the basis that they were essential to practitioners' spiritual welfare as they constituted the sole path to salvation.

While the group had now retreated, turned inward, and thoroughly rejected the established social order, it was not yet in direct confrontation with the outside world. The movement's confrontational stance began unintentionally when the extreme ascetic practices in which Aum had become engaged resulted in the accidental death of a practitioner. This event had profound implications, both internal and external. The death posed an internal challenge to Asahara's charismatic claims as well as to the group's theological claim that its ascetic practices would lead to salvation. When movement leaders decided to cover up the death to protect the group's image, it was in fact in conflict with the state. Only the initial success of the cover-up delayed that confrontation. More ominously, the group reinterpreted its ideology to legitimize the killing by asserting that only the most worthy would be saved. It also became more unstable as its viability now depended on consensual, unanimous secrecy. When a practitioner with knowledge of the initial death threatened to defect, the group decided to eliminate that threat and in the process moved from concealing an accidental death to premeditated murder. This killing, in turn, was legitimized by using the previously developed rationale that coercion of practitioners was justified when it increased the individual's welfare, in this instance by preventing the victim from accruing the bad karma that would derive from discrediting Aum. It now became permissible to kill other individuals, including outsiders, who represented a threat to Aum. That eventuality soon presented itself. When Aum opponents formally organized and their legal representative began investigating Aum, the potential for exposure of past crimes resurfaced. Asahara responded by ordering the killing of the lawyer and his family. The mounting toll of murder victims and the elimination of individuals whose killing would logically be connected to the movement dramatically increased Aum's vulnerability.

At the same time, Aum's efforts to gain legitimacy were self-destructing. The increasing insularity of the group intensified tensions, particularly with relatives of members. Opponents were successful in preventing Aum's attempt to gain legitimacy by registering under the Japanese Religious Corporations Law, although the decision was later overturned. Aum interpreted this rejection on the part of the state and the hostile media coverage as a campaign against the movement. Aum also attempted to increase its public influence by entering candidates in the Japanese parliamentary elections, but was met with a devastating rejection by voters. It was at this juncture that, faced with humiliating electoral defeat, the increasing untenability of preventing disclosure of its crimes, growing tension with the state, and an organized oppositional network, a coterie of Asahara's close disciples commenced the process of developing the chemical weapons that were to be unleashed in the Tokyo underground system.

The movement that came to be known as Heaven's Gate was founded by Marshall Herff Applewhite and Bonnie Lu Nettles (Balch 1982, 1995; Balch and Taylor 1977, 2002). Applewhite had taught music at two universities and Nettles had worked as a registered nurse before the pair met in 1972. Applewhite had been raised a Presbyterian but had been exploring various religious philosophies, while Nettles was active in metaphysical and spiritualist groups. Applewhite and Nettles immediately recognized each other as kindred spirits and became inseparable. The following year after praying and meditating they had a revelation that they were the Two Witnesses referred to in the book of Revelation who were martyred, resurrected, and taken to heaven. Their interpretation of humanity's origination departed categorically from traditional Christian theology. According to Applewhite and Nettles, humans had been placed on Earth by members of the Next Level. The biblical Jesus had been sent to 'harvest' the seeds of creation planted by the Next Level. However, Jesus found that humankind was not yet ready. Now two new individuals had been sent. Following their resurrection (the 'Demonstration'), which would provide incontrovertible evidence that they possessed the secret to overcoming death, those humans who followed Applewhite and Nettles would be transported by spacecraft to the Kingdom of Heaven where they would live as immortal, androgynous beings. They interpreted the cloud that was to transport them to heaven as a spacecraft and heaven as a physical destination that they would reach as living beings.

In order to be able to move to the Next Level, movement members had to abandon all former relationships, possessions, and sexuality. Since they believed that the time remaining before the harvest was short, Applewhite and Nettles began disseminating their message. However, their proselytization campaign was met with derision; the rejection led them to conclude that humans were being influenced by Satan, who was in fact a member of the Next Level who had turned against God; his followers attached themselves to human beings and resisted their attempts to move to the Next Level. Applewhite and Nettles then began to conclude that human civilization might have to be destroyed. When Applewhite was arrested and jailed for failing to return a hired car, he and Nettles concluded that the Demonstration was imminent.

Applewhite and Nettles, who now referred to themselves as Bo and Peep, began drawing on the counter-culture, and were successful at increasing movement membership to 200. To create the proper conditions for movement to the Next Level, Bo and Peep segregated themselves from conventional society, lived a highly encapsulated lifestyle, and focused members' attention on disentangling themselves from their human qualities. When the disappearance of members from their former lives drew hostile media coverage, Bo and Peep interpreted this as a Satanic conspiracy, went into hiding, and concluded that the harvest was imminent. During their period of separation from the group there was a substantial rate of defection.

When Bo and Peep resurfaced, this time as Ti and Do, a number of changes ensued that moved the group in the direction of isolation and withdrawal. Ti and Do announced that the harvest was over. They therefore stopped holding public meetings, and with ongoing defections the group continued to shrink in size. Ti and Do also announced that the Demonstration was no longer going to occur because the pair had been symbolically destroyed by the media, a shift in ideology that meant the group would not have to wait to move to the Next Level. The group continued its highly isolated lifestyle, living communally in rented houses and maintaining distance from outsiders when they accepted assorted jobs to support themselves. They sought to live as closely as possible to the Next Level, organizing the houses as spacecraft, ritualizing daily life to eliminate human tendencies, and spending evening scanning the sky for signs of spacecraft. Some members had themselves castrated in an effort to overcome one of the most difficult attributes of humanness to eliminate, sexuality.

Serendipitously, it appears, Ti and Do concluded that humans were actually members of the Next Level who had been placed on Earth as a training mission rather than as seeds to grow. This insight led members to conceive of themselves as immortal souls who were only temporarily occupying human bodies. This new revelation linked the members more closely to the Next Level as an 'Away Team', and essentially made them aliens on Earth. Another unanticipated event moved the group closer to contemplating departure. When Ti died unexpectedly, the group explained her death as her being recalled to the Next Level when her 'vehicle' (body) had given out. Communication between Do and Ti, now on the Next Level, confirmed that the other members would not necessarily have to make the transit to the Next Level in their physical bodies. The group also began to reinterpret the resistance it was encountering. Alongside the members of the Next Level, members concluded, there were Luciferians, actual beings who were in open combat with the Next Level and who were partly responsible for opposition to Heaven's Gate and human unresponsiveness to their message.

With the group continuing to shrink in size and responses to its public appearances meeting with an almost complete lack of interest, it sought remote locations, both in the United States and abroad, that would allow it to maintain its separateness while it awaited rescue. However, no acceptable location was found. The group began to conclude that the moment had come to depart the planet. It was at that juncture that the Hale–Bopp comet appeared, and it was rumoured that there was a spaceship behind it. The Away Team from the Next Level began its preparations to return home.

In search of a common dynamic

The two cases of violence profiled both have in common apocalypticism, totalism, and charisma, but these attributes are shared with numerous other, non-violent, movements, and yielded one case of internal violence and one of external violence. We argue that the internal characteristics are indeed significant in understanding the slide into violence, which neither group anticipated at the outset, but that it is necessary to specify the dynamic that carries movements along an ever more radical trajectory. We specify three interrelated characteristics that constitute at least one dynamic that is evident in the two cases at hand.

- The movement's goals are articulated so as to make their attainment improbable, leading to activity outcomes that are self-defeating.
- The pattern of internal activity leads to polarization with respect to conventional society, by either creating confrontation or distancing.
- Successive events leading up to the violence episode, planned and unplanned, are incorporated into the movement's ideology and legitimized (and therefore do not become the basis for disconfirmation), thereby creating the basis for more extreme actions leading to either confrontation or distancing.

Both Aum and Heaven's Gate established goals for themselves that were realistically improbable. Aum set international recruitment goals that were unattainable given the group's small size, insularity, and extreme demands on members. Further, a peaceable transition to the millennium could be attained only if the group met those goals, making movement success the key determinant of cosmic history. The movement was thus faced with unattainable goals and a challenge to its legitimacy claims when the goals were not realized. Later in its history Aum sought political influence as a means of exercising influence, despite its small size and unpopularity, with the result that it suffered humiliation at the polls. The most significant series of activities producing polarization for Aum were the planned and unplanned deaths. Moving from an accidental death, to the murder of a member, to the murder of outsiders, the movement placed itself in an inevitably confrontational position once its actions were discovered – as they almost inevitably would be. Arguably the most significant factor in the movement towards confrontation was the way that events were legitimized. The accidental death of the first member was incorporated into the movement's ideology as confirmation that only the most worthy would be saved. The first murder was legitimized on the basis that it increased the victim's welfare, and subsequent murders were justified by extensions of this same logic.

Despite the fact that violence was internally directed, Heaven's Gate presents a similar scenario. Ti and Do presented themselves as key cosmic figures, sent by extraterrestrials from the Next Level, who alone had the capacity to save humankind. There was little realistic probability that a small group with ineffective recruitment techniques and extreme demands for recruits' total commitment to the movement would elicit widespread interest, and in fact the group never grew to more than a few hundred. The group's recruitment failures led to a cessation of recruitment activities and towards more complete isolation and withdrawal, a pattern that repeated itself several times through the movement's history. As the group withdrew from conventional society, it developed a more polarized relationship with outsiders by aligning itself more closely with the Next Level, designing living quarters to resemble a spacecraft, and seeking to eradicate all human characteristics. As events unfolded during the group's final years, these events were interpreted so as to move the group progressively towards separation from earthly existence. Failed recruitment campaigns were attributed to persecution, which led to further separation and isolation. Ti's death, which could have been a disconfirming event, was interpreted as evidence that physical bodies were not necessary for the voyage to the Next Level. The appearance of the Hale–Bopp comet was interpreted as evidence that the moment for an exodus had arrived.

For both groups, then, there was a common dynamic despite the fact that the form the violence assumed differed categorically. In each case, the group engaged in patterns of action that were self-defeating, the patterns of action created a polarized relationship with conventional society, and both planned and unplanned actions were written into an unfolding script in a fashion that subverted the possibility of disconfirmation or reassessment and legitimized progressively more radical action along the same trajectory at the next decision point.

Emerging issues in the study of NRM violence

Given the progress that has been made to date in developing explanatory models for collective violence episodes, we argue that additional advances in understanding violence involving NRMs can follow from the adoption of a more comparative approach. There are several types of comparative theory and research that would be particularly promising: comparing cases in which violence did and did not occur; identifying different types of violence so that theoretical explanations focus on more homogeneous sets of events; interpreting movements as loosely coupled networks; and extending analysis to incorporate violent Islamic movements.

There are a number of cases in which NRM–societal conflict did not escalate into violence, and identifying the factors that headed off such an outcome would be useful in further developing interactional models. The Church of Scientology, for example, has invited conflict with a number of groups, such as professional psychiatric associations, the Internal Revenue Service, INTERPOL, and anti-cult associations. Although its members have engaged in illegal acts in some cases and in provocative harassment in other instances, movement members and affiliated organizations have made use of law and the courts in conflict situations. In response to federal government prosecution of its illegal actions, the movement took disciplinary action against members responsible for those actions and restructured the Guardian's Office to lower the conflict profile. Both The Family and the Twelve Tribes were the targets of police raids against their communities, with The Family experiencing a number of raids in several different nations. In both instances the groups relied on judicial processes to resolve their disputes, and both groups were exonerated of the charges brought against them. Further, both groups reorganized themselves in various ways in the wake of the confrontations. Following its seminal child custody case in England, The Family acknowledged abuses associated with its radical sexual practices, repudiated those practices, and sought reconciliation with former members. The Twelve Tribes reorganized itself by disbanding the Island Pond commune and creating a series of communities across New England as well as reaching out to the local communities in which it relocated. In the case of the Church Universal and Triumphant, the church brought in external consultants, engaged in negotiations with governmental officials, and reorganized itself in a manner that presented a less threatening profile. Such cases need to be scrutinized for factors that distinguish them from other cases in which conflict escalated into violence.

A second aspect to the comparative agenda is to identify different types of violence. The interactional models of collective violence have acknowledged a continuum of cases, with the Branch Davidians constituting the clearest example of external precipitation and Heaven's Gate the comparable case of internal precipitation. However, that continuum has been constructed on the basis of existing cases. It could be argued that the ongoing confrontation between the Falun Gong and the government of the People's Republic of China extends that continuum and constitutes an example of even greater external precipitation. It is clear that the size and resilience of the Falun Gong surprised and threatened government officials, and that those officials have greater unilateral sanctioning capacity than do American officials. The result has been a sustained repression campaign that could not be easily duplicated in most Western nations.

Another aspect of the comparative agenda is to develop theoretical perspectives that interpret movements as networks. It has been well established in the existing literature on NRMs that there frequently are deep divisions within movements. For example, in the Unificationist movement there are substantial differences between the Korean, Japanese, and American branches and between the east and west coast branches in the United States. In the Hare Krishna movement the New Vrindaban community was expelled from the movement for a time for its theological non-conformity and criminal activities; and the Brazilian homes in The Family were placed on probation for non-conformity with the movement's charter. These kinds of differences become relevant in the study of violence because violence may be limited to particular segments of movements, and these differences offer an opportunity for comparative research. It seems clear, for example, that a relatively small number of Aum members were aware of the preparations for the violence that movement leaders were about to unleash, and that the movement's affiliates outside Japan had no knowledge or involvement. Similarly, the Ananda Marga movement was involved in a number of violent incidents in India and Australia, but movement affiliates in Western societies have shown no violent tendencies.

A similar problem presents itself with respect to differentiating among radical Islamic groups. Islam exists not as a single phenomenon, but as a spectrum of widely variant 'denominations' that differ from one another every bit as much as Roman Catholics, Jehovah's Witnesses, and Mennonites differ from one another within the Christian community. Muslims are divided into Sunnis (which exist in Hanafi, Hanbali, Maliki, Shafi'i, and Wahhabi communities), Shiites, Sufis, Ismailis, etc., each of which is further subdivided by national, ethnic, and doctrinal boundaries. Within a Muslim community, the denial of any of the essential beliefs of Islam (such as the declaration of an individual other than Muhammad as a prophet) will quickly push a group to the boundaries of the culture while the adoption of patterns of behaviour that tend to separate one from the local mosque or imams (such as participation in a Sufi brotherhood) will also call a group into question. Given the prominence of Islamic doctrines concerning government, it is not strange that many of the Sunni groupings divide on issues related to their programme for society and are thus often reduced in Western eyes to mere political factions. The Islamist movement is such a set of 'politicized' Islamic groups.

Finally, there is the question of what future studies of a broader range of NRMs, and more specifically those movements involved in violence, can learn from analysis of existing cases in Westernized societies. As discussed previously, the evidence from the cases that have been analysed extensively suggest that factors such as apocalyptic–millennial ideologies, totalistic organization, and charismatic leadership have tended to be associated with high levels of tension between movements and the societies in which they operate. A question that deserves exploration is the extent to which these factors are central in understanding violence by radical Islamic movements. Similarly, the models of interactive violence posit specific dynamics of movement–societal confrontation, and the question remains as to how useful these models will be in interpreting violence in other socio-cultural contexts. To the extent that models developed in response to the incidents of violence beginning with the Peoples Temple and extending through the Movement for the Restoration of the Ten Commandments of God are applicable in other contexts, a more sophisticated and detailed general model may result. Alternatively and probably more likely, scholars may conclude that it is necessary to develop a typology of violent episodes for which related but distinct theoretical explanations are required. In either event, the understanding of violence involving NRMs will be advanced.

Conclusion

In this chapter we have argued that the study of violence involving religious movements has developed historically in response to unanticipated events. The Peoples Temple incident was treated largely as an unanticipated, rare event. The succession of incidents during the 1990s mobilized efforts to develop more general explanatory models. After defining the focal interest as episodes of collective violence and concluding that such episodes were neither common nor unique to NRMs, scholars began exploring both internal factors related to violence and interactional models that incorporated movement–societal exchanges. These models have proven useful in interpreting existing cases of collective violence but may need to be revised in the light of new types of incidents, such as the Falun Gong case in China or radical Islamic movements. We argue that additional attention to internal dynamics is necessary, and propose a specific dynamic that may tie together apparently disparate cases. Finally, we propose that additional insight on collective violence may be gained by adopting a more comparative approach, and we suggest several directions such theory and research might take. It seems likely that the greatest challenge facing scholars will be developing frameworks that connect cases of NRM violence in the West and the rising Islamic movements that constitute the most likely source of violence in the immediate future.

CHAPTER 4

Of 'Cultists' and 'Martyrs': the Study of New Religious Movements and Suicide Terrorism in Conversation

Massimo Introvigne

While many are aware both that Buffalo Bill, Colonel William Cody (1846–1917), tried to mediate in the Ghost Dance incident that eventually led to the infamous massacre of Native American 'cultists' at Wounded Knee in 1890, and that he toured Europe, including England, with his well-known Wild West Show, not many realize that the US government released into his custody those survivors of Wounded Knee who had been arrested. They became part of the Wild West Show, and in the 1890s many in Britain came to see the 'crazy cultists' who had been involved in the Ghost Dance. They were surprised to find the Ghost Dancers quite 'normal'. Some of them were, in fact, Christian (something which would have been less surprising had the media paid some attention to the influence of Christianity, both directly and through Mormon missionaries, on the Ghost Dance movement), and some even ended up marrying British girls in Christian churches. Direct contact quickly debunked the stereotype of the 'mad cultist' (see Maddra 2006, an interesting book whose only fault is to ignore the large literature on Mormon influence on the Ghost Dance.) The same is true of other 'cultists'. It is even true of 'suicide terrorists'.

In 1999, I started a study of Hamas by interviewing religious militants (and extremists) of various persuasions, police and intelligence officers, and scholars in Israel, the West Bank, and Europe. My conclusions were later published as a book (Introvigne 2003.) Contrary to many reports in the news media, I did not find Hamas militants to be 'brainwashed zombies', nor was there any evidence that most of them were mentally disturbed, poorly educated, or desperately poor. Indeed, some who declared their willingness to become 'martyrs' had better schooling, and came from more affluent families, than the average Palestinian. There were sons of doctors, lawyers, and government bureaucrats. They looked, if anything, embarrassingly normal. Some even passed my favourite test for normalcy (at least one I can apply outside the USA), i.e. were familiar with the latest events in international football ('soccer' in America).

My results were by no means unique. Nasra Hassan, a relief worker who wrote an important article in *The New Yorker*, wrote that

> none of the suicide bombers – they ranged in age from eighteen to thirty-eight – conformed to the typical profile of the suicidal personality. None of them were uneducated, desperately poor, simple-minded, or depressed. Many were middle class and, unless they were fugitives, held paying jobs. More than half of them

were refugees from what is now Israel. Two were the sons of millionaires. They all seemed to be entirely normal members of their families. They were polite and serious, and in their communities they were considered to be model youths. (Hassan 2001: 39)

A study by Claude Berrebi (2003) confirmed that, by Palestinian standards, a large majority of suicide bombers have a better than average level of schooling and of income. Alan Krueger and Jitka Maleckova broadened their analysis to include suicide bombers from Islamic groups other than Hamas, and found 'little direct connection between poverty or [poor] education and participation in terrorism' (2003: 144).

Of course, the observations made about Hamas are even more true for al-Qaeda and some other groups engaged in suicide terrorism. Not only is Osama bin Laden's background obviously not rooted in poverty; his deputy, the Egyptian Ayman al-Zawahiri, is a medical doctor whose two grandfathers were presidents of the two main Cairo universities. Mohamed Atta, the leading figure in the 11 September attack, was the son of an Egyptian lawyer and had just earned a degree in urban studies at the University of Hamburg in Germany. Terrorists from Chechnya, most of them female, are often mentioned as exceptions. According to certain Russian propaganda, they are poor peasants, often raped as teenagers, and hence excluded from the conservative local matrimonial market, who find their only alternative in suicide terrorism. Yet one of the few biographies we know of these female terrorists refers to Zarina Alikhanova (1976–2003,) who on 12 May 2003 took with her 60 people in a suicide bombing in Znamenskoye. As reconstructed by two well-respected Russian journalists (Shermatova and Teit 2003), her biography fails to conform to the 'raped peasant' stereotype. Alikhanova was born in Kazakhstan to a Chechen father who had become a Kazakh government officer and an Ingush mother who owned department stores in the Kazakh capital, Almaty. She attended an exclusive German school, developed a passion for ballet, and starred as Juliet in a production of Prokofiev's *Romeo and Juliet* at Almaty's Opera Theatre. She also developed a militant interest in the Chechen Islamist cause, and married a Chechen guerrilla leader who was killed in 1999, prompting her to become one of the 'black widows': candidates for martyrdom through suicide bombing. We may say that themes of romantic love and vendetta interacted here with Islamism; but a marginal peasant Zarina Alikhanova was not (although, of course, the stereotype may include *some* truth in other Chechen cases).

In discussing these findings with colleagues such as Larry Iannaccone, who offered similar conclusions in a paper presented at the 2004 meeting of the American Economic Association in San Diego, and later co-authored with me a book published in Italy on this issue (Iannaccone and Introvigne 2004), we had a clear sensation of déjà vu. Where had we seen all this before? The answer was obvious. During the so-called 'cult wars', 'cultists', particularly these associated with instances of mass suicide and homicide, had been invariably depicted as 'brainwashed zombies', and their deeds were explained as arising from extreme poverty, mental illness, or cultural deprivation. 'Cultism' in general was seen as a phenomenon best explained by deprivation, ignorance, or brainwashing. But academic criticism made these explanations untenable. Empirical data showed that in most cases 'cultists', including those involved in some of the most notorious incidents of 'mass suicide' or homicide, were no more poor, ignorant, or mentally unstable than demographically comparable samples of the general population. The first 'cult wars' of the 1970s and 1980s generated a large number of empirical studies, nearly all coming to the same conclusions. A seminal work, which debunked such mythologies about the followers of Reverend Moon, was Eileen Barker's 1984 *The Making of a Moonie*.

In 1990, the *Fishman* decision, which dealt with accusations of brainwashing allegedly practised by the Church of Scientology, stated that in the United States brainwashing theories were not legally part of generally accepted science, and (although not unanimously confirmed by subsequent decisions) marked a more than symbolic defeat for the brainwashing theorists. What happened in Waco in 1993 did not materially change the situation, because a significant proportion of scholars, politicians, and the media tended to blame the ATF and the FBI for their ill-advised management of the incident. Additional and equally tragic events occurred after Waco, however, and they eventually determined what have become known as the 'second cult wars' in the second half of the 1990s. These included the suicides and homicides of the Order of the Solar Temple in 1994, 1995, and 1997; the gas attack perpetrated by Aum Shinrikyo in 1995 in the Tokyo underground; the suicides of Heaven's Gate in Rancho Santa Fe, California, in 1997; and the homicides and suicides of the Ugandan fringe Catholic movement known as the Restoration of the Ten Commandments of God in 2000 (see Introvigne 2002). Re-energized by these incidents, anti-cult movements again proposed as an explanation brainwashing by 'gurus' who preyed on the mentally unstable, the marginal, and the poor.

Once again, however, facts refused to co-operate. Biographies of members of the Solar Temple, Aum Shinrikyo, and Heaven's Gate were duly examined, and revealed that they were mostly middle class, reasonably well schooled, and apparently 'normal' in all respects. In the case of the Solar Temple, members included millionaires, well-known Swiss socialites and prominent businesspeople, popular doctors, a respected economic journalist, and the mayor of the Canadian city of Richelieu. They did not even live communally: they took care of their respective businesses during the day, and participated in long sessions about hidden Masters, extraterrestrials, and the coming Apocalypse in the evening. Those who met them during their daily business activities did not suspect this other side of their otherwise normal and productive lives (see Introvigne and Mayer 2002). Aum Shinrikyo recruited many of its followers among middle-class Japanese students and young professionals, including some with respected credentials in the field of science (see Reader 2000). The founder of Heaven's Gate, Marshall Applewhite (1931–97), had once been a university professor. Most of the members were middle class and well educated; one, David Cabot Van Sinderen (1939–97), was a millionaire and the son of the former CEO of Southern New England Telephone. Although we do not have enough information about the Restoration of the Ten Commandments of God to profile its average member, it would be a mistake to blame the tragedy on an assumed backward cultural level of the Ugandan Catholic clergy and laity. The most prominent lay member, Joseph Kibwetere (1931–2000), who claimed to have received visions since 1984, was a solid member of the Catholic community in Uganda, who had been a politician and a local leader of the Catholic-based Democratic Party in the 1970s. The movement's ideologue and leader, Father Dominic Kataribaabo (1967–2000), was one the few Ugandan Catholic priests who had been educated in a US college (Mayer 2001).

When, eventually, the dust of these tragic incidents settled, the academic community recognized once again that poverty, schizophrenia, or brainwashing were not sensible explanations for the tragedies, whose origins were rather to be found both in external pressure experienced by the movements, and in internal dynamics rooted in certain specific kind of millenarian ideologies (Bromley and Melton 2002; Wessinger 2000). It is indeed unfortunate that most political scientists who deal with suicide terrorism ignore the debates that took place during the first and the second 'cult wars'. They could probably learn from previous mistakes made by colleagues in other fields, and benefit from a large amount of empirical research on 'cults', including those involved in 'mass suicides' and other violent incidents.

This is not to say that movements such as Hamas or al-Qaeda are similar to the Solar Temple or Aum Shinrikyo. They are different in a crucial respect. 'Cults' in general, and 'cults' involved in violent deeds in particular, are extremely unpopular, and generally not very successful. They may have grandiose plans of converting the millions and influencing world history: but these are never achieved, unless the movement (in this case a 'sect' rather than a 'cult') evolves 'from sect to church' and moves into the mainstream of religion, a process which may require decades if not centuries. Hamas commands the respect of a large segment of the Palestinian population, has won a majority in political elections, and the Palestinian mainstream media routinely depict Hamas suicide bombers as martyrs and heroes. Several Palestinian public schools are named after of these 'martyrs'. A Saudi poll, conducted in 2003 but released in 2004, revealed that almost half of Saudi Arabia's population had a favourable view of Osama bin Laden, although only 5 per cent would like to see him ruling the Arabian Peninsula (Schuster 2004.) In early 2002, the BBC reported that in mainly Muslim northern Nigeria 'there has been a massive increase in the number of baby boys called Osama – after Bin Laden. In one hospital in Kano, where there were celebrations after the 11 September attacks, seven out of 10 babies are said to be being given the name Osama' ('Osama Baby Craze Hits Nigeria' 2002.) By contrast, nobody but their own followers admires the leaders of the Solar Temple or Aum Shinrikyo. No schools are named after them. If anything, their deeds revived a widespread anti-cult sentiment among the general population. When the leader of Aum Shinrikyo, Shôkô Asahara, was sentenced to death in February 2004, virtually all Japanese mainstream media applauded the decision, indicating strong popular support.

In a way, however, this very difference confirms both several elements of the prevailing academic view of new religious movements (NRMs) and its usefulness for scholars of contemporary suicide terrorism. In terms of the sociological theory known as religious economy, which interprets religion through the metaphor of a market where religious firms compete for the allegiance of religious consumers (Stark and Finke 2000), the key distinction is between religious demand and religious offer. Religious demand, the theory suggests, is comparatively stable over time and space. Rodney Stark (2001: 119) argued that 'religious diversity is rooted in social *niches*, groups of people sharing particular preferences concerning religious intensity. … These niches are quite stable over time and quite similar in their fundamental outlook across societies and history.' The different niches are not of equal dimensions. Most religious consumers, absent exceptional circumstances, position themselves in the central, moderately conservative niche (see Introvigne 2004.) There is, however, a small but not insignificant number of people who seek extreme religious experiences, and are ready either to cut themselves off completely from the larger society, or to express their refusal of the social order through violence, terrorism, or suicide. The latter attitude is, of course, significantly different from mere social separatism, and much more dangerous.

From this small, extreme niche of religious consumers seeking ultra-intense experiences arise both members of extremist NRMs such as Aum Shinrikyo, Heaven's Gate, or the Solar Temple and candidates for suicide terrorism joining Hamas or al-Qaeda. They have a lot in common from the point of view of religious *demand*: they belong to the same niche, and share a willingness to seek a kind of religion so extreme that they are ready to die – and kill – for it. Whether or not this readiness translates into actual incidents may depend on societal reactions to the existence of such individuals and groups.

When, on the other hand, we observe that Islamic ultra-fundamentalist suicide terrorists are much more easily recruited than extreme 'cultists', and meet with incomparably more success and social approval, we are shifting our analysis from religious demand to religious offer. If religious niches are comparatively stable over time and history, one should conclude that in many religious cultures and subcultures there is a small number of individuals potentially recruitable into extreme groups (Iannaccone and Introvigne 2004.) Not everywhere, however, does this recruitment in fact take place with the same success and expansion. If this difference is not explained from the side of demand, it should be explained supply side, as indeed religious economy theory would suggest. The religious offer by the ultra-fundamentalist segment of Islamic fundamentalism is rooted in specific local (Hamas) or global (al-Qaeda) grievances, is part of a century-old pervasive fundamentalist subculture, and is very different from the offer proposed by the NRMs in the West. It would seem that in this respect the scholarly study of NRMs has less to offer to those trying to understand Islamic ultra-fundamentalist suicide terrorism. But, at the very least, it has to offer the suggestion of looking, for explanations, to religious *offer* rather than only to religious *demand*. That suicide terrorists are all poor, mentally unstable, or ignorant is a wrong answer that comes from asking the wrong question. The question is not why in a given Islamic country there is a unique pool of recruitable religious extremists. In all probability, such pools exist everywhere. One should rather ask why the *potential* extremists become *actual* extremists in some contexts only, and not in others (see Iannaccone 2004.) Poverty, again, is a truly poor explanation. Rich Saudi Arabia produces more suicide terrorists than poor Mauritania or Niger.

Searching for answers on the supply side suggests that, rather than looking at the individuals and their real or alleged personal, psychological or social problems, we examine the *organizations*, and how they operate. The experience of the study of extreme NRMs may offer here yet another suggestion for the study of suicide terrorism. What makes an organization extreme is not simply the use of strong (or 'totalistic') indoctrination techniques, or the creation of a closed environment which it may be psychologically difficult to leave. This is common to several thousand 'cults' throughout the word, yet only a handful of them end up resorting to violence, terrorism, and suicide. The problem with functionalist interpretations is that they try to understand religious movements by declaring religion irrelevant, and by looking only at how the groups are structured and operate.

In fact, there is no easy way to predict which religious movements may become involved in terrorism, violence, or suicide. All models are purely tentative, and human behaviour is often unpredictable. On the other hand, a comparative study of a number of tragic incidents which took place among NRMs may support the conclusion that trying to predict violence on the basis of purely content-neutral models, focusing only on the persuasion and influence techniques, or the psychological (if not psychopathological) state of the leaders and followers, will probably not lead to any fruitful conclusion. While the study of influence techniques is important, what makes a religious group likely to behave in a certain way is *also* the content of its teachings, and not *simply* how these teachings are imparted to its followers. Social scientists who specialize in NRMs and cult critics are currently finding new ground for dialogue in the United States by focusing, inter alia, on the content of each movement's teachings rather than concentrating solely on their persuasion and socialization techniques. Obviously, the aim of considering the teachings would not be to produce a theological or philosophical evaluation of whether these teachings are true or false, an aim foreign to any value-free scholarly enterprise. However, that certain *doctrines*, or interpretations of doctrines, are more likely than others to lead to self-destruction and violence is a conclusion reached by many scholars of extreme NRMs. It may perhaps help scholars of Islamic ultra-fundamentalism as they try to distinguish between different groups and trends, and to explain why only some of these, by no means all, resort to suicide terrorism and other forms of violence.

CHAPTER 5

In God's Name:
Practising Unconditional Love to the Death

Eileen Barker

In this chapter I consider some of the ways in which those with religious authority might exercise their power by persuading believers to perform actions that they (the believers) would not have dreamed of performing had not justifications been presented to them in the name of religion.[1] There are, of course, reasons other than religion – love and money to take but two obvious examples – that lead people to do things that they would not otherwise have done, but religion would seem to add that extra something (for good or evil) that can inspire people to believe and act with an added fervour, an extra commitment, and an extra disregard for other considerations. If we really believe that it is God who wants us to do something, then we are more likely to do it (or at least feel more guilty if we do not do it) than if George or Tony or even our guru asks us to do it – unless we believe that our guru is God, or is the only one with a direct hotline to Him (or Her). We may even be prepared (in both the active and the passive senses of the word) to kill ourselves and others for what we have come to believe is 'the cause', as happened in a situation described in this chapter.

The term 'brainwashing' has frequently been resorted to in order to explain the control that religious leaders have exerted over their followers. Most scholars have argued against the use of such a term as an explanation of why people join or stay in new religious movements or 'cults'. This is because they see it as little more than a metaphor that expresses the speaker's distaste for the end result of a process of conversion, without actually explaining the process itself. This, however, is not to suggest that people cannot be strongly influenced by others – indeed, the whole exercise of sociology assumes that, to a greater or lesser extent, we are all affected by the social situation in which we find ourselves; we have to take others into account, consciously or unconsciously, in most of the things we do in our everyday lives (Weber 1947: 88). The problem is not usually to declare either that a person is totally free of society or that (s)he is totally controlled by it, but to assess the degree to which the position of each is negotiable as part of an ongoing process of interaction that affects both the individual and the social environment (Barker 1995a, 1995b, 2003).

In the 1970s when the contemporary 'cult scare' was entering public awareness, one of the most frequent explanations of why young people joined a new religious movement was that they had been brainwashed or subjected to some sort of irresistible and irreversible mind-control technique. It was then that I decided to attempt to explore this hypothesis in a somewhat more systematic manner than was being employed by the media, the movements' opponents and/or by those, such as deprogrammers, with a financial interest in suggesting that something had been 'done to' the passive 'victim', rather than any kind of rational choice being involved in a decision by an active agent. I had never been very impressed with rational choice as either an explanatory theory or even a very helpful descriptive tool if it is being assumed that we perform actions because they are the most efficient means to achieve a desired goal. It has always seemed to me that such an explanation must be either a tautology or wrong. Even if we knew what goals people would choose, it is obvious enough that they do not always, or even usually, use the most rational means to achieve their goals. All manner of quirks and moral and religious sentiments interfere with the most efficient means being adopted. One might suggest that infanticide is one of the most rational means of controlling population expansion, but few societies go down that road – and, once we admit all the *ceteris paribus* clauses, we have merely moved to alternative explanations, making the 'rational' element of the choice pretty well otiose.

But this does not mean that the question 'What connection is made between means and ends?' is not an important one. When, for example, I was trying to understand why bright young people from the middle classes who had joined the Unification Church should give up 'everything' to spend long hours witnessing and fund-raising on the streets, one plausible explanation was that these were achievement-oriented young people who rejected what they had come to view as the secular, materialistic rat-race of contemporary society, and that the man whom they saw as the Messiah, the Reverend Sun Myung Moon, had succeeded in persuading them that there was a connection between a religious goal (bringing the Kingdom of Heaven on earth) and mundane, observable means. They could *measure* their achievement – how many dollars they raised and/or how many people they brought to a centre to hear their truth. The trick was that they understood that there was a link between their visible actions and an invisible religious goal – and once the Unificationists had accepted that this relationship existed, it was 'rational' for them to spend long hours fund-raising in the street rather than continuing their university careers – despite the fact that most other people, particularly the parents who had brought them up to be *both* idealistic *and* achievement oriented, considered their behaviour incredibly irrational.

But my main concern was to find out why the Unificationists had joined in the first place – whether they had done so freely or whether, as the media were suggesting, as a result of being subjected to irresistible and irreversible techniques. The first challenge was to 'operationalize' the concept of choice in such a way that it could empirically be recognized as being either present or absent. The definition I used for this purpose was as follows:

A choice would involve reflection (in the present), memory (of the past) and imagination (of possible futures). A person would be an active agent in deciding between two or more possible options when he could anticipate their potential existence and when, in doing so, he drew upon his previous experience and his previously formed values and interests to guide his judgement. (Barker 1984: 137)

This gave rise to four main variables: (1) the individual concerned, with all his/her genetic and psychological characteristics, previous experiences and predispositions (values, hopes, fears, etc); (2) the social environment, which was one over which the Unification Church had near-complete control. It was a residential weekend seminar, which was cut off from the outside world and in which the guests had minimal opportunities to talk among themselves without a Unificationist being present. Even visits to the bathroom were likely to be accompanied. The two other variables were the alternative outcomes: (3) joining the Unification Church; or (4) returning to the wider society.

Having defined the question in these terms, the null hypothesis to be tested was that the environment alone would be responsible for the outcome – that is, that the participants would, as suggested by the media and 'anti-cult' proponents of the irresistible-and-irreversible-brainwashing explanation, all end up as Unificationists. What I found, however, was that 90 per cent of the thousand-plus participants whom I studied did *not* end up as Unificationists, but returned to life outside the movement, thereby proving that the process had not been irresistible. Furthermore, the majority of those who did join went on to leave the movement of their own free will (that is, without the assistance of deprogrammers or other outside interventions), clearly demonstrating that the process, even when it had been successful, was not irreversible. More recently, a quarter of a century later, I have found that the vast majority of the first cohort of second-generation Unificationists have left the religion their parents had joined, indicating that the movement has still not acquired a very effective means of controlling people, even those upon whom it has had the opportunity of imposing their primary socialization. The original hypothesis has, it would seem, been unambiguously refuted.

Looking at patterns of behaviour is an essential part of sociology in that it allows us to see trends and, through comparisons, evaluate the ways in which variables are related to each other. By looking at *all* those who were subjected to the environment of a Unification workshop and seeing that the vast majority did not join (rather than by just looking at those who did join), we were able to conclude that while the workshop might have been necessary for conversions, it was not sufficient).[2]

The next step was to compare the joiners with the non-joiners, and both these groups with people of a similar age and background who had nothing to do with the movement, and by this method to discover some of the characteristics that might predispose someone to join the Unification Church – and some of the characteristics that might 'protect' others from its persuasive influence. Rather than the joiners having weak and highly suggestible characters, as was sometimes assumed, it turned out that the converts were disproportionately white, middle-class youth with somewhat idealistic aspirations to make the world a better place, and they were frequently looking for a religious answer to the world's problems.[3]

A case study

Although the statistical comparison of different groups is an essential part of sociological methodology, we also need to look at individual cases if we want to understand a 'cult career'. Of course, no two cases will ever be the same, but the rest of this chapter concentrates on a terrorist who joined a movement significantly different from the

Unification Church, and whom I have got to know over the past ten years. I shall call her Amy. The question now to be addressed is 'How could she, a well-educated woman in her early twenties from a privileged background, come to be in prison for her role in an attempted hijacking that could well have resulted in her own death, as well as that of several innocent passengers and crew?'

An initial point that should be stressed is that, when looking at any group, even those that claim to be totally democratic, a distinction needs to be drawn between those who exercise power and those who 'go along' with whatever is being suggested. Indeed, there are various finer distinctions that can be made between, say, (a) the leader who defines a goal in religious terms; (b) second-level leaders who translate the goal so that it can be achieved through secular means; (c) followers who draw up a specific plan for practical action; (d) foot-soldiers who execute and/or 'go along' with the plan; and (e) followers who know little, if anything, about what is going on.[4] Members in each of these categories are likely to join the movement for different reasons and to have a different perception of what it is that they are doing and/or should be doing as a member. Understanding what makes the leader tick is unlikely to help us all that much in understanding how the foot-soldier operates (or vice versa).

Amy was a foot-soldier who consciously participated in a terrorist act. However, despite the atrocious nature of the act of which she was a part, I do not believe that it would be helpful to dismiss her as an intrinsically evil person; nor do I believe it would be helpful to label her as a brainwashed zombie. No one pressed (nor, I believe, could they have pressed) a button instantly transforming Amy A (the idealistic but naive young woman) into Amy B (the dangerous terrorist); and Amy C (the mature and exemplary citizen that she is today) did not suddenly become 'reset' to Amy A as the result of some miraculous deprogramming. To understand what happened it is necessary to take into account both the coming together, synchronically, of a number of particular people with particular interests in particular social environments, and, diachronically, a gradual accumulation of processes that contributed to Amy's reaching a stage where she was prepared to play her part in the hijacking.

Joining

There was nothing very dramatic about the way that Amy had come to join her group in the first place. She had not been a seeker in the sense that she had been trying out various new religions before meeting the group, nor was hers a sudden 'Road to Damascus' conversion as sometimes seems to happen (Barker 1984: 171). There were, however, a number of predisposing variables that would seem to have facilitated her joining the movement. These included: (1) her psychological makeup; (2) a number of pushes from the social environment in which she was at the time; and (3) the pull of the attractions that the group appeared to be offering.

According to several criteria, Amy came from a 'good home'. However, she considered her father to be overbearing and she wanted to get away from her family but was not yet quite ready to venture out into the world. In this respect she was not unlike the young people described by Saul Levine in *Radical Departures* (1984), who wanted to get away from their parents but still sought the womb-like protection of a family. Not that Amy had been looking for a group to join, and she would have been unlikely to join most new religions. She had, however, been interested in yoga and Eastern religions, having become disillusioned with traditional religions, so when she saw an advertisement for some yoga classes she went along to try them out.

But Amy had not just wanted to meditate in a passive, navel-contemplative manner; she also had a well-developed social conscience and had been looking for some way in which she could contribute to making the world a better place. She wanted to be someone and to make her mark. Like many other young people in the 1970s, she was critical of the rat-race materialism of capitalism, but she was also critical of the dialectical materialism of communism. She discovered that the yoga classes were being given by a group that offered a combination of spirituality and caring for others, and that it was involved in running projects such as schools for orphans and providing disaster relief in Third World countries.

This commitment to improving the world and the spiritual practices seemed to Amy a perfect combination. 'The ideology fitted my way of thinking *before* joining, took it further and provided the possibility of putting it into practice – as part of an organization rather than as an idealistic individual with no power.' She enrolled in further classes and eventually moved in to live with the group. The fact that the movement had a strict authoritarian structure, with clear guidelines and an uncompromising attitude towards its moral position, might also have resonated with her family background. Reflecting the pattern found in Levine's work, her joining as a rebellion against her father involved moving into an environment that bore some clear similarities to the one from which she was escaping. This was not altogether surprising: in my research into the Unification Church I had found that it was often easier to see the converts as having joined their movement *because of* rather than *in spite of* their family background (Barker 1984: 210 and 1989: 95).

Life in the community

In several ways Amy's movement bore a resemblance to several other new religions that are led by a charismatic leader and have a membership made up of converts rather than those who have been born into and brought up in the movement (Barker 2004). It promoted a dichotomous world-view that made a clear separation between good and bad, godly and satanic, right and wrong, truth and falsity, and Them and Us, part of 'Them' being the converts' biological families. The imposed detachment from family and former friends resulted in Amy's coming to believe that she had nowhere but the movement to which she could turn. However, although initially she had felt that she had joined a friendly and loving community, with the passage of time she found that it was difficult to form close friendships with her new 'brothers and sisters'.[5] Full-time committed membership entailed celibacy and if two people (of the same or a different sex) seemed to be forging too strong a bond they were liable to be separated by sending them to different parts of the world. Although constantly surrounded by other members, life could become very lonely within the movement. 'Everyone had their own problems and didn't want to know about yours.'

The more socially isolated the members were from each other, the easier it was for the leadership to control them. It became increasingly difficult to question and check out reality when it appeared as though her peers all agreed with the beliefs and opinions formulated by the leadership.[6] The special in-group language or jargon that the group employed also served to isolate the members from 'Them' and to direct their thought in a specific direction. Anyone who questioned or deviated from what the leadership decreed had to be 'dealt with' in one way or another. On the rare occasions when Amy expressed any doubts she was told not to intellectualize; she must learn to surrender more completely to gain more spiritual understanding – perhaps she needed to devote more time to meditation until she saw how mistaken she had been. One of the punishments for minor misdemeanours was an extension of the time engaged in the fasting that all members were expected to undergo on a regular basis. This, together with an inadequate vegetarian diet and limited hours of sleep, undermined Amy's health to a certain extent and sometimes left her feeling physically weak.

The hierarchy

As was mentioned earlier, Amy's movement offered not merely a means for gaining spiritual enlightenment but also the promise of creating a much better, more just society. This goal, Amy was taught, could justify whatever means were necessary to overthrow the present bad society. The leadership was granted a special expertise, and followers were expected to be just that: followers.[7] As in the army and elsewhere, the rule was that even if a lower-level leader were to make a mistake, those under him should still follow, rather than each individual doing his or her own thing and, thereby, destroying the strength of the group.

The movement was led by its founder, an Oriental who wielded a charismatic authority over his followers. Unconstrained by either tradition or rules, the guru was both unpredictable and unaccountable to any other authority. Amy had not known about him when she joined, but was introduced to him through pictures and stories related by older members. When she did meet him it was only in the presence of many other devoted followers. She soon, however, came to see him as a parent figure and created in her mind a personal relationship with him. He spoke to her, she believed, in her dreams. 'At that time I'd have followed any one who gave me attention, made me feel important.' The interesting point here, of course, is that the guru not only paid no attention to Amy whatsoever, but was almost certainly in total ignorance of her existence. At the same time, there was a part of Amy that disliked her guru; she told me her first impression on seeing him was how very ugly he was![8]

Beneath the leader there was a well-defined number of hierarchies. Some of these were related to the person's reputed spiritual development, but others were less achieved than ascribed. Orientals were superior to Westerners; men were superior to women; older members were superior to younger members; celibates were superior to those who had been married. Amy soon realized that while she could achieve some 'promotion' (on her path to enlightenment) she would, nevertheless, remain of inferior status because she was a young, female Caucasian.

It was within this general culture and structure that Amy found herself at a special training centre in a remote region of South America, hoping to progress towards enlightenment and to advance her position within the movement. Here she came under the authority of a trainer who would seem to have had not only a lust for power, but also a decidedly sadistic streak in his character. So far as Amy was concerned, her time at the training centre was one of fear, humiliation, and exhaustion. The trainees were subjected to long periods of fasting; they had to engage in continuous periods of devotion that involved dancing and chanting with little sleep. Amy also found herself being sexually abused under the pretext of being taught detachment and submission, but this had the effect not only of humiliating her in her own eyes but also of inducing a state of numbness: 'In the end, I just didn't feel.' At the same time, she was in constant fear of punishment and, above all, of not passing the examinations that would lead her to the next stage in her path towards spiritual enlightenment.

It would seem that her trainer was a past master at manipulating the aspirations, strengths, and weaknesses of those over whom he was in control, to the advantage of both the movement's and his own ends. One girl was encouraged to kill herself as a revolutionary gesture, the trainer helpfully writing the leaflets that were distributed at the time of her death. Others were spurred on to take part in demonstrations and an attempted assassination.

There was a slightly older member of the group of trainees who had attained a higher position in the spiritual hierarchy than Amy and, although not one of the movement's leaders, belonged to a more active category than Amy. She had been an ardent communist, but had undergone a politically radical change when she joined the group, becoming an equally ardent anti-communist. It would seem, however, that this had not amounted to any radical psychological change. To use Amy's phrase, 'she took herself with her'; she would appear to have been what Eric Hoffer (1951) has termed the True Believer. She was determined to fight for the cause and her enthusiasms were undiminished just because the goals she now championed were, in some ways at least, diametrically opposed to those that she had previously espoused. It was she who, with the trainer's encouragement, thought up the scheme to hijack a plane to bring attention to the cause. The plan was that the plane would be forced to land behind the Iron Curtain, when the team leader would commit suicide on the runway. Amy's role was to be an innocent bystander who would write a report of what had happened. She did, however, smuggle an inflammable substance onto the plane in a juice bottle as a potential Molotov cocktail.

Luckily for everyone concerned, the plan failed and the conspirators were overpowered shortly after the plane had taken off. It was acknowledged that Amy had played a minor role and she consequently served considerably less time in prison than her co-conspirators.[9] When she was released she felt that she had nowhere else to go and so, despite having considerable misgivings about the movement, she returned to it, still hoping to pursue her path to enlightenment, although not under the instruction of her previous trainer, who had been removed from his post. Eventually, however, she managed to forge a close relationship with another disillusioned member and together they were able to escape. It took both of them some time to get the group out of their system and to create a life that would fill the gap left by the movement which, they continued to acknowledge, had some very positive aspects.

'Ich kann nicht anders'

There was a point just before the hijacking at which Amy was actually told by a member of the movement, who was of superior status to herself, not to take part; but, she told me, by then she felt that it was too late – she had 'gone too far to stop'; there was no longer a way out – although physically all she had to do was obey the instruction to abort the enterprise.

It might be argued that Amy's conviction that she just *had* to proceed showed that she had been well and truly brainwashed, and it would certainly seem that her mind had been 'bent', if not completely controlled. She had reached a stage in a process of submitting to a religious authority where it would have been extremely difficult for her to extract herself from the influence of the situation. And, of course, she *did* go ahead. We might, however, be in danger of resorting to a dubious kind of hindsight if we were to conclude that, merely because she did it, she *had* to – any more than saying that the one person in ten who converted to the Unification Church had to do so. It is possible that there was still something about Amy herself that prevented her from opting out at the last minute. She still wanted her moment of glory, and admitted this quite freely. People, she said, were going to listen and take notice of her once she explained what the movement had done because of its idealistic beliefs. In other words, the movement (in the persons of the trainer and the team leader) was taking advantage, consciously or unconsciously, of something 'inside' Amy.[10]

Of course, the circular *petitio principii* that Amy could not have done otherwise because she undoubtedly *did* do what she did cannot be countered – except to point out that it does beg the question. I am, however, resorting to my earlier definition of choice by suggesting that it was not *only* the social situation that was the independent variable; there was still something of Amy functioning, albeit at a very diminished level and under a considerable amount of influence from her co-conspirators, and if we want to understand what led her to that final phase of the process, we should not close our eyes to the possibility that there was just a bit of her that was positively collaborating.

Another way in which our understanding of the sense of inevitability that Amy felt might be enhanced is by recognizing that there are other situations when we might feel the odds are overpoweringly against our not 'going along' with the expectations of others, or indeed, ourselves. At the risk of seeming to trivialize the situation, when Amy told me of how she felt she had no longer a way out I was reminded of Susan, who told me that she went ahead with her marriage because, her mother having made all the arrangements and she and her fiancé having received scores of presents from all their friends and relations, she just could not go against their expectations. She had acquiesced for too long and it was just too late. I was also reminded of another, again very different situation – that of Martin Luther when he declared 'Ich kann nicht anders' (I can do no other) at the Diet of Worms in 1521. But many people might think that he was being brave and making a stand just because he *could* have done other. We might also remember that history can provide us with innumerable examples of martyrs who have faced burning at the stake and various other horrible deaths rather than renounce their faith. In recent times there were the Jehovah's Witnesses who were prepared to be killed in Nazi concentration camps rather than submit to the demands of the regime (King 1982).

On several occasions I have come across people who would seem to have been completely under the spell of a guru or leader, or utterly submissive to the group. There has seemed, however, to be a point beyond which they will not go, though that point may not seem entirely 'rational' to outsiders. There was, for example, a young woman who had let her baby die because her husband, the leader of a fundamentalist Christian group, told her it was God's will that she should only breastfeed her baby, although she knew she was unable to provide the needed nourishment. The baby eventually died of starvation, to the mother's deep distress. She, like Amy, had felt that in the circumstances she could not do anything about the situation, yet she also told me that when she was ordered by the group to carry the dead body of the baby round above her head in a ritual, she refused, saying that she just could not believe God would want that. In another instance, a young man who had appeared to be completely under the control of his guru, to the extent that he was physically abusing other members of the group, including his brother, at the guru's command, told me that when he was instructed that he could not wear sandals because God did not like those sandals, he had decided that this was ridiculous and, shortly afterwards, he left the group. Returning to Amy's movement, although the trainer was able to persuade Amy and her fellow believers to carry out several deadly actions, when he had suggested that they should throw one of the group into a fire when she was causing problems, they had refused to do so.

It has not been argued that group pressure might not become irresistible and irreversible under certain conditions for certain individuals. It has been argued that group pressure can be extremely effective. Individuals can be induced to perform actions that they would have strenuously resisted had they not been led along a certain path by those to whom they have accorded (a religious) authority over them. It has, however, also been suggested that it is possible, even in extreme circumstances, that some element of choice may yet remain open to the individual – though whether he or she will decide to exert that choice is a question that may become apparent only after the event. In other words, even when the situation seems as though it is having a well-nigh irresistible effect on the individual, the individual may still, at least in some of the cases I have examined, be capable of resisting the pressure.

Concluding remarks

My limited conclusion is that it is possible to recognize a series of predispositions, values, hopes, fears, actions, reactions, interactions, structures, and processes that can contribute to our understanding of how individuals can find themselves on a path that leads, not inevitably, but understandably, to an outcome that is not only one that they would not have chosen at the start of their journey, but one that would seem to be diametrically opposed to their starting position.

Because each individual *is* an individual, not everyone would respond in the same way to the situations in which Amy found herself. Some might start along the same path, but take a different direction at a later stage. Furthermore, the pressures of certain situations may be resisted by an individual at one time yet sway the same individual at another time. But this does not mean that we cannot discern bundles of characteristics that predispose certain people to follow some more or less well-trodden paths; or that we cannot observe certain patterns of behaviour that tend to lead to more or less predictable outcomes.

The fact that such processes can be recognized might mean that they can become more negotiable. To say the least, we might become more sensitive to a situation and its potential outcomes than we are by simply labelling terrorists (or those involved in other kinds of religious confrontations) as either intrinsically evil people or passive robots who have been subjected to irresistible or irreversible brainwashing or mind-control techniques. But our understanding of how such things come to pass can be increased only by a meticulous charting of a series of journeys from A to B to C to D, recognizing the progress of the individual and his/her relationship to the social environment at each stage in the journey, discovering how the individual *and* the social situation *and* the relationship between them changes as a continuous process.

In short, there is not one straight path to conflict and another to compromise or accommodation; but the journeys to either outcome are not entirely idiosyncratic. Others have travelled recognizably similar paths before and will travel them again – paths along which, in God's name, they have learned to practise unconditional love to the death.

CHAPTER 6

The Terror of Belief and the Belief in Terror: on Violently Serving God and Nation

Abdelwahab El-Affendi

Like William James, I harbour a fascination with the extraordinary and deeply spiritual manifestations of religion. And like him, I consider these manifestations, which border on the 'pathological', to be the more interesting aspect of the religious experience (James 1977: 28–30). In particular, I find the moral compulsion derived from these kinds of experiences (Martin Luther's 'Here I stand, I can do no other'), and the dramatic part it plays in human history, as gripping as it is intriguing. The extraordinary authority of James's '"geniuses" in the religious line' is akin to Max Weber's 'charisma', that mysterious and mysteriously rare 'gift' which inspires awe and devotion to those who manifest it (Spencer 1973). Charisma is often the outer glow of that raging inner fire of conviction and enthusiasm which burns inside the hearts of individuals touched by the 'pure' religious experience. The most salient characteristic of this ultimate religious experience is that paradoxical 'passionate tranquillity', that 'unaccountable feeling of safety', born out of the feeling that whatever may happen, 'one's life as a whole is in the keeping of a power whom one can absolutely trust': 'In deeply religious men the abandonment of self to this power is passionate. Whoever not only says, but *feels*, "God's will be done," is mailed against every weakness; and the whole array of martyrs, missionaries and religious reformers is there to prove the tranquil-mindedness, under naturally agitating or distressing circumstances, which self-surrender brings' (James 1977: 281).

Although charisma and radiant moral conviction are not restricted to deeply religious individuals, as many secular actors do exhibit these traits (Spencer 1973), it is nevertheless noticeable that the 'pure religious experience' and its attendant unbending moral certitude is a rarity in the modern world, often exhibiting itself mainly in fringe groups and cults. For a while I had harboured the belief that the late Ayatollah Khomeini (1903–1989), the leader of Iran's Islamic revolution, was one of the last figures to embody the phenomenon in a modern 'mainstream' context. I was eager, therefore, when the opportunity presented itself, to ascertain this fact. On meeting one of his (admittedly disaffected) former close associates, I asked him whether the man consistently acted from unshakeable convictions and completely un-pragmatic frame of mind. 'I will tell you a story,' he said. 'And you may draw your own conclusions. When I went to discuss with him the students' storming of the American embassy in Tehran in 1980, he said to me: "Who are these people? Throw them out!" However, a few days later, when it became apparent how popular the move was with the masses, he changed his position and gave the students his full backing.'

Later of course, more evidence of pragmatism, even Machiavellianism, in the leadership of the Islamic revolution came to light, including secret arms dealing with the USA and Israel in the notorious Iran–Contra affair during the latter part of the Reagan era. This would not have happened with Muhammad Ahmad ibn Abdullah, the self-proclaimed Sudanese Mahdi (d. 1885), who was probably one of the last figures from the age of unconditional belief. While even the Mahdi was not beyond a pragmatic shift of tactics when necessary (he permitted his followers to use firearms after some initial reluctance), the intellectual universe he inhabited was completely dominated by mystic visions and other-worldly concerns. His motto was: 'I have come [to bring about] the destruction of this world and refurbishment of the Next.' His mission was strictly that: to hasten the Second Coming of Christ and the end of the world. His conduct was dictated exclusively by his mystic visions, which informed him of a duty to purify the world from sin. There was no compromise, no negotiations, and no elaborate plans. People were invited to believe and join the community of the faithful, or await God's wrath, which could come in the form of conquering Mahdist armies, but could be more direct than that. Nothing any human being did was going to change the outcome: it had been decreed.

This feeling of complete assurance of absolute safety, of being in the hands of God, does not preclude death and attaining martyrdom, for that could be part of God's unfathomable plan. Indeed, many of the faithful must die in the course of the *jihad*. For the true believer, such an end should be his dearest wish, since the status of the martyr is the highest there is.

However, groups that stick strictly to the religious imperative tend to die out quickly, as happened to the Mahdist movement in its first phase. After initial defeat and the rise of a new generation, the movement went to the other extreme and became crudely pragmatic, to the extent that its collaboration with the British colonial authorities became the object of fierce criticism from emerging nationalist activists. The Wahhabi movement in Saudi Arabia also went through similar phases of religious zeal, but turned pragmatic after a number of initial defeats and under the new, more flexible leadership of Abdul-Aziz Al Saud (d. 1953).

The celebration of martyrdom is not exclusive to messianic religious creeds, but is present in more sober ones as well. In Protestantism, it has been argued, the 'martyr was, in many respects, successor to the Catholic saint: an exemplary figure whose spiritual heroics helped close the immense gulf separating God from man' (Juster 2005). Even in the secular context, there is not much disagreement that dying for what one believes in is one of the noblest and most quintessentially human acts. To stand up for what you believe to be just and true, and refuse to compromise on your principles even in the face of certain death, is the apex of the human endeavour. Luther's 'Here I stand, I can do no other' is the stuff from which martyrs and saints are made. In the short term, such a stance may earn a person condemnation, derision, persecution, and even crucifixion or burning at the stake, but it usually earns them respect – even veneration – in the long term. Martin Luther King Jr. and Gandhi were murdered, and Nelson Mandela, Vaclav Havel, and many others faced long periods of torment. But few people today doubt their credentials.

Sticking to principles may at times be a sign of narrow-mindedness and fanaticism rather than nobility of purpose. But as long as harm falls exclusively on the person concerned, it can still be respected as an instance of honest and free self-expression. Some acts of self-harm meant to put moral pressure on the perceived oppressors by forcing them to bear the blame for the harm that ensues can be considered extreme, but they still send a powerful message. These include instances of Buddhist monks who used to set themselves on fire to protest against the Vietnam government in the 1960s, Republican prisoners who starved themselves to death in Northern Ireland in the early and 1980s, or Kurdish activists from Turkey who set fire to themselves to protest against Turkish oppression at various times during the last few years.

Fanaticism and terror

Even at this preliminary stage in our discussion, it is clear that there is an important distinction between accepting martyrdom in defence of one's faith or principles (or even engaging in self-immolation to make a point) and the phenomenon we generally describe as terrorism, including suicide terrorism. Suicide terrorism is not about suicide. Neither is it about dying for one's faith. It is about killing for one's cause.

In turn, self-immolation is different from risking one's life to fight for a cause and from undertaking dangerous rescue missions, where the volunteer earns unadulterated praise, becoming more praiseworthy the higher the risk being taken. In these acts of self-sacrifice, in contrast to the deliberate self-harm of protestors or suicide missions, putting oneself in harm's way is not an objective, but an accepted risk.

More generally, being prepared to risk death is somewhat different from being prepared to die, and the latter is again different from committing an act of suicide or a suicidal act (again these two are different things). Professional soldiers (and to a lesser extent policemen or rescue workers) accept the risk of death as a professional hazard. But this does not mean that taking up a job as a soldier indicates a readiness to die. In fact, all soldiers or policemen hope to live long and prosperous lives. At another level, a person who espouses a cause that is dear to him/her and takes up arms (literally or figuratively) in its defence can be said to be ready to die for that cause. Similarly, a soldier who goes on a risky mission or makes a daring assault can be said to be ready to die in the course of fulfilling his duty. But this does not amount to suicidal conduct, since the soldier still entertains the hope of surviving the mission.

Taking such risks is not regarded as an irrational act, and the greater the risk, the more noble and courageous the endeavour is considered. The acts come to be seen as especially rational when they are unavoidable or when the risk of inaction is greater, as was the case for the passengers of United Flight 193 who, once they became aware that they were going to die anyway, made a last-ditch attempt to overpower the hijackers. There might also be rationality as well as nobility in an attempt by a few members of an endangered group to risk their lives in order to save the majority. There is more nobility (but less rationality, depending on how egotistically rationality is construed) in someone who is not in actual or immediate danger risking his/her life to save others who are.

Suicide terrorism differs from these calculated risks in that the perpetrators take the decision in advance to kill themselves, and know that this would be the inevitable outcome of their action. But there is a major difference here between acts of political/ religious suicide and the related act of murder. Suicide as an act of protest, or as a ritual, differs significantly from suicide as a tactic of war. The former, as mentioned earlier, seeks to put the enemy at a moral disadvantage, while the latter aims at inflicting casualties. Suicide as a war tactic is again different from acts of suicide out of despair, such as the recent suicide acts committed by prisoners at the US-run Guantánamo Bay detention centre. Those prisoners apparently decided to kill themselves after losing hope of a quick release and finding the uncertainty in which they existed intolerable. This did not prevent their suicides from being interpreted by a prison spokesperson as falling under the above category of protest suicide, which could not be ruled out.

However, in suicide bombings, suicide is not an objective in itself, nor is it a vehicle of protest, but a means of inflicting damage on the enemy. Just as was the case with the Japanese kamikaze pilots, the death of the actor involved was only thought necessary because it was deemed at the time to be the most effective way of delivering a missile or a bomb. The same task could be fulfilled if it were still possible for the pilot to eject from his plane before it hit the deck of the targeted enemy ship. Similarly, had the suicide bombers in Palestine or Iraq been able to deliver their bombs and then return safely to base, that would have been preferable both for them and their organizations. The point of suicide terrorism is thus the act of killing, not suicide. The latter is quite incidental to the operation.

The focus on the suicide aspect of suicide terrorism may thus obscure the bigger picture, since it neglects the most salient feature of the act. The terrorist is not (in Robert A. Pape's famous phrase) 'dying to win', but killing to win. Pape's analysis brings into focus another major aspect: the distinction between the strategic/political dimension and the 'ethical'/ideological dimension in a suicide terrorist act. The dominant view on the issue (as expressed in the 9/11 Commission's report (2004) and such works as Hoffman (1998), Laqueur (2004) and others) is to distinguish between what has come to be called the 'new terrorism' (or 'fanatical terrorism', 'apocalyptic terrorism' or more directly 'Islamic terrorism') and a more mundane variety. The latter was seen as more 'rational' and pragmatic, being concerned with specific and limited goals, and tailoring its methods for that purpose. The goal is usually to achieve national liberation or to reclaim rights, and the perpetrators are careful not to overdo it lest they provoke an extremely severe reaction or alienate their own base of support.

In 'fanatical' terrorism, by contrast, the perpetrator is said to be motivated purely (or mainly) by his deeply held beliefs, which impel him to hate and seek to eliminate perceived enemies. Since this is a matter of conviction, the terrorist does not need to appeal to a constituency. For such groups, 'terrorism is less of a means to an end than an end itself, serving God or the cathartic self-satisfaction of striking a blow against the hated enemy, for example. Violence is less tailored and as the violence has become more indiscriminate, the terrorists themselves have become more reluctant to claim credit for events' (Hoffman 2001: vi).

The perpetrators of this form of 'apocalyptic, catastrophic terrorism', unlike the more conventional type, 'don't want a seat at the table, they want to destroy the table and everyone sitting at it' (Morgan 2004: 31). Religion is central to this type of terrorism, and we must in this regard 'distinguish religious terrorists from those terrorists with religious components' (Morgan 2004: 30). The main features which distinguish this 'new terrorism' include 'a conception of righteous killing-as-healing, the necessity of total social destruction as part of a process of ultimate purification, a preoccupation with weapons of mass destruction, and a cult of personality where one leader dominates his followers who seek to become perfect clones' (Morgan 2004: 30).

As a result of these characteristics, and because of more recent international developments, including globalization, new technologies, and the decline in the state sponsoring of terrorism, the new terrorist movements have become more freelance, independent, agile, organizationally flexible, and much more lethal and difficult to detect. They are also more fanatical and less squeamish about inflicting mass casualties, not to mention their obsessional quest for weapons of mass destruction.

For many influential commentators, including political leaders such as Tony Blair of Britain, it is not just a question of religious fanaticism, but *Islamic* religious fanaticism. As Blair put it in a recent speech:

> Ministers have been advised never to use the term 'Islamist extremist'. It will give offence. It is true. It will. There are those – perfectly decent-minded – people who say the extremists who commit these acts of terrorism are not true Muslims. And, of course, they are right. They are no more proper Muslims than the Protestant bigot who murders a Catholic in Northern Ireland is a proper Christian. But, unfortunately, he is still a 'Protestant' bigot. To say his religion is irrelevant is both completely to misunderstand his motive and to refuse to face up to the strain of extremism within his religion that has given rise to it. (Blair 2006a)

For Blair then, this threat is very specific: 'The immediate threat is from Islamist extremism. . . . But, this terrorism did not begin on the streets of New York. It simply came to our notice then. Its victims are to be found in the recent history of many lands from Russia and India, but also Algeria, Pakistan, Libya, Saudi Arabia, Yemen, Indonesia, Kenya and countless more' (Blair 2006b). Blair totally rejects the idea that Western policies are to blame for this confrontation, which he sees as inherent in ideology and totally unprovoked.

> I believe its cause is an ideology, a world-view, derived from religious fanaticism and that had we taken no decisions at all to enrage it, [it] would still have found provocation in our very existence. They disagree with our way of life, our values and in particular . . . our tolerance. They hate us but probably they hate those Muslims who believe in tolerance even more, as apostates betraying the true faith. (Blair 2006c)

While recognizing some impact of Western policies, at least in enhancing the appeal of the extremist message, the 9/11 Commission in the USA also takes a similar view which emphasizes the role of religion:

> Usama Bin Ladin and other Islamist terrorist leaders draw on a long tradition of extreme intolerance within one stream of Islam (a minority tradition), from at least Ibn Taymiyyah, through the founders of Wahhabism, through the Muslim Brotherhood, to Sayyid Qutb. That stream is motivated by religion and does not distinguish politics from religion, thus distorting both. It is further fed by grievances stressed by Bin Ladin and widely felt throughout the Muslim world

– against the US military presence in the Middle East, policies perceived as anti-Arab and anti-Muslim, and support of Israel. Bin Ladin and Islamist terrorists mean exactly what they say: to them America is the font of all evil, the 'head of the snake', and it must be converted or destroyed.

It is not a position with which Americans can bargain or negotiate. With it there is no common ground – not even respect for life – on which to begin a dialogue. It can only be destroyed or utterly isolated. (9/11 Commission 2004: 362)

Both Blair and the Commission are reluctant to draw the conclusion that we are in the midst of a religious war, the first since the Crusades (Bar 2004). But other commentators are not that hesitant. As one writer put it, the problem lies not in religion as such, but Islam in particular:

We are at war with Islam. It may not serve our immediate foreign policy objectives for our political leaders to openly acknowledge this fact, but it is unambiguously so. It is not merely that we are at war with an otherwise peaceful religion that has been 'hijacked' by extremists. We are at war with precisely the vision of life that is prescribed to all Muslims in the Koran, and further elaborated in the literature of the hadith, which recounts the sayings and actions of the Prophet. A future in which Islam and the West do not stand on the brink of mutual annihilation is a future in which most Muslims have learned to ignore most of their canon, just as most Christians have learned to do. Such a transformation is by no means guaranteed to occur, however, given the tenets of Islam. (Harris 2004: 9–10)

If the motive of these attacks is clearly and predominantly religious, then the reaction 'must include a religious-ideological dimension: active pressure for religious reform in the Muslim world' and the counter-strategy 'must be based on an acceptance of the fact that for the first time since the Crusades, Western civilization finds itself involved in a religious war' (Bar 2004). This Islamic reform may have to be imposed by force, since dialogue might be ineffective.

While it would be comforting to believe that our dialogue with the Muslim world has, as one of its possible outcomes, a future of mutual tolerance, nothing guarantees this result – least of all the tenets of Islam. Given the constraints of Muslim orthodoxy … for a radical (and reasonable) adaptation to modernity, I think it is clear that Islam must find some way to revise itself, peacefully or otherwise. What this will mean is not at all obvious. What is obvious, however, is that the West must either win the argument or win the war. All else will be bondage. (Harris 2004: 30–1)

It is quite interesting that the belief in the inherently religious character of 'Islamic' terrorism tends to generate in its adherents the very fanatical zeal being decried in the presumed opponent. It is a matter for investigation whether this zealousness and single-mindedness is a natural corollary of the belief, or its source. But we will come back to this matter.

Dogma and strategy

The view that terrorism (and in particular suicide terrorism) is now predominantly of the 'fanatical' religious variety, and more specifically the *Islamic* fanatical variety, has been strongly contested by many researchers. The so-called 'new terrorism', some analysts argue, is neither that new nor that irrational. The truth is that

> fanatical religious terrorism has existed for thousands of years and that the distinction between religiously and politically motivated terrorism is predominantly artificial. The willingness of 'new terrorists' to use more indiscriminate violence is more a continuation of an existing trend than an all-new phenomenon. Terrorism is and always has been a violent business and the trend of increasing deaths per attack initiated in the 1980s, might be down to the need of keeping the media and the world's awareness focused on their grievances. Terrorism is still theatre, just on a much bigger stage, where an act has to be big and shocking to keep the audience's short attention from drifting to other scenes. State sponsorship or support is still part of terrorism today, although it might be less due to financial reasons, take a slightly different form and be less obvious ... Finally the equation of 'old terrorism' = hierarchical structure and 'new terrorism' = network structure is false. Although networks have gained in prominence, hierarchical and network organisational structures are found in both 'old' and 'new terrorism' (Spencer 2006: 24)

Robert A Pape, in particular, has gathered exhaustive data on suicide terrorism which led him to discount the prevalent argument depicting suicide terrorism as 'a non-strategic response, motivated mainly by fanaticism or irrational hatreds' (Pape 2005: 45). On the contrary, these operations invariably form a part of 'large, coherent political or military campaigns,' while the suicide aspect of the operations appears to be a rational precondition for its success.

Pape's data and analysis indicate that there is 'little connection between suicide terrorism and Islamic fundamentalism, or any one of the world's religions. . . . Rather, what nearly all suicide terrorist attacks have in common is a specific secular and strategic goal: to compel modern democracies to withdraw military forces from territory that the terrorists consider to be their homeland' (Pape 2005: 4). This type of terrorism is thus essentially 'a strategy for national liberation from foreign military occupation by a democratic state' (Pape 2005: 45).

Pape's analysis has in turn been challenged by critics who argue that Muslim suicide terrorism must be put in a category of its own, since it appears to be motivated solely by fanaticism and hatred of the West, and nothing that the West could do by way of concessions is likely to influence it. The idea that suicide terrorism is not predominantly religiously motivated and not exclusive to Islam relies too much on statistical correlations which lack the necessary intimate knowledge of the facts, and has also been overtaken by new developments, such as the exponential rise in the incidence of suicide attacks since the invasion of Iraq in 2003 (Atran 2006: 130–2).

> Despite common popular misconceptions, suicide terrorists today are not motivated exclusively or primarily by foreign occupation, they are not directed

by a central organization, and they are not nihilistic. Most suicide terrorists today are inspired by a global jihadism which, despite atavistic cultural elements, is a thoroughly modern movement, filling the popular political void in Islamic communities left in the wake of discredited Western ideologies co-opted by corrupt local governments. Appeals to Muslim history and calls for a revival of the caliphate are widespread and heartfelt. To some extent, jihadism is also a countermovement to the ideological and corresponding military thrust ensconced, for example, in the National Security Strategy of the United States, which enshrines liberal democracy as the 'single sustainable model of national development right and true for every person, in every society – and the duty of protecting these values against their enemies'. (Atran 2006: 139–40)

For the typically secularist mindset of Western observers, proponents of this view argue, the dimension of the 'power of faith' and the specificity of the Islamic case is downplayed. The fact that non-Muslim groups or secular Muslim groups engage in suicide terrorism should not obscure the fact that most suicide terrorist acts in recent years have been perpetrated largely by Islamist groups, which started this wave in the first place. It has taken 'the reworking of an Islamic concept – the idea of martyrdom – to make the initial breakthrough. Islamism is not present in all suicide bombings. But it had to be there at the creation' (Kramer 2005).

Certainly the reality of Israeli occupation was needed to raise the temperature in Lebanon to the point where this breakthrough became possible. But I think it unlikely that secular groups could have reached it independently. Remember, too, that Muslims under long and repressive occupations in the colonial period did not make the leap either. The precondition is the rise of an Islamist sensibility, and its modern utilitarian outlook. Professor Pape has rightly said that suicide bombings require a 'strategic logic' or cost-benefit rationale; a 'social logic' or support system; and an 'individual logic' or personal motive. To this I would add a 'moral logic', which is the entry point for innovative interpretations of Islam. Like the other logics, it is *necessary*, although like them it is not *sufficient*. (Kramer 2005)

Additionally, Pape's critics argue that suicide terrorism as a tactic to force occupiers out has often been either counterproductive or unnecessary, and in many cases appears to be influenced by rivalry among the insurgent groups in areas such as Palestine or Iraq (Kramer 2005; Atran 2006).

The point about the distinction between individual and organizational logic has also been noted by other commentators, such as Fred Halliday, who emphasizes the pragmatic outlook of at least the movements' leaders: 'To adapt Karl von Clausewitz, terrorism is the continuation of politics by other means. The footsoldiers and suicide-bombers of the current campaign may well be fanatics, but the people who direct them have a political strategy. And their vision stretches over years if not decades' (Halliday 2005).

The same point is made by Mia Bloom, who argues that

the perpetrators of suicide terror and the organizations that send them are both acting according to two variants of rational calculation. The organizations strategically adapt to changing circumstances to maximize their popularity and their ability to influence the 'electorate' is based on resonance; specific tactics are either applauded or rejected. This underscores a significant rational calculation – those terrorist groups that are not rational, and do not adjust to circumstances, can lose support and may cease to exist. (Bloom 2005: 85)

All this is common sense, and both sides to the argument appear to concede it. This creates some problems for the argument for a purely, or even predominantly, religious motivation. Proponents of this view also tend to contradict themselves, as does Kramer when he speaks of 'breakthroughs' and 'innovative interpretations of Islam', while the original argument was that the problem was inherent in old extremist interpretations (Ibn Taymiyya etc.). This represents a grudging admission that the actors were in fact responding to their environment and the dynamics of the evolving political situation by creative adaptation of beliefs and ideology, and not rigid adherents to dogma. In fact, there is ample evidence that the main suspects in this drama (from Ibn Taymiyya to Qutb and bin Laden) have been seen in their time as rebels against the prevalent orthodoxy, and consciously so.

Dying for God?

At another level, though, one has to recognize that religious motivation does indeed play an important role in the perceptions of men such as bin Laden. According to both Atran and Kramer, the tendency in modern social science to discount the centrality of religious faith is an indication of secular wishful thinking and self-deception. The idea that terrorist suicide bombers are rational actors who could be influenced and negotiated with is reassuring, Kramer argues. 'No one likes the idea that we may have embarked on a generations-long struggle against growing tides of suicidal fanatics. Professor Pape tells us that it need not be so, that we have it in our power to stop it now' (Kramer 2005). Yet the truth is that mundane calculations are not part of the suicide bombers' repertoire.

> The power of faith is something many understand at home but few deem worthy of consideration for enemies abroad. Yet, responses from jihadis, as well as their actions, suggest that sacred values are not entirely sensitive to standard political or economic calculations regarding costs or payoffs that come with undertaking martyrdom actions, nor are they readily translatable from one culture to another. Especially in Arab societies, where the culture of honor applies even to the humblest family as it once applied to the noblest families of the southern United States, witnessing the abuse of elders in front of their children, whether verbal insults at roadblocks or stripdowns during house searches, indelibly stains the memory and increases popular support for martyrdom actions. (Atran 2006: 139)

Let us overlook here how quickly this analysis has descended into confusing religion with culture, and honour with faith. The two are, of course, distinct and often do clash.

Let us also overlook the absurd suggestion that response to humiliation and oppression is culture specific, and the link between persistent and gratuitous humiliation, which tends to undermine the original argument for religious motivation. But let us go back first to the early distinction between dying for one's beliefs and killing for them. As mentioned before, the suicide attack shares some traits with acts of self-immolation, as well as with braving adversity in defence of cause or principles. It also appears to reflect the courage of a brave soldier defying death in defence of a noble cause.

However, suicide attacks differ in important aspects from all these phenomena. And the central distinctive factor is to do with the target of the suicide bomber, rather than his/her suicide act. And it is in particular the choice of civilian targets that makes this less an act of heroism than an act of brutality. However, criticism often appears to focus less on the terror part and more on the suicide itself. This would appear to be counterintuitive, since the terrorist's suicide should in principle be welcome from the perspective of his victims. Has the terrorist not saved his enemies the trouble by killing himself, leaving people to reflect more on his crime than on his death?

There are several reasons for this apparently puzzlingly misplaced focus. First, the suicide act is frightening and disturbing, mainly because it makes the act of terror more deadly and almost impossible to defend against. Second, the very level of fanaticism, hate, and anger implicit in such an act of angry self-destruction is deeply disturbing psychologically. And, finally, it is also morally unsettling, precisely because it reveals the terrorist's fanatical adherence to his principles. This may cause his victims to feel a strong sense of unease, a perceived threat to one's ethical position, since a person who feels this strongly might just have a cause.

Disturbing also about suicide terrorism is the stealth, the treachery involved. The suicide bomber poses as just another ordinary air traveller or bus or train passenger, thus making every 'ordinary' person suspect, and creating a devastating sense of insecurity and mistrust. This hits right at the fabric of society and the reassurance it affords its members.

In all this, the ethical component of altruistic dedication to cause and principles is eclipsed by the treacherous aggression against unsuspecting non-combatants. The strength of the uncompromising ethical stance of the man of principle, even in its sometimes reprehensible fanatical manifestations, comes from the open declaration made on its behalf. A conscientious objector has to stand out there in the open and declare himself/herself, so to speak. The acknowledged courage of this stance emanates from the very vulnerability of the position, from the knowledge that one is exposing oneself to mortal danger in taking a stand, and deliberately giving up the defence anonymity or the bearing of arms offer. This would not be the case if one only held that position secretly or has taken precautions or launched a 'pre-emptive' strike. A conscientious objector makes his/her point more powerfully, and appeals directly to our moral sensibilities, the more vulnerable he/she appears to be.

The act of suicide terrorism thus loses its moral power precisely because of the many compromises it has to make: by being dishonest and treacherous, and also being reckless and brutal, directed mainly against defenceless non-combatants. It is even worse at the level of organization leaders, where they treat even their own foot-soldiers as expendable.

This is why the analyses that regard suicide terrorism as an act of pure fanaticism, or even an 'ethical act' (as opposed to a political instrumental one), or 'an ethical suspension of ethics' (Devji 2005) miss the point. In particular, what is missed is the important distinction between the personal motives of individual actors and the logic of organizations pointed out by Mia Bloom and others. As Bloom reminds us, 'while individual bombers might be inspired by several – sometimes complementary – motives, the organizations that send the bombers do so because such attacks are an effective means to intimidate or demoralise the enemy' (Bloom 2005: 3).

Similarly, Jessica Stern's field research indicates that over time, and regardless of the original motives of the terror group founders, these organizations acquire a logic of their own:

People first join such groups to make the world a better place – at least for the particular populations they aim to serve. Over time, however, militants have told me, terrorism can become a career as much as a passion. Leaders harness humiliation and anomie and turn them into weapons. Jihad becomes addictive, militants report, and with some individuals or groups – the 'professional' terrorists – grievances can evolve into greed: for money, political power, status, or attention. In such 'professional' terrorist groups, simply perpetuating their cadres becomes a central goal, and what started out as a moral crusade becomes a sophisticated organization. (Stern 2003)

The calculus of salvation

In this regard, Atran's point about 'sacred values' being 'not entirely sensitive to standard political or economic calculations regarding costs or payoffs' may apply to individuals, but not to organizations. For organizations that ignore the cost–payoff logic tend to dissolve very quickly. But even at the individual level complex 'calculations' take place. If we dismiss the cases where some individuals act on impulse (in reaction to a sense of injury, personal humiliation, slight to one's honour, etc.), individuals who are not utterly insane carefully weigh the consequences of their actions. If one believes that martyrdom is the gate to everlasting bliss in Paradise, then choosing a martyr's death may look attractive. However, martyrdom is not the only gate to Paradise, since it is possible for a believer to live a long and prosperous life and still go to Paradise. Most people prefer this second option. Even in the time of the Prophet Muhammad, many good believers displayed this inclination. There is a story told about the plight of the Muslim community when it was under the most traumatic siege by its enemies, when the Prophet asked for a volunteer to go on a spying mission to the enemy camp. In return, he promised to ask God to make this person his companion in Paradise, an honour beyond which there is none for the believer. Not a single volunteer stepped forward to take up this tempting offer in spite of the relatively low risk, since people were too weak from starvation and apparently in great fear.

The widely accepted notion that the universe of the religious person is 'largely immune to the rational calculus' and that 'intense religious commitment springs of nothing less than outright irrationality' has been under some serious revision recently (Iannaccone 1998: 1468). Such notions are now seen as a relic of the nineteenth-century paradigm and the secularization thesis which regarded religion as 'merely a survival from man's primitive past and doomed to disappear' in our scientific era (Iannaccone 1998: 1468). New paradigms, mainly the 'rational choice approach' to the study of religion, have emerged to try to make up for this inadequacy (Iannaccone 1998; Sherkat and Ellison 1999).

Without fully subscribing to this approach, it might still be useful to speak of an 'economy of salvation'[1] which governs the conduct of religious individuals, groups, and societies. The believer thus balances various religious goods against each other: martyrdom against charity or a mystical renunciation of the world; prayer versus fasting; forgiveness versus justice, etc. The religious universe also incorporates a topography that sees the present world as part of a wider universe, and this life as the vehicle to a future one. This in turn requires a policy of 'savings and investments', whereby present sacrifices could secure future gains. In this regard, some writers who follow the Orientalist tradition have tried to posit a fundamental distinction between Muslim and Christian theology (where in Islam a calculus like the one I have outlined works in view of the belief in salvation by works, but not in Christianity where the belief (especially in Protestantism) is that salvation can be attained by Grace alone). This dichotomy is untenable, since it is based on a number of erroneous misconceptions about both religions.

The 'economy of salvation' is in turn embedded in a wider social context. Suicide bombings do not flourish merely on the basis of calculations made solely within the parameters of the 'salvation economy', but a general social acceptance of violence as an option and a realization that other options have little chance of success (Bloom 2005: 85). There must also be a reasonable belief (based on either past experience or other considerations and calculations) that the strategy was going to be effective (Bloom 2005: 83; cf. Pape 2005). This applies even to the most fanatical of groups. One example of this was the Egyptian Gama'a Islamiyya, one of the few groups that espoused '*jihad*' for its own sake. Its leading theorist, Abd al-Salam Farag, argued in his tract *al-Farida al-Gha'iba* (The Neglected Duty, *c*.1979) that *jihad* must be undertaken regardless of prospects for success, since God has ordered it, and it is up to God to take care of the consequences. However, when the group's tactics failed militarily and politically (failing either to topple the regime or gain wide popular support) it decided in 1997 to give up the armed struggle and used the same ideological resources it had used in the past to argue against militancy. In the last few years, its imprisoned leaders have produced several books of 'revision' critical of jihadist tactics, heaping a lot of criticism on groups such as al-Qaeda.

Terrorism and democracy

The way these groups conduct themselves is therefore eminently interactive. That is why Pape's much-criticized argument about the link between suicide terrorism and democracy is quite relevant. Terrorism in general is a problem almost exclusively for democratic societies, if simply because the threat of harming innocent people is not very likely to move brutal dictators (El-Affendi 2005). Some writers even define terrorism in terms of threats directed to democracies (Heymann 1998). In addition, dictatorships have no qualms about using draconian 'counter-terror' measures that are not open to democracies, such as those (extremely effective) tactics adopted by the Marxist regime in Ethiopia in the 1970s or by Syria and Iraq in the 1980s. That is why acts of terror are not often deployed against totalitarian regimes, and if they are, they are quickly defeated.

The incidence of terrorism is also a double pathology in democracies: a sign that something has gone wrong, as well as a reminder that democracies are not cities of virtue, but messy compromises catering for conflicting interests. Violence in general, and terrorism in particular, is often a wake-up call, a signal that the system stands in need of readjustment. It is not a very praiseworthy feature of democracies that only if the cost of unfair policies is significantly raised will compromise be contemplated. Voters in Britain, France, Israel, or the USA have often accepted withdrawal from occupied territories only when the cost of occupation began to significantly outweigh the benefits.

President George W. Bush's ratings were in the 90s when US armies went on the attack against foreign countries with impunity, but plummeted to below Richard Nixon's post-Watergate ratings when insurgencies made these excursions very costly. Israeli prime minster Ehud Olmert basked in approval as Israeli jets pounded the infrastructure of a country that was not at war with Israel and killed hundreds of civilians and displaced hundreds of thousands: over 70 per cent approved of his performance, while (most worryingly) over 90 per cent wanted more. However, it was not the vociferous international calls for restraint that swayed Olmert and his electorate and forced a cessation of hostilities, but the surprisingly robust performance of Hezbollah fighters who stopped the Israeli advance in its tracks and made the whole operation very costly. Olmert's ratings immediately went into a nosedive.

The conduct of Olmert also revealed another related problem of democracies: their vulnerability to extremist pressure, and the tendency of bad coins to chase out the good. Especially in situations of conflict, demagogues and hardliners could easily outbid moderates. Thus 'outbidding' is not only a phenomenon that explains the emergence and proliferation of suicide terrorism in some contexts, such as in Palestine and Chechnya, but also explains the regular ascendancy to power of hardline politicians, from Milosevic in Serbia, to Netanyahu and Sharon in Israel to George W Bush in the USA. More significant, the more moderate leaders are forced to join this outbidding, sometimes with disastrous consequences, as happened to former Israeli prime minister Shimon Peres when he attempted to show how tough he was by launching attacks on Lebanon in April 1996 in the run-up to a general election, and by ordering the assassination of a key Hamas leader at around the same time. The result was the infamous Qana massacre and a spate of suicide operations in Israel, causing Peres to lose the election to his more credibly hardline rival Netanyahu, saddling Israel with problems it continues to grapple with. Similarly, Democrats in the USA are forced to demonstrate that they could be more hardline on security than their Republican rivals if they are to come to power, which pushes them into ridiculous posturing which is far from credible as well as tending to alienate their core constituencies. The same can be seen with some centre-left parties, such as the Labour Party under Tony Blair in Britain, which had to steal the clothes of right-wing parties on security, immigration, and welfare issues, thus driving the whole political spectrum rightwards.

As a result of these developments, the health of democracies has come to depend, ironically, on various insurgencies, including terrorism. Thus it is inconceivable that internal Israeli politics (like US politics, which has become a replica of it) would generate a credible solution to the Arab–Israeli conflict under its own internal dynamic. It has taken the conflict with Iraq in 1990–1 to push the world towards undertaking significant moves in this direction, culminating in the Oslo Accords of 1993, which were repudiated very quickly after a right-wing resurgence in Israel which saw Prime Minister Rabin assassinated and the anti-Oslo Netanyahu elected. This in turn led to a resurgence in the fortunes of Palestinian anti-Oslo factions.

We should also be reminded that terrorism is not always a movement of protest by the weak. It could be a status quo phenomenon, as was the case with the Ku Klux Klan in the USA in the 1960s, the extremist settler groups in Israel, or the death squads in today's Iraq. By the same token, secular groups and even governments may sometimes act in ways that may not fit in with the presumed sharp distinction postulated in social science between the religious and the secular, the rational and the irrational. When it came to defending the United States after 9/11 against what was seen as a mortal threat to the country's security, all economic considerations were thrown out of the window.

Sacred violence

The fascination and puzzlement we experience in the face of suicide terrorism stems from the fact that we are here confronted by a phenomenon that lies at the intersection of a number of fundamental questions which deeply exercise the human mind and conscience. It has to do with the legitimization of violence, which is in turn closely connected to questions of identity, on the one hand, and authority, on the other.

The core question animating the debate on terrorism is the question of authority: who has the right to initiate violence and under what conditions? While it is generally accepted that only a legitimate public authority has the right to initiate violence, this might beg the question when the legitimacy of the state is being contested, or when the conflict is between states. And since ultimate authority flows from God, a person who can claim credibly to speak for God (or the equivalent ultimate authority: party, state, community, etc.) can hope to justify his/her claims of the right to wage violence. However, 'God' (or a 'god') is only recognized as such by a community. There is no point in citing the authority of Jesus to a Jewish community, or the biblical or Islamic God to Hindus. There is thus a circularity between the claim to speak for God and the claim to speak for the community.

The search for justification for suicide terrorism thus takes a complex trajectory, and is reliant on the overall social milieu and the political dynamics of a given situation. The biographies of those involved indicate this. Most jihadists refer to media reports of oppression and violence against fellow Muslims, as well as contacts with militants or listening to preaching about *jihad*. The case of Abu Jandal, a Yemeni man who lived in Saudi Arabia in the 1980s, illustrates this.[2] He joined the *jihad* after being influenced by media reporting of the war in Afghanistan and the Palestinian intifada, and later became bin Laden's personal bodyguard. In addition to media reports, he was also influenced by the general Islamic revival and the spin which the official preachers were putting on the war in Afghanistan as *jihad*. In the end, he was helped along by a donation by a pious lady who wanted to spend money on charity but was told by clerics that the most cost-effective way was to give it to someone wanting to embark on *jihad* (another interesting illustration of how the 'economy of salvation' operates). The existence of *jihad* networks and organizations makes such involvement possible. The way society as a whole regards the endeavour is also decisive.

This points to the problematic influence of religious traditions and doctrines on individual and group action, which is in turn dependent on the way communities relate to their religious traditions. The nearest thing Islam had to suicide terrorists were the Assassins, who belonged to a minority sect that was extremely isolated at the time. And the nearest it had to extremist groups were the so-called *khawarij* (rebels). Both were repudiated by mainstream Islam and regarded as heretics, so no one today can cite either as an authoritative model. By contrast, early Christian martyrs are venerated in mainstream Christianity, while Samson's suicidal revenge forms an important part of Christian/Jewish self-narrative. However, modern secular opinion in both traditions no longer takes those religious traditions seriously, at least not in a direct way, even though Israel's suicidal nuclear programme has been described by one commentator as an adoption of the 'Samson Option' (Hersch 1991). The same could be said about MAD, the Cold War acceptance of mutually assured destruction as the ultimate guarantor of world security.

The motives and actions of the Christian and Jewish martyrs were of course different from those of Samson. The (sometimes fanatical and gratuitous) quest for martyrdom by early Christians (which included beseeching Roman officials to have them executed or jumping into fire to join their fellow Christians who were being executed by burning) was a quest for redemption and resurrection. Similarly, there was so much hankering after suicide among Jews in the Middle Ages that leaders began to worry about the survival of the community (Murad 2005: 69). Samson, however, was different. It was not salvation that he was after, but revenge and the end of humiliating captivity.

The way a community defends its 'gods' or selects and identifies with certain parts of its traditions and not others is part of a complex and dynamic process of inclusion and exclusion. It is therefore often impossible to distinguish between what is religious and what is secular in ethnic conflict. Usually, violence that claims a sacred pedigree is characterized by its intensity and implacability. However, as Juster argues, the question of whether the burning alive of 500 American Indians in Fort Mystic by a Puritan militia in 1637 was a racial or religious killing cannot receive an unambiguous answer.

> The simple, and no doubt the right, answer is that it was both. In early modern Europe, people were defined as much by what believed as by how they looked. … In the British North America colonies, where the 'sacred' had more tenuous material and institutional existence and where legitimacy of any kind was harder to come by, it is nearly impossible to disentangle religious violence from other forms of aggression. (Juster 2005)

The same could be said about the situation in many conflicts today, including the ones where terrorism is a predominant style for some participants. This could lend some credence to the claim cited by Juster 'that all violence is in some sense sacred, that it is rooted in the deepest human desire to defend what is most precious and transcendent' (Juster 2005). This is at least how the perpetrators of massive genocidal violence (from the early American or Buer settlers, through the Nazis to the Khmer Rouge and the Hutus) put it. What is being defended for these groups is deemed so precious, and the threat is so barbaric and cataclysmic, that anything done in the course of this '*jihad*' is legitimate.

It is interesting that the proponents of the 'clash of civilizations' thesis such as Bernard Lewis and Samuel P. Huntington (and their partisans such as Kramer, Bar, and Harris cited above) use a similar language. The dispossession of Palestinian villagers by American and European settlers from Brooklyn or Golders Green, or the subjugation of Iraqis and Afghan partisans, is depicted as a struggle on the frontline in the defence of human civilization: if we do not conquer Falluja or subjugate Helmand province, Osama bin Laden and Ayman al-Zawahiri would be sure to bring Britain under the caliphate and convert America to Islam by force.[3] As Tony Blair put it in a series of recent speeches and press conferences, the battles in Afghanistan and Iraq represent the front line against terrorism, which means that they are the front line for the defence of civilization. And the only key to success was to be as ruthless and determined as the enemy. We are, in short, engaged in a sacred conflict.

Conclusion

The question of whether those engaged in perpetrating terrorist activities in the name of Islam have primarily religious or political motives is both valid and largely irrelevant to the understanding of the current conflict involving terrorism. Religion is certainly involved. Not only do the men of violence use religious rhetoric, but they are personally devout and observant. They genuinely believe that, by engaging in violence, they are doing God's work. Leaders are also charismatic and inspire 'religious' devotion in followers. At times they even exhibit some 'mystical' inclinations, as evidenced by the way in which they set great store by dreams and visions and expect and report 'miracles'. In their self-perception, at least, they do view themselves as 'men of principle', having sacrificed personal gain for the common good of the *umma* (community). Their detractors, and even neutral bystanders, are seen as either traitors motivated by narrow self-interest or blind and deluded individuals who fail to grasp the serious danger facing the *umma*.

With regard to the core issue of targeting civilians, they try to turn the tables on their critics not just by arguing that the enemy also targets civilians, or even that their targets (in particular in Israel and the USA) are not that innocent, but also by pleading an urgent 'humanitarian' imperative: there are innocent victims of oppression who need to be rescued, and this is the only way to achieve this. Thus by one stroke they try to obliterate the key distinction outlined above between terrorist operations and acts of self-sacrifice to rescue or help the innocent.

However, by this very act of pleading on the basis of universal values (defending the 'innocent'), they distinguish themselves from groups basing themselves exclusively on religious norms. As mentioned above, the Egyptian Gama'a Islamiyya is probably, at its inception at least, one of the few groups to take the dogmatic religious view. (There are indications that the Armed Islamic Group in Algeria and some of the affiliates of al-Qaeda in Iraq are taking a similar line). However, such groups tend to splinter quickly, as their narrow interpretations of who is in and who is out causes them to turn on each other. This has happened in Algeria and is happening in Iraq. In Egypt, the hardliners at first divided into two main groups, but later more splintering and defections occurred, and the Gama'a finally made an about-turn, declaring that its original stance was a grave error. This is a recurrent feature of Islamic history, as extremist groups have tended to die out through continuous infighting, not to mention incessant clashes with the authorities and mainstream Muslims, or eventually to accept the path of moderation.

It can be said, therefore, that as far some extremist groups that are motivated exclusively by religion do exist, they are more of a threat to themselves and their immediate communities than to the rest of the world. But the groups that adapt and survive are precisely those groups that do not allow dogma to stand in the way of conducting their little wars. For this, they need to conduct a successful propaganda campaign, which means adapting their discourse not only to appeal to the wider Muslim community, but also to wider international audiences. It also means avoiding the narrow sectarianism characteristic of all religious extremist groups. We find groups such as Hamas not only working happily with the Shiite rulers of Iran, but also with secular regimes where Islamists are heavily persecuted, including Syria (where joining an Islamist party is a capital offence), Saudi Arabia, Egypt, etc. They have also reached some form of accommodation with their secular rivals at home, and dropped key aspects of their Islamist agenda when they came to power – for example, allowing Jericho's notorious casino to continue operating, a decision that would be unthinkable for any Islamist government worth the name.

Thus in so much as they are relatively successful, such groups achieve their success (in terms of effectiveness, popularity, and longevity) by playing down their religious credentials and agendas, so that the only thing that distinguishes them from their secular rivals becomes their effectiveness. It is thus a supreme irony that groups which claim to be, and are described as, primarily religious derive both their legitimacy and political efficacy from other sources, mainly from playing a defined political role and fulfilling a socio-political need, which they can do only by downplaying their religious credentials, or at least by compromising them.

This aspect would have significant implications for policies devised to deal with such groups. We have seen how counter-terror measures premised on the religious nature of the threat tend themselves to advocate reciprocal fanaticism. In the Middle Eastern hotspots of Palestine, Iraq, or Lebanon, the approach of aggressive interventionism appeared to worsen, rather than resolve, the problem. In both Iraq and Lebanon, it has in fact created a problem that was not originally there. What we need in this volatile region is much less fanaticism, not more.

It is the greatest irony that while there is a sense in which all violence is sacred, as people usually go to war as a last resort to defend what is most precious and valuable to them, warriors have no option but to be pragmatic. On the battlefield, every general is a Machiavellian operator for whom the ends justify the means. Both generals and terror masterminds cannot afford dogma, for inflexibility can spell destruction.

One thing that can be said for certain is that an insurgent group primarily motivated by religious dogma cannot last long in the field and does not represent the kind of danger which warrants a world war to combat. If it survives long enough to pose such a threat, then it must enjoy widespread popular support, which is political in nature. It is different with a state possessed by the obsession that it is fighting precisely such a phantom. Movements that sponsor suicide bombings are not themselves suicidal. States possessed by fanaticism can easily become suicidal.

Part II
Religiously Motivated Violence in Specific Contexts

CHAPTER 7

Rituals of Life and Death:
the Politics and Poetics of *jihad* in Saudi Arabia[1]

Madawi Al-Rasheed

In Saudi Arabia jihadism is an underground movement that manifests itself in violent attacks. It is debated in rest places, mosques, private gatherings, poor and crowded neighbourhoods, elite intellectual salons, remote farms, and tents pitched in vast desert areas between major cities. Such debates are clearly illustrated in internet discussion boards and on jihadi websites. Most analysis of jihadism considers it a manifestation of religiously motivated violence. Such violence is often believed to be caused by radical religious interpretations, economic deprivation, anomie, and identity crises among young Muslim men. Although these are important dimensions, they fail to account for the phenomenon. Such analysis offers a description of the world in which jihadism thrives rather than a causal relationship between it and such dimensions. Jihadism is a culture with its own poetics and politics. Understanding it requires one first, to situate it in wider political contexts (global and local) and, second, to consider the performative aspect of violence. *Zaffat al-shahid* (celebration of the martyr) is a ritual of life and death that initiates the suicide novice. This ritual condenses several meanings related to life and death, categories that are often considered separate and deserving of two different rites of passage. The ritual also fuses the personal narrative of the would-be suicide bomber with the local and global political context, thus highlighting the performative aspect of jihadism. These rituals are broadcast on international media and on jihadi websites; both give the ritual a wide coverage.

In the twenty-first century, Saudi society is struggling over religious interpretation, which seems to be at the heart of political activism. As the struggle unfolds, it is accompanied by strife among various groups and confrontation between those groups and the state. Traditional *'ulama*, Sahwi shaykhs, jihadis, and laymen debate religious interpretations; not all subscribe to non-violent dialogue. Since 1990 violence has become the dark side of the Saudi religio-political debate. Various contestants challenge each other in a desperate attempt to control interpretations of religious discourse. The debate intensified after 11 September.

With American military power closing the gates of *jihad* in Afghanistan following the demise of the Taliban regime in 2001, the struggle of Saudis for the way of God came home.[2] Many Saudi jihadis who travelled for the second time to Afghanistan, where Osama bin Laden had lived between 1996 and 2001, returned to Saudi Arabia. After the toppling of the Taliban, the dismantling of al-Qaeda training camps, and the arrest or flight of Saudi trainees, it seemed to many observers that the war on terror, led by the USA and a number of supporting countries, was proving successful. Yet several countries in the region experienced waves of violence. Between 2001 and 2005, Saudi Arabia witnessed the worst violence in its modern history, conducted under the rhetoric of expelling infidels from the Arabian Peninsula and removing the despots, known in jihadi discourse as *tawaghit* of the Land of the Two Holy Mosques.

On 12 May 2003 a major bombing took place in Riyadh; 35 people were killed and hundreds injured. On 8 November 2003 car bombs devastated al-Muhayya residential compound, killing over twenty people and injuring many residents. On 21 April 2004 the building of the security forces in Riyadh was devastated by car bombs. On 2 May 2004 four attackers killed several Western workers in the industrial city of Yanbo. In the same month, another attack on offices and residences of oil company workers took place in al-Khobar in the Eastern Province. Before the end of 2004, on 6 December, the American consulate in Jiddah was attacked. A few days later, a car bomb exploded in the Ministry of Interior buildings in Riyadh.[3] In 2005 regular shoot-outs between jihadis and security forces continued.

These bloody attacks were major events that marked a new stage in the jihadi project: they announced the arrival of the *jihad* campaign in the Land of the Two Holy Mosques, as the jihadis called it. In addition, not a week passed during this period without the government announcing major success in capturing arms and killing suspected terrorists in the major cities, the mountains around Mecca, and the farms of Qasim. Many people, referred to as armed and violent suspects, were killed in shooting incidents between jihadis and the security forces. In 2005, Dammam saw the worst shoot-out between security forces and jihadis, who took refuge in one building. There was no doubt that the struggle for the way of God had returned home after several years in the diaspora.

The rhetoric of jihadis, the legitimizing narrative of violence, drew on the sacred Qur'an and the Prophetic tradition, citing *hadith*s calling upon Muslims to remove associationists or polytheists from the Arabian Peninsula – a reference to Westerners, mainly Americans. It is ironic that the struggle continued even after the USA and the Saudi government announced that most American troops stationed in Saudi Arabia had been moved to neighbouring Gulf states, mainly Bahrain and Qatar, in 2003. However, some American military bases remain in Saudi Arabia. As it unfolded, the struggle proved to be more complex and nuanced than simply a strategy to purify the land of Islam from infidels. The symbolism was, however, potent. The rhetoric of the struggle grew in a specific political context and is inspired by its own politics and poetics.

Throughout the 1990s, while the famous Sahwa *'ulama* were behind bars, a strong indigenous Jihadi trend took shape, which does not represent an external religious tradition, both politically and ideologically, as often mistakenly claimed by the government, traditional *'ulama*, and Saudi media. While several successful scholarly works have attempted to trace the indigenous historical and religious roots of contemporary jihadi discourse,[4] other works dissociate jihadis from the indigenous Saudi–Wahhabi interpretations.[5] In official Saudi discourse, jihadis are often referred to as Kharijites, or those who have gone astray (*al-fi'a al-dhalla*).

The quest to identify the local origins, causes, and intellectual roots of jihadism could have been a legitimate exercise at a time when Saudi Arabia was more isolated from the outside world. However, the country has now been drawn into the political, economic, intellectual, and religious exchanges of other places. Easy travel, the internet (since 1999), satellite television, and the media in general connect Saudis to other places and people. While Saudi Arabia received ideas and religious interpretations from abroad after opening its borders to Islamic trends since the 1960s,[6] it proved to be equally capable of initiating its own transnational religious flows to distant locations, thanks to a vigorous campaign of proselytizing and royal patronage (see Al-Rasheed 2005; Birt 2005). Saudi religious discourse was internalized by a whole generation of students who flocked to Saudi Islamic universities in Medina and elsewhere.[7] It is probably inaccurate to describe religious discourse inside the country since the 1970s as purely Saudi. It is equally unconvincing to describe the Islamic discourse that one encounters in London, Washington, Jakarta, Kabul, and Peshawar as purely Saudi–Wahhabi. At the same time, one cannot argue that jihadism in Saudi Arabia is an alien intellectual trend imported from other Islamist movements and locations.

Whether they draw on local religious tradition or imported politicized religion from other places, all Saudi jihadis make use of locally produced religious knowledge and interpretations. Furthermore, regardless of whether the inspiration for, or even the orders to engage in, violence come from outside – for example, al-Qaeda or other global jihadi movements – it is certain that there is a strong local dimension to the jihadi trend. Religious theoreticians of *jihad* (for example, some *'ulama*), interpreters (Islamist intellectuals), and those who carry out violent acts such as suicide bombers and other young militants are all Saudis, with the exception of a handful of activists who belong to other Arab countries and whose names have appeared on Saudi wanted terrorist lists.[8] To attribute the outbreak of violence in Saudi Arabia in the twenty-first century to outside agents such as a global terror movement is to miss the fact that this violence has its own local religious codes, meanings, politics, and poetics which resonate in some Saudi circles. The violence associated with the jihadi trend affirms that it is part of a 'highly meaningful relationship with divinity'.[9] Violent actors are understood as culturally authentic and significant rather than examples of the absence of such significance.

The terrorist attacks of the 1990s, which increased in frequency and magnitude in 2003–4, are not senseless and aimless acts by a group of alienated youth, often described in official religious and political circles as *khawarij al-'asr* (contemporary Kharijites). Perpetrators of violence are guided by cultural codes that draw on sacred texts and interpretations by religious scholars who claim to return to an authentic Islamic tradition, found not only in *al-kitab wa 'l-sunna* (the book and the deeds of the Prophet) but also in medieval and more recent commentaries on the texts by famous religious authorities among *aimat al-da'wa al-najdiyya* (Najdi religious scholars). Jihadi violence is not at the margin of religious interpretation, but is in fact at its centre; hence the difficulties in defeating the rhetoric of *jihad* in the long term. Jihadi violence, until now dormant in many cultural and religious interpretations, has recently erupted and claimed many lives.

A more fruitful approach to interpreting the jihadi trend and the violence associated with it must start with a number of assumptions. First, jihadism is a cultural expression grounded in strong religious interpretation that is indigenous to Saudi Arabia. Second, even if jihadism in Saudi Arabia is a function of global terror networks and transnational religious and political flows, it grows in a specific local context with its own cultural codes and experiences. Third, jihadism is not an affirmation of alienation, anomie, criminality, economic deprivation, and social marginalization, but an affirmation of a pledge to superiority and the belief in one's ability to change the world by action. It is often understood as a sign of the breakdown of 'traditional' society, loss of identity as a result of increased urbanization and modernization, or self-destruction and annihilation. It may grow in a context characterized by negative conditions of poverty, marginalization, and alienation, but one should not confuse context with cause.

It seems that jihadism, together with the violence associated with it, has been brought from the margins to occupy a central place in the religious map of Saudi Arabia. In jihadi discourse, changing the world by action is not a reflection of defeat, but an expression of empowerment felt by young militants, ideologue *'ulama*, and other Islamist intellectuals. Unless the perpetrator's view forms part of our own understanding, interpreting the jihadi trend will escape us. It is also essential to consider the role played by the Saudi regime in creating a context that allows it to grow. In many respects, the violence of the jihadis represents a mirror reflecting the violence of the state and its official *'ulama*.

Jihad as performance

In a world dominated by media representations, jihadis seem to be well prepared for disseminating powerful messages, iconography, and sounds, thus satisfying a world hungry for images of death, destruction, and devastation. Through several media organizations, one of which is known as Muassasat al-Sahab lil Intaj al-Ilami (Sahab Media Production), the world can see dozens of films of jihadis in training-camps, preparing for the struggle in the way of God. While the majority of this media production is found on the internet, through links to several sites, some important films and video clips are sent to established Arab media satellite stations such as the Qatar-based al-Jazeera channel. Films are also available for purchase from commercial companies, for example Tempest Publishing, a sister organization of IntelCentre, a Washington-based company whose stated objective is 'to assist professionals to understand and fight terrorism'. This company sells films, CD-ROMs, documents, and other material related to *jihad* and terrorism to researchers, journalists, and military and security agencies.[10] Most of the items on the sale catalogue seem to have been produced by al-Qaeda, including the Arabian Peninsula branch.

One controversial film called *Badr al-Riyadh* (The Full Moon of Riyadh, a reference to the 12 May 2003 Riyadh attack), named after the battle of Badr between Muslims and Meccans, was broadcast several months after the Riyadh bombing. According to jihadi sources, between three and four hundred thousand people downloaded the film from the internet in less than five days.[11] To understand *Badr al-Riyadh*, three important dimensions must be considered. The first is the two martyrs. The second is other actors, some meant to inspire and encourage viewers – most importantly Osama bin Laden, Abu Hafs al-Masri, Humud ibn Oqla al-Shuaybi and al-Khattab, *jihad* leader in Chechnya – while others are projected as the 'malicious other', against whom the battle is waged; this category of people includes George Bush, Crown Prince Abdullah (King since 2005), and Minister of Interior Prince Nayef. Third, the film's message is embedded in words and acts.

This film was perhaps one of the most powerful media productions issued by Saudi jihadis, for a number of reasons. It showed the suicide bombers of the attack of 12 May, Ali al-Harbi and Nasir al-Khaldi, in an unusual location – a private house with a sitting-room lined with comfortable cushions and colourful rugs, rather than a military camp with barbed wires and signposts. The cosy setting is a contrast to that often projected in other al-Qaeda films featuring jihadis filmed in training-camps, caves, and rugged mountains. Furthermore, the film portrayed the would-be martyrs in an important event that sealed their fate: *zaffat al-shahid*. The word *zaffa* is usually associated with weddings as in *zaffat al-'arus* (bride) or *'aris* (bridegroom), a common celebration which takes place within the context of Muslim and Arab weddings. The future martyrs, al-Harbi and al-Khaldi, are celebrated in a televised *zaffa* as if they are bridegrooms.[12] They are also shown in what looks like a garage where several jihadis engage in preparing the vehicle, a jeep, for the attack. They are seen painting the jeep and changing its number plate to AZ H 314. A jihadi explains that 314 is the number of the early Muslim fighters who participated in the battle of Badr with the Prophet.

Badr al-Riyadh documents an event best understood as a celebration of life and death interspersed with young men dancing and chanting while sporting a range of weapons around waists, shoulders, and arms. The martyrs, with their bearded smiling faces completely uncovered and with their hair longer than is usual for young Saudi men, dressed in white long shirts, were filmed surrounded by a large number of hooded young men, dancing and reciting verses from the Qur'an and other sources. An unseen interviewer asks them several questions. A sense of camaraderie and solidarity is enhanced by images of the central actors surrounded by supporters and well-wishers.

Although the film shows a celebration of the deaths of the would-be martyrs, they are seen while still alive, and partake in the jubilation. The celebration of life and death and the theme of martyrdom portrayed in the film confirm jihadism as a theatrical performance, in which actors and audience are expected to fuse in a powerful emotional bond. While it is common for societies all over the world to separate birth and death rituals, in *Badr al-Riyadh* the boundaries overlap, and are even blurred. In a single rite of passage, a jihadi passes from life to death, then he returns to life. Death is projected as a temporary liminal phase, neither here nor there, culminating in a return to life. The theme of life and death is best expressed in a song which accompanies the celebration. The song asks participants to 'celebrate the passage of the martyr to his second home in heaven', and 'to celebrate his passage to the afterlife fully clothed, according to the tradition of the Prophet'. Al-Harbi explains that martyrdom is a transaction: God buys the soul of his slave (a human being), who sells it willingly. In a sombre voice, with his head down and his eyes fixed on the floor rather than the camera, al-Harbi recognizes that the martyr may be hesitant to leave his family, friends, and loved ones, but one is under an obligation to perform the noble deed, which is prescribed after the five pillars of Islam. Al-Harbi explains that death is defined as leaving life (*mufaraqat al-hayat*), but the martyr has another life in heaven. Death is a transition from life in a treacherous world to life in a generous world, where the Prophet and his companions reside. He also invokes the inevitability of death, whether 'in bed' or 'in a car accident'. Given this inevitability, he asks a rhetorical question: 'Isn't it more noble to die for the sake of God?'

The martyrs appear in the context of an interview by a fellow jihadi, who asks them questions relating to *shari'a* evidence in support of suicide attacks, the purpose of *jihad*, the target of their actions, and their views on the USA, the Saudi state, the *'ulama*, and the security forces. The interviewer brings to their attention some of the accusations of the Saudi media and officials, which portray jihadis as killing Muslims and generating chaos in the Land of the Two Holy Mosques. The two martyrs are expected to defend the planned suicide attack on Mustawtanat al-Muhayya (the al-Muhayya settlement), a reference to a residential compound mostly occupied by expatriates. Al-Harbi invokes the terminology of 'settlement' to allude to similarities between Jewish settlements in Palestine and foreign residential compounds, inhabited by Americans and Europeans, in Saudi Arabia. The objective of the attack revolves around liberating the Arabian Peninsula from infidels, the establishment of an Islamic state, and revenge for jihadis who are tortured in Saudi prisons or killed by Saudi security forces, such as Turki al-Dandani and Yusif al-Ayri. The martyrs lament the current transformation of the Arabian Peninsula from a land where the message of *tawhid* (monotheism) spread to other parts of the world to one from which infidel armies launch attacks (*himla salibiyya* (a crusade)) on Afghanistan and Iraq.

While the general message of the *jihad* and its purpose reflect well-rehearsed arguments put forward by bin Laden and other jihadi ideologues, both al-Harbi and al-Khaldi fuse the grand jihadi narrative with personal experience, life history, and individual motivation. Asked why he does not go for *jihad* in areas where there is clear argument in favour of the practice, al-Harbi inserts his own personal narrative as one of the primary motivating factors behind his determination to annihilate himself. He explains that the Saudi state is a *kafir* state, practising *nifaq* (hypocrisy). While the state claims that it supports Muslim causes, it punishes those who serve their religion. He went to fight in Bosnia in the 1990s, and when he returned to Saudi Arabia he was imprisoned for a year and three months. He claims that he was tortured, left in a small cell, deprived of sleep, and paraded naked in al-Ruways prison. He was shocked both by the torture of jihadi prisoners, as a result of which some died, and by the verbal abuse experienced in prison. He concludes the narrative of his personal journey to seek death by asking, 'Which Islam is this?'

The second suicide bomber narrates another personal journey. Al-Khaldi recounts several incidents whereby he and his comrades came face to face with Saudi security forces. One encounter took place in Istirahat al-Shifa, where a social gathering of jihadis was taking place. According to al-Khaldi, they were listening to lectures and engaging in recitations when armed security men attacked them. A friend died in the encounter as he was shot by security forces – for no obvious reason, according to the narrator.

In addition to the main suicide bombers, the film invokes the words of famous ideologues. Osama bin Laden's speeches, together with those of his aides, such as Abu Hafs al-Masri, and Saudi religious scholars, such as Shaykh Humud al-Oqla, provide powerful words, inspiring not only the would be-martyrs but a wider circle of viewers as well. The message is to demonize and terrorize the enemy. In a clear declaration, the voice states, 'Yes I am a terrorist,' against a background of chanting:

Crush the Pharaoh with the sorcerers
Kill whoever is an infidel
Make your land a graveyard
For the defeated armies of blasphemy

If ever someone is in doubt of the meaning of terrorism, the chanting then explains:

Prepare bows and arrows for blasphemy
Prepare white swords
Take from our enemies red hearts and necks
Let blood flow on soil
Like a glorious river
Tell the world and repeat
This is the meaning of terrorism

The message of other characters in the film centres on the decriminalization of the perpetrator and the humanization of the martyr. The film blurs the boundary between victim and victimizer, and deconstructs well-rehearsed arguments against *jihad*. The various jihadis in the film face the challenge of responding to Saudi claims that they are criminals, lacking a clear message, and in favour of killing other Muslims rather than infidels. A jihadi responds by asking how someone who spent twenty years defending Muslims in Afghanistan against the Soviets can turn into a criminal targeting Muslims. He adds that 'killing Muslims' in Saudi Arabia would be easier than killing infidels, as the latter reside in well-secured homes and are difficult to reach.

The film also demonizes the other, the enemy, a group of world leaders (such as George Bush) and Arab and Muslim local 'agents' of world powers (for example, Crown Prince Abdullah and Prince Nayef). Speeches by Saudi leaders are played as evidence of their treason, and association with and subservience to infidels. In one speech, the Crown Prince is reported as saying to George Bush that 'a small minority (*al–fi'a al-dhalla*) poisoned our solid friendship and tarnished the image of Islam, but we are determined to fight it with all our means'. Al-Khalidi sends a message to Abdullah asking him to repent and stop privileging secular intellectuals, and associating with infidels. If he does not listen, then he faces the sword.

This film, like many other media clips that flood the internet after every suicide bombing or attack, represents another dimension of contemporary *jihad*, which has so far escaped analysts and commentators. *Jihad* is not only about theological treatises. It is also not solely concerned with purifying the Arabian Peninsula and defeating its despots and pharaohs. *Jihad* is a performance, celebrating heroes in a land where there are none. Saudi youth are denied a symbol for defiance. Their local media is saturated with old preachers calling for total obedience to the ruler, citing Qur'anic verses and *hadith*s discouraging individual opinion, initiative, and interpretation. Such media productions require the viewer to submit, obey, and follow a single interpretation and world-view. Saudi youth surf the internet, downloading *Badr al-Riyadh* and other al-Qaeda productions in search of rebellion, assertion of the self, and individuality, against a well-developed machinery whose main purpose is to censor not only the internet but all alternative visions that may circulate in the public sphere. *Zaffat al-shahid* in *Badr al-Riyadh* is not only a celebration of life and death; it is also a ritual of rebellion and defiance, with a clear message reaching thousands of viewers. In the modern world, *jihad* is the performance par excellence. However, jihadi films are today competing with another genre of video clips and popular culture productions that dominate Arab satellite music channels such as Prince al-Walid ibn Talal's controversial Rotana television channel. The latter proved to be extremely popular among young people, not only in Saudi Arabia but in the Arab world as a whole.

Badr al-Riyadh glorifies a privatized *jihad* in a globalized world where the media create images of a monotonous world, repeat well-rehearsed arguments, and promote one message, despite the fact that globalization was expected to generate diversity and pluralism. At one level, globalization did offer a glimpse of this hoped-for diversity, but at several others it suppressed local culture, authenticity, and tradition. The resurgence of jihadi discourse and practice in Saudi Arabia should be understood as a local response to the challenge of globalization and its alleged discontents using the same weapon that is believed to threaten authentic tradition. This is clearly demonstrated in jihadi views on women, honour, and shame, all believed to be under threat from the champions of the alleged globalized crusade of the unbelievers.

Gendered *jihad*: women, honour, and shame

In Saudi society, women have always been viewed as symbols of the nation's piety, a barometer of its commitment to Islam and Arab tradition.[13] The state enforces this view as it polices public space under the guidance of the Committee for the Promotion of Virtue and Prohibition of Vice, in search of immoral behaviour, potentially generated by the sheer presence of women in the public sphere. Segregated, veiled women in black cloaks have become a symbol of identity in cities indistinguishable from any major cosmopolitan space in Dallas or Houston. On the one hand, the state claims to 'protect' women; it does so for its own purposes, mainly to assert its legitimacy as an Islamic state. Society imitates the state in its obsession with restricting women, but for different reasons – mainly to guard against rapid change and alien intruders. Early in the twentieth century, the majority of Saudis perceived the presence of foreign immigrants as a necessary evil, needed to modernize the country in the absence of local skills and expertise. However, since the 1980s, this presence has become problematic – not only economically, but also culturally and politically. While economic dependence on foreign labour was grudgingly tolerated, reliance on American military assistance has generated heated debate.

Over a very short period of time, Saudi Arabia moved from a small-scale traditional society in the 1970s, in which face-to-face interaction was the norm, to a society inhabiting an urban space shared with a multinational population of Arab, Western, and Asian immigrants, expatriates, and workers, the majority of whom are male. Society responded to the challenge of hosting a substantial foreign population in several ways. It imposed strict segregation on its immigrant population, translated into lavish – and not-so-lavish – residential compounds and neighbourhoods where they were expected to live. It also imposed a strict code of behaviour, limiting interaction between Saudis and foreigners to the workplace, and revisited what is believed to be the last frontier in resisting penetration by the outside world: the female sphere. As a result, women paid a high price: they were seen as the last 'battlefield', to be defended, protected, sheltered, and even restricted, oppressed, and excluded in pursuit of 'guarding' men's honour, and limiting the possibility of 'shame' being inflicted on men as a result of female behaviour or the violation of women by outsiders. Suddenly Saudi society became more restrictive in regulating the female sphere. While men tolerated contact with foreigners in the workplace, they did everything they could to restrict their own women's contact with outsiders, with the exception of course of Arab female teachers, instructors, doctors, nannies (in the case of wealthy women), and other indispensable outsiders, such as male drivers. Society allowed its women to be driven by foreigners, as their foreignness and low status guaranteed their inferiority to Saudi women, but restricted women from entering the public sphere, especially that which has become the sole domain of Saudi and other men. Women who previously worked in markets and fields, where they intermingled freely with men, had to be restrained as this public sphere turned into potentially hostile and alien space.

Instead of creating grounds for the amelioration of the status and rights of women, modernity led to greater restrictions on them. The state restricted female marriages to *ajnabi* (foreigners), a category that included foreign Arabs and Muslims. It also protected the strict sex segregation in the public sphere through its various law-enforcing agencies and modern technology. For example, modern communication technology has allowed strict segregation in universities, where female students see and communicate with male lecturers via videos. Children of women who married outsiders were denied nationality, thus excluding them from citizenship, the welfare state, and its benefits. The state was an active agent in enforcing a restrictive code despite its apparent interest in the welfare and education of women. In 2006 new legislation required shops selling lingerie to employ women only, in a move to appease rising Islamist discontent and ameliorate unemployment rates among women. Outspoken members of the Saudi religious establishment objected to enforcing the law. To resist female employment, they missed an opportunity to Islamize the selling of women's lingerie, a position that brings to mind their objections to women driving.

While the state used women as a token of its piety in a desperate attempt to enhance its own Islamic credentials, jihadis considered women a symbol of their rebellion, defiance, and assertion of Islamic identity, pride, and autonomy. *Jihad* was not only an Islamic duty to defend the land of Islam, it was also a gendered obligation to protect women from the onslaught of alien cultures, corrupting media, state oppression, and Western penetration. In jihadi discourse, *jihad* is not only a defence of Islam and Muslims but is also a resistance to local and global agents who violate men's honour and bring them shame through a systematic violation of Muslim women. Both American troops in Saudi Arabia and the Saudi state are portrayed as contributing to this violation. Examples of American 'aggression' draw on images from Afghanistan, Israel, and Iraq. Israeli and American soldiers searching Muslim women at checkpoints and inside their homes give ample opportunities to illustrate the violation. Saudi state violation of women is represented through a portrayal of the state as an agent of moral corruption and secularization via its support for and sponsorship of a media empire that corrupts the youth of the nation. Jihadis claim that Saudi princes do not respect Islamic tradition, but endeavour to normalize moral laxity, degeneration, and sin. The Jiddah Economic Forums in which women participated in 2004 and 2005 brought about themes relating to the corrupting influence of the state. The picture of Madeleine Albright sitting on an armchair in the front row during the conference, unveiled and with her legs exposed, came to represent not only the 'corruption and moral degeneration' of an 'American Jewish woman' but also the Saudi state. The fact that Saudi women attended these conferences and are now allowed to participate in, for example, the Jiddah Chamber of Commerce and Industry as voters and candidates gives more substance to Jihadi claims.

In jihadi discourse the politics of defiance is not only anchored in Islamic duty, it is deeply rooted in the discourse about women, honour, and shame. A recurrent theme centres on the association between subservience to infidels and the violation of Muslim women. The local despot is not only an oppressor who does not rule according to the revealed message of God, he vigorously contributes to the emasculation of Arab men by *'ahirat al-rum* ('Roman prostitutes'), a reference to the presence of female American soldiers on Saudi soil for over a decade. The fact that Saudi Arabia was defended by American women in the Gulf War was viewed as the emasculation of its male population, especially the armed forces, a theme that is regularly reiterated in jihadi discourse. Such images existed in jihadi literature long before the torture of Iraqi prisoners in Abu Ghraib prison by American soldiers – both male and female – entered the public sphere in 2004. The local despot is often referred to as *dayuuth*, a strong abhorrent term describing a pimp, especially one who trades his own *maharim* (the taboo female relatives such as mother, daughter, sister, etc.). The despot is transferred here from the realm of politics to that of morality, invoking images of sin and punishment resulting from the violation of divine law. Above all, then, the violation of women is attributed to the contribution of two agents: the infidels and the local despot.

Jihadi shaykh Issa al-Oshan (d. 2004), known as Muhammad Ahmad Salim, advised Saudi jihadis against 'going to seek *jihad* in Iraq or elsewhere' and encouraged them to stay at home where they are needed.[14] He elaborates that this is not because the situation in Iraq is confused and unstable and there is no banner to fight under, but because the priority should be the local context. Al-Oshan moves away from the duty to defend the global *umma* to the necessity of guarding against the violation of local women. He mentions a story that brought shame to a Saudi jihadi who was fighting with the Taliban against the troops of the Northern Alliance during the American-led invasion of Afghanistan. Al-Oshan's friend told him that a Northern Alliance soldier asked him why a Saudi Arab was fighting in Afghanistan. The Saudi jihadi answered that he wanted to defend the Muslim emirate of Taliban. The Afghan soldier replied, 'How could you come to Afghanistan while the Americans are with your sister in Saudi Arabia?' At this point in the conversation, the jihadi felt shame. Al-Oshan argues that a Saudi cannot defend the honour of other Muslims while his own house is violated. This is a good reason to 'break the cross first in the Land of the Two Holy Mosques, to set the land on fire so that no cross could feel secure'.

As gendered discourse, *jihad* draws on cultural values, with specific reference to male–female relations, the violation of women, and the obligation to defend one's honour before seeking to do the same for other Muslims. In Saudi Arabia, *jihad* is a response to the emasculation of men, who are subjected to state repression in the context of prison and torture chambers. Al-Harbi, the suicide bomber in *Badr al-Riyadh*, painfully recounts the experience of his friend in al-Ruways prison. He says that during a long and painful interrogation session, his friend and his wife (described as a respectable tribal woman, a *hurra*, a free woman (not a slave)) were subjected to the most humiliating treatment. He claims that his friend, after being paraded naked, was forced to have sexual intercourse with his wife in front of the interrogators. This not only violates the honour of the free woman as a result of an act committed by her husband, who has lost his ability to defend her honour, but also dishonours the man. Rather than being the defender of women's honour, the male prisoner, emasculated and humiliated by state agents, is turned into its violator. He collapsed, sobbing and crying, according to al-Harbi. While it is impossible to verify the authenticity of this story, it is nevertheless a powerful statement in jihadi propaganda that plays on honour and the violation of honour. These images blur the boundaries between protector and violator of women. The helpless Muslim male is portrayed as being forced by the despot to violate his own honour.

The connection between *jihad*, on the one hand, and women, honour, and shame, on the other, invokes the role of women in this duty. Are women expected to join the jihadis? Shaykh Nasir al-Fahad provides a *fatwa* in this regard. He responds to two questions:

Q: what is the nature of female *jihad* and are women required to go out seeking *jihad*? Please answer with regard to defensive and offensive *jihad*.
Sheikh al-Fahad: In general, women are not required to go for *jihad* but their exit with male jihadis to cure the ill and the wounded and to fetch water for the thirsty is permissible. In Ibn Abbas's *hadith*, the Prophet used to raid with women who looked after the wounded and gained booty. Umm Atiyyah confirms that 'we used to go on raid with the Prophet to nurse the ill and there was booty for us'. Also it is permissible for women to fight directly in some situations. This is what Safiyyah bint Abd al-Mutalib did when she hit a Jew with a pole and killed him in battle. Women must get permission from their guardians before going and must be accompanied by a *mahram* [a male chaperon].[15]

While there is no conclusive evidence in support of women directly participating in combat, there is ample evidence to suggest that women must be involved in other capacities, one of which is to support male relatives involved in *jihad*.[16] For this purpose, the al-Qaeda branch in the Arabian Peninsula published *al-Khansa*, a sister electronic magazine to *Sawt al-Jihad*, named after a famous Muslim female poet who lost several sons in *jihad*. The magazine instructs women on how to reconcile *jihad* with family life. According to the editorial board, the magazine is published by an organization called the Women's Media Bureau in the Arabian Peninsula. It owes its publication to the leader of *jihad* in the Arabian Peninsula, Abdulaziz al-Muqrin (d. 2004).[17] The magazine advises women on how to educate their children in the *jihad* culture, in addition to giving instructions in first aid and nursing the wounded, thus echoing the expectation regarding women's participation in *jihad* from an Islamic point of view. The magazine does not, however, exclude women from active combat, as the instructions in carrying and handling arms indicate.[18]

The discourse of the struggle for the way of God which encourages confrontation, resistance, and domination is not only anchored in religion and politics; it is a cultural whole which defines a way of life for the Muslim male, the privatized self in a globalized world. Above all, it tackles the last line of defence, the remaining guarded fortress: women in Saudi Arabia. As gendered discourse, *jihad* not only promises liberation from the domination of 'infidels', but also a defence of the most cherished female, whose violation dishonours and shames men. Violence is generated not simply by adherence to globalized ideologies and movements but through the regional and sub-regional disputes which have their origins in the complexities of local political history and cultural practices (Whitehead 2004). To understand the jihadi trend in Saudi Arabia, one must situate it in the local context. Jihadis are a response to contradictions generated by a political leadership professing adherence to Islam, while the reality attests to something different. Jihadism is today defined as illegitimate violence, but in many respects this violence is a mirror of another type of violence – that of the state. Certain types of violence can be considered legitimate, not only by the Saudi state but also by the international community. In the aftermath of 11 September and under the banner of the 'war on terror', Saudi state violence remains more or less outside the realm of condemnation. Violations of human rights are occasionally mentioned by international organizations, but remain unproblematic for countries that claim to uphold these rights at home and encourage them abroad.

Jihadis narrate their dying for faith through violent acts. The narration takes place in the context of rituals documented in films, poetry, iconography, religious treatises, and art. Whether this violence is religiously motivated but has political purposes is an irrelevant question. Jihadis anchor their violence in religion, but there is more to it than simply being a religious duty. Although they claim they die for faith, they are entangled in a web of local and international politics that attracts heavy media coverage in the contemporary world. To search for the origins of this violence is akin to the futile quest by previous generations of scholars to identify the origins of religion, which they later abandoned in favour of identifying the function, meaning and aesthetic of religion in society. Today the search for the origin of jihadi violence seems to be an equally futile exercise. It is perhaps more productive to examine this violence as a subculture that is struggling to carve a place in a public sphere that demonizes any religious narrative regardless of its message. Jihadis have learned that virtual performative rituals preceding real acts of violence grant them this space in the public imagination, not only in their local communities but also the international arena.

In this respect, as subculture, jihadi violence struggles to become part of the culture, not as an innate attribute of a Muslim tradition or heritage, but as a process that gathered momentum in Saudi Arabia and elsewhere and is continuously fuelled by real acts of state and other global actors' aggression that remain beyond condemnation in the public sphere.

CHAPTER 8

The Islamic Debate over Self-inflicted Martyrdom[1]

Azam Tamimi

A historical context

Until employed in Palestine, the human bomb was seen as alien to the Sunni community within Islam. It had been more commonly associated with Shiism; the Iranians are believed to have been the first Muslims to employ it. They did so quite successfully in the war with Iraq throughout the 1980s. Hundreds of young Iranian men were sent on martyrdom missions along the borders between the two countries to deter the well-equipped and well-armed Iraqi troops, thanks to Western and Arab support. The tactic served the Iranians well because their Iraqi counterparts, many of whom had not been convinced of the legitimacy of the war their government was waging on their neighbour, were not prepared to make similar sacrifices.

The tactic then moved to Lebanon in the aftermath of the Israeli invasion in 1982. The first martyrdom operation within Lebanon took place on 11 November 1982 when Ahmad Qasir, identified as a member of the Islamic resistance, drove his Mercedes into the headquarters of the Israeli military governor in Tyre and detonated its 200 kilograms of explosives, killing 74 Israelis. From then on the human bomb became a routine weapon employed by the Lebanese resistance against Israeli occupation troops. The most memorable of all suicide bombings in Lebanon were the two simultaneous attacks carried out on 23 October 1983 against the US Battalion Landing Team headquarters and the French paratroopers' base situated just 4 miles (6 km) apart in Beirut. The two suicide bombers, both of whom died in the attack, were named as Abu Mazen (26) and Abu Sij'an (24). A previously unknown group called the Free Islamic Revolutionary Movement (FIRM) claimed responsibility for the two attacks, which killed 241 American and 58 French soldiers. FIRM was believed to have been made up of Lebanese Shiite Muslims associated with the Amal militia. Hezbollah had not yet emerged, but FIRM might have been its precursor. Lebanon also produced the first female suicide bomber in the Arab world; her name was Sana' Mhaidli. Her car bombing of an Israeli military convoy on 9 April 1985 was claimed by the secular Syrian Nationalist Party.

The Lebanese Hezbollah, founded with Iranian backing as a Muslim Shiite response to the Israeli occupation of South Lebanon, inherited the resistance and the tactic of the human bomb, which it continued to employ until Israel withdrew unilaterally from South Lebanon in 1999 when the cost of occupation could no longer be borne.

A series of devastating human bomb attacks were launched by the Islamic Resistance Movement (Hamas) in April 1994 in retaliation for the massacre perpetrated on 25

February 1994 by an American-born Jewish settler. Baruch Goldstein, who is believed to have secured the assistance of Israeli troops to sneak into al-Haram al-Ibrahimi Mosque in Hebron, opened fire and threw hand grenades at worshippers as they kneeled halfway through the *fajr* (dawn) prayers, killing 29 of them and wounding scores others.

The series of revenge acts started on 6 April 1994 when Ra'id Abdullah Zakarnah, a Hamas Brigade member, drove a booby-trapped vehicle with an Israeli number plate into Afula bus station and detonated it at around noon. Nine Israelis were killed and more than 150 were injured. A statement issued by Hamas military wing, al-Qassam Brigade, soon afterwards claimed responsibility for the bombing and warned the Israelis to evacuate the settlements in the West Bank and Gaza. With clear reference to what Goldstein had done inside the mosque, Hamas vowed to make Israelis pay for the pain and harassment Jewish settlers inflict on the Palestinians under occupation.[2]

The second attack was carried out on 31 April 1994 by Ammar Amarnah, another member of al-Qassam Brigade. The target this time was an Israeli bus travelling on line 8 at al-Khadirah (Hadera) to the north-west of Tulkarm. Amarnah blew himself up on the bus, killing five Israelis and wounding more than thirty. More operations were carried out that same year; many more were carried out over the years that followed, mostly in response to attacks on Palestinian civilians by Israeli troops or Jewish settlers.

Many Palestinians were initially shocked by the human bomb tactic. Some argued against it from a purely pragmatic point of view; in their assessment it could only harm the Palestinian cause. The operations were also opposed on the ground that they were, by their very nature, indiscriminate and resulted in killing innocent civilians, something the critics believed could not be justified or legitimized under any circumstances. The Fatah-led Palestinian Authority opposed the operations, primarily on the grounds of its commitment to the peace process and the potential damage they could cause to its role in peace-making. Hamas spokesmen, however, insisted that such a tactic was the only means available to the Palestinians to deter the likes of Goldstein from ever attacking the defenceless Palestinian population under occupation. In time, an increasing number of Palestinians accepted that the human bomb was necessary to offset the balance of power, which had been totally in favour of the Israelis, whose military supremacy in the entire Middle East region was guaranteed by the USA and its European allies.

It did not take long for the majority of the Palestinians to express appreciation and admiration of the heroism and altruism of the men and women who volunteered their bodies and souls to go on sacrificial missions on behalf of the cause. The more the Palestinians felt vulnerable the more they supported martyrdom operations, and even demanded more of them. Little effort, if at all, was needed to convince those who had qualms that nothing else seemed to work as a means of self-defence or deterrence. Nevertheless, Palestinian public support for martyrdom operations has varied. Polls conducted at different times gave rise to different results, but rarely has support for these operations dropped below 50 per cent. A poll conducted in the Gaza Strip by the Norwegian pollster Fafo in the first week of September 2005 indicated that a majority of 61 per cent of those questioned agreed with the statement that 'suicide bombings against Israeli civilians are necessary to get Israel to make political concessions'. Fafo conducted a face-to face survey with 875 respondents to monitor Palestinian views on the Israeli withdrawal from the occupied Gaza Strip.[3] The *Jerusalem Post* reported on 16 October 2003 that a poll had shown that 75 per cent of Palestinians supported the suicide bombing of the Maxim restaurant in Haifa on 4 October 2003. The opinion poll was conducted by the Palestinian Centre for Policy and Survey Research in Ramallah.[4] An earlier poll conducted by the Palestinian National Authority's State Information Service between 11 and 13 June 2002 in both the West Bank and the Gaza Strip revealed that 81 per cent of the sample polled objected to the PNA's designation of martyrdom operations as terrorist acts. Fifty two per cent of them said the PNA resorted to labelling these operations as terrorist because of 'international pressure'. The total number of those polled was 1,137 aged 18 years and above, 456 of them from the Gaza Strip and 681 from the West Bank. Incidentally, the poll also revealed that 86 per cent of the sample 'supported military attacks against Israeli occupation troops and Jewish settlers inside the Palestinian territories'. Sixty-nine per cent believed that the objective of carrying out martyrdom operations inside Israeli towns was to force an end to the occupation, while 13.4 per cent believed the objective was to undermine the peace process, and 11.3 per cent said the operations aimed to weaken the Palestinian Authority and embarrass it before the international community.[5]

Elsewhere in the world, the Sri Lankan Tamil Tigers, who struggle for an independent Tamil state, began carrying out suicide bombings in 1987. It is estimated that they have since perpetrated over 200 such attacks. The Tamil suicide bomb attacks were employed primarily to assassinate politicians opposed to their cause. In 1991, they assassinated former Indian prime minister Rajiv Gandhi, and in 1993 they assassinated President Premadassa of Sri Lanka in 1993. In 1999, the Tigers attempted to assassinate Sri Lankan president Chandrika Kumaratunga using a female suicide bomber. While the Tamils tend to prefer female bombers, Islamic groups in Lebanon and Palestine did not deem it appropriate to deploy them until the eruption of the second intifada. Hamas was reluctant to recruit female bombers, but removed the ban under pressure from female members, some of whom threatened to go it alone or in association with other factions. The first female bomber in Palestine was 26-year-old Wafa Idris, who detonated in Yaffa Street in Jerusalem on 28 January 2001. She was followed by ten other female 'martyr bombers', the last of whom was Zaynab Ali, who detonated on 22 September 2004. The campaign was launched by Fatah's al-Aqsa Martyrs Brigade, and was soon joined by the Palestinian Islamic Jihad and Hamas.

The debate

The martyrdom (suicide) operation has been one of the most hotly debated issues in modern times within Sunni circles. Since in Sunni Islam there is no single jurisprudential authority to issue a decisive *fatwa* (legal or jurisprudential opinion) on any matter, and with the opening of new fronts where the tactic of the 'human bomb' has been employed, the debate among specialists and laymen is far from over.

The first and most crucial dimension of the debate relates to whether the act is suicide or sacrifice. The second dimension relates to the problem of the indiscriminate nature of the human bomb that might inevitably, despite all precautions, result in killing innocent civilians, particularly children. The third dimension relates to the repercussions of the tactic on the lives of the community in whose defence such operations are carried out. In the case of Palestine, for example, because the Israelis have both the means and the willingness to respond with air raids, incursions, and all forms of collective punishments, the viability of the human bomb tactic as a means of deterrence or a weapon of retaliation has been a main point of contention. However, Palestinian factions who employed the tactic in the years leading to Ariel Sharon's decision to implement his plan of unilateralism believe they should be credited for forcing an Israeli withdrawal from Gaza. Opponents disagree, and attribute the Israeli decision to other factors, including Israel's concern about demographics and its plan to annex much of the land in the West Bank where large Jewish settlements exist.

Both supporters and opponents of the 'martyrdom operations' support their positions, which in essence are purely political, with evidence derived from the Islamic sources and Islamic historical precedence.

Life and death

Islam teaches that no one but the Creator Himself has the right to take the life of any human being. One of the five essentials Islamic *shari'a* is said to seek to protect is human life itself.[6] Having told the story of the murder of Abel by his brother Cain (the two sons of Adam), the Qur'an concludes: 'On that account We ordained for the children of Israel that if anyone slay a person unless it be for murder or spreading mischief in the land – it would be as if he slew the whole people. And if anyone saved a life, it would be as if he saved the life of the whole people' (Q 5: 32). It is also stated in the Qur'an: 'Take not life which Allah made sacred otherwise than in the course of justice' (Q 6: 151).

It is therefore only in the course of serving justice that authority is given for life to be taken. In such circumstances the taking of life is said to be aimed at saving life itself. 'In the Law of Equality [capital punishment for murderers] there is [saving of] Life to you, O ye men of understanding; that ye may show piety' (Q 2: 179). The Islamic *shari'a* goes into great detail in defining the conditions where taking life is permissible, whether in war or in peace. To avert any attempt at abuse, the Islamic criminal law takes every precaution in order to minimize the need for capital punishment and to ensure that justice is served.[7]

War in Islam is considered a necessary evil; this can clearly be inferred from the Qur'an itself: 'And Allah turned back the Unbelievers for [all] their fury: no advantage did they gain. And Allah has spared the Believers the need to fight. And Allah is full of Strength, Able to enforce His Will' (Q 33: 25). It is from this verse that Shaykh Yusuf al-Qaradawi, one of the most prominent scholars of contemporary Islam, concludes that war in Islam is a necessity that should only be resorted to when it is extremely necessary. 'The rule in Islam is to make peace and to promote it.' In Islam, he explains, if tension could be eased and crisis could be resolved without the need to engage in battle, that would be best. 'The Qur'an describes a situation when God spares the believers the necessity of fighting, as if fighting is a negative thing rather than a positive thing.'[8]

There are two words in the Islamic lexicon that are associated with fighting. *Qital*, which derives from the three-lettered Arabic verb q.t.l (*qatala*), means to kill or to slay. The word *qital* and all its derivatives that mean combat feature in the Qur'anic chapters that were revealed in Medina, that is, in the aftermath of the creation of the Islamic state following migration of the Prophet and his earlier followers from their hometown, Mecca. The word *jihad*, which derives from the three-lettered Arabic verb j.h.d (*jahada*), features in the Qur'anic chapters revealed during the Meccan period, which lasted thirteen years. The word *jahada* may mean: to endeavour, to strive, to labour, or take pains. It may also mean: to overwork, to overtax, to fatigue or exhaust, to strain, to exert, to tire, to wear out or give trouble to, to concentrate on or put one's mind to something. It has also been used as a synonym for *qatala*: to fight.

Jihad

The earliest appearance of the word *jahada* or *jihad* in the Qur'anic revelation was associated with the struggle of the nascent Muslim community against oppression. It was a struggle (*jihad*) for the freedom to worship according to their monotheistic faith and for the right to invite others to embrace it. When first preached to the Arab community within Mecca, Islam was perceived by the town's influential elders as a rebellion aimed at changing the status quo. Those established in power felt threatened by Muhammad's call to the people to reconsider their inherited beliefs and norms; particularly threatening was his powerful critique of the life his kinsmen were leading, one which the Qur'an described as sinful and misguided.

Qur'anic revelations, recited by the few who dared follow the Prophet despite the intimidation, ridiculed idol worshipping and chastised the Arabs for claiming that God had given them authority to commit what Islam considered heinous crimes and sinful acts. The stakes for those in authority were high; this new creed, whose Prophet claimed to be the rightful inheritor of Abraham, the ancestral father of the Arabs and the Israelites, and who presented himself as an endorser of all the messages and prophets that preceded him, was appealing to the weak and the oppressed, to the poor and the destitute, and to all those discriminated against by the Arabs for one reason or another. Throughout the first thirteen years of his mission from around 610 to 622 CE, the Prophet resorted to no means of challenging Arab polytheists apart from engaging them in debate and reciting the Qur'an to them. He attracted the oppressed members of the community who saw in what he preached a promise of emancipation, of deliverance from servitude. His challenge to the mighty and powerful was: 'Allow me the freedom to speak and the people the freedom to choose.'

The 'elders' of Quraysh, the main tribe in Mecca into which the Prophet Muhammad was born around 570 CE, were determined not to allow him to strip them of their prestige or pull the rug of authority from underneath their feet by turning their young men and women and their slaves and servants against them. They orchestrated a defamation campaign against him, claiming he was a charlatan, a magician, a poet, and a soothsayer. People were warned to stay away from him lest they come under the influence of his spell. When that tactic did not work, his opponents used force against him and his followers. The weak among them, who had no solid tribal backing, were persecuted. They were tormented, and some of them lost their lives under torture. At one stage, the entire community of monotheists was banished into a barren valley. Sanctions were imposed on them, and Arabs in and around Mecca were ordered to boycott them for three years. When that too failed to curb the growth of Prophet Muhammad's following, the 'elders' sought to negotiate a compromise with him; they offered to recognize his 'god' provided he recognized their idols; and they suggested: 'Let's worship your god together on one day and our gods on another.'

The Prophet was instructed by the Qur'an not to heed the call for such a compromise: 'Say: O you *kafirun* [those that are thankless or those that reject faith], I worship not that which you worship, nor will you worship that which I worship. And I will not worship that which you have been wont to worship, nor will you worship that which I worship. To you be your Way, and to me mine' (Q 109: 1–6).

The Prophet was advised not to obey them. Instead, he was ordered to perform '*jihadan kabiran* [struggle with the utmost strenuousness] against them with the Qur'an' (Q 25: 52). This verse from Surat al-Furqan (chapter 25) was revealed in Mecca; it comes within the context of the Qur'anic response to the constant endeavour by the polytheists of Mecca to dissuade the Prophet from preaching monotheism. In chronological terms, the verse is believed to be the first Qur'anic reference to *jihad*. Similar to this is the following reference to *jihad* in Surat al-Hajj: 'And strive hard in Allah's Cause as you ought to strive (with sincerity and with all your efforts). He has chosen you [to convey His Message to mankind] and has not laid upon you in religion any hardship: it is the religion of your father Abraham' (Q 22: 78).

Jihad at the time involved no *qital* (fighting or combat); it was an entirely non-violent form of struggle. In fact, throughout the Meccan period, which lasted thirteen out of a total of twenty-three years of Prophethood, the Muslims were forbidden to use force. The prohibition was not self-imposed, but in accordance with a divine commandment. Not even when they suffered persecution or were tortured were they allowed to respond with violence. They were told to be patient, show self-restraint, and withhold their hands.[9]

Observance of patience and self-restraint was hailed as a noble act, a *jihad*, for which the highest of rewards were promised by God in the Hereafter. Consider for instance the reference to *jihad* in the last verse of Surat al-'Ankabut: 'And those who perform *jihad* [strive] in Our [Cause], We will certainly guide them to Our Paths: for verily Allah is with those who do right' (Q 29: 69) It would not be possible to interpret this verse correctly without taking into consideration the first few verses of the same chapter. Verses 1–6 unequivocally associate *jihad* with self-restraint and abstention from the use of violence in response to persecution:

> Do people think that they will be left alone because they say: 'We believe,' and will not be tested. And We indeed tested those who were before them. And Allah will certainly make [it] known [the truth of] those who are true, and will certainly make [it] known [the falsehood of] those who are liars. Or think those who do evil deeds that they can outstrip Us? Evil is that they judge. Whoever hopes for the Meeting with Allah, then Allah's Term is surely coming, and He is the All-Hearer, the All-Knower. And whosoever strives, he strives only for himself. Verily, Allah stands not in need of any of His creation. (Q 29: 1–6)

Despite such a clear origin of the concept of *jihad*, one can hardly find an English-language dictionary that does not suggest 'holy war' as a meaning for it. According to the Merriam-Webster Dictionary, for instance, *jihad* is 'a holy war waged on behalf of Islam as a religious duty'. The dictionary provides two other meanings: 'a personal struggle in devotion to Islam especially involving spiritual discipline'; and 'a crusade for a principle or belief'.

There is nothing whatsoever in the Islamic sources that describes war as holy. The rendering of the word *jihad* as 'holy war' has more to do with the history of Christianity in Europe than with the teachings or the history of Islam. The term 'holy war' is a European Christian invention dating back to around AD 1096, when Rome began preaching a 'Holy Crusade' 'to free the Holy City of Jerusalem from the clutches of heretics and infidels'.

Qital

The ban on fighting was lifted a couple of years after *hijra*, the migration in 622 CE of the Prophet and his followers from Mecca to Medina in search of a safe haven. It was only when the Muslim community of Medina, politically organized by virtue of a constitution known as the Medina Document, needed to defend itself against external threats that permission was given to use force and engage the enemies in battle.

> Permission to fight [against unbelievers] is given to those [believers] who are fought against, because they have been wronged; and surely, Allah is able to give them victory. Those who have been expelled from their homes unjustly only because they said: 'Our Lord is Allah.' For had it not been that Allah checks one set of people by means of another, monasteries, churches, synagogues, and mosques, wherein the Name of Allah is mentioned much, would surely have been pulled down. Verily Allah will help those who help His [Cause]. Truly Allah is All-Strong, All-Mighty. (Q 22: 39–40)

Nevertheless, the licence to fight is not a free one. Only when attacked, or when perceiving a threat of imminent attack, are Muslims allowed to take to arms: 'And fight in [the] way of Allah those who fight you, but transgress not the limits. Truly, Allah likes not the transgressors' (Q 2: 190). And once in engaged in battle, Muslim troops are supposed to abide by a strict code of conduct. The terms of this code are stated clearly in the *hadith* (Prophetic tradition) and are elucidated in the books of *fiqh* (Islamic jurisprudence). It is reported that Caliph Abu Bakr said in a farewell sermon to Muslim troops heading for battle with the Byzantines:

> I recommend to you that you fear Allah and obey Him. When you engage the enemies do not loot, do not mutilate the dead, do not commit treachery, do not behave cowardly, do not kill children, the elderly or women, do not burn trees or damage crops, and do not kill an animal unless lawfully acquired for food. You will come across men confined to hermitages in which they claim to have dedicated their lives to worshipping God, leave them alone. When you engage the pagan infidels invite them to choose between two things. Invite them to embrace Islam. If they don't wish to do so invite them to pay the *jizya* [tax paid by non-Muslims who reside in a land conquered by force]. If they accept either, accept from them and stop fighting. But if they reject both, then fight them. (Basyuni 2003: 35)

In Islamic literature on *hadith* and *fiqh*, when *jihad* is mentioned without further designation it usually refers to *qital*. In this case it does include, in addition to carrying arms and fighting the enemies in the battlefield, contributing money or effort to the cause for which *qital* is undertaken: 'O you who believe! Shall I lead you to a bargain that will save you from a grievous Chastisement? That you believe in Allah and His Messenger, and that you perform *jihad* [strive your utmost] in the Cause of Allah, with your wealth and your persons: that will be best for you if you only knew' (Q 61: 10–11). A great risk is involved in the *jihad*; and Islam motivates its followers to take that risk in anticipation of a great reward in the life after death:

> Allah has purchased of the believers their persons and their wealth; for theirs in return is the Garden [of Paradise]: They fight in His Cause, and slay and are slain: a promise binding on Him in Truth, through the Torah, the Gospel, and the Qur'an. And who is more faithful to his Covenant than Allah? Then rejoice in the bargain which you have concluded: that is the achievement supreme. (Q 9.111)

Believing in the Day of Resurrection, in the inevitability of being brought to account to be asked and then rewarded or punished for one's deeds in this life, is one of the basic tenets of the Islamic faith. To the faithful this life is a temporary abode, a passageway, towards a permanent abode, an eternal life, in the Hereafter. Therefore, a believer has a mission in this life, namely to worship the One and Only God and submit oneself to no authority but His. Submitting to the One and Only God entails freeing oneself from all other deities.

Resisting oppression and striving for a just world is an integral part of a believer's mission in life. According to Tunisian Islamic thinker Rachid Ghannouchi, one of the basic features of the Islamic faith is that it generates within the believer a passion for freedom. Algerian thinker Malik Bennabi had earlier asserted that the Islamic faith accomplishes two objectives: first, it liberates man from servitude and renders him unenslavable; and second, it prohibits him from enslaving others.[10] Many contemporary Islamic scholars and thinkers agree with him and explain that this is exactly what the concept of *jihad* is about. For this reason it is not only on the battlefield that a believer is expected to perform *jihad*, which may be seen as the constant endeavour to struggle against all forms of political or economic tyranny whether domestic or foreign.

Martyrdom
Despite its sanctity in Islam, life can be sacrificed for the sake of ending oppression. Both the Qur'an and the *hadith* (sayings or traditions of the Prophet Muhammad) exhort Muslims to resist oppression and struggle against it by means of *al-amr bi'l-ma'ruf wa al-nahy 'an al-munkar* (enjoining the good and forbidding the evil). On the basis of a *hadith*, which orders Muslims to deter evil with the hand, or with the tongue if that is all they can afford, or with the heart if they lack the power to do much else, Muslim scholars, both past and present, have articulated three levels of resistance or struggle. The minimum level is a psychological process whereby a Muslim prepares himself or herself, by means of boycotting evil and disliking it, for ascending to a higher level. The higher level of resistance entails condemning evil through the use of various non-violent means, such as speaking up, writing or demonstrating, or mobilizing public opinion to identify that which is wrong and endeavouring to change it. The highest level of all is resistance through the use of whatever means of force are available.

What really matters is that oppression should never be given a chance to establish itself in society. A Muslim is supposed to be a conscientious individual responding with appropriate action to whatever injustice may be perpetrated in society provided the chosen action does not produce a greater evil than the one targeted with resistance. A Muslim is thus a force of positive change, a citizen whose faith reinforces within him or her a sense of responsibility to combat oppression. It is understandable that a Muslim may lose his or her life struggling against oppression, and for this he or she is promised a great reward in the life after death. In other words, the effort made is not wasted and the sacrifice is not in vain.

Prophet Muhammad is quoted as saying: 'The noblest of *jihad* is speaking out against an unjust ruler in his very presence.' He also said: 'Hamza [the Prophet's uncle and one of the earlier martyrs in Islam] is the master of martyrs, and so is a person who stands up to an unjust ruler enjoining him and forbidding him, and gets killed for it.'

It would only be right to draw from this Prophetic tradition that martyrdom in the Islamic standard is not failure; a martyr is not a loser but a hopeful human being who offers his or her life for what is much more valuable and, at the same time, eternal. For this reason martyrs are elevated to the highest of all ranks. Muslims pray regularly for the attainment of such status. A Muslim recites at least seventeen times a day in his *salat* (prayer): 'Show us the straight way, the way of those on whom you have bestowed your Grace' (Q 1: 6–7). Those on whom God has bestowed His grace belong to one of the categories listed in another Qur'anic verse which says: 'Those who obey Allah and the Messenger are in the company of those on whom is the Grace of Allah: the Prophets, the sincere [lovers of truth], the martyrs, and the righteous [who do good]. How beautiful is their Company' (Q 4: 69).

By choosing to offer his or her life in the cause of God, a believer, a would-be martyr, enters into a transaction with his Lord, Allah. Such a covenant is referred to at least twice in the Qur'an and is mentioned in quite a few Prophetic traditions as well.[11] Martyrdom, sacrificing one's life for a noble cause, is an Islamic concept par excellence. It is one of only two acceptable outcomes of fighting in the cause of Allah; the other is victory. It would seem, therefore, that from an Islamic perspective life is not the most precious thing because it is highly commendable to give it up for what is more precious, namely, freeing one's self or one's community from the shackles of servitude.

However, martyrdom today is not as simple as it used to be. In the old days Muslims went to war in a *jihad* wishing for either victory or martyrdom. A martyr was one who lost his life because of wounds inflicted on him by the enemy. Furthermore, there was no element of certainty as to which of the two wishes was likely to be fulfilled. Today, many of those who go on a *jihad* are almost certain it is martyrdom they will reap and not victory. On the one hand, they know that the balance of power is not in their favour to dream of a win, let alone anticipate it. On the other hand, one of them is certain about his death because he goes into the 'battlefield' strapped with dynamite; he predetermines his fate when he presses the button. So, rather than be killed by the enemy he chooses to kill the enemy by killing himself. The wars such 'martyrs' fight are not conventional ones. They know they cannot inflict damage on their enemy without exploding in his face.

The 'suicide bombing', or what some Muslims call 'martyrdom operation', was not invented by the Muslims. However, it is today identified with them and with their religion. Precursors of these operations in the Middle East were first introduced by Arab secular leftists, who appear to have imported the idea from elsewhere in the world. During those days such operations did not usually involve strapping oneself with dynamite; mostly, they involved daring attacks from which the attacker had almost no chance of escaping alive. The attack by members of the Japanese Red Army in 1972 at Lod airport in Israel is considered one of the earliest such attacks in the Middle East. However, it was at the hands of the Lebanese Hezbollah, founded in response to the Israeli invasion of Lebanon in 1982, that this modus operandi was refined throughout the 1980s.

Sacrifice or suicide?
The defenders of the human bomb tactic deem it an act of sacrifice, while those who oppose it see the action as nothing but suicide. The defenders judge the perpetrator to be a martyr, a person who offers himself (or herself) for the sake of a noble cause and who ends up reaping the highest of rewards and is designated to the highest ranks in Paradise. From this perspective not only is the act permissible, it is highly commendable and greatly appreciated. Its defenders believe it would not be right to designate the human bomb as 'suicide' simply because suicide is strictly forbidden in Islam. The perpetrators do not resort to killing themselves out of desperation, they argue; otherwise it would be considered a major sin. What they do, in their opinion, is a sacrificial act.

Those who oppose the operations on religious grounds assume that the perpetrators are desperate individuals who prefer to die than live because of having lost hope or patience; they argue that what these individuals commit is nothing but suicide because of their knowledge that what they are embarking on is definitely going to kill them. Thus they conclude that the perpetrator is a sinner who will end up in the Fires of Hell.

The Qur'an is unequivocal in its prohibition of suicide: 'O ye who believe! Eat not up your property among yourselves in vanities: but let there be amongst you traffic and trade by mutual good-will: nor kill [or destroy] yourselves: for verily Allah hath been to you Most Merciful! If any do that in rancor and injustice, soon shall We cast them into the fire: and easy it is for Allah' (Q 4: 29–30). Al-Bukhari reported that Prophet Muhammad said: 'There was once a man before you who suffered a wound; he could not bear the pain, so he took a knife and bled himself to death. The Almighty Allah said: "My servant has taken his own life; therefore I shall deny him admission to Paradise."' The Prophet is also reported to have said: 'Whoever kills himself with an iron instrument will be carrying it forever in hell. Whoever takes poison and kills himself will forever keep sipping that poison in hell. Whoever jumps off a mountain and kills himself will forever keep falling down in the depths of hell.'

A fine thread may separate suicide from sacrifice; which is determined by the intention of the actor. In contrast to suicide, sacrificing one's life for a noble cause is something which Islam enjoins and for which it promises the best of rewards. A person who turns himself or herself into a bomb to thwart or frustrate the enemies is therefore considered a hero who makes the greatest of sacrifices for the sake of his faith, country, or *umma*.

Few Muslim scholars, if any, inside Palestine today subscribe to the opinion that the human bomb is an act of suicide. The official mufti of the Palestinian Authority, Shaykh Ikrima Sabri, has not only considered these operations a noble act of sacrifice for the sake of God, but has also harshly criticized those scholars, mainly from Egypt and Saudi Arabia, who denounced 'martyrdom operations' as suicide. He went as far as accusing them of utter ignorance due to failing to understand the context in which these operations take place inside Palestine. The Palestinian chief judge, Shaykh Taysir al-Tamimi, only concurs.

The attitude of scholars and religious institutions outside Palestine vis-à-vis the human bomb has been varied. Division seems to be prompted by political rather than jurisprudential considerations. As a matter of principle no one denies the concept of self-sacrifice since it is explicitly emphasized in the Qur'an and the *hadith*. Nevertheless, a few establishment scholars, representing government-controlled religious institutions in Saudi Arabia and Egypt, have argued that martyrdom operations are illegitimate. Some deem them to be acts of suicide because of the certainty of death. Others oppose them because they violate the Islamic code of war ethics by the indiscriminate killing of innocent civilians, including children.

However, defenders of the tactic argue that the conflict in Palestine is far from conventional. They emphasize that the Islamic code of war ethics applies to conventional warfare. They refuse to accept that it should also apply in the case of Palestine. They see this situation as an exception to the norm because the unarmed and defenceless people of Palestine have been invaded and oppressed by a power that has exclusive access to some of the most advanced technology and to weapons that kill, maim, and destroy while well out of the reach of their victims. From this point of view, whatever the Palestinians resort to in order to defend themselves and deter their oppressors is seen as legitimate. It is often argued that only when the Palestinians are given access to the sort of weapons the Israelis have, including F16 fighter planes, Apache helicopters, tanks, and armoured vehicles, will it be illegitimate for them to resort to unconventional means of self-defence.

One of the most outspoken scholars against suicide bombings has been the mufti of Saudi Arabia, Shaykh Abd al-Aziz Al Sheikh, who is appointed by a royal decree. Al Sheikh has been quoted as judging these operations to be illegitimate. He said he did not believe them to be a part of *jihad*, and expressed concern that they might amount to suicide. Several scholars in his country have issued statements or *fatawa* that express their opposition to his position. Critics of the mufti discount his *fatwa* on this matter; they suspect that he only issued it in response to a request from the Saudi government, which has indeed come under pressure from its ally the USA to extract such a religious edict from its most senior scholar.

Shaykh Humud ibn Oqla al-Shuaybi has been one of several leading independent scholars in Saudi Arabia to defend martyrdom operations. The shaykh, who commands a considerable following inside as well as outside the kingdom, declared the martyrdom operations that are carried out by the Muslims in Palestine, in Chechnya and in other Muslim countries against invading enemies to be legitimate. He went on to say that these operations are part of the *jihad* in the Way of Allah and are some of the most effective means of *jihad* against the enemies. He concluded his *fatwa* with an explanation about the difference between suicide and martyrdom:

A person who commits suicide kills himself out of desperation, impatience or loss of hope, an act that does not please Allah. A *mujahid* [struggler] executing a martyrdom operation, however, takes the action while in a state of happiness and longing to Paradise; his objective is to inflict harm on the enemy. Therefore, equating a person that commits suicide with a person that offers himself in martyrdom is flawed.

Another outspoken critic of martyrdom operations has been the grand shaykh of al-Azhar, Shaykh Muhammad Sayyid Tantawi, who is appointed by the president of Egypt and reports to him directly. Whereas the Saudi mufti's office has been consistent in its position, Shaykh Tantawi has contradicted himself on a number of occasions on this issue, seemingly reflecting the political mood inside Egypt each time he spoke or was asked to speak. His first *fatwa* was one of outright prohibition, arguing that the operations were illegitimate because of the innocent people they end up killing. He did not seem to object to the use of the operations against military personnel. Then he came out in full support, declaring the attackers to be martyrs of the highest degree. He was quoted as saying: 'When the Muslim explodes himself in the midst of combatant enemies, he only performs an act of self-defence; it is martyrdom because the recompense for an injury is an injury equal thereto. What Israel is doing inside the Palestinian territories would only drive any Muslim to seek revenge and act in self-defence.'[12] He then took a U-turn: speaking at a conference on terrorism in 2003 in Kuala Lumpur he reverted to his original position of outright unconditional condemnation.

Shaykh Yusuf al-Qaradawi, a renowned Egyptian scholar who resides in the state of Qatar, has issued a *fatwa* saying:

> Martyrdom operations are of the greatest types of *jihad* in the Cause of Allah whereby a person sacrifices his soul in the Cause of Allah in full compliance with the Qur'anic verse 'Of the people there are those who trade themselves in pursuit of the Pleasure of Allah.' A person who commits suicide does so out of desperation because of some kind of failure; he is one who seeks to rid himself his life. In contrast, giving oneself to martyrdom is an act of heroism, and act that is deemed by the majority of Muslim scholars to be the greatest form of jihad.[13]

Like al-Shuaybi and al-Qaradawi, most independent scholars have opted for the position of considering suicide operations inside Palestine to be 'martyrdom operations' of the noblest forms of *jihad*. Scholars in Jordan, Lebanon, Saudi Arabia, Egypt, Iran, Pakistan, Malaysia, and Indonesia have been quoted as confirming the legitimacy of resorting to the human bomb tactic in Palestine. A combination of justifications is usually given for supporting martyrdom operations against Israeli targets.

- These operations are not suicide but sacrifices of the highest quality for the noblest of causes.
- Israel is a military outpost and there are no civilians within it to spare apart from children. All men and women in Israel serve in the army. As long as the attackers take every precaution to avoid hitting children, every other target in Israel is legitimate; if children are inadvertently hit it is because it is unavoidable.

- The Palestinians have been left with no other choice since their enemy is armed to the teeth while they are deprived of the basic means of self-defence. So long as this situation continues the Palestinians cannot be blamed for engaging in these attacks. Therefore, the Palestinians are exempt from adhering to the Islamic code of ethics in war.
- If the Israelis want an end to these operations they should accept the offers of truce made to them repeatedly by Hamas and other Palestinian factions. However, to expect the Palestinians to unilaterally stop all resistance in the hope that the Israelis will stop attacking them is unfair and will not do.

More controversy

Suicide or 'martyrdom' operations are by no means restricted to Palestine. As these types of operations are being carried out by Muslims elsewhere in the world, the debate about 'martyrdom' has intensified, with divisions growing wider than ever. Few scholars provide blanket support for any 'martyrdom attack', no matter where or when. It is worth noting that a number of prominent scholars who support 'martyrdom operations' in Palestine were unequivocal in condemning the 11 September attacks in New York; they also condemned the bombings that were carried out later on in Bali, Riyadh, Rabat, Istanbul, Madrid, and London, as well as bombings that target civilians in various parts of Iraq or Afghanistan. They judge these bombings as acts of criminality, not as acts of lawful *jihad*.

In July 2004, Shaykh Yusuf al-Qaradawi, who leads this group of scholars, was invited by the mayor of London, Ken Livingstone, to convene the annual meeting of the European Council for Fatwa and Research at the Greater London Authority. The initiative was intended to be a goodwill gesture on the part of the mayor towards the Muslims of London, who constitute about 10 per cent of the city's population. Shaykh al-Qaradawi seized the opportunity and invited hundreds of scholars from around the Muslim world to come to London during the time of his visit to inaugurate the International Union of Muslim Scholars, a project he had been working on with many of them.

The presence of Shaykh al-Qaradawi in London was condemned by pro-Israel groups in the United Kingdom, which accused him of supporting terrorism. MP Louise Illman and the Jewish Board of Deputies led a campaign to have the shaykh deported, having failed to prevent his visit in the first place. The controversy about al-Qaradawi's visit attracted the attention of the media. The right-wing press focused their attention on the shaykh's position on suicide attacks. Pressed to make his position clear, the shaykh insisted that Palestine was a special case where 'martyrdom operations are legitimate because the Palestinians have no other effective means of self-defence'. Asked about suicide bombings in Iraq, al-Qaradawi explained that although he supported the right of the Iraqi people to resist the US-led invasion of Iraq and to fight to liberate their country from foreign occupation he did not believe that the use of human bombs was justified because, in his judgement, the Iraqis – unlike the Palestinians – had an abundance of means with which to resist foreign occupation and did not have to employ the martyrdom operation, which he described as a weapons of last resort.

When four Muslim men used their bodies to bomb London on 7 July 2005, Shaykh al-Qaradawi, both personally and in the name of the International Union of Muslim

Scholars, condemned the attack. He refused to equate it with what he insisted were martyrdom operations in Palestine. He explained at the time that, unlike the Palestinians whose land is occupied and who suffer because of Israeli occupation day and night, these young men had no justification whatsoever to attack Londoners in the way they did.

There are, however, a few influential scholars, especially in Saudi Arabia, who consider the perpetrators of all 'suicide bombings' as martyrs and their actions to be legitimate. The disagreement in judgement between the two sides is not over the question of whether it is suicide or martyrdom, but rather over which targets are legitimate and which are illegitimate.

Palestinian organizations that resort to martyrdom operations maintain that they never target children. They insist that they primarily target army personnel and that any attacks on civilians are either unintended or inevitable so long as Israel continues to target Palestinian civilians. Additionally, they argue that Israel is a militarized state where every single adult, male or female (apart from the ultra-Orthodox Jews), serves in the army. They explain that when they target buses it is because soldiers travel in these buses and when they target bars and nightclubs it is because these are meeting places for off-duty servicemen and women who earlier in the day would be actively engaged in military operations in the occupied territories.

Consensus among Palestinians regarding the military nature of Israeli society has not been hard to come by. Therefore, the controversy over the target has not been the most difficult issue to tackle. It was the means and not the target that became the subject of theological or jurisprudential investigation. Assessing the nature of the operation was the most important issue, since the legitimacy or illegitimacy of the 'human bomb' was determined upon its outcome. As always in the case of *fatawa*, the difficulty emanates from the fact that in the Islamic religion there is no one spokesperson or single authority to refer to. Furthermore, it is not unusual in such turbulent times as ours today for politics to have a great bearing on the opinion of the religious scholars.

CHAPTER 9

The Radical Nineties Revisited: Jihadi Discourses in Britain

Jonathan Birt

In this chapter I want to attempt to remember the pre-11 September moment more clearly: to recall a time when discourses produced by jihadist Salafi groupuscules in Britain had not been driven underground, when new anti-terrorist legislation to deal with 'international terrorism' had not been enacted (the Terrorism Act 2000 only came into force in April 2001), and when such radical discourses were mostly seen as an annoying, containable irrelevance by most British Muslims, and were the subject of a tacit 'covenant of security' between such groups and the intelligence services, the police and the government.

These radicals were left largely free to operate provided that they caused no harm to the United Kingdom, and in particular would not target Britain for terrorist attack. Some radicals have publicly stated that they understood this tacit agreement to be in place.[1] Former senior British government advisers on security matters have equally noted its existence and questioned its wisdom, as the French were the first to do, contemptuously dubbing the entire arrangement 'Londonistan'.[2] The precise reasons as to why this comparatively laissez-faire arrangement was allowed to continue throughout the 1990s, if not after 11 September, will no doubt remain unconfirmed for some time, but what is relevant here is that during the 1990s there was enough latitude to enable the ideological foundations for a 'grievance theology' to be laid down.

This chapter revisits material collected during fieldwork prior to 11 September among British Muslim communities. The material consists of recordings, interviews, and field notes taken over a period of nine months ending in August 2001, supplemented by published material and audio tapes. Several years on, this material has more the patina of recent history than of raw intelligence; this shift in public perception has coincided with the emergence of memoirs and films by or featuring those seen to have been associated with jihadist trends.[3]

It is important to remember that few, if any, expected or predicted that 11 September would happen, and so any reading back into history to look for causal trends provides a teleological rationale that does not reflect that moment as it ought to be properly recalled. Before 11 September, jihadi Salafis in Britain, existing in small numbers, operated openly. One circle (*halaqa*), always held outside the mosques and the *madrasa*s (supplementary Qur'an schools), was easy for me to access. Even after identifying myself as an academic researcher, I was allowed to attend and record sessions from this circle.

The numbers attending the circle were always small, oscillating between eight and fifteen. A couple of the older men, both in their thirties, acted as mentors to some of the younger men who attended. The circle seemed well connected and had contacts with the Sahwi shaykhs in Saudi Arabia and Abu Hamza al-Masri in London. It could also provide videos of Muslim suffering and heroism from the *jihad*s of Bosnia and Chechnya. It organized paintballing expeditions in the surrounding countryside. Some members of the group had developed a 'look': Pakistani-style shalwar kameez in camouflage, an Afghan hat alongside the obligatory Doctor Martin boots or Nike trainers. This was recognized among local Muslims as the 'jihadi' style.

This groupuscule was largely ignored by the local Muslim community, was seen as extremist, and was not taken terribly seriously. However, the case was very different within the emerging Salafi communities, among whom I conducted my research, which were engaged in a raging re-enactment of similar debates to be found in the Arabian Peninsula and elsewhere between the three main contemporary divisions to be found among the modern-day transnational Salafi movement, described by Quintan Wiktorowicz (2006) as the 'pietists', the 'politicos', and the 'jihadists'. In this city, the Muslim community was largely dominated by British Muslims of Pakistani heritage, who had fostered an Islam largely centred on Sufi reform movements, particularly the Ahl-i Sunnat, or Barelwi, tradition.[4] At the same time, in reaction to this 'default' tradition, a healthy set of dissident traditions had developed a strong presence, such as the Deobandis, the Jama'at-i Islami, and the Ahl-i Hadith. In the younger generation, newer movements such as the Salafi groupuscules or Hizb ut-Tahrir had emerged in the 1990s.[5] All the dissident traditions were engaged in a sharp critique of what they saw as folkloristic, superstitious, and erroneous rural Sufism, which was to be disdained by younger Muslims who saw themselves as better educated than their parents.

It is this context that allows me to observe that the jihadi Salafis defined themselves against most structures of authority, whether credal, political, or community based. To most the *umma* (Muslim supernation) is in error, fallen into political lassitude and credal misguidance, led astray by the godless West; and to uphold her honour, and to establish the rule of religion, the banner of *jihad* must be unfurled. But besides the anti-West rhetoric, which was not so surprising, was an equally strong defiance, albeit less urgently expressed in the formal context of the circle, of Barelwi piety and of the structures of traditional community authority.

At one point after a circle had ended, when I asked one of the mentor figures, Tariq, about what could be done to solve problems within the local Muslim community, he launched into a ferocious diatribe against his own community. Drawing on experience as a youth worker attached to a local mosque, Tariq was very cynical about the prospects for young Muslim men. He described them as 'drugheads' who were being prepared for a life of crime. One 15-year-old in his charge had said that he saw doing time in prison as akin to doing military service for his future criminal career. Tariq was equally contemptuous of the typical parental reaction to drugs: the parents would either send their son back to Pakistan for rehabilitation, costing thousands of pounds, or push him into a marriage with a nice girl from 'back home' who could straighten him out. Neither strategy was particularly effective in his view, ending up creating many unhappy, dysfunctional marriages.

If the youth were going astray, then the community's leadership was irredeemably corrupt. Tariq had a stock of anti-Sufi stories about the corruption of local shaykhs with allegations of the misappropriation of public monies or tales of how ambitious politicians sought to 'make it' without doing anything for their community.[6] As the Muslim community had become morally corrupt, it was necessary to look outside for a grand cause – in this case, the cause of global *jihad*.

To reiterate Johannes Jansen's (1997) point about the 'dual nature' of these discourses, or the utter fusing of politics with religion,[7] it was often hard to distinguish between theological, juridical, ritual, and political concerns in the lessons of the jihadi circle. The preliminary motif was of disassociation – theological and political – which was to be established primarily through the mechanism of *jihad*, almost always used in this context to mean 'just war'. Samir, the other mentor, who read out the lessons, commentated extensively on a commentary of Ibn 'Abd al-Wahhab's *The Three Principles* by the late Saudi jurist Ibn al-'Uthaymin (d. 2001). In the section where the life of the Prophet is epitomized and explained, Samir raised the theme of disassociation with respect to the first command to preach the truth of Revelation in Mecca, or, in the words of the Qur'an, 'to arise and warn'.

> So cut your ties from the people of *shirk* [polytheism], because you can't cut your ties from *shirk*, except that you cut your ties from the people of *shirk*, and that means that any ideology that exists, that ideology can only be carried forward by people holding that ideology as a belief, it can't exist in thin air and in books, somebody has to believe in it and practise it for it to be carried forward, and Shaykh Abdullah al-Azzam said, one of the great *mujahidin* [warriors] of this era, that it's those ideologies and those beliefs, whatever they are, are carried forward by people who believe in them, they sacrifice for them, and they kill for them, and it's only that ideology that people can push forward by people making sacrifices . . . because they believe in it. . . . Allah's Subhanahu wa ta'ala [Glorified and Exalted is He] *din* [religion] will be complete and it will reach every nook and cranny on earth insha'Allah [if God wills], but it doesn't mean that whatever evil beliefs that people hold that they will not try to spread them. So we have to make *bara'* [disassociation] from *shirk*, and from its people.

Here in this passage we can see how disassociation, or *al-bara'* in the modern Salafi lexicon, is attached to the duty to 'warn' people, in this instance, not only from polytheism but also from false political ideologies. The disassociation is a precondition for religio-political mobilization. This discourse moves seamlessly between theology and politics and at the same time promotes the idea of Abdullah Azzam (d. 1989), the chief ideologue of the Afghan *jihad* against the Soviets, that the Islamic 'ideology' can only truly be upheld and promoted through sacrifice and the use of violence, attached surprisingly to a very early Qur'anic verse, well before fighting was prescribed.

The second feature is that *jihad* plays a metonymic role in the jihadi's self-understanding of Islam, as expressed in his explanation of the Prophet's life. The Prophet is both 'the Prophet of mercy and the Prophet of *jihad*' (*al-rasul al-rahma wa'l-rasul al-jihad*). The second pledge of Aqaba, in which the Prophet asked some Medinan tribes to pledge allegiance to him, included a military alliance. This is read in such a way as to reinforce the link between the declaration of faith and the need to sacrifice and uphold the cause of *jihad*:

> The *bay'a* [oath of fealty] was not just for la ilaha illa'Llah [no god but God], straight away they knew that, straight away they knew that this *bay'a* is a *bay'a* of war, of death, of loving, of hating, of fighting, of having peace, but only those whom he [the Prophet] does that with. Whatever he does it with, we do it with. . . . And imagine that, imagine that so many people had come to give the *bay'a* to Rasulullah [the Messenger of God] saw and he says 'Wait, wait – listen to what you are going to let yourselves in for.' Nowadays when somebody says that they want to enter Islam, everybody says 'Get him in, get him in, get him in, let them all in' – without telling them, and it's a crime, about what it requires. You have to give a heavy sacrifice, you have to give a heavy sacrifice. Why shouldn't it be heavy? Allah Subhanahu wa ta'ala demanded from all his believers from the beginning of time up to now, [so] why should it be easier for anybody else? Allah Subhanahu wa ta'ala says 'He has purchased of the believers their wealth and their lives.' If you gave your *bay'a* to Allah, you sold yourself to Allah. That's what Allah Subhanahu wa ta'ala expects from you. You purchase it, that's it. You belong to Allah. And that's how a believer should be, submitting to Allah Subhanahu wa ta'ala. Anything less than that is half-hearted, is half-baked, and you haven't accepted with complete submission.

After establishing disassociation and the linkage of faith with the obligation to wage *jihad* comes the next step: the immediate requirement to migrate in emulation of the Prophet. In contemporary Salafi discourse the duty to migrate is framed more clearly in credal terms, as moving from *dar al-shirk* (land of polytheism) to *dar al-iman* (land of faith), rather than just in the more political sense of moving from *dar al-kufr* (land of unbelief) to *dar al-islam* (land of Islam).

> There's something seriously wrong with someone, especially nowadays if an Islamic state is established that he doesn't make *hijra* [migration], and the shaykh [Ibn al-'Uthaymin] mentions some other points about the alternatives that you have. The alternatives are that you live in *dar al-kufr*, and why would you want to live in *dar al-kufr*? And there's a *hadith sahih* [sound Prophetic report] that you'll be raised with those whom you love, and be raised with those whom you're with, so what does it mean if you insist on being amongst the *kuffar* [unbelievers] all the time? And you love to be here amongst them? What does that mean? That's the alternative. You only have two alternatives – *dar al-islam* and *dar al-kufr*. Anything else is just fooling yourself.

Finally, this particular jihadi circle was not, I believe, propagating the idea of attacking the 'far enemy', the conclusion that Ayman al-Zawahiri, bin Laden's ideological lieutenant, had reached by the late 1990s, in contradistinction to the vast majority of jihadis who remained 'religious nationalists'.[8] Rather, it was still engaged in getting young British Muslims to wage *jihad*s abroad rather more in the spirit of Abdullah Azzam's international vanguard that would champion *jihad* as an individual duty rather than a collective one to be pursued in reclaiming the historical lands of Islam. This vanguard would be a standing, mobile international brigade that would be independently constituted of any nation-state. The Salafi 'pietists' counteracted this with the classic 'Wahhabi' arguments. The first was that sinful Muslim rulers should be tolerated and not overthrown (unless they order disobedience to the *shari'a*); in other words, not to rule by the *shari'a* was insufficient reason for a revolt. The second – also in line with most other mainstream Sunni thought – was that only a properly constituted political authority could legitimately call for a *jihad*.[9] But what is expressed in the following passage allows us to see that the switch from the 'near enemy' or Muslim governments to the 'far enemy' or the West and its allies is merely a tactical switch. Otherwise the political grievances and the theological rationales appear to be already latent in this context. However, latency in and of itself does not provide us with a causal driver, but merely with the insight that the difference between the two positions is quite slight in other respects. Samir continues:

> We know however that the *kuffar* continually wage a war against us, against our belief, against our *'aqida* [creed], against everything that we hold dear, and therefore they will attack you from every possible angle. One of the biggest ways that they are doing it, and we know well we are sitting in the West here . . . we as a small group of minority Muslims living in the West, really in the bigger picture we don't count too much, because what we say and what we do doesn't affect too much what happens in our Muslim world, the Muslim world is what counts, because this is the *kuffar* world, we are in the *kuffar* world, in terms of Islam, we are in ar-Rum, we are in Rome. . . . When we look at our Muslim countries, we see how they are dominated by Western governments implemented [by] puppet regimes, it's a clichéd term that's used often, puppets, [but] I can't find a better word really. . . . They changed the rule of Allah Subhanahu wa ta'ala, they fought the believers and they made friendships with the disbelievers and it's as simple as that.

At this point, it is clear that the Muslim minorities in the West had little to do except migrate and join the greater struggle in the Muslim world if they were to avoid political irrelevance. The West is the decadent new Rome, as a source of moral corruption to be abandoned by Muslim diasporas in favour of a harder struggle in the Muslim world for the establishment of the rule of religion.

Such an unyielding and rigorous position seemed to ask too much of those who attended the circles. Most of the questions asked sought out legal dispensations from the obligation to migrate immediately, as approved by Salafi authorities: looking after an aged parent, pursuing higher education, and preaching Islam. In fact, resistance to migrating and fighting in a foreign *jihad* remained considerable, even if there was no voiced dissent to the appeal put forward by Samir. And this pointed towards an underlying uncertainty that such a Manichaean vision of Islam, demanding all, could therefore potentially get nothing, as seen in this passage:

> Islam is everything – it's a *mushaf* [a copy of the Qur'an] and a sword, it's belief and fighting disbelief, it's love for Allah and hating for the sake of Allah, it's

holding on to the rope of Allah, and it's severing your ties with those who are against the way of Allah, it's the complete religion, it's everything.

So, unsurprisingly, this totalistic vision could also give way to moments of self-reflection and doubt:

This religion that Allah Subhanahu wa ta'ala has given to us, it appeals to people, but it appeals to human beings, not angels. ... Human beings have the loves and hates and the weaknesses and desires...and they want security, and what's the greatest thing of security? I don't want to be with a bunch of losers. I don't want to be with people who are losing all the time. I don't want to be in a place where financially I lose everything and gain nothing. Even though a believer won't say that. A believer will say I lose everything in this *dunya* [world] and this *dunya* is nothing. And in the hereafter that's what counts. But regardless what did we see? Why did people enter Islam in droves? Because victory came with Islam, honour came with Islam, respect came with Islam, security came with Islam.

The tantalizing ambiguity in this passage speaks uncertainly not just of the insecurities of the unbeliever but also of the idealistic young jihadi who is not an angel but a human being, seeking security too, and who, in standing up for justice and against immorality in his community, at home and abroad, hopes that he will not be a loser too but will find honour and victory. The suspicion remains that such appeals are not just about collective struggle for justice and honour, but also for personal fulfilment and recognition as even after the most strident imprecations of sacrificial death there remains the quieter hope that the common decencies of life may be secured too. It is these moments of slippage between the rhetorical exhortation to fight for the *umma* and the realities of daily urban British life that have been much obscured in the wake of 11 September and the brave new world that the 'war on terror' has created, much to the detriment of deeper understanding and, hence, resolution.

CHAPTER 10

al-Shahada: a Centre of the Shiite System of Belief

Fouad Ibrahim

Bertrand Russell, having been asked whether he would be prepared to die for his beliefs, replied: 'Of course not. After all, I may be wrong.'[1]

For more than two decades, the recent version of Shiism devised mainly by Shiite intellectuals has been part of Middle Eastern thought. Their efforts culminated in an essential transformation of Shiism from quietism to activism. However, Shiism cannot be reduced to an ideology of protest, as some scholars have proposed. Nevertheless, although my intention is not to suggest that Shiite Islam encourages violence, the motivation of martyrdom is not necessarily purely religious; other motivations, such as economic deprivation, political and social marginalization, could be crucial in this respect.[2] Generally, one should not de-emphasize the view that Islam is an all-encompassing religion.

For a better understanding of the centrality of martyrdom in the Shiite system of belief, it is important to assert that war is not a sacrament in Islam. There is no such term as 'holy war'. *Jihad* is something different. This distinction, according to Juan Cole (2005: 161), is especially important for Shiites, most of whom until fairly recently held that only defensive holy war could be fought in the absence of the Imam. As I will come back to this point later, I should briefly say that, with the exception of a handful of Shiite jurists, there is a general agreement that offensive *jihad* is the sole right of the impeccable Imam, namely the Mahdi in our times.

There is a view, to which the recent tragic events in America, Afghanistan, and Iraq have lent credence, that martyrdom is tantamount to an act of suicide. However, martyrdom in Islam is subject to religious restrictions, namely that individuals must sacrifice their lives for a heightened objective faith. Generally speaking, there is consensus among nearly all faiths that a martyr is a person who intentionally and determinedly sacrifices his life for the sake of his faith.

Keith Lewinstein (2002: 78–9) contends that the difference between Muslim and Christian in terms of the person earning the title of martyr is that the Muslim martyr does not bear witness or symbolize much beyond the obvious sense of death in the path of God. The Qura'n, he argues, does not know the term *shahid* in its technical sense, though the later exegetical tradition acquired added meanings.

Against this view, Ali Shari'ati (1979) argues that in European and Western languages, a martyr is one who chooses 'death' in the defence of his beliefs where the only way for him to oppose his enemy is to die. But the word martyrdom – 'arise and bear witness' – which exists in Islamic culture to describe or name the one who has chosen 'death' has a quite different meaning from that in the West. In European countries, he argues, the word martyr stems from 'mortal', which means 'death' or 'to die'. One of the basic principles in Islam, and in particular in Shiite culture, however, is 'sacrifice and bear witness'. So instead of martyrdom, i.e. death, it essentially means 'life', 'evidence', 'testify', 'certify'. These words 'martyrdom' and 'bearing witness' show the differences between the vision of Shiite Islamic culture and the other cultures of the world, according to Shari'ati.

Needless to say, the world of Islam in general has been affected by modern disciplines and ideologies. As a result, Shiite revivalists, like their Sunni counterparts, have debated their doctrinal legacy in the light of the new realities, leading to the rationalizing of religious text. The dichotomy between authenticity and modernity manifested itself in nearly all branches of Islam. With regard to the new interpretation of martyrdom, it clearly shows that the intermingling between death and bearing witness is not based on a fixed interpretation of Islamic tradition, but is related to the historical realities that Muslims encountered. In the context of the awareness of martyrdom, one may find indications in the Qur'an and Sunna that connect martyr to bearing witness, though in ambiguous terms.

In Islamic literatures, martyrdom (*al-shahada*) is essentially ingrained in Muslim faith, and is not necessarily associated with a physical act. It contains a number of implications such as certainty, witness, and rightfulness. The Qur'an refers to the word *shahada* and its derivations for various meanings, none of which pertains to killing or death. It mentions the word *shahid* 32 times; *shuhada* 18 times; *al-shahada* 13 times; and *shahada* 21 times, most of which refer to meanings other than killing oneself or death. They refer mainly to witness and presence.[3] Examples are legion in the Qur'an. Muslims are regarded, according to a Qura'nic verse, as witnesses (*shuhada*) to the people and the Prophet is a witness (*shahid*) to the Muslims. In another verse, the Qur'an uses the word *shahada* in case of fasting in Ramadan ('those of you who witness the month are obliged to fast').

In Islamic traditions, the category of martyrs is somewhat loose. Martyrs in Islam denote those were killed in battlefield for the sake of religion, and those who sacrifice their lives in the defence of their faith, property, honour, money, and, by extension, those who die while performing a religious duty, such as pilgrimage (*hajj*) or fasting. They could also pertain to those who die in tragic incidents such as suffocation and drowning. Imam Shafi'i (d. 820) tells the story of a bedouin pilgrim kicked to death by his camel: the Prophet orders that he be buried as a battlefield martyr.

Nevertheless, the Islamic regulations relating to battlefield martyrs per se are very clear. According to Shiite jurisprudence, legitimate *jihad* includes offensive *jihad* (*jihad ebteda'i*) and defensive *jihad* (*jihad defa'i*).[4] Offensive *jihad* is the sole prerogative of the impeccable Imam, while defensive *jihad* is open to all believers, including women and slaves.[5] Those killed in both kinds of *jihad* are considered martyrs and their bodies may be buried without washing. With regard to those who fall into the category of martyrs beyond the front lines, although Islamic traditions grant them the reward of martyrdom, they are not exempted from the regulations related to martyrs, such as burial with their clothes without washing.

This distinction brings our attention to an important aspect, since some scholars allege that Islam is by nature a war-oriented faith. Some argue that the injection of *jihad* into Arabic culture led to the transformation of Islam into a war machine, which once started could not be stopped.[6] This is, however, a misinterpretation and misconception of Islamic tradition and history. The Qur'an (60: 8–9) states: 'As for such [of the unbelievers] as do not fight against you on account of [your] faith, and neither drive you forth from your homelands, God does not forbid you to show them kindness and to behave towards them with full equity: for, verily, God loves those who act equitably.'

Once someone asked Imam 'Ali a question concerning the divine unity just as a battle was about to begin, and he proceeded to answer it. When another person objected, 'Is now the time for such things?' he replied, 'This is the reason that we are fighting Mu'awiya, not for any worldly gain. It is not our true aim to capture Syria; of what value is Syria?'

It should be mentioned that not all warriors to die on the battlefield earn the title of martyr. Two famous reports could be cited in this regard. The first is about a Muslim killed in battle for the sake of plunder, whom the Prophet labelled 'Donkey's Martyr' (*shahid al-humar*). In another report, a Muslim was killed for the sake of a woman called Um Jamil, and he labelled him Um Jamil's Martyr (*shahid Um Jamil*).

Although many examples both in the past and the present clearly show that martyrdom is a reaction to repression, it should be borne in mind that Islamic traditions and jurisdictions are unswerving in prohibiting the taking of one's own life. The Qura'n (6: 151) clearly states: 'And that ye slay not the life which Allah hath made sacred, save in the course of justice.' In another verse (4: 29), it states: 'O you who believe! Do not devour your property among yourselves falsely, except that it be trading by your mutual consent; and do not kill your people; surely Allah is Merciful to you.'

The sole exception to this rule is for those who fight in the way of God. They are encouraged by God through the revealed Qur'an and the sayings of His messenger to submit to death for the sake of defending their faith. Qur'anic verses and Prophetic *hadith*s grant the title of martyr to those who die 'desiring the face of God' or seeking to make the word of God supreme. Although rewards are guaranteed to all warriors, not only to martyrs, the latter would have immediate rewards: their sins will be forgiven, they will be in Paradise immediately after their death: 'Do not say of those slain in God's way that they are dead; they are living, only you do not perceive' (Q 2: 154; cf. 3: 169).[7]

In addition to the odds referred to the person who earns the title of martyr, the historical fact states that from 680AD until at least the 1970s, 'martyrdom' in any Muslim faith was passive.[8] With the end of Islamic conquests in the period between 718 and 750, and the rise of the Islamic empire, which stretched from India to Africa, the emergence of mini-states within it, and the internal fractures and conflicts within the Muslim communities, the decentralization of religious authority followed by the flourishing of numerous schools of thought and jurisprudence, contributed to a decline in the significance of battlefield martyrdom. As a result, the mainstream Muslim community opted gradually for pragmatic quietism for over a millennium, leaving a vast gap between the normative period of Islam and the pragmatic living realities which Muslims encountered. In such a quietist milieu, one could explore how the mainstream

Muslims perceived the concept of martyrdom, as a passive act. It was the jurists who extended the validity of martyrdom to encompass more people.[9]

Over the last four decades a reinvention of tradition has taken place in the major religious centres in Egypt, Iran, Iraq, and elsewhere in the Islamic world, leading to a reinterpretation of Islamic history and legacy.

A reinvention of Shiism

The contemporary reorientation of Shiite tradition marked the transformation of Shiism from quietism to activism. This was primarily a response to opportunities created by changing circumstances in the 1950s. The failure of the Musaddaq–Kasahani movement in Iran leading to the return of the shah to power, the withdrawal of Shiite *'ulama* from the political arena both in Iran and Iraq, and the exposure of Shiite intellectuals in Iran to secular ideologies and Marxist revolutionary literatures via the Tudeh Party in Iran were prime contributing factors for the rethinking of the Shiite system of belief. While Shiite intellectuals in Iran and Iraq recognized the efforts of Sunni movements to manufacture a form of Islamic activism in Egypt and Jordan, they endeavoured to give recognition to what they believe is a revolutionary social change within Shiism. Their effort was broadly geared towards anti-Westernization and pro-religious reform. Jalal al-Ahmad (d. 1969), a former Tudeh Party member, among others, reflected on the extent to which the reform of Shiism can be conditioned by its political and social context. He coined the expression *gharbzadaghi*, to 'denote and condemn those who were awestruck, intoxicated, or bewitched by the West'.[10] It appeared that his critique of Western influence was the prelude to the development of an ideology of protest anchored in Shiite traditions.

The Shiite intellectual generation both in Iran and Iraq seem to have been obsessed with the political and intellectual transformation in Sunni Islam during the 1950s, especially with the emergence of religious and secular liberation movements with anti-Western leanings. The Shiite intellectuals in Iran, who were influenced by Marxist writings, succeeded in attracting an enthusiastic audience among the youth. Jalal al-Ahmad had the added attraction of being the first contemporary Shiite writer to formulate a revolutionary form of Shiism. The impact of Jalal's thought may be observed in the intellectual activities of Ali Shari'ati (1933–77), the ideological father of the Iranian revolution. Shari'ati's intellectual project, which presented Shiism as a revolution, remained dominant and intact until the revolution in 1979. Although Shari'ati left few coherent and systematic written works, his published talks were rich in ideas, ideals, and spirit. The impact of Shari'ati's revolutionary thought, socio-religious analysis, and politico-religious vision on Shiite Islamic movements, in Iran, Iraq, and elsewhere, is undeniable. In his task of formulating an ideology of protest and its relation to Shiism, he resorts to synthesizing religion with modernity.

Shari'ati preached a type of Shiism which was practised by the first three Imams, 'Ali, Hasan and Husayn, aimed at reviving the perceived meanings, symbols, and traditions of the original, revolutionary, version of Shiism. Influenced by Marxism's class dialect, Shari'ati argued that at any point in history, humanity is destined to undergo a class struggle, which will take a static form – that is, a struggle between a chain of polarities: Divine and Satan, rich and poor, good and evil, true and false, oppressors and oppressed, and so on. He maintained (1979: 97–110) that the struggle between Cain and Abel symbolizes the perpetual conflict between two contradictory fronts. Clearly, the goal in this argument is a theology of revolution that can be an effective ideology against oppression. This involved a reinvention, reformulation, and restructuring of the Shiite system of belief. Shari'ati argued that Imam Husayn's revolt was the archetype of the dualistic conflict throughout human history, in which the oppressed rise against the oppressor.

Obviously, this interpretation of Shiism, let alone human history, as a history of class struggle contrasts with Shiite traditions and the expositions of the prominent Shiite *'ulama* of the tenth century. Based on the tradition of dissimulation (*taqiyya*), the traditional *'ulama* called on their Shiite followers to adhere to the principle of waiting (*intizar*), limiting themselves to performing religious observances (*'ibadat*) until the reappearance of the divinely ordained Mahdi.[11]

However, revolutionary Shiism seems to have gained a wide currency among Shiites in general. This can most notably be observed in the works of Shiite *'ulama* and intellectuals in the second half of the twentieth century. The Shiite legacy was revolutionized, reinterpreted, and modernized in the cause of change. Shari'ati's approach is illustrated by his distinction between two types of Shiism: Black Shiism and Red Shiism, or Safavi Shiism and 'Alawi Shiism. Black/Safavi Shiism is used by rulers as a tool to oppress the ruled. It encourages the populace, he argues, to wait passively for the reappearance of the Mahdi, as well as the shedding of tears and mourning on the days of 'Ashura, without comprehending the profound message conveyed in Husayn's martyrdom. On the other hand, the Red/Alawi Shiism calls for revolution by the oppressed, and rising of the downtrodden class against the oppressor and the usurper.[12]

Shari'ati's unprecedented analysis of Shiism has had a great impact upon a large segment of Shiite activists, both in Iran and elsewhere. In distinguishing between the two versions of Shiism, he aimed to develop a paradigm of Shiism that presents it as the religion of martyrdom. He adhered to the view that historical Shiism was an ideology of protest, beginning with 'Ali's rejection of the council's election of Abu Bakr and continuing until the pre-Safavid times. With the advent of the Safavid era in 1497, Shiism, he argues, leaned towards quietism.

Shari'ati's approach to reinventing Shiism was directed to two closely interrelated themes which are inherent in Shiite system of belief and collective consciousness: Husayn's martyrdom and the Mahdi's occultation. The change in one theme affects the other, in other words the new understanding of Karbala has changed the classical belief of the Mahdi, affecting the whole Shiite system of belief. The conventional Shiite view of Mahdi is that he will appear at the end of time to abolish the kingdom of evil and establish a reign of justice on earth. By the same token, he will put an end to Shiite suffering throughout history.[13] This means that as Karbala became a living reality that could be repeated in all times and places, the concept of the Mahdi has dramatically changed from a passive concept to an active one (from mourning, self-flagellation, and *taqiyya* and *intizar*) to spiritual and practical preparation for reform and revolution against the corrupt reality, bearing responsibility to lead society through the election of a noble person on behalf of the occulted Imam.[14]

'Ashura: the paragon of martyrdom

Husayn and his followers were slain on the tenth day ('Ashura) of the Muslim month of Muharram (AH 61/AD 680), at Karbala, in an extremely uneven battle against the army of the Umayyad caliph Yazid ibn Mu'awiya. This tragic episode had an effect on the Shiites' ethos, attitudes, and aims. Until recently it was a passive one, in the sense that it did not instill more than the shedding of tears and the beating of chests. For most of Islamic history, the traditions that elaborated on the 'Ashura episode had reinforced Shiite political passivity and resignation, leading them to perceive themselves as a hopeless, vulnerable, and submissive sect.

The anthropologist Mary Hegland (1983) investigated what Husayn's death meant to Iranian villagers, which in large part reflected both their experiences and what they were being told by the 'ulama. Before the revolution emphasis was placed on Husayn as an intercessor for people with God. However, when 'Ashura was reinvented it turned into a spirit, an energy, and an emblem. As such, it was understood that the grave of Husayn is in the souls of his adherents and beloved ones, according to a widely known Shiite report. It was Shari'ati's school of thought and revolutionary presentation of the episode of Karbala that reversed the classical narrative and perception of 'Ashura. According to the new paradigm, 'Ashura is not an isolated and tragic incident as such; it is the beginning of a cluster of revolutions throughout history. Undoubtedly, no Shiite scholar had previously contemplated the universal dimensions of Husayn's martyrdom in the way that Shari'ati did. Furthermore, no one, including Khomeini, had considered the term *shahada* (martyrdom) in the way that Shari'ati did.[15] His vision of the event embraces all religions and societies. As could be noted, Shari'ati's philosophy of universalism corresponds with the Marxist one, regarding Husayn's actions in Karbala as a 'prototype for all societies and all cultures' (Akhavi 1980: 140).

In his interpretation of Shiism, Shari'ati contends that:

> Like a revolutionary party, Shi'ism had a well-organized, informed, deep-rooted and well-defined ideology, with clear-cut and definite slogans and a disciplined and well-groomed organization. It led the deprived and oppressed masses in their movements for freedom and for seeking justice. It is considered to have been the rallying-point for the demands, distress, and rebellions of the intellectuals seeking to gain their rights, and for the masses in search of justice. (Shari'ati (1979)

In the context of neo-Shiism, martyrdom becomes a cornerstone of its construct. It clearly operates in a non-traditional way, turning not only into a means but into a 'status', and an end; it is a great responsibility, and a valid method for all ages. As faith is faced with threat of collapse, argues Shari'ati, believers should defend it by recourse to *jihad* to secure it as well as their own survival, but if they are unable to resist and have no means of defence or lack resources, then they can preserve their faith, dignity, and future by the use of *shahada*. He considered it an open invitation for all generations in all ages to use this means to secure life.

Shari'ati associates *shahada* and Shiism, asserting that martyrdom is an inherent feature and value of the Shiite school of thought. This value, according to Shari'ati, was overshadowed and nullified by the Safavid Shiism.

Expanding on Salehi Najaf 'Abadi's work on 'Ashura, *Shahid-e Javid* (1982), Shari'ati claims that the martyrs of Karbala convey a different message, that the *jihad* is based neither on capability nor pre-guaranteed victory.[16] It is based on triumph. Death is the tool of *jihad* when triumph with weapons is not possible, and death could achieve victory over enemies. The martyr, the heart of history, is pulsing with life whereas martyrdom is the blood running through the vessels of a society. It gives this society new blood, birth, and movement. The most significant miracle of martyrdom is that it transmits life and blood to the dead parts of the society in order to produce a new generation and belief. The question posed here is: when did martyrdom become not just a means, but a culture and end in itself?

The beginning of the 1980s saw a new perception of Karbala, starting with the eruption of the Iranian revolution and continuing with the Iraq–Iran war, which opened the gateway for the so-called *Karavan* (journey) of Karbala. It is not a coincidence that nearly all Shiite uprisings in the 1980s took place during the 'Ashura processions.

Hezbollah and the culture of martyrdom

The emergence of Hezbollah in 1982, as a response to the Israeli occupation of a large part of Lebanon, is considered a turning point not only in the struggle between Lebanon and Israel but in the destiny, outlook, and position of the Shiites in Lebanon, and perhaps elsewhere in the region.

On 11 November 1982, Hezbollah launched a new strategy in the battlefield, when one of its members, Ahmad Qasir, exploded a truck bomb at the Israeli military headquarters in Tyre, in southern Lebanon. The operation killed about a hundred Israeli soldiers. The perpetrator remained anonymous until 19 May 1985, when Hezbollah revealed its strategy of martyrdom operations, which effectively increased its following among the Shiite community.

One should not ignore the fact that the foundation of this strategy goes back to the pioneering works, activities, and leadership of Imam Mussa al-Sadr, the founder of the Amal movement, who made an essential contribution to transforming the understanding of 'Ashura in the mid-1970s. Like Shari'ati, al-Sadr endeavoured to tackle the main issues within Shiism, with reference to the new interpretation of 'Ashura. He contended that waiting for the occulted Mahdi entails preparation, recruitment, training, and spiritual, psychological, and intellectual preparations.[17]

He critiqued the prevailing Shiite rituals during 'Ashura in his time:

> Let us not be content with ceremonies of pure mourning, and thus have them remain as external, fossilized religious manifestations through which the tyrants can camouflage their crimes, brainwash the populace, and accustom them to passivity. Do not allow ceremonies of lamentation to serve as a substitute for action. We must transform the ceremonies into a spring from which will gush forth the revolutionary fury and the constructive protest. . . . Let me ask you: if Hussain were living with us now and saw that the rights of the people, and justice were being trampled upon by the foot of pride, what would he do? Moreover, he considered those who solely perform 'Ashura rituals are distorting the goals of Hussain's rebellion and lamentations. (Sivan 1990: 61–2)[18]

Al-Sadr emphasizes the significance of martyrdom in the struggle. Martyrdom, he says, transforms an individual into an unbeatable weapon, whereas the martyr becomes like a spring that touches the whole community and spurs its members to reassess their attitude, capabilities, and opportunities of victory.[19] Anchored in 'Ashura narrative, al-Sadr contends that 'our Hussaini's attitude implies defence of our land and bears responsibility on behalf of our people'.[20]

These new interpretations of Karbala led to the transformation of the world-view of the Shiites, making martyrdom a central concept of Shiism. 'The martyrdom of Husayn has become the prototype of every struggle for justice, every suffering. That is where the heart of Shi'ism lies, in this agony which is at one and the same time a revolt and a sign of hope' (Yann 1995: 29).

Sayyid Muhammad Hussein Fadhlallah, a prominent religious authority (*marji' taqlid*), who was considered the spiritual leader of Hezbollah until the late 1990s, states: 'The martyrdom operations are part of the war movement, since the issue of war differs from the issue of suicide. Suicide is the killing of oneself for personal reasons. On the other hand, the martyrdom operation means that a person dies for a greater cause.'

Indeed, the Iranian revolution stressed martyrdom as a key element in Shiism, and this became a crucial factor in the Shiite resistance. In the search for a way out of the passivism impasse, the Shiites in Lebanon and elsewhere found in the new interpretation of 'Ashura a breakthrough towards reforming the Shiite community and system of belief. As a result, the tragedy of Karbala has been transformed into a symbol and guiding star of resistance, victory, and redemption. It might be argued that it served the needs of nearly all Shiite resistance movements, especially in recent times, when the martyrdom of Husayn has vitally shaped the way Shiites understand themselves and their cause.

Hezbollah literatures address martyrdom in conformity with the new exposition advanced by Shiite intellectuals. It says that martyrdom is neither a tragic accident nor death imposed by the enemy on the *mujahid*; rather, it is a conscious choice by the *mujahid*. It could be noted that Hezbollah has cultivated a culture of martyrdom with consistent emphasis on Husayn's heroic act, as the embodiment of the martyr and symbol of martyrdom.

Following the example of Husayn, the death of a man in our age is considered a guarantee for the life of a nation and a factor for the existence of faith, although his martyrdom is also seen as evidence of the great crime, unveiling the deception, tyranny and cruelty that prevails in many societies. It is a 'red resistance' against 'black' dominance, and a cry of anger against the silence of throats, as Shari'ati's suggests. Sayyid Hassan Nasrullah, the secretary-general of Hezbollah, asserts that 'in *jihad* and martyrdom, there are sacrifices and martyrs to safeguard the lives of others. In Lebanon martyrs have fallen to let the others remain alive.'[21]

Within the context of revolutionary Shiism, Sayyid Abbas al-Musawi (killed in February 1992), a founding father of Hezbollah, argued that the example of Husayn is currently the only lesson that inspires the people to rise. Ayatollah Khomeini, he argued, was the first inventor of the weapon of Karbala, as he translated it into the 'prism' (the triumph of blood over the sword). He quoted Khomeini as saying: 'Whatever we have achieved is attributed to the ceremony of Karbala.'[22]

Encountering threats, Musawi argued, hinges on two major prerequisites, one of which is Husayn's spirit. He explains that individuals should challenge the source of the threat, namely Israeli military capabilities. When it comes to religious causes, Islam teaches that Muslims should be courageous regardless of a disparity of power between them and their enemy. He quoted Mussa al-Sadr saying: 'Fight Israel with your fingernails.'[23]

Resistance, al-Musawi argued, is intimately related to religious faith, since eschewing resistance entails renouncing religious faith. He believed that resistance is not a political issue, but a religious duty, which is not affected by political circumstances. Therefore, resistance should continue regardless of the political situation.[24]

This account of the interrelationship between resistance and faith seems to be deeply rooted in Hezbollah literature, attitude, and military operations. Secretary-general Sayyid Nasrullah described martyrdom operations as 'the most exalted and magnificent way of martyrdom in our generation'. He added: '[The] martyrdom operation is the weapon Allah gave this nation [the Islamic *umma*], and no one can take it from us. They [the Israelis and other enemies] can take away our cannons, our tanks, and our planes, but they cannot take away our spirit, which yearns for Allah and which is determined to achieve martyrdom.'[25]

In a speech during a ceremony held at Nabi-Sheit in 2002, Sayyid Nasrullah said: 'The culture of martyrdom finds its expression in the act of *jihad*. Only the culture of *jihad* is capable of bringing about victory. . . . If we lose the culture of martyrdom, then we shall stand before catastrophe. The leadership must abide by the culture of martyrdom.'[26]

During the Islamic Ulama conference, Sayyid Nasrullah made it clear that

resistance is, above all, these young *jihad* warriors who carry guns, fight, assault military posts or carry out martyrdom operations. The main thing that can be achieved in this conference is keeping up the spirit of resistance ... I can tell you in full honesty, that a *jihad* warrior will never forsake the path of resistance, even not if his family is killed, or he is thrown into jail, or beaten with a whip, or threatened with death. [It is] his deepest wish to encounter Allah.[27]

In his statement during the 34-day war in 2006, Nasrullah stated: 'When we chose this way we knew that we were choosing the hard way, the way of martyrdom that makes victory.'[28]

This specific appeal of viewing martyrdom as an indigenous element of Shiism explains the attraction to Hezbollah of Iranian revolutionary literature, which has in a sense helped transform the Shiites of Lebanon into a resistance community.

Nir Rosen, a fellow at the New America Foundation, who is working on a book about the battle of 'Aita al-Sha'ab in the war of July 2006, recorded a significant detail. On 17 September 2006 he attended a memorial service for some of Hezbollah's dead soldiers in 'Aita al-Sha'ab, a border village with Israel. He noted that around a hundred Hezbollah soldiers fought in this town, the majority of whom were not professional soldiers: among them were a high school history teacher; a high school principal; a sweet-shop owner; two high-school graduates about to start studying engineering at university; and a university student home on summer break. They were restaurant waiters, farmers, car mechanics, and bakers. He adds: 'They had completed Hezbollah's boot camp and training and returned to their normal lives, occasionally going for refresher courses, much like our Army reserves or National Guard.'

Most of Hezbollah's soldiers in the most recent war were, he writes, between 18 and 25 years old and had never fought before. Somehow these 100 fighters in 'Aita al-Sha'ab held the town, never surrendering it to the Israeli military. Many of the town's old people stayed behind to cook and care for Hezbollah's soldiers. Other people left their homes and shops open for them. The town was Hezbollah. He concludes by saying: 'As one hears so many times in Lebanon, the entire south is Hizbullah; and "Israel" knew this, hence its war was against the people of the south.'[29]

At the centre of the culture of martyrdom is the remembrance of martyrs – both past and present – who had to sacrifice their souls so that faith could be protected. Every year, Hezbollah celebrates Martyrs' Day. This illustrates the deeply rooted changes in modern Shiite political discourse, the transformation of Shiism from passivism to activism. Martyrdom is now not only a tactic used for a particular purpose in a certain time and place; it has become a culture consisting of values, a way of life, and a variety of choices, means, and an end. Although this culture aims to achieve both mundane and divinely ordained goals, it is open to different types of tactics.

The son of a martyr killed in the battle of Bent Jbil by Israeli troops in Barachit, south Lebanon, said: 'I'm proud of my father. I'm proud he is a martyr' (Peterson 2006). Asked if he was willing to follow in the martyrs' footsteps, the 11 year-old-boy answered without hesitation: 'Yes.' This boy, like many of his generation, was exposed to the culture of martyrdom, which is passed from father to son, unifying the Shiites and solidifying resistance to Israel.

According to a Shiite participant in a martyr's funeral in Lebanon' south: 'It's a very proud moment for the family – now they put [the Hizbollah fighter] in the ground, and send him to God.' He adds: 'This is a moment to mourn – this is death, and they have feelings about it.' He continues; 'After that, it is a moment to celebrate.'

The development of Shiite political awareness and strategies shows that the sense of deprivation fuelled resistance, whereas a culture of complaint turned into a culture of activism. It is the narrative of Karbala that made this drastic change in Shiite thinking and attitude possible. In a practical sense, martyrdom diffused the prevailing concept of death; it became a happy event, like a wedding. Hezbollah communiqués use the word *zaffa*, which applies solely to weddings and to those getting married, to announce deaths in battle.

Despite the destruction and heavy loss of life, a common expression heard from women and children in the southern suburbs of Beirut and southern villages is 'They sacrifice for the sake of Sayyid Hassan and the Muqawamah ['resistance', i.e. Hezbollah].'

While making personal observations during the July–August war in 2006, I arrived in the southern suburbs of Beirut on 14 July, when there was a ceasefire. I asked my Lebanese companion to take me to the so-called the security quarter (al-Muraba' al-Amni), where the Hezbollah headquarters were located. The area had been heavily shelled by Israeli jet-fighters. In our way, we stopped near the compound of Imam Hassan in al-Rwais, which consisted of ten residential buildings, eight of which were levelled to the ground by the shelling of the previous day. I noticed a dozen young people searching for survivors among the ruins of those buildings. The smoke was still emanating from underneath the ruins. A man was shouting: 'Is anybody there?' I asked my Lebanese companion, 'Who are these young men?' He said that they were members of Hezbollah. He added, 'We will see more of them at every corner and entrance of the suburb. They have been here', he said, 'since the beginning of the war, in order to look after the possessions of the residents. They did not let anybody enter the area without proof of identity.' He praised them as heroes, who take responsibility and protect the people despite the risk of death.

As we approached the security quarter, we were told that this part of the area was very dangerous, due to unexploded missiles. I talked to one of the guards, who, I assumed, was a member of Hezbollah, to ask him to allow me to enter the zone. He allowed me in, on condition that I complete my business quickly. As I walked in I noticed that this part seemed to be different from what I had just seen in other parts of the suburb. It was as if an earthquake had hit this part just hours ago; smoke was coming out of the ruins of buildings, many of which had been razed to the ground. As I approached the residence of the leader of Hezbollah, a man in a car with a microphone appeared, calling for an immediate evacuation following a discovery of unexploded missiles. I looked around to see how everyone would react. Although the warning was repeated several times, the residents remained calm and walked around normally.

The reaction of the residents of the suburbs of Beirut and the South following the ceasefire announcement was remarkable: they did not regret the heavy casualties or the destruction of their houses, flats, and shops. Instead, they congratulated themselves on the victory. When the issue of losses was raised, they said: 'God will compensate, the important thing is that we are victorious; stone can be replaced but dignity is not restorable.'

This once again brings to mind a famous Shiite slogan, the Triumph of Blood over Sword (*Intisar al-Damm 'Ala al-Saif*). The significance of this ideal could be explained as follows: the value of martyrdom hinges on the nature of the cause you sacrifice yourself for. According to Ayatollah Mutahhari (1986: 131), *shahada* is 'the death of a person who, in spite of being fully conscious of the risks involved, willingly faces them for the sake of a sacred cause, or, as the Qur'an says, "fi Sabil Allah" [in the way of God]'. He adds: 'The *shahid* can be compared to a candle whose job it is to burn out and get extinguished in order to shed light for the benefit of others.' Indeed, this sums up the philosophy of martyrdom as reflected by the calamity of Karbala. According to this philosophy victory is not necessarily determined by the immediate military results; rather, it is the effect it has on later generations. Speaking of Hezbollah, resistance to Israeli troops had its connection with Imam Husayn. Television clips aired during the recent war showed a Hezbollah fighter shouting 'Ya Husayn!' (Hail, Husayn!) as he attacked an Israeli tank.

Those who die for their beliefs and become martyrs could be compared to seeds transforming into trees after they are buried in the ground, as they transform into a source of inspiration and agitation. In Islamic tradition, those who die in the path of God (martyrs) will not die, but they live in the realm of God.

According to Shaykh Na'im Qawok, the representative of Hezbollah in south Lebanon: 'We celebrate the loss of our martyrs. But in Israel, with their death, with their funerals, they show they are losers' (Peterson 2006). According to a song of Hezbollah,

Lebanon's victory is attributed to martyrs. In another one, Lebanon is secured by blood.

For Hezbollah, resistance is a strategy, an ideology, and a source of legitimacy. If so then the nexus of resistance and martyrdom is essential to understanding the movement's agenda. Its success could be attributed to its dedication to transforming the culture of fear into a culture of resistance and martyrdom, leading to a dramatic change in Shiites' attitude, thought, and strategy. The centrality of the example of Karbala in the popular culture and memory and the remembrance of Husayn's martyrdom became integral to the culture of resistance. In an interview with a Lebanese daily newspaper, Hassan Nasrullah asserted the role of martyrdom, among other elements, as a crucial factor in the battlefield.[30] The effectiveness of the factor could be observed from the warning of Israel's foreign minister, Tzipi Livni, to European ambassadors in Tel Aviv, of the devastating consequences of the religious factor in the conflict between Israel and Islamic resistance movements.

In an interview with a Lebanese satellite channel during the recent war, Nasrullah declared that many leading members of Hezbollah were aiming to gain the title of martyr during the war, as this might be the last opportunity for them. This reminds us of the famous saying of General George C. Marshall: 'It is not enough to fight; it is the spirit which we bring to the fight that decides the issue. It is morale that wins the victory' (De Weerd 1945: 122).

In summing up, martyrdom became a source of inspiration, a tool of mobilization and solidarity. Like Imam Husayn, martyrs of Hezbollah create a deep emotional and political loyalty to the resistance. Martyrdom became a status, which spurred families to encourage their children to set out to the front equipped with the determination to follow in the footsteps of Imam Husayn and those who followed in his steps, the Hezbollah martyrs.

CHAPTER 11

Urban Unrest and Non-religious Radicalization in Saudi Arabia

Pascal Ménoret[1]

And that union, to attain which the burghers of the Middle Ages, with their miserable highways, required centuries, the modern proletarians, thanks to the railway, achieve in a few years.

Karl Marx

The road that crosses the market is very broad; loaded caravans can pass through it.

Anonymous, Nejd, nineteenth century AD

The expressions of dissent in contemporary Saudi Arabia, whether through violent action or ideological and theological constructions, are well documented today. Recent studies have provided valuable information on bombings and incidents between armed groups and the security forces (Cordesman and Obaid 2005). Both the various Salafi discourses that sustain consent to or protest against the Saudi state and the different Islamic movements have also been studied (Al-Rasheed 2007). The very contexts within which violence appears and develops are less well known. It is often said that these contexts are linked with various levels of state violence, the repression of political activities, and the preservation of a status quo through several means of controlling the public sphere. This formula is correct. It grasps the heavy role played by specifically political repression in the radicalization of a whole range of activists who might otherwise have chosen other – more peaceful – means of expression had the circumstances been different. Yet such a way of writing the history of radicalization does not say anything about the thousands of Saudis who do not participate in violent activism or intellectual and political dissent. These ordinary people are often referred to as a 'silent majority'. It remains to be seen whether this silence is due to apathy and inaction or to the fact that such ordinary Saudis, in their effort to channel their discomfort with the system as a whole, use repertoires and dictionaries that do not fall into the Islamic category. It is essential to read and analyse the Islamic discourses and to observe and interpret the history of Islamic activism in Saudi Arabia. Such an elitist focus may nevertheless overlook more discrete events that might explain, more efficiently than the grand narrative of protest, mobilization, repression, and radicalization, the way ordinary people refer to state violence and try to cope with its manifestations on a day-to-day basis.

The people I discuss are young and marginalized male bedouins. They are neither Islamic activists nor intellectuals. They are not totally disenfranchised, although they come from fragile social milieus. Nor are they the most marginalized people in Saudi Arabia, for they live in modern neighbourhoods of the capital, Riyadh, and can at least proudly refer to their tribal heritage. If they have experienced state oppression, it was inside neighbourhood police stations, not in political prisons, and the crimes they were charged with were more linked to petty robbery and violation of driving regulations than with political dissent. Like young women, they are the first target of various disciplinary institutions, such as the regular police forces, the religious police or Committee for the Promotion of Virtue and Prohibition of Vice (Hay'at al-Amr bi-l-Ma'ruf wa-n-Nahi 'an al-Munkar), and the innumerable private security companies that tend to enforce a strict social and gender segregation. Yet these young men's activities can only superficially be described as mere juvenile delinquency. In their own way, they challenge state authority and the official practices that depoliticize the daily activities of ordinary Saudis. They are both a result of de-politicization and a challenge to it.

In other words, we are here going to work on what some may call 'sub-political' phenomena, which deserve in our purview an authentic political analysis. Delinquency, petty robbery, and multiple violations of common rules and regulations have often been overlooked or despised by political science.

> Prevailing definitions, by stressing articulated social change goals as the defining feature of social movements, have had the effect of denying political meaning to many forms of protest. ... The effect of equating movements with movement organizations – and thus requiring that protests have a leader, a constitution, a legislative program, or at least a banner before they are recognized as such – is to divert attention from many forms of political unrest and to consign them by definition to the more shadowy realms of social problems and deviant behaviour. (Piven and Cloward 1977: 4–5)

The apostles of the official Saudi status quo themselves tend to see all forms of protestation – from everyday resistance to public demonstration and to terrorism – as mere social or ideological diseases to be cured by appropriate methods of prevention and repression. By widening the scope of political analysis, we hope to more efficiently grasp the nature of an authoritarian public space where, beyond 'the policeman, the landlord or the "people of worth"' . . . every gesture of revolt proves to be impossible, since the real goal is still unreachable' (Farge 1979: 151).

Tafhit, from oppositional style to 'street terrorism'

Among the 'thousands ways of defying authority, from gibes to sneaky farces and from throwing of excrement to insults and beatings' (Farges 1979: 151), we would like to focus on a truly contemporary way of resisting marginalization and social racism, an authentic 'street culture of resistance' which is 'not a coherent, conscious universe of political opposition but, rather, a spontaneous set of rebellious practices that in the long term have emerged as an oppositional style' (Bourgois 1996: 8). This particular street culture is called *tafhit* or *hajwala*[1] by its aficionados, mainly adolescents and young men living in the peripheral neighbourhoods of Riyadh. Its purpose is 'jumping traffic lights, speeding like crazy, losing the police, slaloming between cars,'³ and doing acrobatic skids at top speed, usually above 200 kmph. The technical goal of *tafhit* is to execute extremely dangerous figures that might be fatal for both the drivers (who are called *mufahhatin*, in reference to *tafhit*) and their fans (the *mushajji'in* or *jumhur*). The most famous of these figures are the *natla* (lateral skid: see fig. 1), the *'ugda* (looping), and the *istifham* or 'question mark' (U-turn at top speed). They might be executed alone or within series, the most widespread being the combination *natla–'ugda*.

Fig. 1: Street heroes. The mufahhat *is executing a* natla *while one of his attendants waves his logo in direction of the overwhelmed public. (Source: www.alb7ri.com)*

The social goal *hajwala* represents is, for every 'skidder', to please his public and become the hero of the day. This can express through various means: by doing *tafhit*, the skidder accumulates social capital (he widens his social networks), economic capital (through the donations he receives from well-off young fans or the advertisements he makes for *tafhit* websites), and, above all, symbolic capital and public respect: senior skidders, such as Bubu, al-Mustashar (the councillor), al-King, al-Khuffash (the bat), or Hitler are as famous amongst youth as international soccer players – or the main figures of the Saudi Islamic movement. In this last sense, 'speeding like crazy' and 'slaloming between cars', sometimes at one's life's expense, is a 'behaviour that appears irrationally violent, "barbaric", and ultimately self-destructive to the outsider' but can be reinterpreted, according to the street culture and the underground economy of symbolic exchange, 'as judicious public relations and long-term investment in one's "human capital development"' (Bourgois 1996: 24).

This highly visible practice is the gathering point of many deviances and forms of delinquency, the first of which is car robbery (the vehicles skidders play with are mainly stolen ones), followed by drug traffic and use (heroin during the 1980s and now hashish and stimulants), alcohol consumption (locally distilled grape alcohol), paedophilia, and homosexual rape. These last practices are perhaps the most emblematic of *tafhit*: in this strictly segregated society, the 'love of younger boys' (*wir'anjiyya*) is both a compensation for the invisibility of girls and women and a mode of socialization amongst youth. The stigmatization – and criminalization in the Saudi context – of skidders as deviant homosexuals is nevertheless assumed by the *tafhit* fans, who recognize blatantly that the social capital they are in search of is first and foremost beautiful boys (*wir'*, pl. *wir'an*). 'Alas! Our love for you [boys] is a sin!' reads a famous slogan, while anonymous street poetry celebrates *wir'anjiyya* as the first purpose of *tafhit*, far ahead of the obvious pleasure of defying police and 'jumping traffic lights'.

> Hamad asked me and told me: why?
> Why do the guys fall into *tafhit?*
> I pointed my finger at him and said: look at you!
> A beautiful boy stretching at the rhythm of the tires![4]

> Put the speed above two-hundred
> Push the engine at six-thousand
> The sexy boys compete for you
> Tell the one you are into.[5]

As a result of these deviances and the very many traffic accidents *tafhit* causes – when a poorly mastered skid ends up among the public, heavy losses are most probable – *hajwala* has been unanimously stigmatized and criminalized by the official institutions. The police are recruiting informers in order to catch the new trends and follow up the main wanted skidders, while the media, the research centres and various Islamic institutions have targeted *tafhit* as both an object of analysis and the goal of many prevention and awareness campaigns. One good example of the way public institutions view *tafhit* can be provided by a documentary shown in December 2006 on national TV channel al-Ikhbariyya. Its director interviewed detained skidders inside police stations under the vigilant gaze of policemen and inspectors, an objectionable bias that tends to diffuse through the public space the repressive spirit of the police and *mabahith*'s (the secret service) methods. The very title of the film, *al-Jarimat al-murakkaba* (The Composite Crime), leaves no space for questioning the social, economic, cultural, or political background of *tafhit*'s fans: besides the terrified interviewed youngsters, the only witnesses the director has called in are a senior police officer and a professor of psychology. *Tafhit* is called 'street terrorism' (*irhab ash-shawari'*) in the film, and has been analysed through the very categories (individual deviance and madness) state propaganda uses against Islamic activism. The social sciences departments also rely on police willingness to provide jailed interviewees in order to analyse *tafhit*. The same methods are indeed implemented by researchers and students, and unsurprisingly lead to the same conclusions, i.e. the identification of street rebellion with mere idiosyncratic troubles and psychological disorders (as-Sayf 1996).

On the other hand, through the 'cultural redefinition' and 'oppositional celebration' of their bad deeds 'as badges of pride' (Bourgois 1996: 130), *mufahhat*s tend to glorify the fear they inspire in governmental institutions. The fascination for the local branch of al-Qaeda and for the Iraqi resistance naturally plays a role in this self-glorification as true 'terrorists', as made clear by the following poem:

> In full dawn
> A Toyota colour of kohl
> Western songs

Iraqi anthems
Terrorist skids.[6]

Tafhit fans are less at ease when it comes to the Islamic institutions that deal with them. Far from being bold and provocative, their reaction to them is a blend of the respect due to the social prestige of the preachers, of the sinner's self-contempt, and of dull hatred and boredom. In East Harlem, Philippe Bourgois observed 'the profound moral – even righteous – contradictory code of street ethic that equates any kind of drug use with the works of the devil, even if almost everybody on the street is busy sniffing, smoking, shooting, or selling' (Bourgois 1996: 41). *Hajwala* fans 'know that *tafhit* is bad'[7] and that 'the end of *tafhit* is either death or repentance'.[8] Their very Islamic way of putting things is somewhat unexpected, especially when it comes from young guys who occasionally use drugs or rape minors. But it is a product of both 'street ethics' and of the aggressive campaigns Islamic institutions wage against them. Preaching groups and Islamic circles are indeed the only official institutions to fight *tafhit* on its very battleground. As well as *tafhit* fans, the preachers have adopted effective means of communication (films, clips, internet or Bluetooth), and sometimes hire rehabilitated skidders (*ta'ibun*) to gather young people and 'save their souls and bodies'.

Yet the Islamic way of dealing with *tafhit* is an exception, for all other institutions have adopted a much more repressive stance towards its perpetrators. These various discourses on deviance and delinquency shall nevertheless not monopolize the observer's attention. As many speeches and narratives produced in the Saudi public sphere, they tend to replace and mime genuine action or effective policy making. Certain sociologists stress that police repression, more than being an organized campaign, is a random enterprise that accommodates the phenomenon and mostly tolerates it. The criminalization of *tafhit* in official discourse cannot hide the loose practices of repression and the continual hesitancy of policemen, uncertain whether *tafhit* is a crime that deserves prison or a simple violation of the traffic regulations.[9] Most neighbourhoods are poorly monitored by police forces that frequently refuse to intervene when *tafhit* occurs, sometimes provoking the indignation of well-intentioned fathers: having called the police because a skidder was disturbing the whole neighbourhood, one of them heard the officer on duty replying: 'Let him skid until he crashes and dies' ('Khallah yifahhat ilen yasdum wa yimut').[10]

Fighting marginalization in Riyadh

Young skidders and their fans are mostly young bedouin men from 15 to 30 years of age.[11] They come from vulnerable sectors of the world of urban bedouins, namely families that have recently emigrated from the countryside to the capital or, worse, split-up families living between some isolated village (*al-dira*), where parents and younger children make a living out of agricultural activity, and the big town, where older sons try to cope with their studies – or give up and end up looking for ill-paid jobs. These individuals and their families live in what one may call the 'bedouin belt', i.e. the neighbourhoods that, from al-Khalij to Nazhim, Nassim and ad-Dakhl al-mahdud, surround Riyadh from the north-east to the south-west near the industrial zones and the huge compound of the National Guard. These families' social capital is scarce and limited to relations with the extended family, without any connection to the outside world of other bedouins or sedentary Riyadh townspeople. The family heads rely mainly on odd jobs in the public sector as soldiers or small-scale contractors for the army or the Ministry of Interior; in a majority of cases, however, they are retired people, and the linguistic and cultural gap between 70- or 80-year-old fathers and their 20-or-so-year-old sons is huge.

Tafhit heroes tend to belong to the very families that never appear on official records: aged and retired fathers are sometimes married four times (*mutazawwij arba'*), and leave the impossible burden of educating up to fifty children to their wives, being both culturally and economically unable to do so themselves. Sometimes they desert their families; when they do not, domestic violence is not rare, and the children tend to live down in the street, coming back home only to eat and to sleep. When the parents are living far away in the steppes (up to 1,200 km away from Riyadh), adolescents and young men who 'came up' to Riyadh for their studies rely on themselves or on some relatives. The discipline required by the university is undermined by the conditions of their lives. It can also depend on moral disposition and cultural capital more than on economic well-being: in the same extended family, for instance, young men in one branch, who are under the protection of educated and strong women, may graduate, while in another branch, wealthier but managed by uneducated men, children will be abandoned once they arrive in Riyadh and will tend to slip into delinquency, giving up studying after several failures and ultimately heading to the street, *tafhit*, and drugs.

Fig. 2: A mufahhat *wearing a* thub *and a baseball cap. (Photograph: Pascal Ménoret)*

The second kind of marginalization is cultural. With the foundation of the modern Saudi state in 1932, bedouins lost their traditional political and cultural preponderance (Pouillon and Mauger 1995). To be a bedouin today means sharing a stigmatized heritage and risking being misunderstood, or even feared, by members of the higher social classes, i.e. the descendants of oasis dwellers, now middle- and upper-class civil servants and businessmen. The bedouin dialects, although perceived as appropriate for poetry, are despised in everyday life as violent, rural, and rather primitive idioms. Clothing and physical appearance is another arena in which young bedouins are despised by sedentary society: 'Their aspect is frightening; they look like crap, as if they came out from under the earth, with their standing hair and their moustaches'.[12] With their tight white clothes (*thub*) and the thousand ways they fold their headdresses (*shmagh*) or mix Arabic costume with Western accessories (such as baseball caps), young bedouins are clearly recognizable (see fig. 2). Even though their clothing style has been imitated by most middle-class adolescents, it remains stigmatized by mainstream society. Young bedouins either frighten the sedentary people or are mocked by them for their supposedly inborn ignorance, anarchy, and violence. Old stereotypes provide a huge repertoire for insults and vexations. *Tafhit* thus is a hopeless rebellion against both the settled way of life and the Saudi norms. An anonymous poem says:

> Go fast, burn tires! Cars make you the 'Antar of this time
> For your time has betrayed you
> The beautiful boys applaud you and prove your value
> The cop beats you
> No wonder he insults you, humiliates you
> Since you failed in everything
> Nothing enhances your position
> You left school and roam with bad boys
> You did not hear your father when he cried because of you
> Nor your mother when she shouted and exhorted you
> You neglected her, you turned your back and you wanted her humiliation
> Go, disappear and let your Lord resolve your crises
> Go fast, burn tires until your ears explode.[13]

Besides having written one of the *Mu'allaqat*, the pre-Islamic bedouin warrior and poet 'Antar is famous for his hostility to the sedentary Banu Tamim tribe, which is today one of the pillars of the modern Saudi state. 'Antar may be viewed as a role model by rebellious young bedouins; they nevertheless know that they have been 'betrayed', and that only their Lord can 'resolve their crises'. No salvation is to come from society.

Economic and cultural marginalization is the fuel of a genuine social and spatial violence. Because of their aspect and behaviour, young bedouins are systematically expelled from most public spaces, malls, and other recreational facilities. Mostly left to themselves, they are utterly vulnerable to the police, the religious police, and the private security companies. Their social capital is clearly at stake: while young middle-class men can avoid the police thanks to their parents' relations (*wasta*), young bedouins are always at risk of having to spend several nights in the police station and endure bad treatment and beatings for having hung out at the wrong place and with the wrong person. As a result, they do not easily 'go down' to the bourgeois central neighbourhoods of Riyadh, such as 'Ulaya and Sulaymaniyya. They sometimes justify their fear of being socially despised by repeating the elders' position on those 'places of moral perdition'. The 'fine neighbourhoods' that reject them are thus one of the most popular goals of *tafhit*:

> Play the horn. Skid and disturb the fine neighbourhood o Bûbû!
> Let the patrols die of disgust and let them give up the chase, give up![14]

Becoming a skidder: the street, the school, and the feeling of deprivation

In the peripheral neighbourhoods of Riyadh, the 'hall of fame' is the street, where teenagers drive the family car very early, notably because of the prohibition on women driving. As the city was designed around use of the car, with a poor public transport system that does not include the periphery of Riyadh, the individual vehicle is both the main condition of freedom of movement and a marker of the social identity of its driver: 'If you have a Lexus, you are yourself a Lexus. If you have a piece of shit, you are a piece of shit.' Furthermore, the configuration of the urban space facilitates risk taking, and straight, long desert highways allow young men to learn acrobatic driving. The openness of urban space is linked with the aggressive strategies of both real-estate investors (since the 1973 oil boom the real-estate market has been the major channel of rent distribution) (Bonnenfant 1982) and car importers, as well as the municipal regulations that require the opening of avenues and connection of electricity before the commercialization of any project. Real-estate development projects (*al-mukhattatat*) have become central in the lives of peripheral residents, who gather, play cards, have dinner, drink alcohol, or take drugs on the vacant lots, while the desert avenues are the skidders' playground. The real-estate boom and the unregulated importation of cars have thus provided the very infrastructures that allowed *hajwala* to thrive. The internet author of a history of hooliganism in Saudi Arabia puts it boldly: 'By the way, they [skidders] don't want to hear about the stock market boom. Why? Because when the share prices go up, the real-estate market stops or slows down. And if real-estate slows down, projects (*al-mukhattatat*) are stopped and with them the opening of new avenues . . . You know how the story ends . . .'[15]

Most parents who retain some authority over their children lock them up at home when they become aware of the modes of deviant socialization in the street. But such youngsters will often join a *tafhit* group during school days. The first step in the world of *tafhit* seems harmless, and consists of accepting from an older schoolmate a master key that will be used to 'borrow' a car. This simple means of admission, added to the excitement of penetrating a new world based on heroism and rebellion, makes it extremely difficult to resist the temptation of *tafhit* in the school environment. Neither the educational institution itself nor the preaching groups that attract young pupils through the organization of soccer tournaments and other playful activities (Ménoret 2005) can challenge the prestige of *tafhit*. 'We were all obsessed by it: you had to become a skidder!' says a ninth grader in a southern Riyadh high school before adding:

A: I feel like . . . 1 per cent of the people are destined for the preaching group. . . . As for *tafhit* groups, they are larger. At the beginning of intermediary school, they distribute master keys to the pupils, those keys we use to steal cars. I remember this one day, I was walking back home and I saw two pupils, fresh ones, they were saying that they were about to steal a car, they had a key. That's their way of recruitment: they distribute keys to the pupils. And they gather important groups.

B: And entering *tafhit* is easier than joining a preaching group. I mean that you are watching them from your window, maybe you're gonna get down in the street and there, in front of the door, you'll find a guy, you'll chat with him, and this guy, maybe, he will let you in his car tomorrow. It's easier![16]

The master key is a challenge to the pupil; if he accepts it, he goes on to other *tafhit*-linked deviances. Should he decline it, he would immediately be confined to a subordinate position in his peer group. From the first step onward, a series of tests leads to the constitution of clear hierarchies inside the group, where dominant positions are the product of a consensus. The attractiveness of *tafhit* groups is all the more difficult to fight because they use extremely efficient media, from flyers to pagers and the internet, the mobile phone and Bluetooth.

The ease of entry does not by itself explain the 'fall into *tafhit*' and the formation of what one might call genuine 'deviant careers' (Becker 1963: 24 ff.). In such a repressive society, how can the individual manage to steal a car and join a group of drug addicts, when both crimes are supposed to be heavily repressed by the state? Young pretenders to the status of skidder provide many justifications for their acts: some talk of blind necessity ('We have only streets and cars, what do you want us to do?'), while others tend to minimize robbery ('We did not actually steal the car; we only borrowed it'). Others will glorify this first step and build a narration of injustice and revenge. These justifications are but *a posteriori* rationalizing. and do not explain what happens during the initial risk taking. The violence of the immediate environment might well explain how young bedouin boys are driven into deviance. A famous preacher and former *mufahhat* tells the story of Abu Hasan, 'former hooligan and drug-addict', whose deviant career began when he was expelled from school for having stolen a sandwich: having experienced at a very young age the *falaqa* (bastinado) torture for an obviously tiny misdeed, Abu Hasan would later declare that 'the school was the beginning of perdition'.[17] Domestic and school violence might thus explain many deviances. However, they do not enlighten the subjective state of mind of young people who are labelled 'deviant'.

Exploring the main feeling expressed by young bedouin men in Riyadh may provide a clue. When asked about *tafhit*, young men are unanimous: 'It is because of *tufush*', a colloquial Saudi word psychologists and sociologists translate by the classical terms 'boredom' (*malal*) (as-Sayf 1996: 107) or 'vacuum' (*faragh*) (ash-Shithri 2001: 170). These translations can be misleading, for *tufush* is more a social than a psychological disorder. *Tufush* is derived from a colloquial verb that denotes the random movements of a drowning man. Being *tufshan* is therefore not only experiencing a 'loss of future' (Bourdieu 1997: 336) or being disappointed or even disgusted by one's own living conditions, but also desperately trying to overcome this experience. While 'boredom' (*malal*) is a mere emptiness, a big nothing', *tufush* is a feeling that 'drives you to do anything and everything, that drives you into being an *'arbaji* [hooligan]',[18] i.e. 'to sell the entire world for a bicycle wheel's price' or 'to take the whole world as a butt and to step on it'.[19] *Tufush* might be analysed as the awareness of the discrepancy between subjective hopes and objective opportunities (Bourdieu 1997: 336), as the feeling of deprivation that results from the odd discovery that the economic and social opportunities Riyadh offers do not improve the young bedouin's social and economic condition. Shortly put, *tufush* is the feeling of being deprived of social or relational capital in a city where all opportunities – especially the economic ones – are within reach, provided that one gets the appropriate 'connection' (*wasta*). It is the rage that overwhelms young bedouins when they discover the essential inequality of the structure of opportunities – an inequality that contradicts the official 'developmentalist' discourse of the Saudi welfare state.

The body capital

The police, the Islamic preachers, and the schoolteachers judge *tafhit* as being *tahawwur wa 'abath*[20] (temerity and nonsense); even young middle-class men share this axiological point of view. It is clearly expressed by a young drag-racing aficionado, who compares his well-off and organized friends with the skidders: 'Us, we have goals, we know what we are doing. Our races are 70 per cent safe. Them, they are acting like fools, it is rabble (*hamajiyya*) and accidents.'[21] Yet *tafhit* is not as confused and anarchic as it first may seem. It is a true discipline that requires of the individual the development of specific skills. A good skidder does not drink, does not smoke, and is dedicated to his excellence as an extreme driver. This ethics of self-control explains why Badr 'Awadh, nicknamed 'al-King', has been the unchallenged hero of *tafhit* in Riyadh for 16 years, while other less careful skidders have been seriously wounded or have even died. This ethics is sometimes justified in very mundane words and in reference to the younger boys that the skidder aims at charming:

> For example, you are working for a company in which there is an outstanding employee. Of course, you want to be better than him. It is the same in *tafhit*. There is the love of younger boys (*al-wir'anjiyya*). But it is a kind of extra reward you get only if you become the best employee. If you enter *tafhit* for the boys' eyes, you will be bad in *tafhit* and lose the boys. You have to get into *tafhit* for *tafhit*'s sake. You have to become the best one, because boys love excellence and dedication.[22]

What is at stake here is an elaboration of a certain type of excellence or capital, the *body capital*, through the instillation of specific 'techniques of the body' (Mauss 1967: 51). The body is a main player in the world of *tafhit* – as well as in marginalized neighbourhoods in Europe or the United States, where the frequentation of gyms and fight-clubs and demonstrations of sheer violence are viewed as a valuable investment. An extreme kind of body capital is thus the 'warrior capital' (*capital guerrier*) that is required in particularly violent environments, such as some American barrios or French *banlieues* (Bourgois 1996: 22–8; Sauvadet 2006: 95–105) and whose main features are 'courage, elegance, mastery, and reputation' (Sauvadet 2006: 99).

Saudi Arabia is characterized by an intense concentration of the various legitimate species of capitals. The political capital (Bourdieu 1994) is monopolized by certain branches of the royal family. The economic capital – which might be seen as an appendix of the political capital – is monopolized by some princes and by their entourage of businessmen and traders. The legitimate cultural capital, although a thin portion of it has been granted to a secular intelligentsia, is almost totally in the hands of the religious elite and has become – because of the limitation of the political capital – the object of an intense competition between various pretenders, including the traditional elite of *'ulama* and preachers, the new counter-elite of the Islamic awakening (*as-sahwa al-islamiyya*), and, more recently, the jihadist movement (Al-Rasheed 2007). Due to the authoritarian seizure of the political and economic capital, the cultural capital is the only legitimate capital open to newcomers. They may acquire it at the university or, more frequently, through membership of an Islamic group, whether pro-government or of a more oppositional nature. The religious field is the only one not to be subjected to a strict reproduction pattern. The people we are studying here have been excluded early from the education system, and belong to this majority of young Saudis who either never entered the education system or drop out of school before completing their secondary or higher education (Prokop 2003: 87). As such they are not only excluded from the political and economic capital. Unless they adopt the asceticism and the peculiar codes of the Islamic groups, they are also deprived of any possibility of acquiring cultural capital. Our hypothesis is that the body capital is the only capital that remains when all other opportunities have been monopolized by specific fragments of society and when no economic, social, or cultural feature of the individual is convertible into social respect, and thus symbolic or real profits.

Fig. 3: Two skidders on a main avenue of Riyadh. For security and symbolic reasons, skidders cover their faces with their shmagh, *just like jihadists do. (Photograph: Pascal Ménoret)*

Holding another type of convertible capital, such as cultural Islamic capital, does not mean that the body capital is not invested. Various body techniques are at stake inside the Saudi religious establishment itself, whose insistence on the multiple details of ritual purification is well known. Young Islamists shorten their clothes and grow their facial hair: they expect these measures to gain them the respect society refuses to ill-born young people. Al-Qaeda in Saudi Arabia is also investing the body as both a weapon and a place of resistance (Al-Rasheed 2007: 156–63). As for young bedouins, the care of the body will first of all accentuate the stigma: the unusual way of wearing *shmagh* (headdress, see fig. 3), as well as the mixture of Saudi dress and Western accessories, are aimed at subverting the refined dress codes of upper Saudi society. Second, the body has to be adjusted to the machine through various exercises in order to confront the risk and the possibility of death. A famous (now closed) *tafhit* website used to propose online training under the slogans: 'al-tadris li-'uyun zahif ma hi khasara' (learning for a *mufahhat*'s eyes is not a loss) and 'al-Funun junun' (madness is an art).[23] Finally, the body is constituted as a weapon: like al-Qaeda supporters (Al-Rasheed 2007: 156), *mufahhat*s are stressing the importance of being thin in a society where obesity is widespread. 'Ezhef, tanhaf!' (crawl, do *tafhit*, you will get thinner), reads a *tafhit* slogan. By its ability to confront death and to distinguish itself from the dominant codes, the body of the *mufahhat* is glorified and allows him to become a hero. The reinterpretations of the common dress code as well as the proclaimed deviant sexual behaviour and the ability to put one's physical integrity at stake in the 'urban jungle' are nothing but symptoms of a rebellion of the body against the dominant norms of Saudi society.

Avenues of participation

The discipline of *tafhit* does not concern only the body. Skidders have also elaborated specific group techniques in order to counter official tactics of repression. A typical *tafhit* session is organized by the fans (*al-mushajji'in*) themselves, who during the afternoon beg a skidder to 'throw the iron' (*siff al-hadid*) or to 'domesticate the steel' (*ta'dib al-hadid*). Fans usually gather money to pay him, while the skidder's 'attendants' (*ta'ziz*), the ones who will ultimately sit in the hero's car, entrust younger members of the network with stealing some cars. Then a central figure, the 'orienteer' (*muajjih*), organizes the night, mobilizing his networks and gathering the largest possible number of spectators in carefully selected places, both well known amongst the *tafhit* fans and relatively new in order to avoid discovery. He also contacts other skidders and manages to organize an attractive panel by choosing both the best places and the most dedicated heroes. The skidders finally head towards the first 'spot', every one of them accompanied by his fans, two or three improvised ambulances driven by the 'supporters' (*musanidin*) in case of an accident, and a crowd of cars, constituted in procession (*mawkib*) and moving very rapidly along the large avenues of Riyadh. In every spot, skidders do several 'shots' (*shut*) of combined figures, while the fans pack the sidewalk, filming, taking pictures, or simply watching. After the show, everyone quickly gets in his car for fear of the police patrols and moves to another spot. These gatherings, which can involve more than fifty cars, usually take place during school exams, holidays, and the month of Ramadan. The golden hour is at dawn, after the *fajr* prayer, between patrols. The most delicate operation is to prevent discovery. This is the task of the 'radar' (*radar*), whose goal it is to gather and update data about the strategies of the police forces, and to inform the 'orienteer', who will react accordingly, either moving the procession from one spot to another or even cancelling the show when danger is at hand.

The hierarchy of *tafhit* is essentially an adaptation to the techniques of surveillance and repression of the Riyadh police. The chaos of a moving procession is in fact the result of meticulous organization and coordination. The appearance of disorder and extreme speed are tactics elaborated against the partitioning and monitoring of an urban area that has become an 'analytical' and 'disciplinary' space, i.e. a space that 'cancels the effects of indecisive repartitions, the uncontrollable disappearance of individuals, their diffuse circulation, their unusable and dangerous coagulation', a space that 'institutes useful communications and interrupts any other form of movement' (Foucault 1975: 168). Speed is the only way of escaping the surveillance of the urban space and its visibility: the large avenues of Riyadh, accessible only by car and monitored by video cameras, hinder the formation of any mass meeting. The 'analytical space' of Riyadh splits up individuals by its very configuration and the many possibilities it offers to the police, so that mass demonstrations on foot are nearly impossible. Only the gathering of numerous cars speeding along the street can allow protesting individuals to escape repression. This method of dissent is embedded in the very 'spatial routines' of the daily life 'that bring large numbers of people together in particular places' (Sewell 2001: 62), these places in Riyadh being cars and highways – moving places – rather than squares or sidewalks. Some techniques familiar to urban walking rioters are used by young drivers, such as the 'swarm' tactics observed during the 1990 revolution in Nepal (Routledge 1997: 76). It consists of a sudden gathering of people at strategic locations, followed by their dispersion when police forces arrive. Many diversion tactics are also used, such as the organization of up to two or three fake parallel *tafhit* shows that mislead the police patrols. In this case, *tafhit* fans don't disperse but force the police to do so.

Space is not only the site of mobilization. Nor is it only its object: it is also an effective cause of the mobilization itself. *Tafhit* 'gives you the sense of time and space',[24] and space in return gives *tafhit* its very signification. As does repression: the confrontation between police forces and young people tend to politicize and organize small-scale or low-intensity dispersed movements (Bayat 1997: 8). The complex pyramidal organization of *tafhit* groups, from 'fans' to 'supporters' to 'attendants', 'radar', 'orienteer', and the skidder himself, is aimed at challenging the various techniques of the police, the most feared of which is the 'web' (*shabaka*) technique, which consists of blocking a whole neighbourhood, tightening the trap, and eventually picking up both the skidders and their fans. The organization's goals are: gathering fans and controlling their movements; watching the police and avoiding arrest; and protecting the skidder in case of massive breakdown. Attracting fans thus bears a double signification and aims at both satisfying a demanding public and potentially hiding the hero in the moving crowd. Protest and resistance are tightly linked. If the police are feared for their repressive tactics, they are also the goal of many provocations, such as throwing insults ('try to follow me, you fag' or 'hey beautiful, do you wanna get in for a ride?'), eggs, and stones at a police patrol (see fig. 4). At some points, retaliation may follow an aggressive police operation: in an eastern neighbourhood of Riyadh, the police station was once robbed and ransacked on the eve of its inauguration by the *amir* of the capital (head of the local administration). Organization is a response to repression; it may also be the backbone of authentic though limited protest actions against the very structures of local power.

Fig. 4: Defying the police. A famous tafhit*'s slogan reads: 'Skid, get drunk and forget the cops' (Fahhet, eskar w-ensa al-'askar). (Source: www.alb7ri.com)*

Urban unrest and non-ideological radicalization

That the peripheral neighbourhoods of Riyadh are first and foremost playgrounds for turbulent children who ride cars in a crazy manner may sound good for the anti-terrorist planners, who look at the south and east of the capital as havens for young terrorists and Islamic extremists. The south of Riyadh notably has a notably bad reputation and is still nicknamed 'the Falluja of Riyadh' or the 'Sunni triangle' for its supposedly peculiar ecology of activism and rebellion. Yet for Riyadh's youth, rebellion's theatre is first of all on the streets. Along the lines of the ancient hatred towards bedouins and the renewed marginalization of young people coming from low-class and rural backgrounds, *tafhit* plays anew the old narrative of bedouins vs. oasis-dwellers. Reviving the moral codes and values of bedouin society, chanting their exploits in poems and songs, risking their lives for the attention of their beloved ones, young skidders imagine themselves as errant heroes of the Saudi urban post-modernity. They attract by their words and deeds far more supporters than the Islamic groups can do with their ascetic conception of the self and their rigid way of painting life. Like the low-riding sub-culture of Los Angeles, *tafhit* groups offer '"cool worlds" of urban socialization for poor young newcomers' from rural areas (Davis 1992: 293), beyond the narrow circle of the family and against the official norms propagated by such local institutions as the school and the mosque. It might be misleading, however, to abruptly oppose 'deviant' and 'Islamic' socializations as two separate poles of attraction. In reality, the politics of deviance has often been an introduction to more organized and effective politics of (Islamic) defiance.

The history of the relations between *tafhit* and Islamic groups is indeed all but a simple one. Like the Saudi Islamic movements, *tafhit* made its first appearance during the 1970s. They have both invested the same spaces: the neighbourhood (*al-hara*) and the school. They both aim at recruiting the largest possible number of members and have launched many propaganda campaigns, using more or less the same media: first the flyer, then the pager, and finally the mobile phone and the internet. The overwhelming success of *tafhit*'s songs, the famous *kasrat* that glorify hooliganism and the street heroes, may be compared with the revival of Islamic hymns (*anashid*), despite the Salafi prohibition of music: this very space also was an arena of competition. *Tafhit* has the obvious advantage of being not only 'cooler' than Islamic socialization, it also addresses more directly the current and immediate problems of the time. It is a rebellion against the very structures of consumption and economic power, while the Islamic movements, in order to reach the same goal, are taking a long detour through religious revival and moralization of the social life. Since the oil boom of 1973, the real-estate market and the monopolies on vehicle sales are two main pillars of enrichment for the royal family's entourage. These very visible elements of power are the first targets of skidders, through the multiple strategies we have been analysing here. The hatred of the 'big shots' who control the Saudi economy of consumption – and thus the Western interests that they are supposedly supporting – is unveiled in the discourse of many *tafhit* fans: 'It is with our oil that you [the West] make cars. And you sell them back to us at top prices. And us, we destroy them.' 'It is a Zionist and American plot. They import cars to destroy us.' 'Rich guys provide us cars and play on us.'[25] The real-estate development projects are also targeted as being a 'killer of youngsters'.

Such longevity in low-intensity rebellion, experienced week after week and season after season in various parts of Riyadh, discovering new playgrounds and spaces, following up the city's astonishing boom and conquering new modes of expression, is rather unusual and tends to contradict the principle according to which 'insurgency is always short-lived' (Piven and Cloward 1977: xxi). This rebellion indeed was not only fuelled by the continuous explosion of real-estate speculation and by the acceleration of the country's heavy dependence on the outside producing world. It was also at the crossroads between two intertwined phenomena. Eager to undermine the first political opposition of the Islamic movements, the Saudi government launched in the 1980s a 'crusade against Evil' and a campaign to enhance the 'moral order' of society. This interpretation of political protest as mere moral and cultural grievances was to become the first and more effective de-politicizing tool of the Saudi state, and was about to radically alter the everyday life of Saudis. Old habits became new deviances; the very notion of public space disappeared almost totally; the economic strategies of the royals and their entourage were hidden behind religious protestations. At the same time, the rising level of corruption and the poorly mastered public expenditures allowed imported goods, the most famous of them being weapons and cars, to flood the country.

Radicalization without an ideology, *tafhit* is but one possible self-destructive response to radical socio-economic conditions. The deviant careers of well-known or more obscure skidders can end up in religious involvement and repentance, or even lead them to violent experiences. One particular group of skidders who were operating in the north-east of Riyadh in the middle of the 1990s is emblematic of these chaotic journeys. Out of ten skidders, two died in *tafhit* accidents; two others are in jail; one has repented and become pious after having killed a man during a *tafhit* accident and having been jailed for several years; two joined the Tabligh movement[26] and preach in the western province of the country. Three of them joined activist groups after a short period of preparation (two to four months) and now fight with the Iraqi resistance.[27] The previous generation of skidders had had the same experience, this time in Afghanistan where 'the story of hooliganism ended up',[28] some of the bolder youngsters of Riyadh heading eastwards to fight the Red Army. From the rebellion of the body against the Saudi codes and monopolies to a rebellion of the body against the 'New World Order', this non-ideological radicalization shows that sometimes suicide fighters do not need to be 'born-again Muslims' in order to participate in a defensive *jihad*: 'The articulate minorities ... arise from a less articulate majority whose consciousness may be described as being, at this time, "sub-political"' (Thompson 1963 59). This less articulate majority, through its tactics of resistance and protest, is training itself to the very gestures of war, and might turn the 'body capital' into an authentic 'warrior capital'. In extreme circumstances, the body may be turned into a weapon, as a means for the individual to achieve his individual fate, to prepare the way for the Islamic state – or for general anarchy.

CHAPTER 12

Bodily Punishments and the Spiritually Transcendent Dimensions of Violence: a Zen Buddhist Example

Ian Reader

Introduction

Perhaps the most intimidating and violent place I have been was the meditation hall of a Rinzai Zen Buddhist temple in Japan, which I visited while conducting Ph.D. fieldwork on Zen organizations during 1981–2. I had spent much of that year at Zen temples, and was used to the austerities associated with Zen monastic life. Therefore I was accustomed to the use of the *kyôsaku*, or 'waking stick' that is carried around the meditation hall by a senior monk, who has been chosen for the task because of his skill in meditation, and that may be used to strike meditating practitioners as a means of 'awakening' them if it appears that their minds are wandering or their posture is poor. Indeed, it is not uncommon for meditating practitioners to request receipt of the *kyôsaku* by holding their hands up as if in prayer; the normal procedure for receipt is for the monk wielding the stick to strike the recipient a number of times either on one shoulder or on the back. However, despite being used to such procedures, I still felt rather intimidated when attending a meditation session open to lay practitioners in spring 1982 at the aforementioned Rinzai temple. The temple appeared almost military in ethos, with strict codes of conduct governing every action and with monks barking out instructions on how to behave and engage in every aspect of the ritualized process of mediation hall life, while sharply castigating those who failed to follow exact procedures. The monk wielding the *kyôsaku* in the meditation hall marched up and down in a brusque, militaristic manner, his footsteps clearly intimidating the numerous lay practitioners in the meditation hall, while he rained down more blows and used the stick more copiously than at any other temple I had ever visited, to the extent that several experienced lay practitioners I met there indicated afterwards that they had felt unsettled by the atmosphere.

This experience in particular, as well as the time I spent in numerous other Zen temples in which the *kyôsaku* was regularly used, brought home to me a seeming paradox between the image of Buddhism as a non-violent tradition, and the prevalence of violence within the context of Zen Buddhist practice, as evidenced by the use of the *kyôsaku* in the meditation hall. Indeed, such usage is widely publicized in Zen contexts as an intrinsic, important, and even appealing aspect of Zen life. The use of the *kyôsaku* is widely emphasized in public depictions of Zen life, with popular Zen publications, including magazines and journals produced by Zen Buddhist sectarian organizations in Japan, frequently focusing on the *kyôsaku* as a seminal feature of Zen discipline and often featuring it in photographic displays intended to highlight and popularize Zen temple life.[1] The violent blows of the *kyôsaku* are just one aspect of the presence of violence in Zen contexts, in which it is depicted as playing an important role in the spiritual awakening of practitioners; numerous stories from the Zen tradition, for example, speak of disciples awakened to enlightenment as a result of the *kyôsaku* or due to sudden blows rained on them by their Zen teachers that cause them to engage in a leap of cognition that is central to Zen experience.[2]

Violence, in such contexts, appears to be accepted and valorized as a worthy act intended to facilitate the attainment of spiritual goals, and as a deed that is valid to enact in order to assist those who are spiritually less advanced, to attain awakening. Equally, those who use such violence are lauded for their deeds, and are perceived as having the right to use violence because of its intentions and because their own spiritual standing is seen as enabling them to act in ways that otherwise might appear immoral. Moreover, the processes through which the violence is enacted – the use of the *kyôsaku* is framed by reverential acts of bowing, while the Zen masters who awaken their disciples by striking them are portrayed as holy figures – appear to sanctify the act and transform it from a mere act of violence into a holy deed. There would appear to be a paradox here, between violence as something commonly viewed as inappropriate and unacceptable, and as something that has a spiritual purpose and that, in certain contexts, may be legitimately used by those of a particular spiritual status as a means of assisting others in their spiritual path, and may even therefore be a sacred deed. It is this seemingly paradoxical aspect of violence as an act associated with sanctity and spiritual awakening that I wish to focus on here. In so doing I will raise questions about the relationship between ascetic practices (which the austere meditative practices of Zen temples are), the body (in Zen, the posture of the body is central, and one aim of using the *kyôsaku* is to alert the practitioner to his/her aberrant posture), and violence, and, since the process of using the *kyôsaku* is accompanied by bows and reverential acts, about the ways in which violence may be sanctified and accorded a ritual and mystical orientation. I will not, however, confine myself to the Zen temple environment, but will also look at how the ways of thinking that legitimized and accorded a spiritual dimension to such acts of violence within the Zen Buddhist tradition extended beyond temple confines and helped facilitate the emergence of Japanese militarism in the first part of the twentieth century, thereby opening the door to greater acts of violence, including murder and military atrocities that were accorded spiritual sanction from within the Zen tradition.

Although, in this chapter, my focus is on Zen, I should note that I am not treating it as an exceptional or aberrant form of Buddhism but as an example of the links that exist in a variety of Buddhist contexts between spirituality and violence. This is an important point to emphasize in wider debates about religion and violence, which have tended to focus on certain types of religious traditions and forms, notably monotheistic and millennial or apocalyptic movements,[3] and which have paid relatively little attention to traditions such as Buddhism. Indeed, to a great degree Buddhism has been a missing element in discussions of the topic, seemingly because of an assumption that it is predominantly peaceful and far less violence-prone than other traditions.[4] The lack of attention paid to Buddhism in such contexts is also, I would suggest, mirrored by a lack of attention to the ways in which violence itself may be seen as a means of inducing spiritual awakening, and may thus be afforded, within the context of religious discourse, a degree of sanctity that both legitimizes its use and can lead to greater violence – themes that also will be discussed here.

Zen and the art of violence

Zen Buddhism is well known for its rich tapestry of stories and narratives that convey images of awakening and of the strivings and sacrifices made by those seeking enlightenment. Often such stories involve or have at their core acts of violence, from blows delivered by Zen masters that result in the sudden awakening of their disciples, to sustained acts of asceticism that punish and purify the body so that the practitioner can be freed from physical restraints and attain spiritual salvation, to acts of mortification through which adepts cast off their worldly attachments in the pursuit of transcendence. D.T. Suzuki, whose extensive writings were influential in popularizing Zen Buddhism in the West in the earlier twentieth century, has introduced numerous accounts of such activities, ranging from the acts of the Chinese master Te-shan (Japanese name Tokushan[5]), who constantly badgered his disciples with phrases such as 'No matter what you say, or what you say not, just the same thirty blows for you!', to Lin Chi (Japanese, Rinzai) whose slap to the face of one monk caused another to experience a sudden awakening.[6] Lin Chi himself had been frequently beaten by his master, Huang-po (Ôbaku) whenever he asked questions about Buddhism; but it was through such violent deeds, according to Suzuki, that he was able to understand the ultimate truth and attain enlightenment, indicating that the violent blows that he received had been delivered 'mercifully'.[7]

In Japanese Zen contexts, the story of Hakuin Ekaku (1686–1769), regarded as one of the greatest and most inspirational figures in Japanese Zen Buddhist history, is well known. Hakuin's awakening was aided by the repeated blows rained on him by his Zen teacher, who on one occasion also pushed him off a veranda, and his ultimate realization of enlightenment came when an old woman (before whose house he was begging) struck him with a broom to make him go away.[8] At no stage is there any hint in the story that the violence dealt out to Hakuin was anything but beneficial. Indeed, Suzuki emphasizes how critical violence was not just to the Hakuin story itself but to the wider Zen aim of stripping away the illusions and delusions that, in Zen thought, cloud the mind and prevent one awakening to the true nature of reality: 'Each slap by Shôju stripped Hakuin of his insincerities. We are all living under so many casings which really have nothing to do with our inmost self. To reach the latter, therefore, and to gain knowledge of ourselves, the Zen masters resort to methods seemingly inhuman.'[9]

Violence, in other words, can be a noble act that is intrinsic to the path of enlightenment. It can also result in bodily mutilations, which are portrayed as worthwhile sacrifices for a higher goal, as in the example of the Chinese master Yun-men (d. 996), who gained sudden awakening after he had visited the temple of Zen master Wen-Yen as a mendicant. Wen-Yen had him thrown out roughly, at which point the temple gate swung back and crushed Yun-men's leg, an event that was the catalyst to Yun-men's attainment of Buddhahood, causing Suzuki to remark that 'the realization now gained paid more than enough for the loss of a leg'.[10]

Sometimes such dismemberments and bodily mortifications may be carried out by the practitioners themselves, with numerous stories in the Zen narrative tradition suggesting that pain, disfigurement, and bodily mutilation may even be necessary prerequisites for attaining enlightenment. Indeed, the traditional founding narrative widely circulated and narrated in Zen contexts – in which the Indian monk Bodhidharma brings the Zen tradition to China, whereupon he retreats to a cave and sits in meditation for nine years – contains several such dismemberments that express a core message about the necessity of pursuing spiritual awakening at all costs and that transmit critical teachings about the nature of Zen as a spiritual path. In the narrative Bodhidharma, the Indian monk accredited, in Zen tradition, with bringing the spirit of Zen to China, meets the Chinese emperor on arrival in that land. Although the emperor regales Bodhidharma with comments about how many temples he has had built, and clearly seeks Bodhidharma's approval for such deeds, the monk has no time for such fripperies, rebuffs all entreaties to pass on his teachings or to submit to the emperor's patronage, and retreats to a cave in order to concentrate wholly on his meditation. Determined not to waste valuable meditation time by sleeping, he then cuts off and casts aside his own eyelids so that he remain permanently awake. Then, because he sits incessantly in the lotus position without moving (Zen legends say he sat thus for nine years), his legs atrophy and rot away. Later, a monk, Huiko, intrigued by the Indian master and desperate to be taught the inner truths of Zen, enters the cave and beseeches Bodhidharma to take him on as a disciple, an entreaty that Bodhidharma initially rejects. Realizing that the master doubts his sincerity and determination to follow the path, Huiko repeats his request, but this time does so by cutting off his own arm and presenting it to Bodhidharma as a demonstration of his determination and willingness to sacrifice all in the pursuit of ultimate truth. Thus convinced of Huiko's sincerity, Bodhidharma acquiesces, and takes on Huiko as his disciple and successor in the Zen lineage of transmission, thereby paving the way for its development in East Asia.

Although these Zen foundation legends are widely recognized as being apocryphal (the Bodhidharma narrative has scant historical basis and is widely acknowledged to be a fictive account), they contain significant messages that affirm critical aspects of Zen teaching. Thus, Bodhidharma's absolute dedication to meditation – so vital that one should make all manner of sacrifices, from dispensing with one's eyelids and forsaking sleep, to losing one's legs – affirms the critical importance of meditation, which is viewed in Zen as the most cardinal of all practices and the key to enlightenment, so crucial, indeed, that one should be prepared to make countless sacrifices (from spurning the patronage of emperors to dispensing with sleep and limbs) for its sake. The example of Bodhidharma's sacrifice and willingness to endure pain and dismemberment in the pursuit of enlightenment resonates through the Zen tradition, legitimizing deeds of mortification – such as the story of the Sung period (960–1279) monk Tzu-ming, who, in a parallel of Bodhidharma's desire to not waste time by sleeping, was said to have pierced his thigh with a drill when he felt sleepy while meditating[11] – while Huiko's sacrifice of his arm in order to be taught by Bodhidharma sends out messages that the pursuit and transmission of Zen teachings are far more important than mere limbs and human attachments. They also articulate in graphic form Buddhist teachings about the necessity of shedding one's worldly attachments in order to attain awakening and escape the world of suffering. As such, Zen stories such as these affirm the view that the external, the physical, and the corporeal are less vital than the internal and the spiritual. As such, ascetic practice can harm, disfigure, and render parts of the physical body useless in the pursuit of higher truths, while the physical body can legitimately be beaten or maimed in pursuit of inner spiritual goals. Since, too, those who engage in such self-mortifications and uses of physical violence to pursue the path of enlightenment are celebrated in the Zen tradition as ideal manifestations of the cardinal Zen determination to attain enlightenment at all costs, one can see embedded in the Zen tradition a legitimization and even a celebration of violence as a worthy spiritual activity in the furtherance of spiritual goals.

Buddhism and the sanctification of violence

The Zen example cited here is indicative of how violence may be mystified, sanctified, and transformed into an act worthy of worship in stories and practices. The *kyôsaku* is itself treated as a sacred object, being placed (when not being carried by a designated and ranked monk) in a special place in the meditation hall and treated with ritual reverence at all times. Before the officiating monk picks it up, he bows to it ritually with hands together in prayer, and when walking around the meditation hall, he holds it upright in front of him, with head slightly bowed; when he touches the person to be beaten, the intended recipient bows prior to receiving the blows and, afterwards, both s/he and the monk who wields it bow again. In such terms, the *kyôsaku* is simultaneously a medium for enacting violence and for punishing the body, a sacred object and a reminder that violence can itself be accorded high spiritual value and sanctified as legitimate – a theme that, as indicated, permeates the Zen tradition with its stories of masters beating disciples and of physical dismemberments and bodily mortifications, all of which are closely linked with spiritual awareness.

It should be stressed that the mystical elevation and sanctification of violence in such contexts is not something that, in Buddhism, is the sole preserve of Zen. In the Tibetan Buddhist tradition, for example, there are numerous stories of those who beseech highly regarded Tibetan Buddhist teachers to take them on as disciples being harshly treated and brutalized, with the underlying message that such violence and brutality can drive away their illusions, and help them cast off their attachments and achieve awakening. Thus the story of the great twelfth-century teacher Marpa, and how he pursued black arts to advance his teachings, and how his harsh treatment of Milarepa helped transform Milarepa into a highly revered and spiritually advanced teacher in his own right, are widely told in the Tibetan Buddhist tradition, and are evidence of a widely accepted notion in that tradition.[12] The Marpa–Milarepa story (along with subsequent stories in which later teachers continue this tradition of harsh treatments as a means of instilling teachings into disciples) expounds the notion that seemingly immoral acts and flagrant breaches of conventional behaviour and mores may be performed by the spiritually advanced in order to assist or force others to achieve higher awakenings. Such behaviour is seen as evidence of the 'crazy wisdom' (Tibetan, *drubynon*) of Tibetan Buddhist masters who are capable of going beyond and breaching normative morality tradition in order to transmit spiritual teachings designed to elevate their disciples.[13]

In other words, the notion that the spiritually advanced can use any means whatsoever, including violence, to help others in their path towards enlightenment is not limited to Zen Buddhism and its stories and examples I have cited earlier, but extends across the Buddhist tradition. If such stories and examples emphasize that spiritual status enables Buddhist teachers to use violence in the furtherance of their teachings – and hence that violence can be a sanctified and exalted deed[14] – they also emphasize important

Buddhist concepts about the body as an impediment to spiritual awakening and as an impure entity that requires purification via austerities, strict disciplines, and even beatings and worse. Whereas, in the stories cited above, the purification of the body may be realized by the performance of austerities and acts of violence that seek to make the adept transcend physical attachments, at times it can, in Buddhist contexts, extend to suggestions that in some contexts getting rid of the body may be a necessary step in overcoming bodily impurity and in order to attain higher realms. This is especially so in the context of gender, an area in which Japanese Buddhism, for example, has widely adhered to the view that women could not attain enlightenment as women because of the sexual and menstrual pollutions that clung to them. Thus death and rebirth as a male were necessary steps on the path, with Buddhist funeral texts indicating that in such contexts death was a form of liberation that enabled women to advance spiritually.[15] Beliefs in the impure nature of the female body even meant that females were excluded from many important Buddhist sites in pre-modern Japan, on the grounds that they would pollute the place and restrict the potential for adepts therein to advance spiritually. When attempts to challenge such restrictions occurred, the results were dire, as is evident in a legend surrounding the mother of Kûkai, the ninth-century founder of Shingon Buddhism in Japan and of its sacred centre at Mount Kôya, one of the places from which females were barred until the modern day. Although she had not menstruated for many years, Kûkai's mother was still forbidden from entering her son's sacred mountain, a ban he himself upheld; objecting to this ban, the mother sought to break the taboo. Kûkai cast his Buddhist robe on the boundary of the mountain for her to walk across, and as she did so, her menstrual blood flowed again, the robe burst into flames, and she was immolated. The upshot of the legend (which exists in a variety of forms) is that the mother was subsequently able to join her son in the next realm as a result of her immolation and death;[16] a fiery death, in other words, was a necessary stage in her liberation and in order to rid her of the impediment of a polluted (female) body. In other words, the violence done to her body – and her sudden death – are not so much punishments for the misdeed of challenging female taboos, but necessary events that led to her potential salvation, which could be achieved after the barrier to her salvation, her body, was immolated.

Zen and the art of war

As the above discussion has suggested, in Buddhism in general, and Zen Buddhism in particular, one can find plentiful evidence to suggest that violent acts may be revered and accorded a mystical dimension, in which the very implementing of violence may be seen as a testimony to and affirmation of the spiritual status of those who commit it, and in which physical pain and loss of life may be interpreted as good and beneficial events for the greater spiritual good of those who lose their lives. As such, violence to the body, and even death, thus may be essential aspects of the journey to higher spiritual realms in Buddhist contexts, sending out messages that external physical reality is of lesser importance than the internal spiritual realm, and that those who mete out or preside over such violence are justified in so doing for the betterment of those they afflict.

Problems can arise in this context, however, when the thinking that operates within the confines of a tradition or, for example, within a monastic environment, extends out beyond such arenas into the wider public domain – an issue that is amply illustrated by the ways in which Zen Buddhism, in the first half of the twentieth century, became a driving force in the rise of Japanese militarism and played a crucial role in helping the Japanese state embark on a path of aggressive nationalism and in legitimizing acts of murder, colonial subjugation, and warfare. Zen Buddhism had long had a close history of association with the state, and especially with the military classes, before the twentieth century, and its austere and martial disciplines were deeply influential in the development of martial culture among the samurai warrior class in medieval Japan. In this fusion of Zen, the warrior class, and the martial arts, Zen Buddhist ideals and ethical orientations became tied to the legitimization of militaristic activities and helped sustain and support a culture of warfare.[17] While this relationship between Zen, militarism, and the warrior class was a significant feature of pre-modern Japan, it came to the fore again as a potent force in the 1920s and 1930s, as Zen concepts of austerity and discipline, coupled with Zen's implicit sanctification and justification of violence as a means of self-improvement, impacted on the attitudes of leading lights in the Japanese Imperial Army.

Studies of Zen influences in the earlier parts of the twentieth century indicate how Zen ideas about discipline, austerities, and the value of using violent acts to bring about awakening and spiritual purity were incorporated into the ethics of Japanese militarism, and how an idealized vision of the soldier as an adept of Zen, and of the Zen adept as a military figure, emerged as a key force in the military thinking of the era.[18] In this dynamic, Zen notions sanctifying violence as a spiritually empowered and mystical deed helped create, promote, and justify the deeds of violence, murder, and atrocity that were carried out in the name of Japan by its militarists as they first sought to exert their influence over the Japanese government and state, and later as they waged war and sought to subjugate other countries and peoples under the Japanese yoke.

Brian Victoria, for example, has discussed the activities of prominent Japanese Zen Buddhist priests as well as Zen proponents such as D.T. Suzuki, whose writings have been commented upon earlier in this chapter, who played an important role in the promotion of Japanese militarism and in helping to justify acts of violence, and even transform them into dutiful and even sacred acts on behalf of the country. As Victoria shows, there were close links between Zen and the Imperial Army, with many senior military figures undergoing Zen training and austerities which helped familiarize them with the notion that violence was a viable means of instilling 'spirit' into the military. Zen training practices were thus adopted by senior army officers as a means of providing 'spiritual education' and for bolstering morale and adherence to regimented discipline in the armed forces.[19] The harshness of Imperial Army discipline and culture has been highlighted in recent times by a number of studies and documentaries produced in Japan, in which former soldiers of the period have spoken about a culture of martial discipline that was in effect based on violence and beating and that owed much to the aforementioned Zen notions of beating as a means of enlightening and training others, which was prominent in the Army from the 1930s onwards, contributing significantly to the culture of brutalism that typified Japanese militarism of the period.[20]

Prominent Zen priests and teachers of the period played major roles in creating the cultural environment in which such martial views could flourish and through which acts of violence could be legitimized, imparted with a spiritual dimension, tied to notions of nationalist superiority, and aligned with concepts of a sacred or holy war that legitimized Japan's subversion of democracy and its attacks on other nations. Thus Ômori Sôgen – a highly ranked Zen master, calligrapher, swordsman, and writer, who in the post-1945 period became well known in the West as a Zen teacher – expressed ultranationalist and militaristic sentiments from the 1920s onwards and promoted the concept of the nation as a sacred entity consisting of the one indivisible body of the emperor, as father and god, and of his subjects, the people, who were his children.[21] Ômori viewed democracy as antithetical to these aims, and participated in various attempts to eliminate it via such acts as political assassinations, including an anti-Western, anti-democratic plot in 1933 that sought to restore imperial rule and that he presented in a sacred guise, describing it as a 'holy war' directed against inimical forces – the rule of law, democracy, individualism, and liberalism – which Ômori saw as un-Japanese and as products of the West.[22]

Other Zen teachers of the age also played a role in fomenting a climate in which deeds of assassination and violence in furtherance of militaristic nationalism were seen as legitimate – indeed, even sacred and mystically charged – acts. The prominent Zen teacher Fukusada Mugai, for example, was a spiritual mentor to Aizawa Saburô, a Zen adept who was also one of a number of militant young army officers who strove in the 1930s to promote an aggressive nationalism centred on emperor veneration and who sought to 'purify' the army and country by eradicating those who, in their view, impeded this aim. Aizawa had been encouraged by various Zen teachers, including Fukusada, under whom he trained from 1917 onwards, to fuse his Zen discipline with his military endeavours on behalf of the Emperor and the nation, and had become convinced as a result of the righteousness of killing the enemies of the Emperor. One such, in the view of Aizawa and his fellow militant young officers, was Major-General Nagata Tetsuzan, the director of the Military Affairs Bureau at the Japanese War Office; after unsuccessfully attempting to persuade Nagata to resign his office, Aizawa assassinated him on 12 August 1935. He was court-martialled, sentenced to death, and executed, but not before Fukusada had spoken up for him in court and later offered further supportive statements that imparted a spiritual dimension to Aizawa's murderous deed. According to Fukusada, Aizawa was committed to the Zen way of destroying the false and establishing the true, while the 'incident' (as Fukusada referred to the murder) was 'truly a reflection of the purity of mind' Aizawa had acquired, as he 'was burning with the ideal of destroying the false'.[23] Fukusada later wrote that Aizawa had transcended life and death and had sacrificed himself for the sake of the nation in the act of a man of pure character and self-sacrificing devotion.[24] Murder, in other words, when committed by someone fired by the ideals of Zen, was not a heinous crime but an act of purity and spiritual transcendence.

Japan's path to aggressive, imperial-centred nationalism, militarism, and war was not spurred on by rampantly nationalistic Zen Buddhists alone, but they were, as both Robert Sharf and Brian Victoria have demonstrated, highly influential in the process.[25] They clearly helped create a context in which violence was (as with the murder of Nagata) seen as a legitimate and spiritually purifying act in line with Buddhist thinking, and in which the harsh disciplines that brutalized the military were accepted and promoted as valid. They also helped reinforce and strengthen the rampant nationalism of the period, along with its underlying ethos that Japan – and the Japanese – were culturally and spiritually superior to those they sought to colonize or fight against, and hence that Japan's military aggression and its repercussions were therefore legitimate acts carried out in the noble cause of civilization. Certainly since the late nineteenth century the Japanese had produced large amounts of literature and rhetoric on this subject that argued that Japan, as an advanced country, had a duty to help its neighbours along the path of civilization (an argument that, in effect, sought to legitimize Japanese ambitions to develop a colonial empire, and to justify its annexation of Taiwan in the 1870s and of Korea in 1910).[26]

Many Japanese Buddhists underlined such arguments by claiming that Japanese Buddhism was the pre-eminent form of Buddhism in Asia, and hence Japan had a duty to extend its influence so that Japanese Buddhists could help 'awaken' their Asian counterparts. In 1943, for example, Yasutani Hakuun (1885–1973), a leading Sôtô Zen teacher who in the post-war period became widely known in the West, wrote a book in which he portrayed Japanese expansionism in war as a means of saving Asia from the 'treachery' of the USA and Britain, in which he eulogized the 'spirit of Japan' as something unique and as supported by Japanese Buddhism, which taught the duty of sacrificing oneself for the Emperor, and in which he described Japan's annexation of Korea and Taiwan as the 'practice of a bodhisattva', which was grounded in compassion and ensured the greatest happiness for the people of those countries.[27] The aforementioned Ômori Sôgen expressed similar views through the scroll he hung up at his Zen training centre, and which bore the phrase 'Tekikoku kôfuku' ('Enemy countries surrender!').[28] Subjugation and colonization, in other words, appeared to be, to the eyes of such Zen Buddhists, noble ways of restoring or enhancing the spiritual standing of their fellow Asian Buddhists.

Not only did militant Zen priests such as Yasutani, Ômori, and Fukusada provide succour for militarism and help wrap it in a spiritual cloak, they also helped provide reasons why the Japanese could or even *should* kill those they fought against, while arguing that such killing would not violate Buddhist precepts. Yasutani, for instance, argued that by engaging in war Japan and its soldiers were in reality confronting and seeking to remove evil influences from the world – and hence killing as many of the enemy as possible was thus a good thing in line with, rather than contradictory to, Buddhist precepts. Indeed, it was those who failed to kill the enemy who were truly in breach of the precepts, for they would be enabling evil to continue.[29] As I have showed elsewhere, such thinking has been a recurrent theme in the production of religiously impelled violence, surfacing, for example, in the teachings of Asahara Shôkô, the founder of Aum Shinrikyô, who developed the notion that it was the duty of highly advanced spiritual practitioners – such as his disciples – to kill those who had not awakened to the spiritual truths he taught; to kill them was to save them from the greater evil of continuing to accumulate bad karma in this world through ignoring the truth, and it also served to eradicate the evils of this world by removing those who opposed what Asahara postulated as the truth.[30]

Sawaki Kôdô, another Sôtô teacher who attained a large following in the post-war period, also justified the killing of others in war, claiming that such acts were carried out independently of the individual's will, and therefore that they were not culpable deeds or violations of Buddhist precepts.[31] Suzuki, too, emphasized the sacred dimensions of Japan's war activities, claiming that Japan had the right to pursue its ambitions, that anyone or any nation that stood in its way should be punished, and that such punishment (which of course amounted to destruction and killing) was in itself a religious act.[32] In 1937, too, Hayashiya Tomojirô and Shimakage Chikai, two Japanese scholars affiliated with the Sôtô Zen sect and teaching at Komazawa University (a university controlled and run by the sect), produced a book arguing that wars could be compassionate affairs when fought for the sake of the enemy, who would be killed and saved, and when such a war could remove the defilements afflicting a country; this, indeed, they indicated, was what Japan was doing with regard to China, and hence Japan's military engagement with that country was in fact a war of compassion.[33] When Japan started to face defeat and invasion, too, Zen teachers such as Harada Daiun lined up to encourage the populace not just to fight and take the lives of their would-be invaders, but to sacrifice their own lives with honour in the cause if need be; thus Harada urged his fellow countrymen not only to observe what he termed the 'cardinal points of Zen' by killing the enemy and destroying the false, but to be prepared to die themselves in the cause.[34]

Concluding comments

In such ways Zen teachers helped justify and sanction assassination, war, and violence. Their arguments were grounded in concepts of spiritual superiority, in the belief that strict ascetic practices were an appropriate means of instilling spiritual disciplines for the betterment of all, in claims that the spiritually superior had the right to beat and punish those who were less advanced, and in assumptions that such punishments were in fact purifying acts designed to root out evil and to enable those who were punished to progress spiritually. Such arguments, in effect, are an extension of the practices that centre around the use of violence in Zen asceticism and the meditation hall and in the underlying beliefs that surround them, and through which violence is sanctified as a means of leading the beaten to higher spiritual realms. As I indicated earlier, the use of the *kyôsaku* in the meditation hall is based in the assumption that physical discipline is necessary in order to purify and mould the body so as to open up the path to awakening, and that those who occupy what is believed to be a higher spiritual status (such as the monk wielding the *kyôsaku*) have the spiritual 'right' to force others to experience awakenings. It presupposes that those who are claimed to have an advanced spiritual standing are not bound by normative bonds or constraints: when the Zen master beats and cajoles, rather than infringing moral standards, he transcends them because of his own standing as an advanced spiritual practitioner. Therefore the act of violence becomes one of compassion – an argument that was transposed, along with the harsh disciplines that underpinned it, onto pre-war Japan in ways that helped shape the militaristic ethos of that era.

By extension, the violence of Zen temple life and its underlying meanings permeated into the public sphere, with Zen teachers justifying and encouraging assassinations, war, and the subjugation of others, in the name of spiritual awakening and – as various Zen teachers who were involved in promoting Japanese militarism and nationalism indicated – for the spiritual advancement of the nation. This process in turn imparts a mystical dimension to violence while promoting the notion (inherent in the act of the monk or Zen teacher striking an adept in order to provoke an 'awakening') that the spiritually superior have both the right and the moral duty to commit acts of violence for the benefit of others. Thus, violence can be committed in the name of the sacred, even leading – as the rhetoric of some Zen teachers in early twentieth-century Japan shows – to the justification of warfare and the subjugation of others as holy deeds.

Such a process also fuels the righteousness of those who carry such deeds out, a point I have made elsewhere in my studies of how the members of Aum Shinrikyô who committed that movement's atrocities in Japan felt that being chosen for such tasks was a sign of their spiritual advancement, while being able to carry such deeds out with equanimity indicated how well they had mastered the Buddhist skill of detachment. As such, being asked to kill an opponent of the movement was not just an exercise in eradicating an opponent of the truth or of 'saving' that person (since, like the Zen Buddhists who justified killing in war, Aum also framed its killings of others in a rhetoric of salvation), but a statement and manifestation of the righteousness and spiritual stature of the perpetrators.[35] I would suggest that Zen teachers who were used to an environment in which beating adepts and using harsh disciplines to help save or enlighten such disciples was a norm that affirmed their own spiritual status as being advanced enough to use violence yet not be committing a moral wrong, similarly extended such arguments beyond the confines of the meditation hall, and that by sanctioning murder and war as compassionate and spiritually beneficent activities, they equally were affirming their own sense of righteousness and spiritual superiority.

I should emphasize again here that I am not intending to single Zen Buddhism out as a special and exceptional case here, or as an aberrant form of an otherwise non-violent tradition. Indeed, as was noted earlier, one could draw on a variety of strands within the wider Buddhist tradition to show how acts of violence may be sanctioned and indeed celebrated because they revolve around spiritually powerful teachers who use harsh methods to help or force the spiritual awakening of their disciples, and point to how seemingly brutal and even immoral acts may be seen as legitimate because they help others on the path to spiritual advancement and because they are committed by spiritually advanced teachers who have gone beyond normative moral boundaries. As I have already noted, too, similar themes and patterns of sanctification and justification of violence can be found in Aum Shinrikyô's turn to violence, a turn that was initially impelled by the use of coercion and violence to make disciples carry out harsh austerities that were designed to awaken them, and that was underpinned by the belief that those who regarded themselves as spiritually advanced had the right – and duty – to coerce others in the name of salvation. In formulating its understandings of this process, and of what it saw as the legitimate use of violence, Aum drew on Buddhist examples, most particularly from Tibetan lamas who beat their disciples for their own spiritual good, but also from Zen and its use of force as a means of encouraging meditation.[36]

My aim is, in other words, to point out that even supposedly 'peaceful' and non-violent traditions such as Buddhism also can foment, encourage, and legitimize violence, and that such violence may indeed be intrinsic to their normative everyday modes of behaviour. As the Zen example demonstrates, violent images are embedded in the core of the tradition, intrinsic to its founding stories, and widely utilized – in the context of spiritual advancement and training – in its meditation halls, and it shows us how readily a specific tradition can utilize violence in its spiritual practices and transform such violence into an act of spiritual merit. It also points to an area I have touched on in this chapter but that, for reasons of space, have not been able to adequately explore, namely the connections between asceticism, bodily austerities, and violence. As the examples of Zen practice I have cited earlier indicate, there is a close connection between the promotion and legitimization of a culture of violence and the practice of asceticism; this is a point I have made elsewhere, when discussing how the ascetic practices of Aum Shinrikyô played a formative role in developing a culture of violence within that movement,[37] but it is an issue that requires further study and more consideration than it has thus far been given in the context of the relationship between religion and violence. Here I will just note that there is a link between notions of the body as an impure entity that requires ascetic endeavour in order to purify it and enable the practitioner to achieve higher spiritual states, and the idea that violence is itself a sanctifying dynamic that can purify and elevate those against whom it is directed, and that simultaneously elevates the perpetrator of violence while affirming his/her spiritual transcendence and power.

Especially since the horrors of 11 September 2001, there have been frequent attempts – from the pronouncements of politicians and clerics to the claims of some scholars of religion – to argue that 'true' or 'real' religions do not produce or promote violence, and that when a religion does become involved in such activities and becomes 'evil' it in effect ceases to be true religion and becomes perverted into something else instead.[38] Yet such attempts are, in essence, highly problematic, not only because they create seemingly artificial categories of 'true' and 'false' religion that are based in a particular (and, I would argue, narrow and subjective) view of what religion 'ought' to be like, but because they assume that 'true' religion is somehow not involved with violence in any way. Yet such claims would appear untenable judging by the examples I have focused on in this chapter; I have looked at ascetic practices and notions of spiritual transformation and transcendence, all of which would normally be considered to be religious in nature, and shown that these may well be deeply linked to (and may at times even be inseparable from) acts of violence. In such terms, indeed, not only is religion inherently associated with violence, but violence is, de facto, an innate characteristic of 'true' religion. Not only does religious practice in pursuit of supposedly higher goals, such as enlightenment in Zen, facilitate the expression of violence, but it provides the most profound legitimizing process for expressions thereof. It also provides, through rituals and practices, the means of transforming the potential of violence into actuality, and the means of justifying and affirming the right of those who see themselves in spiritually advanced positions to inflict violence on others, for the betterment and spiritual welfare of those so afflicted.

There may be a long distance in conceptualization between the simple act of violence in order to improve the spiritual status of the beaten (as in the case of the Zen monk and the *kyôsaku*) and the mass murders that have been a feature of recent religiously associated acts of violence such as those seen in Tokyo in March 1995 and the USA in September 2001, but I would suggest that they are intimately connected by a thread that is at the very heart and core of religion. That thread relates to concepts of spiritual advancement and the notion that there are those who are spiritually advanced and who thereby have the 'right' to act outside normative moral frameworks and to use violence as a means of purifying others. That thread is present – as my example of Zen Buddhism and its links to warfare and to physical violence in Japan have shown – in the supposedly 'peaceful' tradition of Buddhism just as it is in other traditions that have more commonly been the focus of discussions about the relationship between religion and violence. It is therefore important to include Buddhism in studies of this relationship, rather than overlooking it due to the often spurious assumption that it is non-violent; as I have shown, it also provides examples of how violence, as in the beating of meditating practitioners, may occur within the context of religious practice, and offers examples of how violence may not only be justified in the name of spiritual awakening but may also be viewed as a spiritual act in itself. Through the example of Zen Buddhism, in other words, one can see how close the spiritual and the violent may be and how deeply embedded violence may be in the practices of religion and in the pursuit of the spiritual. In such terms, it is foolish to think of 'true' religion as being somehow nothing to do with acts of violence. Indeed, if one accepts that the pursuit of spiritual awakening and practices related to asceticism are truly religious activities, it is not difficult to recognize that truly spiritual religion can be truly violent.

CHAPTER 13

Jewish Millennialism and Violence

Simon Dein

Introduction

In this chapter I describe several instances of violence among Jewish groups 'fuelled' by messianic tension. The first part of the chapter examines violence among religious extremists in Israel with an emphasis on Gush Emunim, a messianic and fundamentalist religious Zionist group whose beliefs are based heavily on the teachings of Rabbi Abraham Kook and his son, Rabbi Tzvi Yehuda Kook. The second part examines increasing tensions in Lubavitch, a group of Hasidim largely based in the USA with offshoot groups in London, Israel, and Belgium. Until his death in 1994 the group was led by their spiritual leader, the Rebbe Menachem Schneerson. These instances exemplify the relationship between violence and millennialism in different contexts with different implications.

In the case of Gush Emunim, plans to destroy the Dome of the Rock were based on the notion that the redemption needed to be active to the extent that it was dependent on human action, not miracles, and involved a theocratic government centred on the Temple Mount and a country that controlled the Sinai, Jordan, Syria, and parts of Lebanon and Iraq. The redemption of Israel was 'stopped' on the Temple Mount, and not until its expurgation could the grand process be renewed. This group appeals to the notion of 'forcing the end'. In this particular case, had the Dome of the Rock been blown up, the event could have escalated into a third world war. In the case of Lubavitch, violence ensued between two groups – messianists and anti-messianists – essentially surrounding the belief that the dead Rebbe is the Jewish Messiah. Messianic tension has run high in this group for the past twenty years or so, and the group is known for its attribution of messianic status to the now deceased Rebbe, Menachem Schneerson.

Jewish millennialism

Jewish eschatology is concerned with a number of related themes: the Redemption; the Jewish Messiah; and the *olam haba* (the world to come). The idea of a future Messiah who will arrive to redeem the world is mentioned in a number of biblical passages such as:

> And in thy seed shall all the nations of the earth be blessed; because thou hast hearkened to My voice. (Genesis 22: 18)

Therefore the Lord Himself shall give you a sign: behold, the young woman shall conceive, and bear a son, and shall call his name Immanuel. (Isaiah 7: 14)

Rejoice greatly, O daughter of Zion, shout, O daughter of Jerusalem; behold, thy king cometh unto thee, he is triumphant, and victorious, lowly, and riding upon an ass, even upon a colt the foal of an ass. (Zechariah 9: 9)

Seventy weeks are decreed upon thy people and upon thy holy city, to finish the transgression, and to make an end of sin, and to forgive iniquity, and to bring in everlasting righteousness, and to seal vision and prophet, and to anoint the most holy place. Know therefore and discern, that from the going forth of the word to restore and to build Jerusalem unto one anointed, a prince, shall be seven weeks; and for threescore and two weeks, it shall be built again, with broad place and moat, but in troublous times. And after the threescore and two weeks shall an anointed one be cut off, and be no more; and the people of a prince that shall come shall destroy the city and the sanctuary; but his end shall be with a flood; and unto the end of the war desolations are determined. (Daniel 9: 24–6)

Messianic themes are also discussed in the Babylonian Talmud, which contains a long discussion of the events leading to the coming of the Messiah: 'R. Johanan said: When thou seest a generation overwhelmed by many troubles as by a river, await him, as it is written, when the enemy shall come in like a flood, the Spirit of the Lord shall lift up a standard against him'; which is followed by 'And the Redeemer shall come to Zion' (Tractate Sanhedrin).[1]

Conceptualizations of Jewish messianism are closely allied with those of 'exile' and 'redemption'. The Jewish concept of exile refers not just to a historical displacement from the homeland, but a spiritual state of distance from God. This state will be terminated following the arrival of the Redemption. At the religious/spiritual level, the traditional perception of Exile and Redemption was that Exile (diaspora) was a punishment for the people's sins and therefore a punishment from Heaven. While Exile was nevertheless to be temporary, Redemption could come only with the advent of the Messiah, and with the Almighty's will. One had to come to terms with an enduring exile until redemption from Heaven. Following his arrival, the Messiah will perform a number of tasks: build the Third Temple (Ezekiel 37: 26–8); gather all Jews back to the Land of Israel (Isaiah 43: 5–6); usher in an era of world peace, and end all hatred, oppression, suffering, and disease (Isaiah 2: 4); spread universal knowledge of the God of Israel; and unite humanity as one (Zechariah 14: 9).

Ravitsky (1996) points out how the messianic idea in Judaism has always been marked by inner tensions and profound disagreements.[2] These disagreements have a long historical legacy and go back to the Talmudic era where we find significant differences of opinion on the subject of eschatology: what is the role of human action in preparation for the messianic era – in particular, can we 'force the end'? Will the yearned-for Redemption occur gradually or break forth all at once? Will the Talmudic Redemption depend solely on the Jews' repentance, or also on divine decree? Will Redemption necessarily evolve around the human figure of a personal Messiah? Will the messianic era result in any change in the Torah and Halakhah (Jewish law)?

Specifically in relation to forcing the end, the Talmud and Midrashim condemn these acts, both through decree and through oath. The Talmud states 'that Israel not ascend the wall from the exile, 'that they not rebel against the nations of the world' and 'that they not force the End' (*Ketubot* 111a). These oaths have been invoked at various stages throughout history as an argument against *aliya* (emigration to the land of Israel), which has been seen by some as forcing the end.

Much of this disagreement has centred on the role of political emancipation and the liberation of the Jewish people from subjugation to the 'great powers'. At one extreme there is a hope for cosmic redemption and a profound change in nature itself, which will result in an entirely new world order, literally 'a new heaven and a new earth' (Isaiah 65: 17). Included in this group are Rabbi Isaac Abravanel, Rabbi Judah Low and the Maharal of Prague, who took a somewhat apocalyptic view. In contrast, Maimonides' code describes national redemption in purely natural historical worldly terms: 'Let no one think in the days of the Messiah any of the laws of nature will be set aside or any invasion introduced into creation . . . do not think the King Messiah will have to form signs or wonders or bring anything new into being' (Hilkhot Melachim11:3).

The notion of Israel as a Jewish state is intimately related to discussions of Jewish messianism, and there has been much contention among rabbis relating to the issue of Zionism. On the one hand, there are those who condemn modern Zionism as 'forcing the end' and interfering with the divine plan for history. Examples include the Satmarer Hasidim and groups like Neturei Karta (lit. 'Guardians of the city'), who reject any form of Zionism and the state of Israel. As the Satmarer Rebbe stated: 'I have become the object of scorn and contempt . . . no force in the world shall move me from my stand to accept, God forbid, the [Zionist] heresy, from which the Merciful One must save us' (Kaplan 2004: [165]). For these groups the ingathering of the exiles and liberation from subjugation to the great powers are expectations whose fulfilment should depend solely upon transcendental and miraculous divine activity, not by prayer or more positive corporeal activity; for them, Zionism is a denial, rather than a fulfilment, of messianism. It is a blatant violation of the oath sworn by the Jewish people to wait till the end of days for this to occur.

Many Haredi (ultra-Orthodox) groups are against the pre-messianic state of Israel. Their leaders condemned Zionism from its very onset, criticizing the secularity of the state with its repudiation of religious practice. They saw the settlement of the land of Israel by Jews as a threat to the theological interpretation of the Jewish history. The Lubavitch movement in the 1920s, led by Rabbi Shalom Dovber Schneerson, argued that Zionism was a denial of messianism, and wrote that 'those who assist the Zionists will pay at the Day of Judgment, because they are causing the masses to sin'. The last Lubavitcher Rebbe, Menachem Schneerson, adopted a more moderate position but nevertheless refused to call the state by name, claiming that the holy land exists independent of any authority that sees itself as sovereign over the land. He further criticized feelings of nationalism connected to the state of Israel, claiming that the only thing that unites Jews is the Torah, not a secular state that happens to be planted on holy land.

On the other hand, there are religious Zionists who see the state of Israel not only as practically necessary for Jews but also as religiously meaningful and as an essential step in bringing the Messiah. This trend is exemplified by groups such as Gush Emunim, who see Jews returning to their 'homeland' as the beginning of a redemptive process. I shall examine this group in more detail below.

Judaism, millennialism, and violence

The potential association between millennialism and violence is borne out by numerous historical examples (Talmon 1996). To date, much of the academic literature on millennialism and violence has focused on catastrophic millennialism – a belief in the imminent and catastrophic transition to a millennial kingdom. Wessinger (2000) has well argued how this type of millennialism is responsive to repeated disasters and that millennial beliefs may function to assuage distress and provide salvation. The fact that catastrophic millennialists so often hold that the imminent millennial kingdom will be earthly may result in direct conflict with civil authorities, and they may appeal to a messianic figure or God to overthrow this order. Alternatively, they may attempt to overthrow the existing social order themselves through violent means. There may be other motives underlying such millennial violence. Rapoport (1988) has argued that both messianism and terrorism imply extra-normal behaviour predicated on the conviction that traditional conventions of behaviour are no longer binding. Under certain conditions, when the expected millennium fails to materialize, believers might resort to violence, either because they want to prove to themselves that the redemption remains relevant or because they want to convince God that this is indeed the case.[3] However, messianic fervour is by no means always precipitated by feelings of catastrophe. In some instances it may be heightened by feelings of success, and spread. Such is the case for groups such as Gush Emunim and Lubavitch, as Ravitsky (2000) has argued.

The association between Judaism and violence is complex. Like most religious traditions, Judaism justifies violence to some extent, at least in cases of righteous warfare. Juergensmeyer (2000) emphasizes the fact that the Jewish Bible is replete with violent images – 'The Lord is a warrior' (Exodus 15: 3) – and there are many scenes of desolation caused by divine intervention. By comparison, later Judaism is largely non-violent, but at the level of statecraft the rabbis did sanction warfare. Depictions of God and war exist alongside another body of rabbinic literature which in most cases condemned war making. The rabbis distinguished 'religious' war from optional war. The former was based upon a moral or spiritual obligation to protect the faith or defeat God's enemies, whereas the latter was waged for reasons of political expediency.

Reports of violence in the Middle East are commonplace in the media. Compared to other countries in the Middle East, the Jewish state was for many years perceived as an island of democracy, secularism, pragmatism, and non-violence. Sprinzak (1998) makes the important observation that events of the late 1980s and early 1990s raised the question of whether, within its borders, Israel was in fact isolated from the atmosphere of political violence in its neighbouring countries. Though largely peaceful, Israeli politics have never been devoid of extremism. Far from arguing that Zionism is inherently violent, or that it is the principal cause of the fighting in the Middle East, as some have argued (e.g. Rose 2005), there is some truth in the fact that some readings of Jewish nationalism fail to take into consideration the legitimate claims of Palestinian Arabs. Ruether and Ruether (2002 []), who agree with this view, point out in relation to Zionism:

It has become less a 'light to the nations' of exemplary social justice and equality than an expression of militarism and intercommunal discrimination and hatred. ... The ultra-Orthodox have become the source of extremely dangerous kinds of political violence in their fanatical efforts to create settlements in the midst of sites holy to Muslims, such as Hebron, or to occupy the Temple Mount in preparation for the rebuilding of the Jewish Temple. Thus religious messianism, far from being healing and unifying, has become one of the major sources of inter-Jewish violence, as well as violence with Palestinians.[4]

I now move on to discuss several high-profile cases of religious violence in Judaism which have to greater or lesser extents have been influenced by Jewish millennial ideas.

Baruch Goldstein and Yigal Amir

The first instance relates to Baruch Goldstein, a religious settler, doctor, and a graduate of a prestigious yeshivah (Jewish seminary), who massacred 29 worshippers in the Ibrahimi mosque in Hebron on the feast of Purim in 1994, an incident which has been referred to as the Cave of the Patriarchs Massacre. Goldstein was a member of the Jewish Defence League, a right-wing terrorist organization now outlawed by the Israeli government. It was founded in 1966 by Rabbi Meir Kahane, a right-wing extremist who adhered to the belief that Palestinians have no right of existence in Israel, regarding them as disparate and unrelated Arab clans with no distinct ethnic identity. He thought Israel should limit citizenship to Jews and adopt Jewish law in public life. Goldstein had suffered from a number of crises prior to this event, including increasing doubts about the future of Judaea and Samaria (the West Bank) as well as the escalation of Palestinian violence. Both led him to believe that only through a dramatic act could the course of history and the redemptive process be put back on course. For him this act of violence was *kiddush hashem* (sanctification of God's name).

In a second incident the following year, Yigal Amir assassinated Yitzhak Rabin, the Israeli prime minister. Although he was not a member of an organized messianic movement he came from a similar cultural background to Gush Emunim and Meir Kahane's Kach movement, and had studied at the Gush Emunim yeshivah. It appears that the impetus for the attack derived from the signing of the Oslo peace agreement in September 1993 by Shimon Peres and Yassir Arafat, which he took to be governmental treason. His anger was intensified by an unprecedented series of Hamas and Islamic Jihad suicide bombings inside Israel for which he (and several prominent rabbis) held Yitzhak Rabin personally responsible, and felt betrayed by him. For him, killing Rabin was the only way to save the state of Israel. Following his imprisonment he gained a wide following, and received a considerable amount of fan mail from ideological supporters and teenage girls from a religious camp in Israel. Lifton, a psychiatrist who has written extensively on religious violence, underscores the role of messianic belief in this act of violence: 'Like Goldstein (and in a sense like McVeigh), Amir considered himself "an agent of the Redemption," obligated to "change history and return the messianic process to its course"' (2003: 13). Amir claimed that he was acting upon a long-antiquated Talmudic precept of *din rodef* – the duty of a Jew to kill another Jew designated a traitor because he has given away Jewish land or imperilled the lives of Jews.

In both of these cases religion explains and provides the motivation for violent acts. It also provides a sense of conviction – a belief that this is what God *really* wants.[5]

Gush Emunim and Kach

According to members of Gush Emunim the conquests of Israel by secular Zionists had unwittingly brought about the beginning of the messianic age. For their supporters the coming of the Messiah can be hastened by Jewish settlement on land which they believe God has biblically allocated to Jews. The group, which was established in 1974, held that the state of Israel and its secular institutions are an essential, though nascent, stage in the process of Jewish redemption. The group's beliefs are derived from the teachings of Rabbi Abraham Kook and his son, Rabbi Tzvi Yehuda Kook, who believed his father would see the conquest of the entire biblical land of Israel, including the West Bank and Gaza, as part of the messianic fulfilment. Its leaders argued, contrary to numerous other rabbinic authorities, that the military victory of 1967 must be seen as a harbinger of messianic times. All political decisions thus were to be considered strictly in terms of their ability to bring forward the advent of the Messiah, and thus territorial compromise violated this essential tenet.

Their theology is both eschatological and messianic, and assumes the imminence of the coming of the Messiah, when the Jews, directly under God's influence, will triumph over the Gentiles and rule them (for the latter's own benefit) forever (Shahak 1995). All current political developments can be interpreted by the leaders of the sect as destined to bring this end nearer, or to postpone it. The messianic ideas within the group build on the Kabbalistic concept of two Messiahs. The first is a militant figure called the Son of Joseph, who would have the task of preparing the material preconditions for the redemption. The second Messiah would be the spiritual Son of David, redeeming the world by spectacular miracles. However, Rabbi Kook changed this notion by identifying the Son of Joseph with his own group, which perceives itself as a collective incarnation of the first of the two divinely ordained Messiahs, who redeem the Jews – at least as far as they are capable of being redeemed. Members of Gush Emunim see their purpose as bridging the gap between themselves and the rest of society by involving themselves in the latter and sanctifying it.

Although the original theology did not advocate the use of violence, and the founders held that in the aftermath of the 1967 victory the Arab enemies were no longer a threat (and are expected to accept Jewish dominance over the Holy Land), they exhibit a twofold hatred against non-Jews and secular Jews. They are against any peaceful coalition with Arabs. According to them Israel will commit apostasy the day the agreement with the PLO takes effect: that day will mark the end of the Jewish Zionist era in the sacred history of the land of Israel. Some rabbis belonging to the group argue that Israel is a new sinful Canaanite Palestinian state and therefore cannot be a foundation of God's throne on earth. Those who lead their fellow Jews into that sin no longer deserve any divine protection. Some members of the group even advocate that the murder of a non-Jew by a Jew is exempt from human judgement, and has not violated the prohibition of murder. Gush Emunim rabbis have often said that Jews who have killed Arabs should go unpunished.

The group obtained notoriety when some of its members were arrested in 1984 for planning to blow up the Dome of the Rock. They belonged to the Gush Emunim

Underground, sometimes called the Jewish Terror Organization, a militant organization formed by prominent members of Gush Emunim, which existed from 1979 to 1984, who held that destroying the Dome of the Rock would bring about the advent of the Messiah, hence 'forcing the end'. As one of the perpetrators stated during police interrogation:

> The demolition of these mosques would have infuriated the hundreds of millions of Muslims in the entire world. Their rage would inevitably lead to a war which, in all likelihood, would escalate into a world war. In such a war the scale of casualties would be formidable enough to promote the process of Redemption of the Jews and of the land of Israel. All the Muslims would by then disappear, which means that everything would be ready for the coming of the Messiah.

This violence was by no means accepted by all members of the group, and several revered rabbis were critical of the proposed terrorism of the Gush Emunim Underground, and warned them never to consider it again.

Another group which warrants brief discussion is Kach, established in 1971 by Rabbi Meir Kahane, and by far the most violent of all Israeli religious groups to express hostility towards the secular leadership of Israel on account of its 'Gentile-like sinful behaviour'. Theologically they are located between Haredim and Gush Emunim. Like Gush Emunim, Rabbi Kahane recognized the hand of God in the creation of the state of Israel and was enthused by the success of the Six Day War. For him both these events signified the beginning of the messianic era where 'the gates of heaven were opened wide'. Kahane taught that the establishment of the state of Israel was to prove the might of God by showing that Jews can humiliate Gentiles (who had previously humiliated them) by the use of physical force, which was sanctified and glorified for its own sake. His followers were encouraged to resort to violence against Israel's enemies and to feel good about it. The group has been engaged in protest, conflict, and street hooliganism.

For Kahane, the redemption could come in one of two ways: by turning to faith and forcefully removing the Arabs from Israel; or by trials and tribulations, bloodshed, and suffering. Kahane's Kach maintained two central political views. The first was the proposed forced transfer of Arabs from the borders of Israel, including Israeli Arabs who did not accept the conditions of *ger toshav* (a Gentile who fulfils the seven Noahide commandments). The second was the establishment of a theocracy in Israel, namely a state in the borders of Eretz Yisrael (the biblical land of Israel) ruled by traditional Jewish law (Halakhah). The group has never recruited more than several hundred activists. Today in Israel being a member of Kach is deemed illegal.

Messianism, schism, and violence among Lubavitcher Hasidim

I now turn to a hitherto unexplored area within messianism. Specifically, I examine how messianic beliefs may cause schism within a religious group and potentially lead to violence. Lubavitch is a worldwide movement of Hasidic Jews, whose main centre is in Brooklyn, New York.[6] The organization is also called Chabad, an acronym deriving from the first three Kabbalistic *sefirot* (divine emanations) *chochma*, *binah*, and *daath*. It is estimated there are about 200,000 members of Lubavitch worldwide. Until his death in

1994 from a stroke, the movement was led by the spiritual leader Menachem Schneerson, the seventh Lubavitcher Rebbe. Lubavitcher communities exist on a worldwide basis, the main ones being in Israel, Great Britain, the United States, and Belgium.

Unlike other Orthodox Jewish groups, Lubavitch places a central focus upon the teaching of mystical concepts to all members of the community through its core text, *Tanya*. Written by the founder of Lubavitch, Rabbi Schneur Zalman, it emphasizes the close relation between the physical and spiritual worlds. The Lubavitcher world-view is grounded in the traditional belief that the arrival of the redemption is contingent upon human efforts related to the teachings and dissemination of Torah teachings and meticulous observance of the *mitzvot* (the commandments God gave to the Jewish people in the Torah). Every individual Jew has the potential to elevate himself spiritually through the performance of good deeds. Hence much of the everyday activity of Lubavitch centres around returning non-practising Jews to orthodox practice through sending out emissaries (*schluchim*) globally.

The group is administered by an organization called Aggudat Chassidei Chabad, based in the USA. The British organization is led by Rabbi Sudak, who is the Rebbe's representative in London and responsible for major decisions about Lubavitch. The overall organization has a huge budget, estimated at $1 billion in 2002, which is derived mainly from private sponsors, many of whom are wealthy non-Hasidic Jews. The British organization is financed by private donations, local council and European grants, and from revenue collected from members, such as tuition fees for schooling.[7] It is far from surprising, then, that the image the group presents to outsiders is of considerable importance.

A unique facet of Hasidism, and the way in which it differs from other ultra-Orthodox groups, is the idea of the *zaddik* or rebbe, a perfectly righteous man who is the spiritual leader of the group. The 'current' Rebbe, Menachem Schneerson, was born in 1900 and commenced leadership of the movement in 1950. Known throughout the Jewish world as a great scholar, he was seen by his followers (and many continue to do so) as a miracle worker, an intermediary between God and man. For Lubavitchers the Rebbe was central to their lives, and for many he still is very influential. Every major decision was made through him by writing to him or, eventually, by faxing or e-mailing him. Until his death in 1994 his followers would regularly have audiences with him at his residence, '770' in Brooklyn asking for help with problems ranging from health, wealth to marriage and education (Littlewood and Dein 1997).

Messianic ideas in Lubavitch

Like those of other Orthodox Jews the messianic ideas in Lubavitch derive from the medieval Jewish scholar and physician Maimonides, who taught that the obligation of every Jew is to expectantly await the coming of Mosiach – the Messiah. The topic of messianism has always been central to Lubavitcher discourse. Indeed throughout his career Schneerson emphasized spreading awareness of the coming of Mosiach as a fundamental Jewish duty, including the idea that the era of redemption was close and could be brought on by the fulfilment of *mitzvot*. In response to the question 'What remains to be done to bring Mosiach?', he would characteristically answer, 'Acts of Goodness and Kindness.'

Since the inauguration of the 'current' Rebbe, this messianic interest has been growing in intensity. In the early 1980s Lubavitch began a 'We-want-Mosiach' campaign to popularize the belief in the imminent arrival of the Messiah. This campaign increased in momentum over the next few years, with frequent advertisements appearing in Jewish newspapers across Europe, Israel, and America. Mosiach became a major topic of discussion, and there was an escalation of messianic excitement in Lubavitcher communities in Europe and America (Dein 2001).

Despite suffering a stroke in March 1992 which paralysed him on the right-hand side of his body and rendered him speechless, his followers continued fervently in their belief that he was the Messiah. They interpreted the illness as a necessary prerequisite for the messianic arrival and quoted Isaiah 53, asserting that the Messiah must be someone acquainted with pain and suffering. Despite the fact that following this stroke he was unable to give 'Dollars', his followers continued to write to him for blessings. His secretary would read the letters to him, following which he would indicate an answer by moving his head up or down. In Brooklyn, he would be seen frequently but unpredictably at prayer services, sometimes twice a day and sometimes less than once a week. In order to ensure that his followers would be present when he came out, they carried 'Mosiach' bleepers which flashed 'MHM [Melech ha Mosiach – King Mosiach] is on the platform'.

Far from reducing the messianic excitement, discourse relating to the Messiah increased rapidly in Lubavitch communities following his first stroke. Although some Lubavitchers were reluctant to admit it publicly, many held that Schneerson was the Messiah, and they were waiting for him to reveal himself. In fact, in 1993, a group of women in Brooklyn prepared to crown the Rebbe, an event that other members found shameful. There was much excitement in the Stamford Hill community and many people spoke of the Messiah being in our midst and of redemption being imminent. There is little to suggest that Schneerson condemned this messianic excitement.

Although many Lubavitchers privately admitted that the Rebbe was Mosiach, the official response of Lubavitcher Hasidim when asked whether this was the case was to carefully stop short of claiming outright that the Rebbe was or will be revealed as Mosiach. When questioned by outsiders the invariable reply was threefold: all Jews are required to believe in the coming of the Messiah; the Talmudic sources say that the Messiah will arise from among the people; and 'Do you know of anyone alive today who fits the bill better than the Rebbe?'

Messianic activity following the Rebbe's death

The Rebbe died on 12 June 1994, following a second major stroke from which he never regained consciousness and remained comatose for several months. Outsiders predicted mass depression and suicide among members of the movement, given their strong attachment to and dependence on him. As part of 'Operation Demise', police, psychiatrists, and trained counsellors were recruited to avert a potential tragedy. Yet it is striking how well the Lubavitch coped with the death of the Rebbe. Far from diminishing the activity of Lubavitch, in the decade following his death, the influence of the movement has continued to grow, with about 15,000 adherents in Crown Heights alone, near its headquarters. The movement is currently involved in approximately $100 million worth of construction projects around the world. The number of outreach programmes has significantly increased in the past ten years, with Lubavitch Houses being established in a number of countries. According to the official Chabad website[7] there are more than 3,300 Lubavitch institutions worldwide. Lubavitch continues to bring Orthodox Jewish practice into the mainstream consciousness of world Jewry by its emphasis on sending out *shluchim*.

Violence surrounding the messianic belief

Before the Rebbe's death virtually the whole community believed that he was Mosiach. Following his death, Lubavitch has divided into two factions: messianists and non-messianists. In one sense all Lubavitchers are messianists, as anticipation of the coming Messiah is a central principle of their faith. However, in recent years the term has come to take on a more specific meaning, referring to those who believe that the Rebbe is Mosiach, with those who are antagonistic to this belief deemed anti-messianists. There has been increasing tension between the two groups over the past few years. Beyond simply disagreeing over Schneerson's messianic status, there has been much animosity aroused by struggles over whether this claim should be publicized, and the implications of doing so for outsiders. The extreme messianic faction not only continues to proclaim publicly that Schneerson is Mosiach, it asserts that he is alive and uses the term '*yehi*' (he lives) when referring to him, a practice that has caused much embarrassment to the anti-messianist faction. Both the messianists and the anti-messianists claim to be true to the Rebbe's vision. The situation is complex since he had no heir, and named neither a successor nor a governing body to act after his death, no one is authorized to resolve the dispute.

The mainstream organization has been particularly influential in discouraging its members from identifying the Rebbe as Mosiach and from publicly promoting this claim. In 1996 Aggudat Chassidei Chabad–Lubavitch (the umbrella organization of the worldwide Lubavitch movement) stated:

> With regard to some recent statements and declarations by individuals and groups concerning the matter of Mosiach and the Lubavitcher Rebbe, Rabbi Menachem Schneerson, of sainted memory, let it be known that the views expressed in these notices are in no way a reflection of the movement's position. While we do not intend to preclude expressions of individual opinion, they are, in fact, misleading and a grave offence to the dignity and expressed desires of the Rebbe. (Chabad newsletter [1996])

The Central Committee of Chabad rabbis in the United States and Canada condemned similar pronouncements in 1998, stating that 'the preoccupation with identifying the Rebbe, [may merit protect us], as Mosiach is clearly contrary to the Rebbe's wishes.'

Over the past few years there has been escalating conflict between the two groups about propaganda, with rival publishing houses, magazines, bookstores, and even radio talk shows being established. The ultra-messianists hold that they can hasten the Rebbe's return by persuading as many people as possible that he is Mosiach, and they promote these ideas in the street. The conflict has resulted in vandalism, physical fights, arrests, and even secular court. The past five years have seen skirmishes between the messianic and non-messianic factions of Lubavitch largely centred around the synagogue at 770

Eastern Brooklyn, which today is in the control of the messianic faction. Violence has ensued surrounding a plaque which was put up eight years ago by the anti-messianists and bears the inscription 'of blessed memory' after the Rebbe's name, referring to him in the past tense. Fights have broken out at the site of the plaque, security guards have even been hired to protect the cornerstone, arrests have been made The feud has moved beyond Crown Heights and spilled into secular court. This vandalism, along with other defacements through the years, is seen to be the work of young Israelis who believe that the Rebbe is the messiah, and not an organized effort. Several young Lubavitcher men wrenched the defaced plaque off the wall and tried to put up their own, using the honorific '*Shlita*', an Aramaic abbreviation for 'He should live for many long years', which conventionally follows the name of a living sage.

There is still much animosity between the two rival factions, although actual violence is rare. It remains to be seen how (if ever) this conflict will be resolved and its effects on the wider Jewish community.

Conclusion: what really happens when prophecy fails?

Festinger et al. (1956) in their classic text *When Prophecy Fails* argue that disconfirmation of prophecy results in an intensification of religious belief and increased proselytization with a view to spreading that belief. Far from individuals rejecting belief and leaving the movement, religious activity is reinvigorated. At times this process may culminate in violence. Occasionally believers may go 'over the top' in an attempt to persuade God that his most faithful servants do not deserve to be deserted, as Rappoport (1988) has argued.

For Gush Emunim and Kach and for Baruch Goldstein and Yigal Amir, political processes were perceived as interfering with the messianic course, and their elimination was considered imperative if the messianic process was not to completely fail. They all felt they had to force the hand of God to bring the End. Although Lubavitcher violence is far less extreme and occurred at a local level, a similar process of messianic disconfirmation occurred following the Rebbe's death. Far from giving up their beliefs, they held more strongly to the conviction that he was (and for many still is) Mosiach. This resulted in increased proselytization and, ultimately, a schism in the movement revolving around messianists and non-messianists. The former group hold that the Rebbe is still alive, an assertion which has caused extreme embarrassment to the non-messianic group and, ultimately, increasingly frequent skirmishes between the two factions. All these groups underscore the fact that messianic belief may at times provoke and justify violent processes.

Part III
Reporting Religiously Motivated Violence

CHAPTER 14

Sacral Violence:
Cosmologies and Imaginaries of Killing

Neil Whitehead

Mission accomplished

How to win a war is infinitely more complex than how to start one, and we face this truism not for the first time in our current engagements with an Iraqi insurgency that seems set to disable our mission of democracy in Baghdad. But addictive though the exercise of violence in the cause of truth and justice is for us we will have to acknowledge sooner or later that the violence we deploy to punish the brutality of others itself powerfully validates violence, and thus may only serve to license the further use of the very violence that it was our original intention to suppress. However, like all addicts, we believe that more of the same will somehow resolve our hungry need for redemptive violence against terrorist violence and the enemies of democracy. This has also been a bitter lesson for others, such as both the British and Israeli governments, as they have spent the last 30 years trying to suppress 'terrorism'.

In turn, it is our conception of how violence is produced that drives the political, economic, and military interventions our governments make – we can see violence as indicating the urge to democracy and Western liberal freedoms, as in our former imagining of bin Laden as the enemy of Soviet totalitarianism. Alternatively, we can understand it as emanating from a world-wide terror conspiracy that is poised to undermine our values and way of life – as in our current imaginings of bin Laden and the insurgents of Iraq. Our own tradition of violence thus feeds off and is used to picture the external violence of the terrorists and dictators at the political and economic margins of Western democracies. However, at those 'margins' acts of insurgency and terrorism are culturally expressive acts directed towards the centre – *us* – no less than to the immediate victims who suffer the bodily dismemberments and bloody consequences of such acts. At the same time our institutions of military and politico-economic intervention – the UN, NATO, the World Bank, the IMF – are themselves predicated on the existence of crisis and conflict and so have a vested interest in the social, political, and economic structures of globalized international relations that produce the violence they exist to suppress.

Indeed, this is well understood by the agents of genocide and terrorism, and the all-seeing eyes of CNN, the BBC, or other global media such as al-Jazeera too often become necessary participants in the performance of the violence that they so readily deplore as beyond explanation. Such violence is beyond the explanation of these institutions for the very reason that they are unwittingly complicit in its production. For terrorism to be effective it must be known about widely, and the extreme 'visibility' of the 11 September attacks was part of the reason they were so effective in achieving that aim. But such is our addiction to violence that images of political terror have to vie for our attention with enactments of crime, murder, disease, and supernatural horror in the kaleidoscope of movie events, TV dramas, and crime specials. America, by its own admission, will never be the same again after 11 September – not just because of what was done to us, but also what we then do to ourselves.

Alongside the overt political and military commitments that are made when we go to war there are also hidden effects and consequences – no less predicable than the obvious results of war wounded, war dead, and spiralling economic cost is the expansion of institutions of police and security, the enactment of patriotic laws, and the glamourization of military violence though stirring appeals to national fantasy and our sense of duty and fair play. Equally, Western military theory, grounded in ideas as ancient as the classical world of Greece and Rome itself, still clings to ideas of victory and vanquishment that deeply mark our thinking about war, military violence, and its redemptive possibilities. Total war, total victory, no surrender, no mercy, shock and awe, mission accomplished – so the script has run from the ancient times, recently subtly re-inscribed through movies such as *Troy, Alexander,* and the *Star Wars* cycle.

How could Western history, itself so marked by the very acts of torture, killing, and genocide that we now so promptly deplore in others, not see in the exercise of violence profound, even if ambiguous, possibilities? Punish the wicked, smite them with rods of iron and purge the body politic of its terrorist and infidels. The surgical and professional violence of the high-tech highly trained modern military are in this kind of rhetoric the perfect means through which the rational order of democracy can be infiltrated into the tribal and ethnic chaos of a collapsed state. Of course this noble undertaking is contingent on a perception of our own interests, which are apparent in some places such as Somalia, Haiti, Bosnia, Afghanistan, and Iraq, but apparently not in others, such as Rwanda, Sudan, or Palestine. But all these engagements, missions of democracy and social development, whatever their eventual success and however that might be measured, share a key characteristic. Moreover, this characteristic has been with us since the very inception of war: Lycurgus, law giver of the Spartans, warned them not to battle their enemies more than one season, or the enemy would come to know them intimately enough to defeat them.

So today this fundamental but muted aspect to violent military encounter – that it draws us closer and ties us into an ever-increasing intimacy with the enemy – is the unspoken nightmare of counter-insurgency operations of modern times. This is how the short sharp war against rebels, insurgents, guerrillas, dictators, oppressors, and all their kind ineluctably results in that familiar quagmire of political indecision which, field commanders so rightly note, seems to defeat the best efforts of civilian politicians to comprehend and control. The one clear lesson to be drawn from anthropology's contemplation of war through all human time and cultures is that death and killing do not banish the enemy but make us all the more dependent upon and attuned to that enemy. This intimacy is not measured in just the war dead and wounded, on both sides, but also in the youth and life forever entailed and damaged by the exotic and frightening death-scapes of Fallujah, Najaf, the Sunni triangle, the Baghdad green zone – and so on . . . and on. These are places we never even knew were there but which have now become the sites of grief and mourning forever etched into the minds of both the grief-stricken and us – the silent but consenting witnesses of the media portrayal of our troops in Iraq. However, paying close attention to the cultural forms and meanings of violence may yet improve our interpretation of shocking and troubling instances of conflict and killing, since as I mentioned before those interpretations directly contribute to and are indissolubly linked to the way in which the violence of ourselves and others occurs.

What then are the immediate implications of this emphasis on the often ignored cultural meaningfulness of violence? Principally it allows us to appreciate that perhaps it was not a 'war on America' that was intended by the 11 September attacks, but rather an attack on the US government (the Pentagon) and the institutions of global finance (the World Trade Center). Terrorists might have chosen a packed ball-game or a subway full of commuters, so we have to ask the question: what was the meaning of the attack on these specific locales and not others? In turn when, as in Madrid or London, terrorists did choose to inflict mass casualties amongst commuters, is this just to be understood as mindless terror or a rather more pointed message as to the consensus as to a war on terror that living in a liberal democracy implies? Terrorist theory, as evinced in the writings of various political leaders throughout the last century, would argue that it is the psychological effects of a violent act, not its inherent destructiveness, that is key to a successful operation. In this sense the collapse of the twin towers and the horrific number of deaths that ensued actually changed the political meaning of the act, and it could then become precisely an attack not just on the state but also US society. In turn the mimetic violence of the 'shock and awe' bombing of Baghdad was not read by Iraqis as a punishment for 11 September, for they were not involved, but it did make insurgents out of them.

Twentieth-century war showed us that armed conflict has become a total relationship – between societies, not just armies. As a result the civilian population, especially where it is held complicit in military matters due to its democratic participation in government, becomes a legitimate target for terrorist violence. Thus terrorism, unlike warfare, aims to split off state and society, to cause the political breakup of social consensus over the direction and forms of government. The US government, in declaring war on al-Qaeda, signalled its determination to make a military solution, and our impatience for revenge was the political context in which the path of war – even an 'infinite justice' – was chosen. Among the bitter lessons we can learn from 11 September and Iraq must be that we will resort to brutality and killing if we think it necessary, and so will others unless our openness to political persuasion is evident. Such an openness may result from a more complex view of the process of war and how violence might be managed. We prefer to see violence as a pathological problem affecting individuals, and even the sanctioned violence of war as the product of individual heroism or irresistible necessity. If we are to develop a more adequate pedagogy of violence then new approaches must be taken that are alert to the meaningful nature of violence and its role as cultural expression. Violence is not a unique facet of Islamic culture, and no amount of teach-ins or travelling lecture tours that 'contextualize Islam' will meet the need to understand the reasons for the form and intent of the 11 September attacks and our entanglement in Iraq – the problem is not Islamic fundamentalism but rather how violent cultural expression is legitimized, and how we can affect that process.

Violence and the cultural imagination

Terror and violence occupy central places in our contemporary cultural imaginary, and we all die many times before our deaths as we contemplate and, even more crucially, anticipate the possible consequences of terrorist attack. This constant imaginative rehearsal of certain forms of death and dying reflects not just some greater awareness of the use of shocking and outrageous forms of violence as a means of political and cultural assertion, but also the avowedly conscious construction of violent strategies of such assertion. This has occurred most notably in the context of post-colonial conflicts such as Bosnia, Sri Lanka, and Rwanda, as well in contexts of 'terrorist' actions, particularly suicide bombings, in Chechnya, Iraq, and Israel/Palestine. Such violence is overtly designed to achieve an impact on the cultural imagination of the 'West'.

Revelations of prisoner abuse and humiliation by US forces at Abu Ghraib in turn pointedly raise the issue of whether this torture was an outcome of individual psychopathology or part of a systematic military policy for interrogation. Such revelations also underline the importance of understanding how violence works, both as part of the individual imagination and as part of the cultural order, since the form of abuse practised by individual US soldiers reflected particular kinds of cultural values emphasizing certain forms of sexualized humiliation rather than, say, gross physical injury. It is part of the teaching of interrogation techniques that torture and abuse in these senses simply do not work as effective means of intelligence gathering. It thus follows that the purpose of such abuse must be analysed by reference to the way in which the cultural meaning of the 'war on terror' in Iraq, and the cultural place of the military in US society, interrelate. In this light 'homeland security' and preparedness for terrorist attack are no less part of a cultural performance of our own violent socio-cultural order through the 'software' of our imaginations than the constant display and homo-erotic appreciation of the 'hardware' of Hummers, tanks, automatic weapons, precision rockets, and bombs.

However, the media dominance of Euro-American commentary on 'violence' and 'terrorism', as well their supposed ideological and psychological bases, in 'radical Islam' or other unfamiliar political ideologies, can be considered part of that violence for the way in which it directly feeds the cultural imaginary of media consumers around the globe. From comic books, to movies and music, no less than news and media analysis TV, the imagination of violence and terror is not just about violence but is actually integral to it. The physicality of violent assault cannot not be limited to its destruction of human bodies but, necessarily, must also be related to the way violence persists as memory, trauma, and in the intimate understanding of one's self-identity.

Violent acts may embody complex aspects of symbolism that relate to both order and disorder in a given social context, and it is these symbolic aspects that give violence its many potential meanings in the formation of the cultural imaginary. This is a particularly important point when we consider the violent acts taken by peoples around the world in the name of a particular religion, or in a belief that these acts conform to a set of 'moral' or 'patriotic' teachings directly linked to specific ideologies. When atrocity or murder take place they feed into the world of the iconic imagination. Imagination transcends reality and its rational articulation, but in doing so it can bring further violent realities into being.

Ethnographically anthropology has proved hesitant to try and understand the ferocity and forms of such violence, since witnessing such acts is problematic in itself – to say nothing of the direct challenges to the practice of ethnography that violent cultural practices inherently present. The ethnographer can just as easily be a victim of violence as an observer of it, and observation itself contributes to the cultural meaning of violent acts, no less than their perpetration. The papers collected in this volume clearly show the importance of attempting to grapple with these issues since they all emphasize in varying degrees the relevance of changing global conditions to the violent contestation of nationalism, ethnicity, and state control. Crucially they also address the question as to why such violence might take particular cultural forms – such as specific kinds of mutilation, 'ethnic cleansing', or other modes of community terror. Such an approach has not been adequately integrated into wider anthropological theory despite the pioneering work of relatively few authors, but it is only in this way that the links between acts of violence and their imagination and anticipation can be drawn out. The significance of this linkage should not be underestimated, and has been a key focus in this volume. As was the case under early modern European regimes of torture, simply to be shown the instruments of torment was often sufficient to produce the required confession of heresy or apostasy. So today, simply to be shown the aftermath of 'terrorism' invites each citizen to rehearse their complex political commitments to 'freedom' and 'democracy' which in turn sustain those regimes of political power that locate and identify the terrorist threat at the very gates of society, political stability, and economic prosperity.

This kind of approach requires a more explicit anthropology of experience and imagination in which individual meanings, emotive forces, and bodily practices become central to the interpretation of violent acts. This also implies a recognition of the need to interpret violence as a discursive practice, whose symbols and rituals are as relevant to its enactment as its instrumental aspects. How and when violence is culturally appropriate, why it is only appropriate for certain individuals, and the significance of those enabling ideas of cultural appropriateness to a given cultural tradition as a whole are therefore among the key questions that have been addressed in this volume. Until now there have been few attempts to map how cultural conceptions of violence are used discursively to amplify and extend the cultural force of violent acts, or how those violent acts themselves can generate a shared idiom of meaning for violent death – and this discursive amplification is precisely what is meant by the poetics of violent practice. By bringing together questions as to how violence is legitimized, and by relating the contest for such legitimacy to a wider field of cultural meaning and imagination, the papers here take an important step forward in developing such an anthropology of experience.

Anthropological research on violence also has the potential to make an important impact on anthropology's understanding of neo-liberal development and democratization more widely, since it is in those economic and political margins of the global order that violence becomes an inevitable and legitimized form of cultural affirmation and expression of identity to counter or compensate for a felt loss of 'tradition' or challenge to collective identity. Unless anthropology can develop ethnographic approaches and theoretical frameworks for engagement with such violent contexts, it risks being intellectually marginal to both the subjects and consumers of its texts.

In many popular and conventional presentations of indigenous or 'tribal' life ways the more or less overt message is normally to the effect that the lives being witnessed are subject to the kinds of arbitrary violence and terror that Western liberal democracy has otherwise banished from our everyday existence. Of course other kinds of trope are used in the myriad of programming on TV which suggests a more positive aspect to the lives of others – their harmony with nature, the beauty and satisfaction derived from tradition and custom – but even here the implicit meaning of the representation is that it is an anachronistic route to human happiness and contentment. Accordingly, the pervasive threat of the Hobbesian condition – a war of all men against all men – with the inevitable consequence – that the life of most men is nasty, brutish, and short – repeatedly ensues.

This mode of representation, and the imagination of other's subjectivities it entails, is particularly evident in the treatment of topics such as sorcery and witchcraft, and other televisual dioramas of 'traditional' violence, such as initiation ceremonies, mystical practices of self-mutilation or pain endurance, and so forth.[1] What such portrayals neglect in their urgent concern to convince us of the degree to which such lives are immured in superstition and fear is that we too live in a state of constant fear and terror, kept active in public consciousness by such devices as government-issued threat levels, civic exercises in preparedness for attack or disaster, and the nightly news bulletins and TV dramas. For even if we are somewhat defended against the terrorist of yesterday, the potential for similar violent disruptions of normalcy are nevertheless constantly rehearsed in crime dramas, documentaries, and reportage on the imminence of all kinds of natural and social disaster.[2]

However, as the chapters here suggest, not only (of course) is this to overlook the way in which states of terror and acts of violence are entangled with the social and political order, but also how those apparently negative and undesirable conditions are nonetheless valorized as the context for the expression of ultimate cultural value – be that heroism and self-sacrifice or physical endurance and indifference to pain. Moreover, the meanings of the televisual contrasts between savage and violent others and our pacific and sophisticated selves are not just linked to an implicit endorsement of a 'Western way'. They are also linked to the effacement of our own social and cultural capacities for, and institutions of, violence, with a resulting enfeeblement of the individual in the face of – or prospect of – the exercise of violence. We sit entranced by the sights and sounds of 'terrorist violence' – the twisted piles of metal and rubble, the wailing of women, the shouting of men, and the shots of tell-tale blood pools which visually confirm the overriding importance of this kind of violence as a token of the perpetrators' barbarity, and the occasion for our condemnation. In this way we are implicitly invited to infer the relative insignificance of our own counter-violence, rarely itself so starkly presented, in defeating the monstrous perpetrators of such acts. We also learn that we are dependent on the professionals of violence to achieve that end.

This is partly why the visual materials emanating from the torture camp at Abu Ghraib prison were so shocking and incommensurable with our understanding of the meaning of violence when we deploy it. Although US cultural values were overtly shaping the forms of violence – all the torturers wore plastic gloves, focused on sexualized humiliation, and generally gave off the impression that this was merely a frat party or hazing event – it was the automatic response of commentators that either the perpetrators were individually psychopathic or that higher authority was aberrant, but understandably so, since the aim of defeating terror was a far more important political goal. Moreover, even recent liberal-inspired commentary focuses on a validation of US government and the nation's body politic by suggesting a balancing out of the 'mistakes' of Abu Ghraib by the process of free journalistic inquiry and a Freedom of Information Act that uncovers the 'truth' of such abuse and torture – presumably then the detainees at Guantánamo Bay are doing just fine.[3]

Of course the latest terrorist pandemonium is in many ways just a re-inscription of pervasive and limitless threats that were earlier evident in the supposed imminence of total global holocaust that was constantly paraded during the era of nuclear confrontation between the United States and Soviet Union. Now 'weapons of mass destruction' are back in vogue again to suggest the imminent possibility of terrorist catastrophe in the vein of the 11 September attacks, if not the emergence of a Cold War-style stand-off with North Korea or Iran. Clearly though, certain forms of violent 'terrorist' action cannot serve this cultural purpose, since such responses to Timothy McVeigh's bombing of a federal building in Oklahoma have been noted but not introduced into the wider public discourse on the 'war on terror', precisely highlighting the difference between personal safety and national security as relating to different realms of political thinking and priority. Security is the politico-military prerogative of government, while safety remains a culturally diverse and individualized idea. 'Safety' in this sense can only be realized by the occupation of a different kind of space to that of threat and terror. Perhaps a nostalgic retreat, as in the sudden popularity of American folk music and the movie *O Brother Where Art Thou?* in the immediate wake of 11 September, and also in the remaking and recycling of movie/TV formats from or about the 1950s and 1960s.

Nonetheless, the interest of the authors in this volume in the imagination of terror and violence suggests that there is no geographical limitation on how such discourses travel, or at least only those of the medium in which they are expressed. My own discussions of a relatively obscure form of terror – the kanaimà – underscores this de-location, since despite regional use of the idea it has not connected with a global discourse of terror in the way that other local imaginings have already done, as in the case of the vampire, zombie, or werewolf. Such discourses also proliferate and expand locally through rumour, gossip, and imagination to constitute a cultural imaginary, and in particular they provide a sustained demonstration of the relevance of a comparison of sorcery with terrorism and how the field of sorcery is a key historical site for the understanding of violent social and cultural transformations.

In the contemporary 'West' the figure of the 'suicide bomber', more than the 'sorcerer', holds a key place in cultural imaginary, serving as a token of the illegitimacy of political causes that generate such acts. In Chechnya, Iraq, Sri Lanka, and Palestine, the 'suicide bomber' evokes the imagination of an irrational and unreasoning violence whose motivations are buried in the obscurity of religious cultism. It important to note therefore that the 'suicide bomber' is a Western media formulation, and that martyrdom and self-sacrifice – or fighting to the death – are much closer to the ideas that activate perpetrators. Valuable though recent studies are (see, e.g., Reuter 2004), they do not adequately engage the multiple cultural imaginaries from which such acts emerge. In Japan, Iraq, Chechnya, Sri Lanka, and Palestine such acts acquire meaning from quite distinct traditions and practices of violence. Just as is the case for an older idea of terror, cannibalism, it transpires that the apparent behavioural similarity of these acts actually belies their distinct cultural meanings and trajectories. This is very strikingly borne out by Ohnuki-Tierney's (2002) study of Japanese kamikaze, whose motivations were formed more through an admiring contemplation of Western modernity than as a remnant of anachronistic and traditional samurai ethics.

In many ways the figure of the suicide bomber also makes dramatically overt the identification of our bodies with the body politic. Through the social order of power, our bodies are shaped, and defined. They are also joined to locations and landscapes such that destruction of sites of civic identity become felt as bodily invasions, from which the invader must be repelled, purged, and cleansed. So too in the absence of specific kinds of bodies – suspects, offenders, terrorists – or in the lack of physically distinguishing features for such categories, the site of a 'war on terror', or against other kinds of 'enemies within', must become internalized as an aspect of 'mind' and 'attitude'. In this way we can come to appreciate how acts of violence are necessarily, and sometimes only, acted out in imagination.

This volume has emphasized the fruitful link to be made between 'traditional' forms of terror and violence, such as sorcery, and the contemporary depictions of terrorists, suicide bombers, and other anti-social threats; but earlier commentators on sorcery were no less aware of the significance of the imaginative order. As one missionary in Guyana wrote:

> At times I was warned that they were going to 'piai' me, that is, to cause sickness or death by their art; information which gave little uneasiness. For though the Obiah men of the negroes, and these Piai sorcerers of the aborigines, do *often cause sickness and sometimes death by the terror their threats inspire, they can only have this effect on minds imbued with a belief in them.* In order to injure others they must resort to actual poison, as in compassing the death of Mr. and Mrs. Youd [my emphasis]. (Brett 1881: 53)

The subsequent expansion of global media has ensured that many more minds can become imbued with a conviction of the reality of present terror, just as previously an elaborate theatre of public punishment and execution imbued minds with a lesson as to how the destruction of the bodies of the condemned was integral to the reproduction of society, paradoxically achieving the incorporation of society through the exclusion of its victims.

It is also significant, then, that colonial depictions of other rituals of bodily destruction, particularly as encountered in the colonial occupation of America, put great stress on the collective participation of the community in the destructive production of the victim. This was done as a way of illustrating the barbarity of the ritual exercise of 'cannibalism', so that both commentators and illustrators repeatedly alluded to the participation of women and children in the cannibal moment. It is striking that it was this community participation in the incorporating cannibal moment that shocked the early modern Europeans, not its cruelties and torments. By contrast, an exclusion, not inclusion, of the victim is envisaged in the European tradition of torture and execution as an adjunct to judicial process. Such is now the fate of detainees at Guantánamo

USAF base in Cuba, whose marked bodies and tortured minds leave them in a limbo of non-being, excluded from the society of human rights and law.

A violent and fetishized control of human bodies – both live and dead, imaginatively and physically – is a way of engendering political power, and the taste of death and desire that such fetish violence conveys is apt to make cowards of us all. But through careful thought about such imaginative experience we might also begin to understand how our own deep traditions of violence and sexuality structure and motivate a mystical and imaginative search for a final, ultimate triumph of progress over the terror and violence of barbarity . . . a desire and longing, 'an urge to surge', which actually can never be realized.

CHAPTER 15

Journalists as Eyewitnesses

Noha Mellor

If the third millennium will be remembered for anything, it will probably be for its momentous share of terror and pain. The first four years of this millennium alone have witnessed 80 per cent of the total number of the suicide attacks committed since 1968 (Atran 2006). In particular, news media have been assigned a key role in mediating such terrorist acts. News reports are usually examined for their credibility and impartiality, not only through their representation of hard facts about the causes of pain and violence, but also through their integration of particular cases of sufferers in an interwoven narrative of the objective world and subjective emotions, urging the audience's commitment (Boltanski 1999). For example, Chouliaraki (2004) argues that the news on the 11 September attacks managed to trigger the Danish audience's sympathy for the victims, while inviting them to denounce the perpetrators and to reflect on the sublimation of suffering as a universal emotion.

Thus, it is acknowledged that journalists carry a huge moral responsibility in reporting on terror and violence, particularly the way they manage to help the audience identify with a distant Other. This chapter examines these challenges on the role of journalists as mediators and, in particular, how the media incorporate this moral responsibility of reporting suicide attacks into their own market logic. I argue that the ethical task of reporting is a product of the market logic itself. The market gain of this sympathy lies in the news value of identification or personalization, that is, to humanize and popularize the story. This news value also serves to brand the journalist as an authentic eyewitness who communicates the hardship of a distant Other to a local audience. However, I do not see this value as a manifestation of the globalization of conscience; rather, I point to the scarcity of comparative research that could unravel the way journalists, cross-culturally, perceive their moral obligation in reporting terror and violence, and how they reconcile this type of reporting with a diverse market and institutional constraints.

The aim of the following discussion is to open up a new research agenda that focuses on the role of journalists as mediators of the news on terror as well as the audience as consumers of this news. I call for an expansion of our research agenda to account for the mechanisms by which journalists and audience alike respond to the news on terror and violence, and for how they apply and respond to the news value of identification. The chapter unfolds as follows: first, I discuss the convergence of moral and market logic in light of Sznaider's (1998, 2001) distinction between market compassion and moral compassion. I argue that the moral logic is closely linked to the market logic of the news on terror and violence, and I discuss the news value of identification as an illustration of this convergence of market and moral values. Then I discuss the role of journalists as eyewitnesses, and how this role consolidates the power of journalists as cultural authorities, drawing on examples of debates among Arab and British journalists. Although the roles of journalists as mediators and the audience as receivers are of paramount importance, I point to the concentration of the recent research on the textual representations rather than on these roles.

Market compassion

Sznaider (2001) analyses the relationship between compassion and the rise of humanitarianism, on the one hand, and the liberal capitalist system, on the other, distinguishing between what he calls moral compassion and market compassion. While the former is concerned with human rights and with spreading liberal democratic values, the latter is concerned with the means by which capitalism has unintentionally helped spread the concern for the Other. This view departs from, for example, neo-Marxist as well as Frankfurt theorists, who link the rise of the market society with a new set of constraints on solidarity and equality that in turn foster conflicts rather than empathy among individuals (Sznaider 1998: 118).

Compassion, as Sznaider (2001) argues, is at once an individualistic as well as a collective emotion, a paradox of late modernity that manages to reconcile modern individualism with humanitarianism, uniting market compassion with moral compassion. Market compassion, according to Sznaider (2001), has given rise to humanitarian movements such as those aiming to abolish slavery, to enhance child welfare, or to combat domestic violence. This view echoes Norbert Elias's view of the market society as a means to civilize human behaviour (Wilkinson 2005: 113). Consequently, the modern age has witnessed the paradox of accumulating individual wealth while increasing interaction with the Other and the spread of the ideals of egalitarianism and compassion (Levy and Sznaider 2004: 147).

The press, Barnhurst and Nerone (2001: 71) argue, helped advance the market revolution by spreading market news, and promoting goods through advertising. Thanks to the market society, the news media have turned from private publishing ventures into large conglomerates, thereby promoting the news itself as a commodity. The readers have then turned into 'paying customers', and hence it has become the duty of the news media to publish what is appealing to their customers (Barnhurst and Nerone 2001: 105).

The movement towards market economics had an impact on newspapers; Gans (2003: 23) argues that the shrinking audience has forced the news media to increase their soft news sections in order to attract, or at least maintain, their share of the audience. Accordingly, Western news media have witnessed an increase in the so-called human-interest news, a tendency that has existed for several decades, starting with the introduction of this type of news in weekly supplements, and then as an integral part of the daily editions. The market value of the news lies in personalizing its content by focusing on ordinary people as subjects of the news and hence increasing the audience's identification with the news stories. The market ideology has thus unintentionally led to the increasing visibility of the Other. In late modernity, visibility has particularly gained a new status thanks to the technological advances that render irrelevant the distances between nations and peoples (Thompson 2005: 35).

The sine qua non is that the increasing interconnectedness among world nations and the fast circulation of world news in transnational channels have, for better or worse, had an impact on public opinion both in the West and in the East. The increasing globalization and the accelerated technological advances have added a moral dimension to the profession of journalism. The shrinking distance between sufferer and spectator (including reporter and audience) has enforced the feeling of being *there*, being close to the scene of suffering – hence the importance of live reporting. The journalist has also gained the role of an eyewitness and observer who not only mediates distant events but also continuously engages in drawing moral boundaries.

Several scholars (e.g. Postman 1985; Bird 1998) accuse the media of personalizing the news in order to increase their share of the audience, and hence of advertising, rather than fostering a rational debate. According to this view, it is unlikely that the news media can reconcile their commercial interest with their moral task in society. As I argue below, however, the news value of identification or personalization combines the market and moral values of the news: It brings a distant event and actor closer to the audience's attention, while retaining the viability of the news story as a commercially appealing commodity. What is more important, I argue, is that this news value is a manifestation of the role of the journalist as an eyewitness, engaging with the Other and bringing news of their hardship to a distant audience.

The news value of identification

The incoming news on violence and conflicts is subjected to the logic of news selection based on its worthiness as well as its market value (McManus 1994: 114 f.); in particular, news reports tend to be popularized in order to attract a large segment of the audience while serving the interest of stakeholders such as advertisers. Combining moral and market logics is not necessarily intricate, for the process of mediating suffering, far from being based merely and only on an ethical relationship, is also a commercial commodity. Kleinman and Kleinman (1997) hammer home this point in their discussion of how the images of suffering may be valued as aesthetic objects, competing not only for the sympathy of the audience, but also for professional prizes such as the Pulitzer Prize.

Furthermore, the choice of images and even words is bound not only to the ethics of the news institutions, but also to the market value of the news. For instance, when al-Jazeera decided to show images of dead American soldiers and/or to broadcast interviews with captured soldiers in Iraq, this decision was partially justified by the need for the channel to compete with other media outlets in bringing the *news*, which boils down to the commercial, rather than the ethical, dilemma in dealing with the representation of pain (Zayani 2005: 25).

The news value of identification illustrates this convergence of market and moral logics. On the one hand, it has a commercial value in making the news stories more popular by incorporating the voices of ordinary people as eyewitnesses, while on the other hand, it consolidates the position of the journalist as a cultural authority by stressing the moral responsibility of reporting. This news value renders intelligible the acts of violence by invoking near contexts of pain, and incorporating the voices and images of laypeople into the news stories. For instance, the use of ordinary citizens as sources is deployed particularly in terrorism news (Atwater and Green 1988: 970), and one common question for survivors of violence is 'how they feel', which means that feeling has become more important than reporting pure facts. It is the bodily and emotional experience that is important to mediate, even before counting the number of casualties. Coleman (2000: 48) argues that the increasing reliance on ordinary citizens as an integral voice in the news can be a means of 'restoring a moral voice to society' or of scrutinizing the role of the journalist as a 'moral decision maker'.

Popular media tend to appropriate the tales of suffering through mundane details and characters, for example, the story of a family who survived an attack or by focusing on the destiny of a child who may have lost its family in the attack. In so doing, a distanced victim is brought closer to distant viewers by journalists zooming in on her plight as a fellow human being – that is, a mother, daughter or a sibling, rather than a world citizen.

As they serve as our eyes and ears in the distant hotspots, journalists also inevitably acquire the status of authentic witnesses. Thus, the act of witnessing is no longer confined to survivors or perpetrators; rather, journalists contribute to the process of writing history by providing their own testimonies to reconstruct acts of violence. Crucial for the testimony of the reporters, moreover, is the *authentic* aura that renders legitimacy to the mediated signs.

Journalists as eyewitnesses

For their testimony to be more authentic, broadcast journalists make use of live coverage as a means of giving the audience a sense of immediacy of action. Live coverage, as Peters (2001: 719) argues, 'serves as an assurance of access to truth and authenticity'. Thanks to the technological advance in newsrooms, covering an event as it unfolds has become a customary feature of news coverage. As live coverage has increased in the electronic media, so has weblogging on the internet, relying more on the individual voice of reporters as the source of its credibility.[1] Thus, the more the news report is personalized via the presence of the reporter, the more authentic it is for the audience.

The authentic testimony is also spatially bound, as one has to witness it via bodily pain. For instance, al-Jazeera presenter Ghassan Ben Jeddou put on public display his personal emotion when he reportedly shed a tear while reporting the news of the assassination of the Lebanese journalist Samir Qassir.[2] This physical emotionality has been seen as an indication of an authentic testimony and tribute to Qassir, which was the reason why some of the audience showed interest in learning more about him.[3] The physical experience may then be mediated along with the verbal and visual text to contribute to the 'authentic' experience of 'being there', as illustrated by another al-Jazeera journalist, Taysir Alluni, during his live coverage of the Afghanistan War as the only international correspondent in Kabul in 2001: the audience could see him reporting live with his gaze alternating constantly between the camera lens and the battlefield behind him, while occasionally bending his head in an attempt to protect his body from the bombs and rockets flying over him.

Journalists, then, serve as trustworthy eyewitnesses, a necessary character in this uncertain world, or as Thompson (2005: 46) argues, the context of the recent changes in political, social, and journalistic cultures has inevitably led to increasing uncertainty, and hence the quest for trustworthiness:

> People become more concerned with the *character* of the individuals who are (or might become) their leaders and more concerned about their *trustworthiness*, because increasingly these become the principal means of guaranteeing that political promises will be kept and that difficult decisions in the face of complexity and uncertainty will be made on the basis of sound judgment.

In sum, the task of journalists as gate-keepers embraces more than just hard facts and information about events such as suicide attacks; their responsibility now encompasses the gate-keeping of feeling, emotions, and suffering. In covering violence, reporters feel the power of their mediating role as eyewitnesses: the suffering to which they are witnesses depends on their professional effort as communicators to make it meaningful to their audience, far away from the heart of events. Crucial here is the possibility of setting shared 'objective' rules for journalists worldwide, if their mediation depends on their 'subjective' closeness to the Other. Let me illustrate this point with examples of recent debates among Arab and British journalists.

The guardians of conscience
To a question whether he served as a model of an emotional reporter, al-Jazeera correspondent Taysir Alluni, whose arrest and recent trial by the Spanish authorities made the headlines in the global media,[4] responded that his tone might have changed as a result of his interaction with events/wars and with victims in Afghanistan and Iraq. This change of tone occurred because, he argues, 'I am a man of flesh and blood, I do not claim to be the role model for television correspondent[s], but like my colleagues I interact with the event which I cover, but without violating my professional or objective codes.'[5]

This view is shared by other Arab journalists such as Diana Mouqalled (Future TV) and Walid al-Emari (al-Jazeera), who see as part of the journalist's duty a moral responsibility to reveal victimization, particularly in covering terror and violence (Hamidi 2004: 209 ff.).

This debate is not confined to Middle Eastern practices. In Britain, the former journalist Martin Bell, who served as a war correspondent at the BBC before embarking upon a short career in politics, distinguished between two types of reporting: bystander journalism versus journalism of attachment (Bell 1998: 15 f.). The former is concerned with the facts and figures of wars, such as casualties, rather than with 'the people who provoke them, the people who fight them and the people who suffer from them (by no means always the same categories of people)'. The latter, on the other hand, is concerned with precisely the representation of pain as human feeling, and in so doing, this type of journalism 'cares as well as knows', which Bell situates in the heart of the journalistic profession. The two types of reporting do not exclude one another; rather, they can be seen as available tools for which the reporter might opt, or, as Bell (1998: 18) puts it, 'There is a time to be passionate and a time to be dispassionate – a time and season for all things; and I would not report the slaying of innocent people in the same tone and manner that I would use for a state visit or a flower show or an exchange of parliamentary insults.'

What these journalists share, then, is the view that the journalist's task must include a touch of 'humanity' by personalizing conflict news in order to enable the audience to sympathize with the victims, lest we become complicit in evil (Bell 1998: 22).

On the other hand, other Arab journalists see emotionality as an impediment to the ideal of journalistic objectivity: as one of al-Jazeera's renowned presenters once said: 'If we let free our emotions, we would not interview Israeli [sources] and my colleague may refrain from entering into a dialogue with someone he [sic] does not like, or with the opposition in his country. . . . We should at least try to distinguish between feelings and the journalistic practice.'[6]

Also, Talal al-Haj, director of Arabiya and MBC offices in Washington, warns precisely against following one's emotions; for him, journalism should be based on fairness, which is the sum of detachment in coverage while bounded by the agreed-upon professional ethics (cited in Hamidi 2004: 234).

Moreover, David Loyn, a BBC correspondent, rejects the role of journalists as participants, arguing instead that journalists have only one task, that is, to 'witness the truth' (Loyn 2003: 1). Unravelling the truth, then, in a rational rather than an emotional manner, becomes the strength of the journalistic profession.

Broadcast journalists in particular tend to assign themselves the responsibility of orchestrating the audience's sensibility towards violent events, a responsibility that seems to blur on the internet, where the audiences, rather than the journalists, have the main responsibility for the deliberate act of screening and watching. For instance, when the South African Broadcasting Corporation took the decision to air footage showing the beheading of the American hostage Eugene Armstrong in Iraq, the consequence was widespread criticism and a fine, while the full video of the beheading was made available online to a global audience, whose personal reasoning would guide their free choice of whether to watch this video.[7]

Thus, on the one hand, traditional media serve a public that is not fully capable of taking moral and sensible decisions such as what to watch, whereas new media such as the internet are uncontrollable, lying beyond the manageability mechanisms in other electronic and print media. Audiences, then, are at once subjectified as rationally capable of taking the right decision and objectified as a cohort susceptible to damaging signals (verbal and visual), from which the media professionals can protect them.

In sum, the above debate illustrates the divergence of opinions about journalists' subjective role as eyewitnesses versus their traditional role as objective observers. Journalists seem to agree that they indeed possess the responsibility for eyewitnessing events, but they differ on the outcome of this responsibility: should journalists be responsible for arousing the audience's sympathy towards the subjects of the news or should they confine their responsibility to the role of informers by providing mere statistics of injuries?

As I argue below, it is potentially difficult to universalize such roles cross-nationally, not to mention the difficulty of generalizing the response of audiences to the news value of identification, which may be contingent on external factors. In fact, there is little evidence as to whether providing knowledge about the suffering following suicide bombings or violence would necessarily trigger the audience's sympathy or indifference towards the Other.

Knowledge versus action

As Boltanski (1999: 31) argues, knowledge alone as the basis of an ideal public sphere where citizens meet to discuss social issues rationally does not guarantee the citizens' emotional commitment to act upon their knowledge. Thus, the verbal testimony of reporters as active witnesses does not necessarily revoke the audience's sympathy with the victims, for words cannot be equated to the real experience of pain (Peters 2001: 710). Some scholars (Thompson 1995; Sznaider 2001; Chouliaraki 2006) argue therefore that imagination is indeed the key faculty needed to cultivate this morality disposition; it is only when the audience put themselves in the place of the Other 'as if' they were the victims that they can feel the plight of the Other and the urge to alleviate it. Compassion, then, has the capacity to transcend spaces and unite distant individuals, thus departing from the old tradition for which interpersonal communication and mutual presence are the keys to feeling with the Other.

But imagining the pain of, for example, terror victims assumes the ability to feel that particular pain in that particular situation; hence, one may argue that we can only feel with those who are like ourselves rather than with an Other who is situated beyond our immediate contexts. For instance, could we argue that the Israeli audience (and reporters) perform that as-if operation when watching the victimization of Palestinians under an officially justified Israeli attack? Conversely, could the Palestinian audience and reporters manage the same operation upon watching the pain of Israeli victims following a Palestinian suicide attack?

For Nossek and Berkowitz (2006: 691), the news of terrorism is particularly characterized by journalists' ability to 'retell the *master narratives* of a society', thereby reflecting specific cultural values. Journalists, then, are not 'super citizens' who can part company with their nationalistic and collective sense of belonging in order to encourage a rational debate among the audience; rather, they show personal involvement, as they are at once the producers and the audience of the news. Such master narratives are particularly apparent in crisis situations, and their main function is to ensure coherence (Nossek and Berkowitz 2006: 704). For instance, Nossek and Berkowitz analysed the reporting on two suicide bombings, one targeting a shopping mall in Tel Aviv and the other a campus of the Hebrew University in Jerusalem. They showed that the reports on the bombings were based on the master narratives of the Holocaust and anti-Semitism. Thus the journalists depended on the news value of identification to evoke shared narratives or history and thereby appeal to their core audience. If this were the case, however, how would it be possible to define one set of ethical rules to guide journalists worldwide in reporting suicide attacks and violence?

What is more, the global and regional media are indeed a site of struggle over legitimacy as well as visibility, and hence it is crucial to analyse the distribution of power among media actors and journalists on the global media scene. Each media institution then occupies a certain position vis-à-vis other institutions according to its weight and power on the media scene (Bourdieu 2005). So the pan-Arab media, for instance, would derive their power from their position vis-à-vis certain Western media outlets which may serve as a professional yardstick. Consequently, professional principles can be contingent on the power possessed by each media institution, rather than being based on a universal sense of morality.

Multiplicity of morality

Moreover, the call for humanizing the news seems to take the audience's response to the value of 'identification' for granted, assuming that humanizing any news of terror or violence would automatically trigger the audiences' sympathy towards its victims. This implies that there is a shared sense of morality, as well as justice, that grounds this feeling of sympathy, rather than seeing the possibility of having a range of moral stances towards witnessing others' hardships (see, e.g., Tester 2001, chap. 3). Studies among audiences could show different responses to different disasters, or even different expressions of indifference. For instance, Höijer (2004: 521) shows how Swedish audiences respond to images of victims from Macedonia according to their perception of the 'ideal victim' such as children. Audiences' compassion may also be subject to their justification of violence as a logical consequence of victims' irrationality; as one Swedish interviewee commented, 'I think they [victims of the Kosovo War] only have themselves to blame. There have been problems in the Balkans ever since World War I. They are no angels!' Moreover, Tester (2001, chap. 3) and Höijer (2004: 525 ff.) point to the possible differences among an audience's reaction according to gender; thus, women may be applying a care perspective that denounces acts of violence for their inevitable human losses, while men may be applying a justice perspective that justifies violence if conducted to take retribution.

One example of these different perspectives was a debate among Arab audiences about the definition of terrorism,[8] which showed the discrepancies between some male and female participants. Some male participants preferred the political frame of their definition, leaning on the principle of justice to rationalize events labelled as terrorist. For instance, an Egyptian male hailed the Iraqis' 'resistance' to what he labelled 'Western terrorism' in Iraq, while an Iraqi male questioned the killings of women and children as a legitimate means of resistance. Thus both participants reflected on the issue of justice in defining terrorism, and on whether it was just to carry out resistance action in Iraq. On the other hand, some female participants talked from a 'caring' perspective, preferring to define terrorism as lack of care for the less privileged. For instance, one Syrian female saw terrorism as 'a product of the rich countries that live in comfort ignoring the poverty which invaded three quarters of the world', thereby stressing the significance of the solidarity with the Other. Another Kuwaiti female, moreover, regarded terrorism as 'the confiscation of the other's opinion and freedom'.

This brings us back to Sznaider's views on moral and market compassion, discussed in the beginning of this chapter. What is implied in Sznaider's account is that the market revolution has increased interaction with, and hence compassion for, strangers. The commercialization of news as a commodity has indeed ensured the visibility of the Other and increased our knowledge of their dilemmas. However, to conclude that this has inevitably resulted in the globalization of compassion is to undermine the multiplicity of morality and cultural repertoires among different social groups, as Michele Lamont (2000) demonstrates in her comparative research among American and French workers.

Lamont argues against this shared sense of morality, and shows how morality, as a yardstick, is framed differently among American black workers compared to their white counterparts. For instance, the white workers identify the goodness in others through the concept of the 'disciplined self', based on work ethics, while black workers seem to favour the concept of the 'caring self' as their means of self-evaluation. Lamont went further to compare the moralities of black and white American workers with those of French white and North African workers: the French white workers tended to exclude the North African workers due to the latter's 'lack of civility'; thus civility and culture, rather than wealth and work ethics, were the foundations of the white French workers' morality. One important contribution of Lamont's work is that it refutes the presence of one universal standard of dignity or morality; rather, there exist different interpretations among social groups according to their class, race, and, indeed, gender. These multiplicities of morality are used for self-definition but also, more importantly, to 'draw the line that delimits an imagined community of "people like me"' (Lamont 2000: 3).

This is where there is a need for comparative studies among journalists in order to validate the normative view that the moral logic of reporting can be subjected to one universal set of rules applicable to journalistic practices worldwide. Future studies can address how the issue of professionalism may be interpreted and applied differently cross-culturally, and how this may be 'employed to accomplish the same normative goals' (Reese 2001: 178). Such studies may also designate the principles that guide journalists' personalization of the news – for example, which testimonies to draw on and why.

Likewise, there is a need to carry out more studies among audiences in cross-cultural contexts to see how the audiences make sense of news on terror, how they respond to the news value of identification, and whether this value really contributes to fostering the audiences' moral disposition vis-à-vis the Other. We need to examine the means by which these moral dispositions are construed, not only among 'privileged' Western audiences and professionals gazing at a distant Other in a turbulent area, but also how audiences and journalists from the less privileged areas cultivate the same dispositions vis-à-vis a privileged Other (for example, 11 September). In other words, could compassion be a Western indulgence inapplicable to other less privileged contexts, where local people themselves are too engulfed with suffering to feel the pain of others in distant contexts? Debating these issues would be a feasible basis for the global ethics project.

Conclusion

News media are assigned a huge moral responsibility in reporting on suicide attacks and violence. This responsibility is one outcome of the market ideology, which made it imperative for reporters to make their news stories appealing to laypeople by humanizing the content. As I argue above, the market ideology may have unintentionally led to the increasing visibility of the Other, as illustrated in the news value of identification or personalization, that is, humanizing the story, and hence popularizing the news while regarding the journalist as an authentic eyewitness. However, the global reach of the news media may not necessarily result in the globalization of conscience, for we know little of how journalists interact with the subjects of the news, and how this may differ cross-culturally.

Scholars' concern for morality and ethics has focused particularly on news texts as the main catalysts for cultivating our moral sensibility vis-à-vis the Other. The aim of the above discussion, however, is to broaden our research agenda to examine the power of journalists as mediators of pain in order to unravel the way journalists, cross-culturally, conceive of this moral task. Comparative research among journalists will then complement and support the textual and visual analysis of news texts, illustrating the incorporation of emotions and reason as analytically connected categories, in the process of both encoding and decoding the news. The importance of conducting comparative research lies precisely in unravelling whether the moral responsibility in mediating and digesting this type of news is related to a universal concept of morality, which may then serve as a guideline to journalists worldwide, or rather to a 'multiplicity of morality' tied closely to the experiences of both the producers and consumers of this news.

CHAPTER 16

Understanding Religious Violence:
Can the Media be Trusted to Explain?[1]

Mark Huband

The primary role of most Western media during the period between the 11 September attacks and those in London almost four years later has been to provide definitions: what it is to be of one nationality or another; what it is to be democratic; what it is to be Muslim; what it is to be a suicide bomber; what it is to be 'hate-filled'. Without these characteristics, the 'war on terror' would have no shape.

To meet this formidable challenge required the media was itself to be extremely well informed. Not only would it have to accurately identify the source and purpose of the terrorist threat, but also accurately describe the nations that were being threatened. Why do they hate us? It was a question the media had to be able to answer accurately and without hesitation.

In these endeavours most media has completely failed. In fact, most have never sought to provide such a service to the public.

'Why do they hate us?' In the wake of the 2001 terrorist attacks on New York and Washington, this was a question that many Americans asked themselves, each other, and anybody who was prepared to listen. The question has brought a range of answers. Some are as simple as: 'Because we give them lots of reasons to do so.' Equally, the answer could be: 'Because they hate each other and possibly even themselves. But they are looking for somebody else to blame for their woes.' Whatever the answer, since that day when the United States found itself forced to face the consequences of its foreign policy choices, the difficulty its people, its thinkers, and its policymakers have had in understanding what is confronting them has grown rather than diminished.

Far from being contained or consigned to the margins as a 'radical minority' or an 'extremist fringe' or a group that 'hates our success and prosperity', the suicide bombers, extremist preachers, and radicalized groups that together amount to the 'global *jihad*' are presenting a challenge that is likely to prove as profound and enduring as any in history.

'Why do they hate us?' was once the plaintive cry of a people that reckoned the trauma would eventually pass. National strategies would and could be put in place to deal with the consequences. Life would return to normal. The survival of the nation was – ultimately – not at stake. But to convince themselves that there was no mortal threat to a way of life whose value ultimately lies in the opportunity to take it for granted, Americans cocooned themselves in a web of lies, deceits, and misinformation about themselves and their place in the world.

Meanwhile, on the other side of the Atlantic Ocean, the opposite appeared to be true. In Britain the assumption since 11 September had been that one day the counter-terrorism effort would fail and that the bombers would slip through the net and commit their crimes. The British knew they would be attacked, and prepared themselves.

That it took until 7 July 2005 for the attackers to achieve their aims – after numerous plots aimed at Britain had been foiled – provided ample opportunity for the British to examine their national psyche. They talked of their *sang-froid*, their stoicism, and referred to the qualities that had seen them through IRA terrorism during the 1970s and 1980s. But not only were the British rumoured to be made of sterner stuff than their American allies; they also seemed to have the courage to admit that whatever measures were taken to thwart a plot, it was bound to happen sooner or later. Empowered by their realism, the British embarked on the process of waiting – a process that ended with the 7 July bombings in London.

Against this background, the primary role of most media in both countries during the period between the 11 September attacks and those in London almost four years later was to provide definitions: what it is to be American or British; what it is to be democratic; what it is to be Muslim; what it is to be a suicide bomber; what it is to be 'hate-filled'. The media has facilitated the process of defining what the people involved in this drama are: some people are terrorists; some people are intelligence officers; some people are apologists while others are either moderates or extremists; some people are senior al-Qaeda operatives, while other people are foot-soldiers; some people are victims; other people are Western allies, while some are 'not with us, so they are against us'.

For the media, as for the political establishment with which its agenda is so closely entwined, everybody has had to become something. Without allotted roles, the 'war on terror' would have no shape. A shape was needed in order for bulletins and news reports to have a beginning, a middle, and an end, for headline writers to grab the readers' attention for yet more of the same story, and for nations to feel that they were winning, that the 'war' was moving, and that all this would one day come to an end so that we could all get back to living normal lives.

Just as the people of America wrapped themselves in the Stars and Stripes, so the British sought to prove their *sang-froid* was not a hackneyed cliché but a national characteristic with real substance. But to really believe this of themselves they required the media. Unless the media flew the flag, the people would not know how to respond to the threat to the nation. Thus, the media had the role of defining the nation of which the people under threat needed to feel a part. The media would define who was a part of the nation and who was not. Those who were a part were the heroes; those who were not could be rightly reviled. In short, the media would become the window through which the people would see the correct version of themselves and their enemy.

To meet this formidable challenge required that the media was itself extremely well informed. Not only would it have to accurately identify the source and purpose of the terrorist threat, but also describe the nations that were being threatened. Why do they hate us? It was a question the media had to be able to answer accurately and without hesitation, because to explain why a bomb had been detonated or a person shot or a plot revealed, the media had to be able to provide context, historical perspective, and genuine, well-judged, well-informed, and sober explanation.

In these endeavours most media have completely failed. In fact, most have never sought to provide such a service to the public. This is either because having realized they were not up to the task they chose to deny it was ever their role, or because they could not conceal the superficiality of their self-appointed *expertise* on the issues that have arisen – without making it obvious that they simply did not know what they were talking about. In place of information they opted to become the voices of popular indignation.

Among the more experienced journalists there has been a trend towards trying to avoid being the 'media' at all. Peter Preston, former editor of *The Guardian*, made this clear in 2004 when he wrote:

> There is no limit to the targets that may be chosen by terrorists who expect to die but know that they will make a splash in the process. There is no limit to the soft touches that cannot be anticipated or defended. Frontiers are meaningless, because pictures have no frontier. Fear needs no visa.
>
> Two bleak things follow. One is that – whether or not it exists on any organised level – we shall gradually come to identify a force called international terrorism, a force defined not by the coordination of its strikes or creeds but by the orchestration of its inhuman propaganda. I manipulate, therefore I exist.
>
> The other thing is self-knowledge for media-makers and media-watchers. If the malignant message is itself a device, a weapon of mass hysteria, how do we defuse it? By a suppression that undermines free society, that gives terror its victory? Or by the realisation that we are not puppets, that we must see and explain for ourselves? That we have a duty of understanding. (Preston 2004: 15)

It seems to me that Preston is admitting a confusion that exists within the media, by suggesting ultimately that the terrorists only really do what they do because they know the media will report what they do. He further emphasizes the confusion he clearly feels as a media professional by pointing out that the media have a 'duty of understanding' which necessitates that they do report what has taken place and thus risk becoming tools in the terrorists' propaganda war.

But would the terrorist threat die if the media started to ignore it? Of course it would not. For Preston to imply that the jihadist–Salafist threat and the campaign that is currently under way under its banner could somehow be halted if Western media – for it is they to whom he is addressing his comments – ignored them, betrays a major failure in the 'duty of understanding'.

There is no doubt that al-Qaeda and its affiliates are using the media to get their messages across. But the medium is not the message. The message is something far more profound. This is because it is a message that is ultimately directed not at the West but at Muslims in the heartland of Islam. A decision by Western journalists to self-censor, or not, would make little difference in the big scheme of the jihadists' campaign because the real target of that campaign remains the Muslim world itself.

This fact is the source of the second major failing of the Western media. The determination of the Bush administration to portray al-Qaeda's campaign as *primarily* rather than *secondarily* a campaign against the United States has been a key test of the media's ability to distinguish propaganda from fact, fiction from political clap-trap, truth from lies. The 'malignant message' referred to by Preston is one that has powerful repercussions in the West because the West has the most dynamic and advanced media: most global television channels are controlled by Western interests and are omnipresent.

In order to engage viewers and readers, Western media need to portray stories as essentially *relevant* to the West. Even though there is no doubt the West is under attack, this relevance is strengthened by portraying attacks on Western targets and in Western cities as being the *primary* ambitions of the terrorists and as attempts to destroy Western civilization and all it stands for. In fact, this has not been the terrorists' aim, though the emergence of 'homegrown' terrorists in Western Europe may eventually make it so.

In the wake of the London bombings of 7 July 2005, Ayman al-Zawahiri made it clear – and not for the first time – that al-Qaeda's focus was not the West but the West's role in the regions of the world the jihadists define as the Muslim heartland. In a statement broadcast by al-Jazeera television al-Zawahiri said:

> O nations of the crusader alliance, we proposed that you at least stop your aggression against the Muslims. The lion of Islam, mujahid Sheikh Osama bin Laden, may God preserve him, offered you a truce until you leave the lands of Islam. Has Sheikh Osama bin Laden not informed you that you will not dream of security until we live it in reality in Palestine and before all infidel armies leave the land of [the Prophet] Muhammad, may peace be upon him? You, however, shed rivers of blood in our land so we exploded volcanoes of anger in your land. Our message to you is crystal clear: Your salvation will only come in your withdrawal from our land, in stopping the robbing of our oil and resources, and in stopping your support for the corrupt and corrupting leaders.[2]

Being prepared to believe such statements is essential if those in the West who are engaged in defining and countering the terrorist threat are to be successful. But their task has been greatly complicated by the determination of the Bush administration to exploit the threat and use it as a mechanism for expanding Western influence. The invasion of Iraq under the pretext that the war was a response to 11 September and a necessary way to fight al-Qaeda amounted to the most flagrant example of this opportunism.

Far from being a plot to overthrow Western civilization, the 11 September 2001 attacks were a result of the anger that had accumulated among generations of Arabs over several decades. Those who carried out the attacks saw them as a *reaction* rather than an *action*, justifiable in Qur'anic terms as a *defensive* act and not as an act of aggression. For Americans, whose ignorance of the world around them has become legendary, the 11 September attacks came out of the blue; to much of the rest of the world they were seen as the appalling price a country can pay for numerous cack-handed policies and – specifically – successive US administrations' unquestioning support for Israel's policies towards the Palestinians.

The extent to which the Bush administration relied on the media was made clear by Stefan Halper and Jonathan Clarke in their book *America Alone*. The following extract is informative:

> The administration seemed intent, from the early stages of the war [in Afghanistan], to sell a policy that relied as much on the media as on the official statements of government officials. In waging a war of words to provide the basis for a war of weapons, the media was of paramount significance, and the extent to which the media outlets underpinned the successful formulation of neo-conservative foreign policy was of great importance. . . . Beyond the presentation of policy objectives, this process had the effect of diminishing and marginalizing dissenting voices arising from other sections of the policy community. It created in effect an echo chamber, in which the administration's rationale was repeated and sustained in primary and secondary circumstances, such that opinion was formed and then reinforced through endless repetition of neo-conservative themes. . . . Thus, by the time that speechwriters and neo-conservative officials within the administration began to construct the notional discourse, half the task had already been completed by the overwhelming and sensational coverage from much of the American media. (Halper and Clarke 2004: 194–5)

It is without doubt that the failure of the US media to break free of political loyalties, proprietorial influence, and personal prejudice contributed to the intensity of the shock Americans felt when their country came under attack on 11 September 2001. They did not know what had hit them because they had been kept in the dark for so long about how their country's activities abroad were being regarded by those on the receiving end. By doing so, the US media greatly contributed to the sense of confusion that continues to prevail among Americans.

The July 2005 bombings provided an opportunity for the UK media to detach the threat to Britain from the experience of the USA. But the UK media's ability to rise to the occasion first necessitated that the public rapidly forget much, if not all, of what they had read in newspapers during the months that preceded those terrifying moments in London.

Three weeks before the bombings – on 17 June 2005 – the *Financial Times* had made great and uncritical play of a statement by the opposition Conservative Party's legal affairs spokesman in a story headlined: 'Threat of terrorism has been overstated, says MP'. The story then quoted the MP, Dominic Grieve, as saying that the introduction of control orders intended to place known radicals under intense surveillance 'appears to confirm our suspicion that the anti-terror bill before the general election was a cynical election ploy rather than a genuine attempt to protect British people'.[3] Similar politicization of the issues was undertaken by other media seeking to force the terrorism threat through the political prism.

But of perhaps greatest concern has been the calm authoritativeness among the 'quality' newspapers, which have sought to project an image of well-informed 'expertise' in reporting and analysing the threat from religious radicals. On 7 November 2002, the *Sunday Times* published a now infamous story on its front page in which it stated that Algerian terrorists had been thwarted in their plans to carry out a 'gas attack' on the

London underground.[5] The claims in the article were a concoction by the newspaper, comprising elements that had been brought together disingenuously: there had been concern among security officials about Algerian Islamists; the London underground was widely regarded as a potential target; some forms of gas – like the sarin used in a terrorist attack in Tokyo – were thought to exist within the al-Qaeda arsenal. But no security officials had brought these elements together: the newspaper's staff had done this for themselves. Even so, the truth behind the issues barely mattered: the article set the news agenda for the following couple of days, and the *Sunday Times* never published a correction.

But if the media is not concocting stories of its own, it is accusing governments of doing so. On 13 March 2005, *The Observer* published a long analysis by its chief reporter. The theme of government exaggeration of the terrorist threat was given substantial space, though in the form of the views of its reporter himself rather than as a report of the views of an opinionated politician or informed security official. 'The threat to Britain from Islamic militancy is far less serious than the government is telling us', the strapline in the story informed readers. This particular assessment of the terrorist threat to the UK as seen through the eyes of a journalist is informative in several ways. The reporter – Jason Burke – wrote:

> As you read this, there are no 200 'Osama bin Laden-trained volunteers' stalking our streets, as is claimed by the government. Nor are there al-Qaeda networks 'spawning and festering' across the country. Nor are Islamic militants cooking up biological or chemical weapons. Nor indeed are there any 'terrorist organisations', as Charles Clarke, the Home Secretary, calls them, nor are there 'hundreds of terrorists', as the Prime Minister told Woman's Hour. Nor are there legions of young British Muslims, enraged by perceived injustices in the Islamic world and by the supposed iniquities of Western policy towards their co-religionists, preparing to mount violent attacks.[6]

Several important issues arise from these assertions. The key one is that the bombings of 7 July and the attempted bombings of 21 July 2005 disproved all the claims made in the article regarding terrorist organization and motivation.

A second issue regards the number of 'volunteers'. The article implies that the reporter himself knew how many such 'volunteers' there were in the UK at that time, which of course he did not and cannot know. In the months prior to the July bombings there were far more than 200 investigations under way in the UK relating to the terrorist threat. The bombings showed that there was meanwhile a clear process of 'spawning and festering' under way, and that without any doubt there were – and probably still are – 'terrorist organisations'.

In my view the core reason why this article is such a travesty of what reporting ought to be about is that it pretends to know what it cannot know. It then uses unproven assertions to attack the government for daring to think in a manner that does not correspond to the half-baked views of a reporter seeking to promote himself as a better-informed 'expert'.

The London bombings offered the British public an opportunity to see just how little the numerous *experts* within the media actually know about *the* major global issue currently facing the world. But just as it took the British media to invent all sorts of scenarios to keep their readers convinced that it was in *their* newspaper that the exclusive stories and privileged insights would be published, so it took some within the media to highlight the ill-informed nature of much of what was being printed. The internal mechanism of self-justification that exists within the media became clear, as the more cerebral commentators began to point out how spurious much of the reporting had been, either as fact or interpretation.

Matthew Parris, columnist with *The Times*, was early in his identification of the trend. In a critique published on 23 July 2005, he vilified the media in general and specific terms to a point where the reader could only be left wondering whether there was any real point in relying on journalists to ever report anything resembling the truth. Parris wrote:

> At times of national emergency, the habit of the news media to drop a story or a lead in mid-air when it seems to be going nowhere unsettles the public. The media betray a sort of sheepish wish to 'move on' from an erroneous report, hoping that their audience will not notice. Rather than acknowledge this, they publish a new report, leaving us to compare it with what had previously been said – and draw our own conclusions. Or they start barking up a different tree, the inference being that the last tree may have been the wrong tree. (Parris 2005: 21)

But if this is the best that the more thoughtful and intelligent of the UK's commentators can come up with, it is no surprise that when the truth of the bombings emerged the nation was taken by surprise. The truth was that Britain had produced its own suicide bombers, though with some help from operatives abroad. The question was: how and why? A media that had generally decided to believe that 'we' could not have done this to 'ourselves' had by then led the public so far in one direction that it was unlikely that it would have the capacity to turn the spotlight on Britain itself and ask awkward questions about the fragile state of British society. So it turned the issue into a manhunt, a criminal investigation, a race against time, and a flag-waving exercise that warned al-Qaeda that Britain would not be cowed, as *The Express* made clear on 5 August after Ayman al-Zawahiri had issued a fresh threat. 'Threats won't defeat us', a headline said above the newspaper's leader column.

Two important lessons will nevertheless have been learned from the appalling events in London. First, the terrorists' capacity existed within the UK despite all the efforts to thwart it. Second, the jihadist–Salafist ideology propagated by al-Qaeda had become entrenched in the UK in its purest form – in the creation of the suicide bomber – implying that efforts to dilute it by countering its message with the propagation of 'moderate' alternatives have had only limited success.

In such circumstances, the media has a vital role to play: not in identifying 'our values' and explaining how they must and should be protected, but in informing people about the reality of the society in which they live and why it is that the way we live has spawned such antipathy. It would be wrong, however, to imply that 'society' was to blame for producing the 7 July bombers: they made their own decisions to kill. But the sentiments that have developed into extremism and the readiness to kill and die are now a part of what Britain has become.

It is the role of the media to explain what we are, not what we would like to be. But how good is the media at confronting the public with reality, after so many years of exploiting the freedoms democracies enjoy in order to turn truth into a political weapon?

'Attack is the best defence against terror',[7] the *Sunday Telegraph* announced in an editorial on 10 July 2005. The editorial revealed very clearly the ambiguities that prevail within the media, seeking as it does to ally a perception of the factual reality with the preferred political perspective of the newspaper. The *Telegraph* argued:

> There is in fact no foreign policy initiative that will make the slightest difference to the murderous intentions of the people responsible for last week's bombs. Indeed, there is no policy of any kind that will make any difference at all – short of adopting the extreme, Wahaabi version of Islam advocated by Osama bin Laden and his supporters. That is why it is also a mistake to believe that fundamentalist-inspired terrorism can be stopped if only we address its 'causes'.

Then the newspaper concluded:

> The reality is that we cannot address the 'causes' of terrorism, for the simple reason that no one knows what they are: no one knows why people decide to become mass murderers, or how to prevent them from doing so. The only defence we have is to penetrate and destroy the terrorist organisations themselves: to identify, arrest and imprison the terrorists and their leaders.

But the *Telegraph*'s assertion that measures 'to identify, arrest and imprison the terrorists and their leaders' will address the root problem is spurious: arrests have happened, but the threat remains.

On both sides of the Atlantic Ocean, the confusion of the West in trying to discern what that phenomenon is has been made far more difficult by a media that does not know whether it should be running towards the gunfire to find out more about those who are doing the shooting, or running away from it as part of a 'patriotic duty' to condemn.

It is very difficult for Western media commentators and pundits to address the profound issues arising from the challenge presented by al-Qaeda and its affiliates. But this is primarily because of the lack of understanding of where or why anti-Western sentiment actually fits into the ideology of the jihadis.

The simplistic explanation for jihadist violence in the West itself – as opposed to in Iraq or elsewhere – is that the perpetrators are seeking to subvert 'our' way of life. It is a simple way of deriding the jihadist terrorists' ideological position. The purpose of taking this line – and all media have done it, either by condemning the jihadists for being 'anti-democratic' or by stirring feelings of nationalism – is to avoid seeking real answers to the perennial question to which few have the courage to admit there is an answer: why do they hate us?

Notes

Introduction: Between Death of Faith and Dying for Faith: Reflections on Religion, Politics, Society and Violence, *Madawi Al-Rasheed & Marat Shterin*
1. Interview with Andre Girard, *Le Monde*, 6 November 2001

Chapter 1: Apocalypse, History, and the Empire of Modernity, *John R. Hall*
1. For a comparison of these events and 9/11, see Bousquet (2006).
2. Two other notable cases – the Solar Temple and Heaven's Gate – involved a different basis of collective suicide – travel from this 'spiritually failed' world to a better one. In their vision, participants achieved heaven not on earth, but through orchestrated collective death as rebirth.
3. STRATFOR, 'Emerging Bush doctrine reshaping U.S. strategy', http://www.stratfor.com/standard/analysis_view.php?ID=203273, 25 February 2002.

Chapter 5: In God's Name: Practising Unconditional Love to the Death, *Eileen Barker*
1. I would like to thank the Nuffield Foundation and Leverhulme Trust for their support for the research upon which this chapter, a slightly different version of which first appeared in Ahlbäck 2007, is based.
2. In fact, it was not even necessary. I have met a few Unificationists who joined after having themselves read the movement's scripture, *Divine Principle,* without ever attending a workshop.
3. Further details of these findings can be found in Barker (1984).
4. The vast majority of grass-root members of Aum Shinrikyo were totally unaware that the leadership was planning to deposit sarin gas in the Tokyo underground.
5. It is a common feature of close-knit religious and political communities that the members refer to each other as brother or sister, with leaders frequently being referred to as Mother or Father and the group as a whole as The Family.
6. The influence of peer pressure on an isolated individual was classically illustrated by experiments conducted by Solomon Asch (1959) in which a roomful of students all said that the second-longest of a series of lines drawn on a blackboard was the longest. In a significant number of cases the last student to be asked (who was not privy to the fact that all the others had been told to pick the second-longest line) would also say the second-longest was the longest, either not wanting to be the odd man out, or actually doubting the evidence of his own senses. When one other person chose the longest line, then the 'naive' student would be far more likely also to choose the correct one.
7. Some experiments by Stanley Milgram (1974) illustrated how a significant percentage of subjects would be prepared to administer painful, in some cases apparently lethal, electric shocks to others when they were told to go ahead by an 'expert' dressed in a white coat.
8. I have used the term 'charismatization' to describe a process whereby followers seem to conspire together to build up a picture of their leader, according him (or, occasionally, her) a special charisma which authorizes him/her to have an unfettered control over all aspects of their lives (Barker 1993).

9.   She was given six months for aiding and abetting, most of which she had already spent on remand by the time she was sentenced.
10. The extent to which the trainer's manipulation of those in his charge reflected the movement's policy and culture cannot be explored in detail here. Suffice it to say that he was given a position of authority that he undoubtedly abused. When his superiors learned of some of the things that he had done in overstepping his authority, they first chastised him and then, when his behaviour did not change, they removed him from his post. Amy heard later, however, that he had been reinstated and had returned to some of his earlier practices.

Chapter 6: The Terror of Belief and the Belief in Terror: on Violently Serving God and Nation, *Abdelwahab El-Affendi*
1.   For a more detailed discussion of this point see my forthcoming book *The Terror of Spin*.
2.   The memoirs of Abu Jandal (alias Nasir al-Bahri), who now lives in Yemen after having been released from prison there, were serialized in the London-based *al-Quds al-Arabi* from 17 March 2005.
3.   I am not making this up: read page 51 of the *9/11 Commission Report*, which argues that al-Qaeda's demand is that 'America should abandon the Middle East, convert to Islam and end the immorality and godlessness of its society and culture'.

Chapter 7: Rituals of Life and Death: the Politics and Poetics of *jihad* in Saudi Arabia, *Madawi Al-Rasheed*
1.   This chapter is based on research on Saudi Islamist movements. A full treatment of the topic is found in Al-Rasheed (2007).
2.   After Palestine, the Afghan *jihad* remains the second and most important experience that captures the imagination of jihadis in their literature. Recently, other locations have become equally important for the second generation of jihadis – for example, Bosnia, Kashmir, Chechnya, and, more recently, Iraq.
3.   For a chronology of violence in 2003 and 2004, see *Arab News*, 26 April 2004. For an analysis of violence from a security perspective, see Cordesman and Obaid (2005: 109–36). A more nuanced interpretation is Meijer (2005).
4.   The assessment of the intellectual origins of jihadis polarized the scholarly community, journalists, and intelligence services. Among academics, there are those who argue that jihadism originates from Wahhabi sources (Abukhalil 2004; Algar 2002). There are also those who argue that the ideology and practice of jihadism is alien to Saudi Arabia; for example, Natana DeLong-Bas (2004) absolves Wahhabism from any responsibility for the intellectual roots of jihadi thought. Maha Azzam (2003) also argues that the jihadi thought of al-Qaeda is rooted in the Egyptian radical Islamist trend rather than in Wahhabi sources. Other analysts differ in their assessment of the origins of jihadism. A Saudi convert from jihadism to 'rational' Islam argues that jihadi thought has its roots in the local Wahhabi tradition (al-Noqaydan 2003). I am more inclined to agree with this assessment, although it must be admitted that transnational influences are extremely important.
5.   Traditional Salafi publications dissociate jihadism from Wahhabi Salafi thought and insist that it derives from the Muslim Brotherhood and Qutbist agendas. See Oliver (2002).
6.   Gilles Kepel (2004: 152–96) sketches the process by which Saudi Arabia became host to the exiled Egyptian and Syrian members of the Muslim Brotherhood in the 1960s. However, hosting members of a political party with its own intellectual Islamist heritage and activism may not always translate into actual endorsement of all this group's ideas. The cross-fertilization of religious ideas between Saudi Wahhabi thought and that of the Muslim Brotherhood, which arrived in Saudi Arabia with the flight of its persecuted members, is more complex than is often acknowledged. It is certain that Saudis benefited from the

modern organizational skills of twentieth-century Islamist movements, but they brought their own tradition into the complex Islamist scene of the last half-century.

7. For details on British Muslims studying at Saudi religious universities, see Birt (2005). For a general overview of Saudi transnational religious networks in London see Al-Rasheed (2005).

8. After 11 September Saudi Arabia started issuing its own lists of wanted terrorists. The first, containing 19 names, appeared on 7 May 2003. On 6 December 2003, it issued a list with 26 names of wanted terrorists. Saudi security forces killed more than half of the men mentioned in both lists. See *al-Riyadh*, 7 December 2003. For an English version of these lists, together with the names of suicide bombers who perished after each attack, see Meijer (2005: 301–11).

9. Anthropologist Neil Whitehead offers a nuanced interpretation of violence as a cultural phenomenon; see his remarks in Strathern, Stewart, and Whitehead (2005: 10). He argues that it is perfectly obvious that culture is relevant to violence since violence is part of human action. But he rejects the notion that violence might be integral or fundamental to cultural practice. See Whitehead (2004: 8).

10. IntelCenter Tempest Publishing: see http://www.intelcenter.com.

11. *Sawt al-Jihad*, vol. 11.

12. One Saudi commentator argues that jihadis lure young Saudi men by invoking *zaffa*, a happy celebration for a bridegroom-to-be, thus playing on youthful sexual frustration and sensational themes. See the minister of the interior's spokesman, Saud al-Musaybih (2005). See also 'Amer al-amir al-kabt al-jinsi bayn al-jana wa al-nar', http://daralnadwa.com/vb/showthread.php?t=153503, accessed 21 April 2005. Some Saudis argue that bin Laden and other jihadi *'ulama* use the glorious and sensual description of heaven in the Qur'an to lure sexually frustrated youth into holy war. They suggest that lifting sex segregation in society would be beneficial in fighting terrorism. Novelist Turki al-Hamad plays on the same theme in his 2005 novel *Rih al-janna* (The Wind of Heaven). Saudi anthropologist Saad al-Suwayan expressed a similar opinion. Biographies of dead jihadis reveal that most of them are married, thus making the sexual frustration theory implausible.

13. Eleanor Doumato (1992) interprets gender in the context of national identity and monarchical rule in Saudi Arabia.

14. Muhammad Ahmad Salim (n.d.). This view echoes a document by 26 Saudi Sahwi *'ulama* who declared resistance in Iraq a legitimate *jihad* but were hesitant regarding the involvement of Saudi youth. See http://www.yaislah.org/vboard/showthread.php?t=116031.

15. For Nasir al-Fahd's views on the participation of women in *jihad*, see al-Fahd (n.d.). The role of women in *jihad* is also discussed by Shaykh Yusif al-Ayri (n.d.).

16. Shaykh al-Ayri (n.d.). explains women's involvement in *jihad* by drawing on *shari'a* evidence.

17. *Al-Khansa, Jihad Magazine for Women*, 24 August 2004; see BBC News, http://news.bbc.co.uk/go/pr/fr/-/2/hi/middle-east/3594982.stm.

18. The Saudi-sponsored al-Arabiyya satellite channel reported a story about a female Saudi jihadi. Um Usama admitted that she was active in supporting *jihad* through participation in internet discussion forums, promoting jihadi thought, and encouraging other women to recruit for al-Qaeda. The story cannot be cross-checked. See http://www.alarabiya.net/articlep.aspx?p=10527, accessed 27 February 2005.

Chapter 8: The Islamic Debate over Self-inflicted Martyrdom, *Azam Tamimi*

1. This chapter derives its contents from chapters 7 and 8 of Tamimi (2006).

2. Settling Jewish immigrants on land confiscated from the Palestinians within the areas occupied by Israel in 1967 was meant to enhance Israel's security. However, Jewish settlements have proven to be a heavy burden on Israel and a source of constant provocation

for the Palestinians. One of the main reasons for the failure of peace making between the Palestinian Authority under Yassir Arafat and successive Israeli administrations had been the existence of these settlements.

3. For full details of the poll and its results visit http://www.fafo.no/gazapoll/summary.htm.
4. See http://www.pcpsr.org/survey/survey.html.
5. See http://www.sis.gov.ps/english/index.html.
6. According to al-Imam al-Shatibi (d. 1388), Islamic *shari'a* is aimed primarily at protecting the five essentials: life, faith, progeny, property, and sanity
7. See El-Awa (1993).
8. Shaykh Yusuf al-Qaradawi, interview with the author in Doha, Qatar, 19 October 2005.
9. Prominent commentators (scholars of Qur'anic exegesis) al-Tabari and al-Qurtubi both agree in their commentaries on this verse that Prophet Muhammad was instructed to challenge the unbelievers with the Qur'an and to perform *jihad* against them by reading it and conveying its message to them. Al-Qurtubi goes further and criticizes 'those who claimed that the Prophet was ordered in this verse to perform Jihad against the unbelievers of Quraysh with the sword'. He argued that this was a Meccan verse; fighting with the sword had not yet been allowed.
10. For more discussion of the opinions of both thinkers on this issue see chapter 3 of Tamimi 2001.
11. See Q 9.111 and Q 61.1–6. Both al-Tirmidhi and Ibn Maja reported that the Prophet peace be upon him said that a martyr receives seven rewards: he will be forgiven for all his sins; he will be able to see his place in Paradise; he will be saved from the ordeal of the grave; he will be secured from the Day of Great Fear (Day of Resurrection); on his head will be placed the crown of dignity in which a single gem is better that life and what exists in it; he will be married to 72 wives of the Hur al-'In; and he will be granted permission to intercede on behalf of 70 of his relatives.
12. Quoted in *al-Hayat*, 4 August 1997.
13. The *fatawa* of both Shaykhs al-Shuaybi and al-Qaradawi are quoted in *Filastin al-Muslimah*, March 2002 edition.

Chapter 9: The Radical Nineties Revisited: Jihadi Discourses in Britain, *Jonathan Birt*

1. As in the case of Omar Bakri Mohammed: see Wiktorowicz (2005: 9, 215, 216), although it remains unclear just how much this public rhetoric was designed solely for public consumption.
2. See the remarks of a former intelligence officer and adviser to the Cabinet Office (1998–2002): Black (2005: 31)
3. E.g. Michael Winterbottom's film about the Tipton Three, *The Road to Guantanamo* (2005); Moazzam Begg's memoir (Begg 2006); and Taseer (2005).
4. See Khan (2006); McLoughlin and Khan (2006); and Werbner (2003).
5. See Birt (2005a); Geaves (1996, 2000); Hamid (2007); Lewis (1994); McLoughlin (2005); and Taji-Farouki (1996).
6. Pnina Werbner (2003) provides a detailed British case study.
7. See chapter 1.
8. See Gerges (2005: 26–7 and chapter 3).
9. See Birt (2005b) and Commins (2006: 185).

Chapter 10: *al-Shahada*: a Centre of the Shiite System of Belief, *Fouad Ibrahim*

1. Quoted from Encarta® Book of Quotations (1999).
2. Ayatollah Khomeini emphasized these motivations indirectly by praising the recruiters of Iranian troops during the 1980–8 war with Iraq by saying: 'To which class of society do these heroic fighters of the battlefield belong? Do you find even one person among all

of them who is related to persons who have large capital or had some power in the past? If you find one, we will give you a prize. But you won't.' The same can be said of the Amal movement, which Mussa al-Sadr established in the mid-1970s, which consisted of the deprived (*mahrumin*), many of whom subsequently joined Hezbollah and became part of the project of martyrdom. This extends to Sayyid Muqtada al-Sadr's Mahdi Army, whose members belong to the downtrodden class. He identifies his movement as *taiyyar al-mahrumin* (the deprived trend).

3. See, for example, Tabari (1988, III: 106) ad Q 3: 140 ('So that God may know who are the believers, and may take witnesses (*shuhada*) from among you'), and v. 162f. and Q 4: 69 ('Whoever obeys God and the Messenger – they are with those whom God has blessed, prophets, just men, *shuhada*', the righteous; Good companions they!').

4. Kashif al-Ghita (n.d.: 381).

5. Al-'Amili (1983, II: 379, 382).

6. See e.g. Nafziger and Walton (2003: 207).

7. See Lewinstein (2002: 80ff.).

8. See Charles (2005).

9. See Lewinstein (2002: 82).

10. See Momen (1985: 62).

11. See al-Asfahani (1987:16 ff.).

12. See Shari'ati (2002: 145, 166).

13. See Sivan (1990: 52).

14. See Shari'ati (2002: 311).

15. According to Abrahamian (1993: 27), Khomeini rarely used the word *shahada* before the 1970s.

16. According to Hamid Enayat (1982: 194 ff.), Najaf 'Abadi's work allowed Shiite revolutionaries to relate to and emulate Imam Husayn's experience, rather than viewing it as something humanly impossible.

17. Speech delivered by Mussa al-Sadr on the anniversary of the birth of Imam Mahdi in al-Yamouna village, in Beqa' district; available at http://www.moqawama.org/_lemoussakhitab. php?filename=2005112611380544. Accessed 23 November 2006.

18. See also speech on 'Ashura in Yater village in South Lebanon on 2 February 1974, available at http://www.moqawama.org/_lemoussakhitab.php?filename=2005112611380435. Accessed on 12 November 2006.

19. Sermon by Musa al-Sadr on the occasion of 'Ashura, 12 January 1976, available at http://www.moqawama.org/_lemoussakhitab.php?filename=2005112611380422. Accessed 12 November 2006.

20. Quoted in *al-Nahar*, 27 January 1975.

21. Al-Manar TV, 24 March 2002.

22. See http://www.moqawama.org/_leabbaskhitab.php?filename=2005112612163415. Accessed on 23 November 2006.

23. Ibid.

24. Biography of Sayyid Abbas al-Musawai, available at http://www.moqawama.org/_leabbassera.php?filename=20050601184813. Accessed on 23 November 2006.

25. *The Culture of Martyrdom and Suicide Bombers*, al-Arabiya TV special, 22 July 2005.

26. Al-Manar television, 16 February 2002.

27. Al-Manar television, 9 January 2002.

28. Al-Manar television, 26 July 2006.

29. Nir Rosen, Hizb Allah, Party of God, available at http://www.truthdig.com/report/item/200601003_hiz_ballah_party_of_god/. Accessed 28 November 2006.

30. *As-Saffir*, 5 September 2006.

Chapter 11: Urban Unrest and Non-religious Radicalization in Saudi Arabia, *Pascal Ménoret*

1. Thanks to all those who have agreed to share the stories of their young lives. Many thanks to Dr Yahya ibn Junayd, Dr Awadh al-Badi (KFCRIS), and Dr Bernard Haykel (New York University) for having been supportive of this fieldwork.
2. The colloquial bedouin verbs *fahhata*, *hajja*, and *tafasha* denote flight or running. *Hajwala* is still used as a synonym of 'confusion', 'anarchy'; a *muhajwel* is a tramp. Young people reverted the term: a *muhajwel* is a tough guy, a street hero.
3. Interview with a *tafhit* driver, 28 January 2006.
4. *Al-Mustashar* web page, available at http://www.saher4.com/vb/printthread.php?t=28760. Accessed 18 April 2005.
5. Interview with a skidder, 18 January 2006
6. See http://www.saher4.com/vb/printthread.php?t=28760.
7. Interview with a skidder, 28 January 2006
8. Interview with fans, 20 August 2005.
9. Interview with a Saudi sociologist, 24 January 2006.
10. Iman Kamel, 'Tafhit as-sayira min hiwaya ila idman intahi li-l-shabab al-khaliji bi-l-mawt', reader's commentary, *al-'Arabiyya*, 14 August 2005, available at http://www.alarabiya.net/Articles/2005/08/14/15875.htm.
11. We rely here on personal observations by both authors. They provide general trends rather than a precise photography of the social reality of peripheral Riyadh neighbourhoods.
12. Interview with a sedentary drag-racing fan, 26 May 2006.
13. Available at http://www.saher4.com/vb/printthread.php?t=28760.
14. 'Songs for Bûbû', available at www.moon15.com. Accessed 22 March 2004.
15. Rakan, 'al-'Arbaja, nash'atuha wa namûha', available at www.alqasir.net. Accessed 8 January 2004.1
16. Interview with bedouin pupils, 2 March 2006.
17. Abu Zegem, *Min qisas at-ta'ibin Abi Zegem wa Abi Hasan*, video CD bought on the street in Ta'if, 28 December 2005.
18. Interview with a fan, 7 March 2006.
19. Anonymous, 'Akhiran, al-kitab al-mamnu': 'al-hajwala fi 'ilm al-'arbaja'', available at http://www.ksayes.com/forums/showthread.php?t=1561. Accessed 9 May 2005.
20. Badr al-Mutayri, *Liqa' ma' ashhar al-mufahhatin*, video CD bought in Ta'if, 28 December 2005.
21. Interview with a drag-racing fan, 26 May 2006.
22. Interview with a fan, 23 February 2006.
23. See www.za7ef.net. Accessed January 2006.
24. Interview with a skidder, 28 January 2006.
25. Interviews with fans and skidders, 25 and 28 August 2005; 27 April 2006.
26. The Jama'at al-Tabligh was founded on a Sufi basis in the 1920s by an Indian scholar, Muhammad Iliyas. It penetrated Saudi Arabia during the 1960s and focuses mainly on social and moral issues, notably drugs, alcohol, and road delinquency.
27. Interview with an ex-fan, 28 August 2005.
28. Rakan, 'al-'Arbaja, nash'atuha wa namuha'.

Chapter 12: Bodily Punishments and the Spiritually Transcendent Dimensions of Violence: a Zen Buddhist Example, *Ian Reader*

1. For example, the Sôtô Zen sect – the largest Zen Buddhist sectarian organization in Japan, with over 15,000 temples, including around 30 monasteries at which meditation is a central part of daily life, and several hundred more temples at which priests and laity alike can

practise meditation – publishes numerous magazines that highlight meditation and monastic life and that feature images and texts depicting the use of the *kyôsaku*, portraying it as an intrinsic element in Zen life, and a key to Zen spiritual disciplines. See, for example, *Zen no Kaze*, 1981, 1982, and 1983; *Zen no Kaze* ('the wind of Zen') is the annual magazine publication of the Sôtôshûshûmuchô, the head office of the Sôtô sect in Japan. The popular Japanese Buddhist magazine *Daihôrin*, too, often features articles about Zen meditation and temple life in which the use of the *kyôsaku* features prominently; see, for example, 'Zazen no susume', *Daihôrin* (1981) 7: 94–167 (special feature on Zen meditation), esp. pp. 100 and 109.

2. See, for example, Suzuki (1975: 339–40).

3. On the links of monotheism and violence see, for example, Schwartz (1997); on millennial and apocalyptic movements and violence, see Hall et al. (2000) and Wessinger (2000a, 2000b).

4. This point came across to me most clearly when discussing the Japanese movement Aum Shinrikyô, whose acts of violence are well known. Aum insisted it was a Buddhist movement, yet I have often had people tell me that Buddhism is non-violent and therefore Aum could not have been Buddhist. Indeed, Aum used this very argument to defend itself when it was first accused of the 1995 Tokyo underground attack, stating that it was Buddhist and therefore could not have committed such a murderous deed: see Appleby (2000: 313, n.25). Appleby appears to have largely gone along with the pattern of separating Buddhism out from other traditions in this context, saying that it is 'the least fertile ground of any of the major religions' for developing a violent hermeneutic and suggesting that when violence occurs in association with Buddhism, it does so in conjunction with other (e.g. ethnonationalist) factors (2000 131–6).

5. While Chinese and Japanese use the same ideograms in their writing, the readings of the ideograms differs depending on the language; hence the readings of Chinese Zen teachers' names will differ according to whether they are being read in a Chinese or Japanese context.

6. See Suzuki (1975: 276, 306).

7. See Suzuki (1975: 306–7).

8. See Suzuki (1975: 339–40); see also Stevens (1993: 66–9), which emphasizes the severity of Hakuin's teacher.

9. See Suzuki (1975: 341).

10. See Suzuki (1975: 22).

11. See Suzuki (1965: 10).

12. See, for example, Snellgrove (1987: 498–9).

13. For an excellent discussion of this concept and the ways in which it has been manifest also in contemporary Tibetan Buddhism in the USA and elsewhere see Bell (1998).

14. In Reader (2005) I give a fuller and more comprehensive discussion on mystically charged violence and its legitimizations, in which I examine a variety of cases in which adherents of movements ranging from Aum Shinrikyô to medieval millennial movements utilize concepts of spiritual superiority in ways that transform violence into a mystical activity replete with religious meanings.

15. See Moerman (2005: 213).

16. See Moerman (2005: 209–10).

17. See, for example, Aho (1981: esp. 127–41), where Aho discusses how Zen in particular contributed to the development of the Japanese samurai ethic and its related traditions of warfare and martial arts; and Victoria (1997: esp. 129–44), which discusses the links between the imperial state and Zen in the twentieth century.

18. See, for example, Victoria (1997: 97–129, esp. 116–21), where Victoria shows how a prominent Japanese army officer came to be regarded as a prime example of the Zen–military ideal.
19. See Victoria (2003: 17–26).
20. Similar themes were expressed in a British documentary *The Real Tojo* (about General Tojo, Japan's wartime prime minister who was executed in 1948 for war crimes), which was aired on Channel 4 on 12 December 1998, in which ex-soldiers talked about how beatings were an intrinsic part of the army's attempts to forge discipline and strength.
21. See Victoria (1997: 47).
22. See Victoria (2003: 52–4).
23. These comments by Fukusada are cited in Victoria (2003: 33–4).
24. See Victoria (2003: 34).
25. See Sharf (1993) and Victoria (1997).
26. See Oguma (2002) for a comprehensive discussion of such literature and discussions in Japan from the late nineteenth century until the Second World War.
27. Yasutani, cited in Victoria (2003: 69–72). As Victoria shows also (pp.73–4), Yasutani was also virulently anti-Semitic.
28. See Victoria (2003: 51).
29. Yasutani, cited in Victoria (2003: 72).
30. I discuss such issues in Reader (2000).
31. See Victoria (1997: 35–6).
32. See Victoria (1997: 25).
33. See Victoria (1997: 86–91).
34. See Victoria (1997: 138).
35. See Reader (2000: 150–1).
36. See Reader (2000: esp. 138–40).
37. See Reader (2000: 137–8, 232–3).
38. An example of this genre is Kimball (2002).

Chapter 13: Jewish Millennialism and Violence, *Simon Dein*
1. Maimonides, in his commentary on Tractate Sanhedrin of the Babylonian Talmud, states: The Messianic age is when the Jews will regain their independence and return to the land of Israel. The Messiah will be a very great king. He will achieve great fame and his reputation among the gentile nations will even be greater than that of King Solomon. His great righteousness and the wonders he will bring about will cause all people to make peace with him and all lands will serve him. Nothing will change in the Messianic age, however, except that Jews will regain their independence. Rich and poor, strong and weak, will still exist. However, it will be very easy for people to make a living, with little effort they will be able to accomplish very much … there will be a time when the number of wise men will increase … war shall not exist, the nations shall no longer lift up swords against nations. … The Messianic age will be highlighted by a community of the righteous and dominated by goodness and wisdom. Be ruled by the Messiah, a righteous, honest king, outstanding in wisdom, close to God. Do not think the ways of the world and the laws of nature will change, this is not true. The world will continue as it is.
2. See e.g. Scholem (1971); Werblowsky (1969).
3. The area of millennial violence is a relatively new one, provoked by several high-profile cases: the Peoples Temple in Guyana; the Branch Dravidians at Waco; the Order of the Solar Temple; Aum Shinrikyo; Heaven's Gate; and the movement for the Restoration of the Ten Commandments of God. Understanding this millenarian violence is a multi-disciplinary

endeavour. While it is generally accepted that several factors inherent within millenarian groups themselves may predispose them to become violent or volatile, they are not sufficient causes in themselves. Robbins (1997) and Robbins (2002) describe three broad interlinked sets of predisposing factors, including: the inherent violence and antinomianism of millenarian ideologies; the volatile nature of charismatic leadership; and, finally, the fact that such groups are often totalistic organizations in re-socializing their members. However, these endogenous factors themselves are not sufficient to cause violence. Bromley (2002) draws attention to the role of cultural opposition in such cases.

4.   Sprinzak (1998) describes how conflicts between different Jewish groups in Israel itself have resulted in militancy and violence. These have been conflicts between ultra-Orthodox and secular Jews; Sephardi and Ashkenazi Jews; and between the Israeli left and right over the borders of the state of Israel and its relationships with Arabs. All warrant separate discussion, which is not possible here.

5.   Lifton (2003) points out how apocalyptic visions underlie much of the terrorism in the Middle East. Palestinian Hamas suicide bombers, for instance, have an immediate political goal: interrupting any progress in the peace process, which they strongly oppose. But the group's larger vision is of a holy war in which the Jews of Israel are the designated victims. Hamas's charter declares that 'Allah is [our] goal, the Prophet its model, the Qur'an its Constitution', jihad its path, and death for the cause of Allah its most sublime belief'. It speaks of a world-ending mystical process of purification in which even rocks and trees 'will cry O Muslim! There is a Jew hiding behind me, come and kill him!'

6.   Some of this discussion derives from S. Dein and L. Dawson, The "Scandal" of the Lubavitch Rebbe: Messianism as a Response to Failm Prophecy", *Journal of Contemporary Religion* 23, issue2: 163–180.

7.   Chabad.org 2004.

Chapter 14: Sacral Violence: Cosmologies and Imaginaries of Killing, *Neil Whitehead*

1.   A recent series of programmes on such topics made for the Discovery Channel was thus entitled 'Culture Shock Week'

2.   Carolyn Nordstrom (2004) has aptly termed this 'the Tomorrow of Violence'.

3.   See the review of Danner (2004) by Andrew Sullivan in the *New York Sunday Book Review*, 23 January 2005.

Chapter 15: Journalists as Eyewitnesses, *Noha Mellor*

1.   In fact, Wall (2005) presents a survey among the readers of news blogs that suggests that the popularity of these weblogs is due to the audience's view of them as a more credible source of information than the mainstream news media.

2.   Samir Qassir was assassinated on 2 June 2005, less than four months after the assassination of the former prime minister Rafiq al-Hariri, and both assassinations fuelled huge demonstrations inside Lebanon, accusing Syria of plotting both acts. Qassir was known for his anti-Syrian writings, which appeared in the widely distributed *an-Nhar* daily; he called for the withdrawal of all Syrian troops from Lebanon and for reforms inside Syria.

3.   Source: MEB Journal, available at http://www.mebjournal.com/index.php?option=com_magazine&func=show_article&id=53. Accessed 25 May 2006.

4.   Taysir Alluni was known for interviewing Osama bin Laden. He was arrested in Spain in connection with the railway bombing, and was later sentenced to seven years in prison for supporting al-Qaeda.

5.   These remarks were made in a special episode of *Open Dialogue* on the occasion of the seventh anniversary of al-Jazeera. The episode included commentaries from al-Jazeera journalists as well as other Arab journalists from other media outlets. Available at http://www.aljazeera.

     net/programs/open_dialog/articles/2003/11/11-6-1.htm. Accessed30 November 2003.

6.   Mohamed Krishan, al-Jazeera. Available at http://www.aljazeera.net/programs/open_dialog/articles/2003/11/11-6-1.htm. Accessed6 November 2003.

7.   See 'Is linking to beheading video OK on web, not TV?' Available at http://www.poynter.org/column.asp?id=31&aid=72830. Accessed 25 May 2006.

8.   See http://news.bbc.co.uk/hi/arabic/partnership/newsid_4486000/4486298.stm. Accessed 12 December 2006

Chapter 16: Understanding Religious Violence: Can the Media be Trusted to Explain?,
Mark Huband

1.   This chapter is based on an essay which appears in Kassimeris (2007).

2.   Ayman al-Zawahiri, statement issued on al-Jazeera TV, Doha, in Arabic, 12.02 GMT, 4 August 2005. Source: BBC Monitoring.

4.   'Threat of terrorism overstated, says MP'. *Financial Times*, 17 June 2005. p. 4.

5.   'MI5 foils poison-gas attack on the Tube'. *Sunday Times*, 17 November 2002, p. 1.

6.   'Be afraid, perhaps. But very afraid? No: The threat to Britain from Islamic militancy is far less serious than the government is telling us, says Jason Burke'. *The Observer*, 13 March 2005.

7.   'Attack is the best defence against terror', *Sunday Telegraph*, 10 July 2005, p. 22.

Bibliography

Introduction: Between Death of Faith and Dying for Faith: Reflections on Religion, Politics, Society and Violence, *Madawi Al-Rasheed & Marat Shterin*

Balch, Robert W., and David Taylor (2002). 'Making sense of the Heaven's Gate suicides', in Bromley and Melton (eds.), *Cults, Religion, and Violence,* pp. 209–28.

Barker, E. (1984). *The Making of a Moonie: Brainwashing or Choice?* Oxford: Basil Blackwell.

Barker, E. (2002). 'Watching for violence: a comparative analysis of the roles of five types of cult-watching groups', in Bromley and Melton (eds.), *Cults, Religion, and Violence,* pp. 123–48.

Bromley, D.G., and J. Gordon Melton (eds.) (2002). *Cults, Religion, and Violence.* New York: Cambridge University Press.

Cohen, S. (1972). *Folk Devils and Moral Panics.* London: MacGibbon & Kee.

Devji, F. (2005). *Landscapes of Jihad: Militancy, Morality, Modernity.* London: Hurst & Co.

Eckert, J. (2005). *The Politics of Security.* Max Planck Institute for Social Anthropology Working Paper No. 76.

Galanter, Marc (1989). *Cults: Faith, Healing and Coercion.* 2nd edn., Oxford: Oxford University Press.

Gerges, F. (2005). *The Far Enemy: Why Jihad Went Global.* Cambridge: Cambridge University Press.

Girard, A. (1977). *Violence and the Sacred.* Baltimore: Johns Hopkins University Press.

Hall, J. (1987). *Gone from the Promised Land: Jonestown in American Cultural History.* New Brunswick: Transaction Books.

Hall, J., P. Schuyler, and S. Trinh (2000). *Apocalypse Observed: Religious Movements and Violence in North America, Europe and Japan.* London: Routledge.

Introvigne, M., and J.-F. Mayer (2002). 'Occult masters and the Temple of Doom: the fiery end of the Solar Temple', in Bromley and Melton (eds.), *Cults, Religion, and Violence,* pp. 170–88.

Juergensmeyer, M. (2000). *Terror in the Mind of God.* Berkeley: University of California Press.

Levine, S. (1984). *Radical Departures: Desperate Detours to Growing Up.* San Diego: Hartcourt Brace Jovanovich.

Mayer, J.F. (2001a). 'Field notes: the Movement for the Restoration of the Ten Commandments of God'. *Nova Religio* 5: 203–10.

Mayer, J.F. (2001b). 'Cults, Violence, and Religious Terrorism: An International Perspective', *Studies in Conflict & Terrorism,* 24: 361-376.

Pape, R. (2005). *Dying to Win: The Strategic Logic of Suicide Terrorism.* New York: Random House .

Picard, E. (1993). *The Lebanese Shia and Political Violence.* United Nations Research Institute for Social Development Discussion Paper 42.

Rapoport, D.C. (1984). 'Fear and trembling: terrorism in three religious traditions'. *American Political Science Review* 78 (3): 658–77

Reader, I. (2000). *Religious Violence in Contemporary Japan: The Case of Aum Shinrikyo.* Richmond: Curzon Press.

Richardson, J., (1994), 'The Ethics of "Brainwashing" Claims About New Religious Movements', *Australian Religious Studies Review,* 7: 48-56

Richardson, J. (2001). 'Minority religions and the context of violence: a conflict/interactionist perspective'. *Terrorism and Political Violence* 13 (1): 103–33.

Robbins, T. (1997). 'Religious movements and violence: a friendly critique of the interpretative approach'. *Nova Religio* 1 (1): 13–29.

Robbins, T. (2002). 'Sources of volatility in religious movements', in Bromley and Melton (eds.), *Cults, Religion, and Violence*, pp. 57–79.

Robertson, R. (1992). *Globalization*. London: Sage.

Weber, M. (1978). *Economy and Society*. Berkeley: University of California Press.

Wessinger, C. (1997). 'Millennialism with and without the mayhem: catastrophic and progressive expectations', in T. Robbins and S.J. Palmer (eds.), *Millennium, Messiahs and Mayhem: Contemporary Apocalyptic Movements*. New York: Routledge, pp. 47–57.

Wessinger, C. (2000). *How the Millennium Comes Violently*. New York: Seven Bridges Press.

Wessinger, C. (2006), "New Religious Movements and Violence", in E. Gallagher and W. Ashcraft (eds.), *New and Alternative Religions in America*, V. 1, Westpoint, Conn.: Greenwood Press, pp. 165–205.

Whitehead, N. (ed.) (2004). *Violence*. Oxford: James Currey.

Wright, Stuart A. (ed.) (1995). *Armageddon in Waco: Critical Perspectives on the Branch Davidian Conflict*. Chicago: University of Chicago Press.

Chapter 1: Apocalypse, History, and the Empire of Modernity, *John R. Hall*

Benjamin, Walter (1968 [1940]). 'Theses on the philosophy of history', in Walter Benjamin, *Illuminations*. New York: Harcourt, Brace, & World, pp. 253–64.

Bousquet, Antoine (2006). 'Hiroshima, September 11 and apocalyptic revelations in historical consciousness'. *Millennium* 34: 739–64.

Coward, Martin (2005). 'The globalization of enclosure: interrogating the geopolitics of empire'. *Third World Quarterly* 26: 855–71.

Eisenstadt, S.N. (1999). *Fundamentalism, Sectarianism, and Revolution*. Cambridge: Cambridge University Press.

Fukuyama, Francis (1992). *The End of History and the Last Man*. New York: Free Press.

Habermas, Jürgen (1987 [1981]). *The Theory of Communicative Action, Vol. 2: Lifeworld and System*. Boston: Beacon Press.

Hall, John R. (1978). *The Ways Out: Utopian Communal Movements in an Age of Babylon*. London: Routledge.

— (2003). 'Religion and violence: social processes in comparative perspective', in Michele Dillon (ed.), *Handbook for the Sociology of Religion*. Cambridge: Cambridge University Press, pp. 359–81.

Hall, John R., with Philip D. Schuyler and Sylvaine Trinh (2000). *Apocalypse Observed: Religious Movements and Violence in North America, Europe, and Japan*. London: Routledge.

Hechter, Michael (1975). *Internal Colonialism*. London: Routledge.

Mannheim, Karl (1936). *Ideology and Utopia*. New York: Harcourt, Brace, & World.

Merleau-Ponty, Maurice (1969 [1947]). *Humanism and Terror*. Boston: Beacon Press.

Partner, Peter (1982). *The Murdered Magicians: The Templars and their Myth*. Oxford: Oxford University Press.

Schmalenbach, Hans (1977). 'Communion – a social category', in Hans Schmalenbach, On Society and Experience. Chicago: University of Chicago Press, pp. 64–125.

Schutz, Alfred, and Thomas Luckmann (1973). *The Structures of the Lifeworld*. Evanston: Northwestern University Press.

Wagner, Peter (1994). *A Sociology of Modernity: Liberty and Discipline*. London: Routledge.

Weber, Max (1978 [1922]). *Economy and Society*. Berkeley: University of California Press.

Chapter 2: Martyrs and Martial Imagery: Exploring the Volatile Link Between Warfare Frames and Religious Violence, *Stuart Wright*

Aho, James (1995). *This Thing of Darkness: A Sociology of the Enemy.* Seattle: University of Washington Press.

bin Laden, Osama (2005a). 'Declaration of *jihad*', in Bruce Lawrence (ed.), *Messages to the World: The Statements of Osama bin Laden.* London: Verso, pp. 23–30.

bin Laden, Osama (2005b). 'Terror for terror: October 21 2001', in Bruce Lawrence (ed.), *Messages to the World: The Statements of Osama bin Laden.* London: Verso, pp.106–29.

bin Laden, Osama, and Ayman al-Zawahiri (2005). 'The World Islamic Front: February 1998', in Bruce Lawrence (ed.), *Messages to the World: The Statements of Osama bin Laden.* London: Verso, pp. 58–62.

Chomsky, Noam (1991). *Deterring Democracy.* New York: Hill &Wang.

Flynn, Kevin and Gary Gerhardt (1989). *The Silent Brotherhood.* New York: Signet.

Franklin, Jonathan (1997). 'The good soldier'. *Spin Magazine*, April, pp. 136–43.

Gamson, William (1992). 'The social psychology of collective action', in Aldon D. Morris and Carol McClurg Mueller (eds.), *Frontiers in Social Movements.* New Haven: Yale University Press, pp. 53–76.

Grossman, Lt. Col. Dave (1995). *On Killing: The Psychological Cost of Learning to Kill in War and Society.* Boston: Little, Brown.

Hedges, Chris (2002). *War is a Force that Gives us Meaning.* New York: Public Affairs.

Hunt, Scott A., Robert D. Benford, and David A. Snow (1994). 'Identity fields: framing processes and the social construction of movement identities', in Enrique Larana, Hank Johnston, and Joseph R. Gusfield (eds.), *New Social Movements: From Ideology to Identity.* Philadelphia: Temple University Press, pp. 185–208.

Johnson, Chalmers (2000). *Blowback: The Costs and Consequences American Empire.* New York: Henry Holt.

Juergensmeyer, Mark (2000). *Terror in the Mind of God.* Berkeley: University of California Press.

Klare, Michael T. and Peter Kornbluh (1988). *Low Intensity Warfare: Counterinsrugency, Proinsurgency and Antiterrorism in the Eighties.* New York: Pantheon.

Kraska, Peter B. (2001). *Militarizing the American Criminal Justice System.* Boston: Northeastern University Press.

Kraska, Peter B., and Victor E. Kappeler (1996). 'Militarizing American police: the rise and normalization of paramilitary units'. *Social Problems* 44 (1): 1–18.

LaShan, Lawrence (1992). *The Psychology of War.* New York: Helios.

Lincoln, Bruce (2003). *Holy Terrors: Thinking about Religion after September 11.* Chicago: University of Chicago Press.

Marshall, Jonathan, Peter Dale Scott, and Jane Hunter (1987). *The Iran Contra Connection: Secret Teams and Covert Operations in the Reagan Era.* Boston: South End Press.

'McVeigh's April 26 Letter to Fox News, Thursday April 26, 2001.' Accessed online at http://www.foxnews.com/printer_friendly_story/0,3566,17500,00.html.

Snow, David A., and Robert D. Benford (1992). 'Master frames and cycles of protest', in Aldon D. Morris and Carol McClurg Mueller (eds.), *Frontiers in Social Movements.* New Haven: Yale University Press, pp. 133–55.

Snow, David A, E. Burke Rochford, Steven Worden, and Robert Benford (1986). 'Frame alignment process, micromobilization, and movement participation'. *American Sociological Review* 51: 464–81.

Stern, Jessica (2003). *Terror in the Name of God: Why Religious Militants Kill.* New York: HarperCollins.

Wiktorowicz, Quintan, and John Kaltner (2003). 'Killing in the name of Islam: al-Qaeda's justification for September 11'. *Middle East Policy* 10 (2): 76–92.

Wright, Stuart A. (2007). *Making War: Patriots, Politics and the Oklahoma City Bombing.* Cambridge: Cambridge University Press.

Chapter 3: Violence and New Religions: an Assessment of Problems, Progress, and Prospects in Understanding the NRM–Violence Connection, *J. Gordon Melton & David G. Bromley*

Anthony, Dick, and Thomas Robbins (1997). 'Religious totalism, exemplary dualism and the Waco tragedy', in Thomas Robbins and Susan Palmer (eds.), *Millennium, Messiahs, and Mayhem.* New York: Routledge, pp. 261–84.

Balch, Robert W. (1982). 'Bo and Peep: a case study of the origins of messianic leadership', in Roy Wallis (ed.), *Millennialism and Charisma.* Belfast: Queen's University, pp. 13–72.

Balch, Robert (1995). 'Waiting for the ships: disillusionment and the revitalization of faith in Bo and Peep's UFO cult', in James R. Lewis (ed.), *The Gods Have Landed: New Religions from Other Worlds.* Albany: State University of New York Press, pp. 137–66.

Balch, Robert W., and David Taylor (1977). 'Seekers and saucers: the role of the cultic milieu in joining a UFO cult'. *American Behavioral Scientist* 20 (6): 837–60.

Balch, Robert W., and David Taylor (2002). 'Making sense of the Heaven's Gate suicides', in David G. Bromley and J. Gordon Melton (eds.), *Cults, Religion, and Violence.* New York: Cambridge University Press, pp. 209–28.

Bromley, David G. (2002). 'Dramatic denouements', in David G. Bromley and J. Gordon Melton (eds.), *Cults, Religion, and Violence.* New York: Cambridge University Press, pp. 11–41.

Carroll, J., and B. Bauer (1979). 'Suicide training in the moon cult'. *New West,* 29 January.

Chidester, David (1988). *Salvation and Suicide: An Interpretation of Jim Jones, the Peoples Temple, and Jonestown.* Bloomington: Indiana University Press.

Coser, Lewis (1974). *Greedy Institutions.* New York: Free Press.

Dawson, Lorne (2002). 'Crises of charismatic legitimacy and violent behavior in new religious movements', in David G. Bromley and J. Gordon Melton (eds.), *Cults, Religion, and Violence.* New York: Cambridge University Press, pp. 80–101.

Dornbusch, Sanford (1955). 'The military academy as an assimilating institution'. *Social Forces* 33: 316–21.

Galanter, Marc (1978). 'Why cults turn to violence'. *US News & World Report,* 4 December: 23–9.

— (1989;.rev. edn. 1999). *Cults: Faith, Healing and Coercion.* New York: Oxford University Press.

Hall, John (1987). *Gone from the Promised Land: Jonestown in American Cultural History.* New Brunswick, NJ: Transaction.

Hall, John, with Philip Schuyler and Silvia Trinh (2000). *Apocalypse Observed: Religious Movements, the Social Order, and Violence in North America, Europe and Japan.* New York: Routledge.

Kanter, Rosabeth (1972). 'Commitment and the internal organization of millennial movements'. *American Behavioral Scientist* 16: 219–44.

Kerns, Phil, with Dough Wead (1979). *Peoples Temple, People's Tomb.* Plainfield, NJ: Logos Inernational.

Kilduff, Marshall, and Ron Javers (1978). *The Suicide Cult: The Inside Story of the Peoples Temple Sect and the Massacre in Guyana.* New York: Bantam Books.

Krause, Charles, and Frank Johnston (1978). *Guyana Massacre: The Eyewitness Account.* New York: Berkeley Books.

Levi, Ken (1982). *Violence and Religious Commitment: Implications of Jim Jones's People's Temple Movement.* University Park: Pennsylvania State University Press.

Melton, J. Gordon (1979). 'Jim Jones, Charles Manson, and the process of religious group disintegration'. Paper presented at the Society for the Scientific Study of Religion, San Antonio, Texas.

Melton, J. Gordon (1998). *Encyclopedia of American Religions* (6th edn.). Detroit: Gale Research.

Mills, Jeannie (1979). *Six Years with God.* New York: A&W Publishers.

Moberg, David (1978). 'Revolutionary suicide'. *These Times,* 6 December, 3, p. 1a.

Moore, Rebecca, and Fielding McGehee (eds.) (1989). *New Religious Movements, Mass Suicide, and Peoples Temple: Scholarly Perspectives on a Tragedy*. Lewiston, NY: Edwin Mellen Press.

Reader, Ian (2000). *Religious Violence in Contemporary Japan: The Case of Aum Shinrikyo*. Honolulu: University of Hawaii Press.

Richardson, James (1980). 'Peoples Temple and Jonestown: a corrective comparison and critique'. *Journal for the Scientific Study of Religion* 19: 239–55.

Robbins, Thomas (1986). 'Religious mass suicide before Jonestown: the Russian Old Believers'. *Sociological Analysis* 44: 1–20.

Robbins, Thomas (2000). 'Apocalypse, persecution and self-immolation', in Catherine Wessinger (ed.), *Millennialism, Persecution and Violence*. Syracuse: Syracuse University Press, pp. 205–19.

Weber, Max (1964). *The Theory of Social and Economic Organization*, trans. A.M. Henderson and Talcott Parsons. New York: Free Press.

Wessinger, Catherine (2000). *How the Millennium Comes Violently: From Jonestown to Heaven's Gate*. New York: Seven Bridges.

White, Mel, with Paul Scotchmer and Marguerite Shuster (1979). *Deceived: The Jonestown Tragedy: What Every Christian Should Know*. Old Tappan, NJ: Fleming H. Revell.

Chapter 4: Of 'Cultists' and 'Martyrs': the Study of New Religious Movements and Suicide Terrorism in Conversation, *Massimo Introvigne*

Barker, Eileen (1984). *The Making of a Moonie: Choice or Brainwashing?* Oxford: Basil Blackwell.

Berrebi, Claude (2003). 'Evidence about the link between education, poverty and terrorism among Palestinians'. *Princeton University Industrial Relations Sections Working Paper* no. 477 (September): 1–65.

Bromley, David G., and J. Gordon Melton (eds.) (2002). *Cults, Religion and Violence*. New York: Cambridge University Press.

Hassan, Nasra (2001). 'An arsenal of believers'. *The New Yorker*, 10 November: 36–41.

Iannaccone, Laurence R. (2004). 'The market for martyrs'. Paper presented at the 2004 meeting of the American Economic Association, San Diego, California.

Iannaccone, Laurence R., and Massimo Introvigne (2004). *Il mercato dei martiri. L'industria del terrorismo suicida*. Torino: Lindau.

Introvigne, Massimo (2002). '"There is no place for us to go but up": new religious movements and violence'. *Social Compass* 49 (2) (June): 213–24.

— (2003). *Hamas. Fondamentalismo Islamico e terrorismo suicida in Palestina*. Torino: Elledici, Leumann.

— (2004). *Fondamentalismi. I diversi volti dell'estremismo religioso*. Casale Monferrato (Alessandria:) Piemme.

Introvigne, Massimo, and Jean-François Mayer (2002). 'Occult masters and the Temple of Doom: the fiery end of the Solar Temple', in Bromley and Melton (eds.), *Cults, Religion and Violence*, pp. 170–88.

Krueger, Alan B., and Jitka Maleckova (2003). 'Education, poverty and terrorism: is there a causal connection?' *Journal of Economic Perspectives* 17 (4) (Fall): 119–44.

Maddra, Sam A. (2006). *Hostiles? The Lakota Ghost Dance and Buffalo Bill's Wild West*. Norman: University of Oklahoma Press.

Mayer, Jean-François (2001). 'Field notes: the Movement for the Restoration of the Ten Commandments of God'. *Nova Religio: The Journal of Alternative and Emergent Religions* 5 (1) (October): 203–10.

'Osama baby craze hits Nigeria' (2002). BBC News, 3 January. Available at http://news.bbc.co.uk/1/hi/world/africa/1741171.stm.

Reader, Ian (2000). *Religious Violence in Contemporary Japan: The Case of Aum Shinrikyo*. Richmond: Curzon; Honolulu: University of Hawaii Press.

Schuster, Henry (2004). 'Poll of Saudis shows wide support for bin Laden's views'. CNN, 9 June. Available at http://www.cnn.com/2004/WORLD/meast/06/08/poll.binladen/.

Shermatova, Sanobar, and Aleksandr Teit (2003). 'Juliettas with explosives'. *Moskovskie Novosti*, 4 November.

Stark, Rodney (2001). *One True God: Historical Consequences of Monotheism*. Princeton and Oxford: Princeton University Press.

Stark, Rodney, and Roger Finke (2000). *Acts of Faith: Explaining the Human Side of Religion*. Berkeley, Los Angeles, and London: University of California Press.

Wessinger, Catherine (2000). *How the Millennium Comes Violently: From Jonestown to Heaven's Gate*. New York and London: Seven Bridges Press.

Chapter 5: In God's Name: Practising Unconditional Love to the Death, *Eileen Barker*

Ahlbäck, Tore, with Björn Dahla (2007). *Exercising Power: The Role of Religions in Concord and Conflict*. Åbo: Donner Institute.

Asch, Solomon E. (1959). 'Effects of group pressure upon the modification and distortion of judgement', in Eleanor E. Maccoby, Theodore Newcomb, and Eugene L. Hartley (eds.), *Readings in Social Psychology*, 3rd edn. London: Methuen, pp. 174–83.

Barker, Eileen (1984). *The Making of a Moonie: Brainwashing or Choice?* Oxford: Basil Blackwell.

—— (1989). *New Religious Movements: A Practical Introduction*. London: Her Majesty's Stationery Office.

—— (1993). 'Charismatization: the social production of an ethos propitious to the mobilization of sentiments', in Eileen Barker, James T. Beckford, and Karel Dobbelaere (eds.), *Secularization, Rationalism and Sectarianism*. Oxford: Clarendon Press, pp. 181–202.

—— (1995a). 'The cage of freedom and the freedom of the cage', in Eileen Barker (ed.), *LSE on Freedom*. London: LSE Books, pp. 103–18.

—— (1995b). 'The scientific study of religion? You must be joking!' *Journal for the Scientific Study of Religion* 34 (3): 287–310. Available at http://www.cfh.lviv.ua/Barker.doc. Accessed 18 October 2005.

—— (2003). 'And the wisdom to know the difference? Freedom, control and the sociology of religion'. *Sociology of Religion* 64 (3): 285–307.

—— (2004). 'What are we studying? A sociological case for keeping the nova'. *Nova Religio* 8 (1): 88–102.

Hoffer, Eric (1951). *The True Believer: Thoughts on the Nature of Mass Movements*. New York and London: Harper & Row.

King, Christine (1982). *The Nazi State and the New Religions*. New York and Toronto: Edwin Mellen Press.

Levine, Saul (1984). *Radical Departures: Desperate Detours to Growing Up*. San Diego and London: Harcourt Brace Jovanovich.

Chapter 6: The Terror of Belief and the Belief in Terror on Violently Serving God and Nation, *Abdelwahab El-Affendi*

9/11 Commission (2004). *The 9/11 Commission Report*. New York: W. W. Norton & Co.

Atran, Scott (2006). 'The moral logic and growth of suicide terrorism'. *Washington Quarterly* 29 (2) (Spring): 127–47.

Bar, Shmuel (2004). 'The religious sources of Islamic terrorism'. *Policy Review* 125 (June–July). Available at http://www.hoover.org/publications/policyreview/3438276.html.

Blair, Tony (2006a). 'Clash about civilisation foreign policy speech I', 21 March 2006. Available at http://www.number-10.gov.uk/output/Page9224.asp. Accessed 13 January 2007.

—— (2006b). 'Global alliance for global values speech', 27 March 2006. Available at http://www.number-10.gov.uk/output/Page9245.asp. Accessed 13 January 2007.

—— (2006c). 'Speech to the Los Angeles World Affairs Council', 1 August 2006. Available at http://www.number-10.gov.uk/output/Page9948.asp. Accessed 13 January 2007.

Bloom, Mia (2005). *Dying to Kill: The Allure of Suicide Terrorism*. New York: Columbia University Press.

Devji, Faisal (2005). *Landscapes of Jihad: Militancy, Morality, Modernity*. London: Hurst &Company.

El-Affendi, Abdelwahab (2005). *The Conquest of Muslim Hearts and Minds? Perspectives on US Reform and Public Diplomacy Strategies*. Brookings Project on US Policy towards the Islamic World, Working Paper, September 2005.

Halliday, Fred (2005). 'Terrorism and world politics: conditions and prospects'. *OpenDemocracy.net*, 18 January 2005. Available at http://www.opendemocracy.net/globalization/article_2309.jsp. Accessed 8 September 2006.

Harris, Sam (2004). *The End of Faith: Religion, Terror, and the Future of Reason*. New York: W.W. Norton.

Hersh, Seymour M. (1991). *The Samson Option: Israel's Nuclear Arsenal and American Foreign Policy*. New York: Random House.

Heymann, Philip B. (1998). *Terrorism and America: A Commonsense Strategy for a Democratic Society*. Cambridge, MA: MIT Press.

Hoffman, Bruce (1998). *Inside Terrorism*. London: Victor Gollancz.

— (2001). 'Foreword: twenty-first century terrorism', in James M. Smith and William C. Thomas (eds.), *The Terrorism Threat and US Government Response: Operational and Organizational Factors*, INSS Book Series, March 2001. Colorado: USAF Institute for National Security Studies. Available at http://www.usafa.af.mil/df/inss/TerrorismBook.pdf. Accessed 4 September 2006.

Iannaccone, Lawrence (1998). 'Introduction to the economy of religion'. *Journal of Economic Literature* 36 (3): 1465–95.

James, William (1977). *The Varieties of Religious Experience: A Study in Human Nature*. Glasgow: Collins Fount Paperbacks.

Juster, Susan (2005). 'What's 'sacred' about violence in early America?' *Common-Place* 6 (1). Available at www.common-place.org/vol-06/no.01/juster/index.shtml.

Kramer, Martin (2005). 'Suicide terrorism: origins and response'. Presentation at the Washington Institute for Near East Policy, 8 November 2005. Available at http://www.geocities.com/martinkramerorg/PapeKramer.htm. Accessed 6 September 2006.

Laqueur, Walter (2004). 'The terrorism to come'. *Policy Review* 126 (August). Available at http://www.policyreview.org/aug04/laqueur.html. Accessed 23 September 2006.

Morgan, Matthew J. (2004). 'The origins of the new terrorism'. *Parameters* 34 (1) (Spring): 29–43.

Murad, Abdal-Hakim (2005). 'Bombing without moonlight: the origins of suicidal terrorism'. *Islamica* 12 (Spring): 59–79.

Pape, Robert A. (2005). *Dying to Win: The Strategic Logic of Suicide Terrorism*. New York: Random House.

Sherkat, Darren E. and Christopher G. Ellison (1999). 'Recent developments and current controversies in the sociology of religion'. *Annual Review of Sociology* 35: 363–94.

Spencer, Alexander (2006). 'Questioning the concept of "New Terrorism"'. *Peace Conflict & Development* 8 (1) (January): 1–33. Available at www.peacestudiesjournal.org.uk.

Spencer, Martin E. (1973). 'What is charisma?' *British Journal of Sociology* 34 (3) (September): 341–54.

Stern, Jessica (2003). 'The protean enemy'. *Foreign Affairs* 82 (2) (July–August): 27–40.

Chapter 7: Rituals of Life and Death: the Politics and Poetics of *jihad* in Saudi Arabia, *Madawi Al-Rasheed*

Abukhalil, As'ad (2004). *The Battle for Saudi Arabia*. New York: Seven Stories Press.

Algar, Hamid (2002). *Wahhabism*. New York: Islamic Publications International.

al-Ayri, Yusif (n.d.). 'Dawr al-nisa fi jihad al-ada'. Available at http://www.hakayk.org/vb/showthread.php?t=1665. Accessed 5 November 2005.

Azzam, Maha (2003). 'al-Qaeda: the misunderstood Wahhabi connection and the ideology of violence'. London: Chatham House, briefing paper 1.

Birt, Jonathan (2005). 'Wahhabism in the United Kingdom: manifestations and reactions', in Madawi Al-Rasheed (ed.), *Transnational Connections and the Arab Gulf*. London: Routledge, pp. 168–84

Cordesman, Anthony, and Nawaf Obaid (2005). *National Security in Saudi Arabia: Threats, Responses, and Challenges*. Westport: Praeger Security International.

DeLong-Bas, Natana (2004). *Wahhabi Islam*. London: I.B.Tauris.

Doumato, Eleanor (1992). 'Gender, monarchy and national identity in Saudi Arabia'. *British Journal of Middle Eastern Studies* 19 (1): 31–47.

al-Fahd, Nasir (n.d.). 'Minbar al-tawhid wa al-jihad'. Available at http://www.alsunnah.info/ r?i=996. Accessed 26 February 2004.

Kepel, Gilles (2004). *The War for Muslim Minds*. Cambridge, MA: Belknap Press.

Meijer, Roel (2005). 'The "cycle of contention" and the limits of terrorism in Saudi Arabia', in Paul Aarts and Gerd Nonneman (eds.), *Saudi Arabia in the Balance: Political Economy, Society, Foreign Affairs*. London: Hurst & Co, pp. 271–311

Muhammad Ahmad Salim [Issa al-Oshan] (n.d.). 'La tathhabu lil iraq' (Don't go to Iraq), *Sawt al-Jihad*, vol. 7

al-Musaybih, Saud (2005). *al-Yawm*, 17 January

al-Noqaydan, Mansur (2003). *al-Riyadh*, 11 May.

Oliver, Haneef (2002). *The Wahhabi Myth*. Victoria: Trafford.

Al-Rasheed, Madawi (2005). 'Saudi religious transnationalism in London', in Madawi Al-Rasheed (ed.), *Transnational Connections and the Arab Gulf*. London: Routledge, pp. 149–67.

Al-Rasheed, Madawi (2007). *Contesting the Saudi State: Islamic Voices from a New Generation*. Cambridge: Cambridge University Press.

Strathern, Andrew, Pamela Stewart, and Neil Whitehead (eds.) (2005). *Terror and Violence: Imagination and the Unimaginable*. London: Pluto Press.

Whitehead, Neil (ed.) (2004). *Violence*. Oxford: James Currey.

Chapter 8: The Islamic Debate over Self-inflicted Martyrdom, *Azam Tamimi*

Basyuni, M. Sharif (2003). *al-Watha'iq al-dawliyah al-ma'niyah bi huquq al-insan* (International Documents on Human Rights), vol. II. Cairo: Dar al-Shuruq..

El-Awa, Mohamed S. (1993). *Punishment in Islamic Law*. Indianapolis: American Trust Publications.

Tamimi, Azam (2001). *Rachid Ghannouchi: A Democrat within Islamism*. New York: Oxford University Press.

— (2006). *Hamas: Unwritten Chapters*. London: Hurst.

Chapter 9: The Radical Nineties Revisited: Jihadi Discourses in Britain, *Jonathan Birt*

Begg, Moazzam (2006). *Enemy Combatant*. London: Free Press.

Birt, Jonathan (2005a). 'Locating the British Imam: the Deobandi 'Ulama between contested authority and public policy post-9/11', in Jocelyne Cesari and Sean McLoughlin (eds.), *European Muslims and the Secular State*. Aldershot: Ashgate, pp. 181–96.

Birt, Jonathan (2005b). 'Wahhabism in the United Kingdom', in Madawi Al-Rasheed (ed.), *Transnational Connections and the Arab Gulf*. London: Routledge, pp. 168–84.

Black, C. (2005). *7/7, the London Bombs: What Went Wrong?* London: Gibson Square.

Commins, David (2006). *The Wahhabi Mission and Saudi Arabia*. London: I.B.Tauris.

Geaves, Ron (1996). *Sectarian Influences within Islam in Britain with Rreference to the Concepts of 'Ummah' and 'Community'*. Leeds: Department of Theology and Religious Studies, University of Leeds.

— (2000). *The Sufis of Britain: An Exploration of Muslim Identity*. Cardiff: Cardiff Academic Press.

Gerges, Fawaz A. (2005). *The Far Enemy: Why Jihad went Global.* Cambridge: Cambridge University Press.

Hamid, Sadek (2007). 'Islamic political radicalism in Britain: the case of Hizb-ut-Tahrir', in Tahir Abbas (ed.), *Islamic Political Radicalism: A European Perspective.* Edinburgh: Edinburgh University Press, pp. 145–59.

Jansen, Johannes J.G. (1997). *The Dual Nature of Islamic Fundamentalism.* Ithaca: Cornell University Press.

Khan, Muzamil (2006). 'Devotional Islam in Kashmir and the British Diaspora: The Transmission of Popular Religion from Mirpur to Lancashire'. Ph.D. thesis, Department of Theology and Religious Studies, University of Liverpool.

Lewis, Philip (1994). *Islamic Britain: Religion, Politics and Identity among British Muslims.* London: I.B.Tauris.

McLoughlin, Sean (2005). 'The state, "new" Muslim leaderships and Islam as a "resource" for public engagement in Britain', in Jocelyne Cesari and Sean McLoughlin (eds.), *European Muslims and the Secular State.* Aldershot: Ashgate, pp. 55–69.

McLoughlin, Sean and Muzamil Khan (2006). 'Ambiguous traditions and modern transformations of Islam: the waxing and waning of an "intoxicated" Sufi cult in Mirpur'. *Contemporary South Asia* 15 (September): 289–307.

Taji-Farouki, Suha (1996). *A Fundamental Quest:* Hizb ut-Tahrir *and the Search for the Islamic Caliphate.* London: Grey Seal.

Taseer, Aatish (2005). 'A British jihadist' (interview with Hasan Butt). *Prospect* 113 (August):18–24.

Werbner, Pnina (2003). *Pilgrims of Love: The Anthropology of a Global Sufi Cult.* London: Hurst.

Wiktorowicz, Q. (2005). *Radical Islam Rising.* Lanham, MD: Rowman & Littlefield.

—— (2006). 'Anatomy of the Salafi movement'. *Studies in Conflict & Terrorism* 29 (April–May): 207–39.

Chapter 10: *al-Shahada*: a Centre of the Shiite System of Belief, Fouad Ibrahim

'Abadi, Salehi Najaf (1982 [1968]). *Shahid-e Javid: Husayn ibn 'Ali.* Tehran: n.p.

Abrahamian, Ervand (1993). *Khomeinism: Essays on the Islamic Republic.* Berkeley: University of California Press.

Akhavi, Shahrough (1980). 'Shariati's social thought', in Nikki R. Keddie (ed.), *Religion and Politics in Contemporary Iran: Clergy—State Relations in the Pahlavi Period.* New York: Yale University Press, pp. [[page extent?]].

al-'Amili, Zain al-Din (al-Shahid al-Thani) (1983). *al-Rawdah al-Bahiya fi Sharh al-Lum'a al-Dimishaqiya.* Beirut: Al-Ta'aruf Lil Matubu'at. 10 vols.

al-Asfahani, Sayyid Mohammed Taqi (1987). *Wadhifat al-'anam fi zaman ghaybat al-Imam.* Beirut: Dar al-Wilayah.

Charles, Robert (2005). 'Martyrs and language'. *Washington Times,* 2 June.

Cole, Juan (2005). *Sacred Space and Holy War.* London: I.B.Tauris.

De Weerd, Harvey Arthur (1945). 'George C. Marshall, selected speeches and statements'. *Infantry Journal:* 220–1.

Enayat, Hamid (1982). *Modern Islamic Political Thought.* Austin: University of Texas Press.

Hegland, Mary (1983). 'Two images of Husain: accommodation and revolution in an Iranian village', in Nikki R. Keddie (ed.), *Religion and Politics in Iran: Shi'ism from Quietism to Revolution.* New Haven: Yale University Press, pp. 218–35.

Kashif al-Ghita, Jafar (n.d). *Kashf al-Ghita 'an Mubhamat al-Shari'a al-Ghara.* Isfahan: Intisharat Mahdawi Bazar.

Lewinstein, Keith (2002), 'The revolution of martyrdom in early Islam', in Margaret Cormack (ed.), *Sacrificing the Self: Perspectives on Martyrdom and Religion.* Oxford: Oxford University Press, pp. 75–87.

Momen, Moojan (1985), *An Introduction to Shi'i Islam: The History and Doctrines of Twelver Shi'ism*, New Haven: Yale University Press

Mutahhari, Murtiza (1986). 'Shahid', in Mehdi Abedi and Gary Legenhausen (eds.), *Jihad and Shahadat: Struggle and Martyrdom in Islam*. Houston: Institute for Research and Islamic Studies, pp. 131ff.

Nafziger, George F., and Mark W. Walton (2003). *Islam at War: A History*. Westport: Praeger

Peterson, Scott (2006). 'Funerals in Lebanon's south foster culture of martyrdom'. *Christian Science Monitor*, 9 August.

Richard, Yann (1995). *Shi'ite Islam*, trans. Antonia Nevill. Oxford: Blackwell.

Shari'ati, Ali (1979). *On the Sociology of Islam*, trans. Hamid Algar. Berkeley: University of California Press.

— (2002). *al-Tashaiou' al-'Alawi wa al-tashaiou' al-Safawi*, trans. Haidar Majid. Beirut: Dar al-Amir.

— (2006) Red Shi'ism: The Religion of Martyrdom, Black Shi'ism: The Religion of Mourning, at http://www.shariati.com, accessed on 29 May 2006.

Sivan, Emmanuel (1990). 'Islamic radicalism: Sunni and Shiite', in John L. Esposito (ed.), *Voices of Resurgent Islam*. Albany: State University of New York Press, pp. 46–66.

Tabari (1988 [1408]). *Jāmi' al-bayān*. Beirut: Dar al-fikr.

Chapter 11: Urban Unrest and Non-religious Radicalization in Saudi Arabia, *Pascal Ménoret*

Bayat, Asef (1997). *Street Politics: Poor People Movements in Iran*. New York: Columbia University Press.

Becker, Howard S. (1963). *Outsiders: Studies in the Sociology of Deviance*. New York: Free Press of Glencoe.

Bonnenfant, Paul (1982). 'La capitale saoudienne: Riyad', in Paul Bonnenfant (ed.), *La péninsule arabique d'aujourd'hui*. Paris: CNRS éditions, vol. II, pp. 655–705.

Bourdieu, Pierre (1994). 'La variante "soviétique" et le capital politique', in Pierre Bourdieu, *Raisons pratiques. Sur la théorie de l'action*. Paris: Seuil, pp. 31–5.

— (1997). *Méditations pascaliennes*. Paris: Seuil.

Bourgois, Philippe (1996). *In Search of Respect: Selling Crack in El Barrio*. Cambridge: Cambridge University Press.

Cordesman, Anthony and Nawaf Obaid (2005). *National Security in Saudi Arabia: Threats, Responses, and Challenges*. New York: Praeger.

Davis, Mike (1992). *City of Quartz: Excavating the Future in Los Angeles*. London: Vintage Books.

Farge, Arlette (1979). *Vivre dans la rue à Paris au XVIIIe siècle*. Paris: Julliard.

Foucault, Michel (1975). *Surveiller et punir. Naissance de la prison*. Paris: Gallimard.

Mauss, Marcel (1967). *Manuel d'ethnographie*. Paris: Payot.

Ménoret, Pascal (2005): "Le cheikh, l'électeur et le SMS. Mobilisation électorale et pratiques de vote en Arabie Saoudite", *Transcontinentales* 1: 19–33.

Piven, Frances Fox and Richard A. Cloward (1977). *Poor People's Movements: Why they Succeed, How they Fail*. London: Vintage Books.

Pouillon, François and Thierry Mauger (1995). 'Un Etat contre les bédouins: l'Arabie Saoudite'. *Maghreb-Machrek* 147: 132–48.

Prokop, Michaela (2003). 'Saudi Arabia: the politics of education'. *International Affairs* 79: 79–90.

Al-Rasheed, Madawi (2007). *Contesting the Saudi State: Islamic Voices from a New Generation*. Cambridge: Cambridge University Press.

Routledge, Paul (1997). 'A spatiality of resistance: theory and practice in Nepal's revolution of 1990'. in Steve Pile and Michael Keith (eds.), *Geographies of Resistance*. London: Routledge, pp. 66–86.

Sauvadet, Thomas (2006). *Le capital guerrier. Concurrence et solidarité entre jeunes de cité.* Paris: Armand Colin.

as-Sayf, Muhammad (1996). *al-Zhâhira al-ijrâmiyya fî thaqâfa wa binâ' al-mujtama' as-su'ûdî, bayna at-tasawwûr al-ijtimâ'î wa haqâ'iq al-ittijâh al-islâmî.* Riyadh: Markaz Abhath Mukâfaha al-Jarîma.

Sewell, W.H. (2001). 'Space in contentious politics'. in R. Aminzade (ed.), *Silence and Voice in the Study of Contentious Politics.* Cambridge: Cambridge University Press.

ash-Shithri, Abdelaziz (2001). *Waqt al-farâgh wa shaghluhu fî madînat ar-Riyâdh. Dirâsat maydâniyya.* Riyadh: Jâmi'at al-imâm Muhammad bin Su'ûd al-Islâmiyya.

Thompson, Edward P. (1963). *The Making of the English Working Class.* London: V. Gollancz.

Chapter 12: Bodily Punishments and the Spiritually Transcendent Dimensions of Violence: a Zen Buddhist Example, *Ian Reader*

Aho, James A. (1981). *Religious Mythology and the Art of War: Comparative Religious Symbolisms of Military Violence.* Westport: Greenwood Press.

Appleby, Scott (2000). *The Ambivalence of the Sacred: Religion, Violence, and Reconciliation.* New York: Rowman & Littlefield.

Bell, Sandra (1998). '"Crazy wisdom", charisma, and the transmission of Buddhism in the United States'. *Nova Religio* 2 (1): 55–75.

Hall, John R., with Philip D. Schuyler and Sylvaine Trinh (2000). *Apocalypse Observed: Religious Violence in North America, Europe, and Japan.* London: Routledge.

Daihôrin (ed.) (1981) 'Zazen no sesume', *Daihôrin* 1981 Number 7: 94–167

Kimball, Charles (2002). *When Religion Becomes Evil.* San Francisco: HarperSanFrancisco.

Moerman, D. Max (2005). *Localizing Paradise: Kumano Pilgrimage and the Religious Landscape of Premodern Japan.* Cambridge, MA: Harvard University Asia Centre.

Oguma Eiji (2002). *A Genealogy of 'Japanese' Self-Images.* Melbourne: Trans Pacific Press.

Reader, Ian (2000). *Religious Violence in Contemporary Japan: The Case of Aum Shinrikyô.* Honolulu and Richmond: University of Hawaii Press and Curzon Press.

— (2005). 'Religion, radicalisation and terror in contemporary and historical contexts',. Paper presented at the conference on *Religion, radicalism and terror*, University of Aberystwyth, 26 November.

P *International Politics.*

Schwartz, Regina (1997). *The Curse of Cain: The Violent Legacy of Millennialism.* Chicago: University of Chicago Press.

Sharf, Robert (1993). 'The Zen of Japanese nationalism'. *History of Religions* 33 (1): 1–43.

Snellgrove, David (1987). *Indo-Tibetan Buddhism: Indian Buddhists and their Tibetan Successors,* vol. II. Boston: Shambala Press

Stevens, John (1993). *Three Zen Masters: Ikkyû, Hakuin, Ryôkan.* Tokyo: Kodansha.

Sôtôshûshûmuchô (ed.) (1981–83) *Zen no Kaze* (annual magazine of the Sôtô Zen sect). Tokyo: Sôtôshûshûmuchô.

Suzuki, D.T. (1965). *The Training of the Zen Monk.* New York: University Books.

— (1975 [1949]). *Essays in Zen Buddhism,* vol. I. London: Rider.

Victoria, Brian (1997). *Zen at War.* New York: Weatherhill

— (2003). *Zen War Stories.* London: Routledge.

Wessinger, Catherine (2000a). *How the Millennium Comes Violently.* New York: Seven Bridges Press.

— (2000b). 'The interacting dynamics of millennial beliefs, persecution, and violence', in Catherine Wessinger (ed.), *Millennialism, Persecution, and Violence: Historical Cases.* Syracuse: Syracuse University Press, pp. 3–39.

Chapter 13: : Jewish Millennialism and Violence, *Simon Dein*

Bromley, D. (2002) 'Dramatic denouements', in D.G. Bromley and J.G. Melton (eds.), *Cults, Religion and Violence*. Cambridge: Cambridge University Press [11-41].

Dein S. (2001). 'What really happens when prophecy fails'. *Sociology of Religion* 62 (33): 383–401.

Dein, S., and Dawson, L. (forthcoming). 'The scandal of the Lubavitch rebbe: messianism as a response to failed prophecy'. *Journal of Contemporary Religion*.

Festinger, L., H. Reicken, and S. Schachter (1956). *When Prophecy Fails: A Social and Psychological Study of a Group that Predicted the Destruction of the World*. New York: Harper & Row.

Juergensmeyer, M. (2000). *Terror in the Mind of God: The Global Rise of Religious Violence*. Berkeley and Los Angeles: University of California Press.

Kaplan Z. (2004). 'Rabbi Joel Teitelbaum, Zionism and Hungarian ultra Orthodoxy'. *Modern Judaism* 24 (2): 165–78.

Lifton, R. (2003). *Superpower Syndrome*. New York: Thunder's Mouth Press/Nation Books.

Littlewood, R. and S. Dein (1997). 'The effectiveness of words: religion and healing among the Lubavitch of Stamford Hill'. *Culture Medicine and Psychiatry* 19: 239–83.

Rappoport, D. (1988). ' Messianic sanctions for terror'. *Comparative Politics* 20 (2): 195–213.

Ravitzky, A. (1996). *Messianism, Zionism and Jewish Religious Radicalism*. Chicago: University of Chicago Press.

Ravitzky, A. (2000). 'The messianism of success in contemporary Judaism', in S.J. Stein (ed.), *The Encyclopaedia of Apocalypticism*, vol. III: *Apocalypticism in the Modern Period and the Contemporary Age* . New York: Continuum, pp. 204–29).

Rose, J. (2005). *The Question of Zion*. Princeton: Princeton University Press.

Robbins T. (1997). 'Religious movements and violence: a friendly critique of the alternative approach'. *Nova Religio* 1: 13–29.

Robbins, T. (2002). 'Sources of volatility in religious movements', in D.G. Bromley and J.G. Melton (eds.), *Cults, Religion and Violence*. Cambridge: Cambridge University Press, pp. 57–79.

Ruether, R. and H. Ruether (2002). *The Wrath of Jonah: The Crisis of Religious Nationalism in the Israeli–Palestinian Conflict*. Augsburg: Fortress Press.

Scholem, G. (1971). *The Messianic Idea in Judaism and Other Essays on Jewish Spirituality*. New York: Schocken.

Shahak, I. (1995). 'The ideology of Jewish messianism from race and class'. *Journal on Racism, Empire and Globalisation* 37 (2): 81–91.

Sprinzak, E. (1998). 'Extremism and violence in Israel: the crisis of messianic politics'. *The ANNALS of the American Academy of Political and Social Science*, Vol. 555, No. 1, 114-126.

Talmon, Y. (1966).'Millenarian movements'. *Archives Europeennes de Sociologie* 7: 159–200.

Werblowsky, R. (1969). 'Messianism in Jewish history', in H. Ben Sasson and S. Ettinger (eds.), *Jewish Society through the Ages*. New York: Schocken [30-45].

Wessinger, C. (2000). *Millennialism, Persecution and Violence: Historical Cases*. Syracuse: Syracuse University Press.

Chapter 14: : Sacral Violence: Cosmologies and Imaginaries of Killing, *Neil Whitehead*

Brett, William (1881). *Mission Work in the Forests of Guiana*. London and New York: SPCK and E. and J. B. Young & Co.

Danner, Mark (2004). *Torture and Truth: America, Abu Ghraib, and the War on Terror*. New York: Review Books.

Nordstrom, Carolyn (2004). 'The tomorrow of violence', in Neil L. Whitehead (ed.), *Violence*. Oxford and Santa Fe: James Currey and School of American Research Press, pp. 223–42.

Ohnuki-Tierney, Emiko (2002). *Kamikaze, Cherry Blossoms, and Nationalisms: The Militarization of Aesthetics in Japanese History*. Chicago: University of Chicago Press

Reuter, Christoph (2004). *My Life is a Weapon: A Modern History of Suicide Bombing*. Princeton: Princeton University Press.

Chapter 15: : Journalists as Eyewitnesses, *Noha Mellor*

Atran, Scott (2006). 'The moral logic and growth of suicide terrorism'. *Washington Quarterly* 29 (2): 127–47.

Atwater, T. and N.F. Green, (1988). 'News sources in network coverage of international terrorism'. *Journalism Quarterly* 65: 967–71.

Barnhurst, Kevni and John Nerone (2001). *The Form of News*. New York: Guildford Press.

Bell, Martin (1998). 'The journalism of attachment', in Matthew Kieran (ed.), *Media Ethics*. London: Routledge, pp. 15–22.

Bird, S. Elizabeth (1998). 'An audience perspective on the tabloidisation of news'. *The Public* 5 (3): 33–50.

Boltanski, Luc (1999). *Distant Suffering: Morality, Media and Politics*, trans. Graham Burchell. Cambridge: Cambridge University Press.

Bourdieu, Pierre (2005). 'The political field, the social science field, and the journalistic field', in Rodney Benson and Erik Neveu (eds.), *Bourdieu and the Journalistic Field*. Cambridge: Polity, pp. 29–47.

Chouliaraki, Lilie (2004). 'Watching 11 September: the politics of pity'. *Discourse and Society* 15 (2–3): 185–98.

— (2006). *The Spectatorship of Suffering*. London: Sage.

Coleman, Reita (2000). 'The ethical context for public journalism: as an ethical foundation for public journalism communitarian philosophy provides principles for practitioners to apply to real-world problems'. *Journal of Communication Inquiry* 24 (1): 41–66.

Gans, Herbert J. (2003). *Democracy and the News*. Oxford: Oxford University Press.

Hamidi, Asef (ed.) (2004). *The Radio and TV Journalism: Keys to Success and Creativity*. Abu Dhabi: n.p. (in Arabic).

Höijer, Birgitta (2004). 'The discourse of global compassion: the audience and media reporting of human suffering'. *Media, Culture & Society* 26 (4): 513–31.

Kleinman, Arthur and Joan Kleinman (1997). 'The appeal of experience; the dismay of images: cultural appropriations of suffering in our times', in A. Kleinman, V. Das and M. Lock (eds.), *Social Suffering*. Berkeley: University of California Press, pp. 1–24.

Lamont, Michele (2000). *The Dignity of Working Men: Morality and the Boundaries of Race, Class, and Immigration*. Cambridge, MA: Harvard University Press.

Levy, Daniel and Natan Sznaider (2004). 'The institutionalization of cosmopolitan morality: the Holocaust and human rights'. *Journal of Human Rights* 3 (2): 143–57.

Loyn, David (2003). 'Witnessing the truth'. *Open Democracy*, 20 February. Available at http://www.opendemocracy.net/media-journalismwar/article_993.jsp.

McManus, John (1994). *Market-Driven Journalism: Let the Citizen Beware?* Thousand Oaks: Sage.

Nossek, Hillel and Dan Berkowitz (2006). 'Telling "our" story through news of terrorism'. *Journalism Studies* 7 (5): 691–707.

Peters, John Durham (2001). 'Witnessing'. *Media, Culture & Society* 23: 707–23.

Postman, Neil (1985). *Amusing Ourselves to Death*. New York: Viking.

Reese, Stephen D. (2001). 'Understanding the global journalist: a hierarchy-of-influences approach'. *Journalism Studies* 2 (2): 173–87.

Sznaider, Natan (1998). 'The sociology of compassion'. *Cultural Values* 2 (1): 117–39.

— (2001). *The Compassionate Temperament: Care and Cruelty in Modern Society.* Lanham, MD: Rowman & Littlefield.

Tester, Keith (2001). *Compassion, Morality and the Media.* Buckingham: Open University Press.

Thompson, John B. (1995). *The Media and Modernity.* Cambridge: Polity.

— (2005). 'The new visibility'. *Theory, Culture & Society* 22 (6): 31–51.

Wall, Melisaa (2005). '"Blogs of War": weblogs as news', *Journalism* 6 (2): 153–72.

Wilkinson, Iain (2005). *Suffering: A Sociological Introduction.* Cambridge: Polity.

Zayani, Mohamed (ed.) (2005). *The Al Jazeera Phenomenon: Critical Perspectives on New Arab Media.* London: Pluto Press.

Chapter 16: Understanding Religious Violence: Can the Media be Trusted to Explain?,
Mark Huband

Halper, Stefan and Jonathan Clarke (2004). *America Alone: The Neo-conservatives and the Global Order.* Cambridge: Cambridge University Press.

George Kassimeris (ed.) (2007). *Playing Politics with Terrorism: A User's Guide.* London: C. Hurst & Co.

Parris, Matthew (2005). 'I name the four powers who are behind the al-Qaeda conspiracy'. *The Times*, 23 July.

Preston, Peter (2004). 'Writing the script for terror: media makers must defuse these weapons of mass hysteria'. *The Guardian*, 6 September.

Index

This list does not include names of authors cited. Full references are in the bibliography.